A SPECIAL

RELATIONSHIP

A Special

Relationship

THE UNITED STATES AND

MILITARY GOVERNMENT IN

THAILAND, 1947–1958

Daniel Fineman

UNIVERSITY OF HAWAI'I PRESS

HONOLULU

02 01 00 99 98 97   5 4 3 2 1

Library of Congress Cataloging-in-Publication Data
Fineman, Daniel, 1962–
   A special relationship : the United States and military government
in Thailand, 1947–1958 / Daniel Fineman.
      p.   cm.
   Includes bibliographical references and index.
   ISBN 0-8248-1818-0 (alk. paper)
   1. Thailand—Politics and government.   2. Thailand—Armed Forces—
Political activity.   3. United States—Foreign relations—Thailand.
4. Thailand—Foreign relations—United States.   5. United States—
Military relations—Thailand.   6. Thailand—Military relations—
United States.   I. Title.
DS586.F56   1997
327.593073'09'045—dc20   96-25657
                                       CIP

Designed by Paula Newcomb

CONTENTS

ACKNOWLEDGMENTS

A ny research project depends on the help of many people, and this book has relied on its fair share. Here I'd like to thank those who have helped my work over the past five years.

Several organizations supported my research and writing financially. The Luce Foundation funded much of my language study, and the Yale Center for International and Area Studies and the Yale Council on Southeast Asian Studies gave grants for my research in the United States, England, and Thailand. The Yale Graduate School provided a generous write-up fellowship for the dissertation on which this book is based, and the National Research Council of Thailand handled many of my contacts with Thai government agencies. The assistance I received from each of these organizations eased my work considerably.

The librarians and archivists I met while researching were almost invariably helpful, knowledgeable, and eager to share their ideas. I'd like to thank in particular Dane Hargrove of the United States National Archives for his time and attention and Director Sakarin Wisetsaphan and Section-Head Aranya Rodkun of the National Archives of Thailand for allowing me to see documents still being processed. I'm especially grateful to the staff of the National Archives of Thailand for their friendship and delicious noodle soup. Archival research can be lonely work. Thanks to people like Kornwipha Kornsin and Phenphan Wathanasunthornsin, I never suffered for lack of companionship.

I owe the greatest debt to those whose advice and instruction contributed to the writing of this book. Without the help of Kannikar Chinachote, I never would have acquired the Thai language skills I needed to conduct my research. Kannikar combines patience and intense interest in her students with a deep understanding of linguistic theory. I believe her to be one of the world's great language teachers. The instruction I received from Dr. Sydney Nathans, Dr. Thomas Robisheaux, and Prof. David B. Davis, though in fields unrelated to Thailand or U.S. diplomatic history, has strongly influenced my work. Any analytical and writing skills I now have I gained from these three teachers. Other friends and scholars have contributed directly to the writing of this book. I'd like to thank for their helpful advice Prof. Robin Winks, Dr. Chai-anan Samudavanija, Dr. Kusuma Sanitwongse, Prof. David Wyatt, Dr. Andrew Rotter, Dr. Wiwat Mungkandi, Michael Montasano, David Strechfuss, James LoGerfo, Surachat Bamrungsuk, Kruamat Bamrungsuk, Prof. Benedict Anderson, Dr. Chairat Jaroensin-olan, Prof. Alfred McCoy, Dr. E. Bruce Reynolds, Dr. Prudhisan Jumbala, Dr. Kasian Tejapira, Dr. R. Sean Randolph, Asst. Prof. Narong Phuangphit, Dr. Chakhrid Chumwathana, and Prof. Thamsook Numnonda. On my dissertation examination committee, I was lucky to have as readers two leaders in the fields of Thai political history and U.S. diplomatic history, respectively, Dean Thak Chaloemtiarana and Prof. Gaddis Smith. Their advice in the initial stages benefited my project enormously.

Most of all, I'd like to thank my dissertation adviser, Ben Kiernan. Dr. Kiernan's knowledge of Southeast Asian history is considerable, and, though a Cambodian specialist, he was able to advise me on points of Thai politics and American foreign policy as well as larger conceptual issues. At times, I initially disagreed with his criticisms, but in the end, I always found him to be right. His recommendations shaped my thinking in countless ways.

Finally, I'd like to thank my parents and sister for their love and support. Although they would have preferred me to write about a place closer to home, they encouraged my work throughout. My greatest joy in completing this book is knowing that, in a small way, it will make them proud.

NOTE ON TRANSLITERATION

AND THAI NAMES

Several systems are commonly used for transliterating Thai, providing endless confusion for specialists and nonspecialists alike. Some systems copy spelling, while others reproduce sound. This book follows the sound-based "General System" of transliteration in the *Romanization Guide for Thai Script* (Bangkok: Royal Institute, 1982), with some variations introduced to clarify differences in pronunciation. Readers need only note here that *ph* is pronounced as the *p* in Peter, not as an *f*, and that *th* is pronounced as the *th* in Thomas, not as in that. In keeping with local tradition, I refer to Thais by their given (i.e., first) names, not their surnames. I will also, on occasion, include aristocratic or honorary titles, if they appear frequently in Western writings. I use only three titles—*Luang, Phraya,* and *Krommameun.*

Often, westerners refer to Thais by abbreviated names or names transliterated according to spelling. Thus, although in this book the reader will encounter the name Sarit, he or she will also find, in a few U.S. diplomatic records, reference to the same person as Srisdi. The latter transliteration reproduces the spelling, not the pronunciation, of the name. Where widely divergent spellings are common, I will use the more prevalent form, providing alternative spellings in parentheses in the first reference to the figure in question.

Before 1939 and from the end of World War II to 1949, Thailand was officially called Siam. I refer to the country as Thailand and the people as Thai throughout, though many quotations from primary sources use the terms Siam and Siamese.

ABBREVIATIONS

ANZUS	Australia–New Zealand–United States Treaty Organization
BPP	Border Patrol Police
CIA	Central Intelligence Agency
CID	Criminal Investigation Department, Thailand National Police Department
FRUS	*Foreign Relations of the United States*
ICA	International Cooperation Administration
JCS	Joint Chiefs of Staff
JUSMAG	Joint United States Military Assistance Advisory Group
KMT	Kuomintang
MAAG	U.S. Military Assistance Advisory Group
NATO	North Atlantic Treaty Organization
NSC	National Security Council
OCB	Operations Coordinating Board
OIR	Office of Intelligence Research, State Department
OPC	Office of Policy Coordination, CIA
OSS	Office of Strategic Services
PARU	Police Aerial Reconnaissance (Resupply) Unit
PRC	People's Republic of China
PRO	Public Record Office, London, England
PSB	Psychological Strategy Board
RG	Record Group
SEATO	Southeast Asia Treaty Organization
SPANSA	Office of the Special Assistant for National Security Affairs
TFML	Thailand Foreign Ministry Library
TNA	Thailand National Archives
USIS	United States Information Service
USNA	United States National Archives
VDC	Volunteer Defense Corps

A SPECIAL

RELATIONSHIP

INTRODUCTION

President Gerald Ford and Secretary of State Henry Kissinger faced a troubling dilemma in May 1975. The new Khmer Rouge government of Cambodia had just captured an American merchant vessel, the *Mayaguez*, in international waters, and fears ran high as to the fate of the ship's crew in the hands of the unpredictable Khmer Rouge leadership. Ford and Kissinger wanted to recapture the *Mayaguez* by force, but the only American military bases close enough to launch an attack were in neighboring Thailand, and that country's fragile, two-year-old civilian government had refused the Americans permission to mount the operation from Thai territory. Without the use of the Thai bases, the United States had little hope of rescuing the detained seamen. But all was not yet lost for Ford and Kissinger. The Thai military, though it had been forced to relinquish its control of the government two years earlier, still jealously guarded its prerogatives against the civilian leadership, which it was, in any case, about to overthrow. Ford and Kissinger, therefore, simply ignored the elected government and got permission from the army to launch the attack. Then, even as the American ambassador in Bangkok informed the civilian prime minister that the United States would respect Thai sovereignty, American forces working out of Thailand proceeded with the rescue—losing more lives in the process than they saved. The elected Thai government's protests proved futile.[1]

More than just a panicked response to a momentary crisis, this U.S. decision to defy the elected government of Thailand and rely on the army was the legacy of twenty-five years of intimate American relations with a corrupt, undemocratic, and often brutal Thai military. The United States, over that period, provided arms, money, and political support to a succession of military regimes in Thailand, and, in return, those governments backed American diplomacy and collaborated in a variety of military operations. In the 1950s and 1960s, Thai paramilitary police supported CIA covert activities in Burma and Laos. In the Korean War, Thai soldiers fought alongside the American army. During the Vietnam War, almost fifty thousand U.S. servicemen pursued most of the air war against North Vietnam from a string of air and naval bases in Thailand. The American military presence in the country in the 1960s was so extensive that political scientist Benedict Anderson has called the period the "American Era" of Thai history.[2] After the Vietnam War, although the United States withdrew its troops, the American and Thai militaries remained close. Throughout the 1970s and 1980s, the United States provided arms and training to the Thai military, and Thai and American troops participated annually in joint exercises on Thai soil. In important ways, the United States has retained its special relationship with the Thai military.

To understand why this special relationship has endured—why the Thais sent troops to Indochina, why the United States provided billions of dollars of arms to a corrupt and inefficient Thai military, why Thai leaders allowed tens of thousands of foreign troops on their soil, why successive American administrations supported repressive military regimes—we must turn to the time when it all began, the period from 1947 to 1958. Bounded by two important political events, the return to power of the army through a coup in November 1947 and the assumption of complete control of government by the military in October 1958, the twelve years from 1947 to 1958 formed a watershed in Thai history. The period both brought the establishment of a form of military government that would survive intact until 1973 and witnessed a transformation in Thailand's foreign policy. In the late 1940s and 1950s, the Thai government slowly acquired the closed and repressive qualities it would retain throughout the 1960s and early 1970s. At the same time, the country abandoned the flexibility it had previously maintained in its foreign relations and forged an alliance with the United States that would last for decades. By the end of the period, in late 1958, a military dictatorship ruled the country, and the basis for all future cooperation with the United States had been laid. With that, modern Thailand was born.

This book seeks to show that the two processes at work in Thai politics and foreign affairs from 1947 to 1958—the extension of the military's control of government and the movement toward closer relations with the United States—were intimately related. While the military would have interfered in politics whether Thailand maintained an alliance with the United States or not, America's actions strengthened the existing tendency toward repressive military government. At first unintentionally, later intentionally, U.S. policy in the late 1940s and 1950s encouraged military leaders to tighten their control over the government and suppress dissidents. Likewise, although Thailand and the United States probably would have maintained close relations no matter what the military's political role, only a military government would have aligned itself so firmly with the United States and participated in the myriad covert operations the Americans sponsored. The Thai-American alliance of the 1950s was built on the rock of repressive Thai military government, and the military's success in establishing its authoritarian regime resulted, in part, from that same alliance.

In examining this interdependence of military and American interests in Thailand, I have abandoned the conventional model of Thai-American relations. Published studies by Raymond Sean Randolph and Donald Nuechterlein and numerous dissertations by both Thais and Americans all focus on the importance of the Cold War to the Thai-American alliance. Such works portray the Thai-U.S. relationship as a partnership of ideological soulmates: the Thais feared the Communists; the Americans did too. By necessity, therefore, the two worked together.[3] All aspects of the relationship, according to this model, focused on national security concerns. "Beginning in the 1950s and continuing through the present, then," Randolph concludes, "themes of security and of American commitment have dominated Thai-American relations."[4] While this interpretation might appeal to Americans and Thai scholars trained in the United States, however, the Cold War paradigm explains little from the perspective of Thais of the time. It neither answers why Thai foreign policy took the direction it did nor accounts for inputs into Thai policymaking other than security concerns. Throughout the period, traditional, nonideological policy aims, not doctrinal anticommunism, informed Thai policy. Even regarding U.S. policy, the Cold War model distorts American aims and attitudes. It at once oversimplifies the reasons for American support for military governments in the country and obscures Thailand's role in America's disputes with its European allies. Significantly, none of the published studies and only two of the dissertations on Thai-U.S. relations in the period use Thai or American archival sources. And one of those two dissertations, by Arlene Becker Neher, concentrates on economic relations in the 1940s. The other, by Apichart Chinwanno, though ultimately upholding the conventional model, shows signs, especially in his chapter on the initiation of American military assistance to Thailand, of analyzing Thai policy in terms other than of anticommunism.

Most seriously, the Cold War model fails to explain the role of the military and military-controlled governments in the alliance. In focusing on national security issues, the proponents of the Cold War model assume that political considerations mattered little to Thai foreign policymaking. The need to find a defense against the Communists drove the military government of the late 1940s and 1950s to seek out the alliance with the United States, and, presumably, the foreign threat would have forced a democratic administration, had civilians stayed in power after 1947, to do the same. Domestic politics and the form of government, from this viewpoint, had little impact on Thailand's stance toward the United States. Likewise, the United States, recognizing the importance of national security concerns to Thai leaders, took limited interest in trying to shape Thai political developments. According to the Cold War model, American support for military governments in the country arose not out of a desire to manipulate Thai foreign policy, but from the belief that the country needed strong leadership to defend itself from Communists. In any case, the United States could do little, the Americans supposedly believed, to influence the course of internal events. Intensification of military rule and the movement toward closer relations with the United States proceeded independently.

Rather than considering Thailand's alliance with the United States as separate from internal politics and driven by the novel and imported ideology of anticommunism, as the Cold War model assumes, we should view the country's domestic politics and foreign policy, as the Thais themselves did, as closely connected. Small, weak, and underdeveloped, Thailand in the late 1940s and 1950s was susceptible to outside pressure at several key points. Various outside powers—including the United States—recognized this vulnerability and endlessly pushed the Thai government to set domestic policy in line with their own interests. The competing pressures from the United States and other powers regarding treatment of dissidents and ethnic minorities, in particular, made government conduct toward these internal groups foreign-policy issues. Such pressures had a profound impact on the repressiveness of the military regime. At the same time, the structure of the Thai military governments of the period induced Thais themselves to draw foreign powers into the Thai political arena. Factious, lacking a broad political base, and enjoying uncertain legitimacy, the military rulers of the period badly needed support from wherever they could get it. Because of the relative lack of anti-Western sentiments in Thailand, they sought such political support from outside powers. When working in unison, the military leadership looked to foreign help to strengthen the military institutionally; individually, military leaders sought outside aid for their personal political interests. Thus at once confronting the inevitability of foreign intervention in internal affairs while also seeking it, Thais of the late 1940s and 1950s treated domestic politics and foreign policy not as separate, but as highly interdependent. Political developments, Thai leaders understood, often had consequences for the country's foreign relations. And foreign-policy decisions almost always affected domestic politics.

Significantly, although the various international-relations-oriented studies of the Thai-American alliance neglect this crucial point, students of Thai domestic politics offer support for an approach emphasizing the importance of internal political events. Thak Chaloemtiarana, the leading scholar of Thai politics of the late 1940s and 1950s, has commented that "Thailand's involvement with the United States after the Second World War could be viewed as one prompted by domestic political concerns of the Thai leaders."[5] Similarly, J. L. S. Girling, author of one of the best recent surveys of Thai politics, *Thailand: Society and Politics,* describes the U.S.-Thai relationship as an outgrowth of Thailand's patronage political system.[6] Because of their focus on Thai domestic politics, neither scholar elaborates on these brief observations, but I take Thak's and Girling's comments as an analytical base for my own study of the U.S.-Thai alliance.

This book, therefore, is as much political as diplomatic history. In part, it should be seen as an update of Thak's study of the politics of the 1940s and 1950s in *Thailand: The Politics of Despotic Paternalism.*[7] My examination of Phibun's ambiguous attitude toward the coups and accumulation of power by the military in the period should, in particular, contribute to a reevaluation of this important figure's role in developing the modern Thai political system. At the same time, it is hoped that this book will add to the growing body of studies of American relations with developing countries, best represented by George McT. Kahin's book on American involvement in Vietnam and Bruce Cumings' examination of the Korean War, analyzing U.S. policy in terms of the domestic politics of the nations in question.[8] Only through such an approach can the full meaning of the Thai-American alliance be understood.

Fortunately, sources for conducting a wide-ranging study of Thai politics and the alliance with the United States in the late 1940s and 1950s now abound. In the United States, fairly comprehensive records of the State Department and meetings of the National Security Council are held in the National Archives and the Eisenhower and Truman libraries and appear, in part, in the published *Foreign Relations of the United States* series, the various versions of the Pentagon Papers, and the microfiche collection of documents released under the Freedom of Information Act, the *Declassified Documents Reference System.* Personal papers of two American ambassadors to Thailand, Edwin F. Stanton and William J. Donovan, housed in the University of Bridgeport Library in Connecticut and the Army War College in Carlisle, Pennsylvania, respectively, are similarly illuminating.

In Thailand, the National Archives and the Foreign Ministry Library retain important records—many never before researched—of the cabinet, Supreme Command, Foreign Ministry, Defense Ministry, and Interior Ministry. Newspapers held in the National Library, transcripts of parliamentary debates in the National Assembly library, and proceedings of the Juridical Council (Kritsadika) at the Juridical Council's library are revealing of both Thai domestic politics and foreign policy. The Phibunsongkhram Memorial Library at the Chulachomklao Military Academy in Nakhorn Nayok province also contains helpful, though limited and unorganized, materials, and masters' theses from Thai universities often provide useful descriptions of important events. In England, British Foreign Office documents at the Public Record Office offer an added perspective on both Thai and American policies and shed light on Britain's crucial role in the development of Thai-American relations in the late 1940s and early 1950s.

Each of these source materials is deficient in some respects. On the Thai side, a number of Thai-language newspapers from the late 1940s and 1950s have not been preserved, and the records of the various ministries suffer from huge gaps, both chronological and topical, for no apparent good reason. Even where newspapers are available and official records abundant, the Thai sources are often silent on those items of greatest interest because so many important decisions and events were made and occurred in back-room settings involving no note-keeping. On the American side, documentation is more extensive, but the reviewer responsible for declassifying the State Department records from the 1955–1959 period released significantly fewer documents than reviewers for the earlier years. For all periods, the American records contain almost no references to the CIA, possibly the most important American agency operating in Thailand in the 1950s.

Luckily, however, materials from one source often compensate for weaknesses in another. Although the official Thai records at times give no indication of the behind-the-scenes maneuvers critical to the politics of the period, a careful reading of contemporary newspapers can be most revealing. Where such newspapers are missing, U.S. and British embassy reports on press opinions often fill the gaps. Likewise, because important Thai political figures regularly consulted American and British diplomats about domestic events, the State Department and Foreign Office dispatches provide a great deal of information unavailable in the Thai records. And while the American records are mostly silent about CIA activities, the Thai documents are, at times, strangely open about both American and Thai covert operations. Perhaps most helpful in this respect have been the numerous interviews conducted for this study with former Thai diplomats and military leaders and American CIA and State Department officials. When pieced together with the documentary evidence, such interviews supply important insights into both the development of covert operations in Thailand and the personal aspects of the alliance.

From these various sources, a picture of Thai-American relations from 1947 to 1958 emerges in which American fortunes in Thailand, far from being independent of the country's domestic politics, were bound directly to the strength and repressiveness of the military government. Initially, the Americans responded negatively to the military's overthrow of the elected government in November 1947, but, as the military consolidated its rule over the next three years, relations between the United States and Thailand improved. The formation of the de facto alliance in 1950 coincided exactly with the diminution of civilian control over the foreign-policymaking process. Then, as the military tightened its grip over the country in the early 1950s, eliminating its rivals and repressing dissidents, relations grew even closer. The United States in these years expanded its aid to the military, intensified its operations in the country, and strengthened its commitment to fight for the government's survival. When, from 1955 to 1958, the government instituted democratic reforms, freeing dissidents and allowing political parties to form and compete in elections, relations with the United States deteriorated. Disputes between the two countries emerged, and both Thais and Americans reevaluated the prospects for continuing the relationship. Only the imposition of an absolutist military dictatorship in 1958 restored the alliance.

Although, superficially, this correspondence of American policy successes and military accumulation of power appears merely coincidental, more was at work here than happenstance. The problem, simply put, was that American policy aims and Thai democracy were incompatible. The Americans sought a massive increase in Thai military power, insisted on the repression of criticism of the United States, and enhanced the military's ability to conduct covert operations without outside interference. In a country where a military tending toward authoritarianism already intervened in politics and construction of a public consensus on foreign policy was nearly impossible, such policies could not help but conflict with the forces for democracy. Likewise, American policies would have enjoyed little chance for success had civilians been allowed to criticize government foreign policy and over-see covert activities and the military expansion.

Therein lies the tragedy of the Thai-American relationship of the late 1940s and 1950s. When, in 1958, the Americans finally embraced outright military dictatorship in Thailand, they had not lost faith in democracy. They still believed that civilian participation in government strengthened Thailand. By then, however, their own policy concerns simply mattered more to them.

THE SETTING

Thailand is a Texas-sized country with a tropical monsoon climate set in the middle of mainland Southeast Asia. It shares borders with Cambodia to the east, Laos to the north, Burma to the west, and Malaysia to the south. Neither China nor Vietnam is contiguous, but parts of both lie within one hundred kilometers of Thai territory. Much of Thailand's border, except where the Mekong River forms the boundary with Laos, is poorly demarcated.

Measured by population and economic development, Thailand ranked in the top half of Southeast Asian nations of the late 1940s and 1950s. In 1947, it had a population of more than seventeen million, a gross national product of about $700 million, and a per capita income of approximately $42.[9] Eighty to 90 percent of the population in the period farmed. Although tenancy was on the rise, more than 80 percent of all farmers cultivated their own land. The country's main exports, in descending order, were rice, rubber, teak, and tin. Bangkok, the capital, formed the only major urban area.

Land forms and drainage divide Thailand into four geographically and linguistically distinct regions. The central region, including Bangkok, is the richest, most densely populated, and most developed. The fertile soil of the Chao Phraya River valley has made it the rice bowl of Thailand, and its hub, Bangkok, handles most of the country's international commerce. The most populous region, the northeast, is the poorest. Underdeveloped and relatively dry, it depends on rice cultivation, but, unlike the central region, usually supports only one crop per year. The south, a narrow peninsular region, has an economy and climate more like Malaysia's than those of the rest of Thailand. Rubber remains its major agricultural product, with tin-mining contributing income in the 1940s and 1950s. The north, a mountainous region, is the most thinly populated. Its inhabitants are concentrated in the rice-growing alluvial valleys. Each of these four regions has its own dialect. The central dialect is the official language.

Ethnically, Thailand is the most homogeneous nation of Southeast Asia but contains significant minorities. Small numbers of non-Thai, primarily migratory "hill tribes," live in the mountains of the north. These tribes mix little with the ethnic Thais of the lowlands. In the four southernmost provinces, Muslim Malay speakers form the majority, and Khmer (Cambodian) speakers predominate in some northeastern border provinces. A few Indians and Europeans live in Bangkok and larger towns. Most important, some 10 to 15 percent of the population is of Chinese ancestry. Although Chinese have occupied a prominent place in Thai society for centuries, most arrived from the late nineteenth to mid-twentieth centuries, and many remained unassimilated in the late 1940s and 1950s. Chinese of the time controlled almost all the country's domestically owned industry, commerce, and banking. Despite the prominence of some minorities, however, ethnic differences never troubled Thailand as much as they did its neighbors. More than 80 percent of the population in the period could be classified as Thai, and, because the Chinese quickly adopted their hosts' religion, more than 90 percent practiced Thais' syncretistic form of Theravada Buddhism.[10]

PART ONE

LEARNING TO LIVE WITH PHIBUN,

1947–1948

The return to power of Thailand's wartime strongman, Field Marshal Plaek Phibunsongkhram, in a coup overthrowing the elected government in November 1947 could not have more exasperated the United States. During the war, Plaek—known in the West as "Phibun"—had assumed dictatorial powers, established social and political institutions modeled on those in fascist countries, and struck an alliance with Japan against the United States and Great Britain. As a State Department release at the time put it, this "man who had declared war on the allies" was "extremely unpopular" with the U.S. government.[1] But the Americans found it hard to bear a grudge. Gradually, their passions cooled, and by April 1948, American thinking had reached the point where one official could describe Phibun as a democrat "deeply concerned with how he shall go down in history." Not all on the U.S. side gave such a glowing assessment, but support for Phibun had grown by leaps and bounds. By May 1948, the United States had embraced the former dictator as the best hope for both Thailand and American interests in Thailand.[2]

The revolution in American attitudes toward Phibun represented the first step on the road to partnership for the United States and the Thai military. At first, the Americans resisted Phibun's return to power not merely because they disliked him personally but because elements in the military trying to oust the civilian government looked to him as their leader. To oppose Phibun, most American officials believed, was to support democracy. By later accepting him, they also endorsed, to a large extent, military control of government.

Although the transformation in American policy toward Phibun occurred over a mere matter of months, the change came with difficulty. The ambiguity of the initial response to the November 1947 coup in no way reflected uncertainty regarding Phibun. The United States badly wanted him back into retirement. The coup, however, caught the Americans off guard, and the coup-makers' skillful diplomacy limited U.S. ability and willingness to oppose Phibun once enough time had passed for a careful consideration of policy options. By the spring of 1948, changes in U.S. policy in the region made maintenance of friendly relations with Thailand imperative. The United States then felt it had to accept the civilian government's downfall.

As painful as the decision to support Phibun was, however, American policymakers must accept some blame for having to make it. Although the United States wanted civilian government to succeed in Thailand, American policymakers, both passively and actively, helped bring about its failure. At the same time that they proclaimed their support for the freely elected government in the months before the 1947 coup, they also displayed their favor for politicians aligned with military elements seeking its overthrow. And, while the Americans protested the ouster of the elected government in November 1947, they did nothing to help it return to power. Despite their effusive praise for civilian rule and outward concern for Thai independence and sovereignty, American policymakers courted individual military leaders, involved themselves in internal political disputes, and stayed silent when the military suppressed those civilian politicians the Americans found objectionable. The dilemma facing the United States here was never whether to intervene in Thailand's politics. It was already doing that. Rather, the question was whether the Americans would stand firmly behind the democratic process or selectively intervene on behalf of the elected government's opponents. They chose the latter, and democracy paid the price.

Chapter One

PRELUDE TO THE COUP,

JANUARY 1947–NOVEMBER 1947

As it had for fifteen years, the struggle for power between soldiers and civilians in Thailand in 1947 revolved around a personal contest between Phibun, champion of the army, and Pridi Phanomyong, leader of the main civilian faction. Controversial figures, largely because of the mutual recriminations surrounding their rivalry, Pridi and Phibun defy easy description. The length of time each was involved in politics renders simple characterizations of their careers impossible. As complex and contradictory as their political legacies are, however, their importance to twentieth-century Thai history is undeniable. Either together or separately, they dominated the Thai political scene continuously from 1932 to 1957. No other figures in this century had as great an impact on the style, substance, and intellectual foundation of Thai politics.

Of the two, Pridi was the more impressive personally. Forceful, articulate, occasionally called brilliant, Pridi had overcome relatively humble provincial origins and part-Chinese ancestry to gain his position of prominence in the country's affairs. His career was unique in modern Thai history. In a political system where privilege, wealth, and brute force determined success, Pridi depended on his charisma and ideas, and, unlike leaders of the fluid, shifting, ever-changing political groupings then prevalent in the country, Pridi enjoyed the heart-felt loyalty of most of his followers. To be sure, Pridi was no saint. He was not above using heavy-handed methods, and, though himself untainted, he tolerated corruption in his supporters. From the beginning, however, he bound his fate to parliamentary supremacy and civilian control of the country's affairs. On his shoulders rode the fate of civilian government in Thailand in 1947.

Phibun, by comparison, appears a much less imposing figure than the cerebral Pridi, but the complexity of his character and his greater political success reflect a deep reserve of cunning. Although never very intellectually inclined, Phibun, the son of a prosperous but not wealthy orchard owner near Bangkok, had performed well enough in school and afterwards to rise to power from origins as obscure as Pridi's. Certainly, any deficiency Phibun suffered in raw intelligence never prevented him from thinking broadly and with vision. Phibun's modest, self-effacing demeanor appears, rather than an indication of low self-esteem, to have derived from a calculated effort to mask his soaring ambition and pride. In any case, such was the effect on people of his unpretentious charm. Despite his well-known admiration for Napoleon, self-aggrandizement, and occasionally brutal political methods, even his harshest critics, after meeting him for the first time, at least considered the possibility that they had prejudged him unfairly. This capacity for carefully measured self-control helped make Phibun the longest serving prime minister in Thai history. Equally important, his bold and decisive leadership and relentless promotion of army interests made him one of the most popular commanders ever. As much as prospects for democracy depended on Pridi's success, so did the army's fortunes in 1947 rest with the wily and persistent Phibun.

Despite their later rivalry, Pridi and Phibun began their careers as friends and rose to power together. The two met in the 1920s while on Thai government scholarships. Phibun was training in military science in Paris, and Pridi was studying law at the Sorbonne. Together, they joined with several other young Thais studying in France to plan for a "revolution" to overthrow the absolute monarchy and modernize the country. Back in Bangkok several years later, Pridi and Phibun's group recruited a number of mid-level bureaucrats and military officers to the revolutionary cause. In June 1932, these combined forces mounted a bloodless, lightning coup that forced the king to cede effective power to the coup "Promoters" and grant the country its first constitution and parliament.[1] Quickly, Phibun and Pridi emerged as the new government's most powerful figures. Pridi acted as the Promoters' intellectual leader, and, after decisively quelling a conservative countercoup in 1933, Lieutenant Colonel Phibun assumed control of the group's powerful army faction. Although the potential for conflict between Phibun and Pridi increased in these years, their continuing friendship, a neutral and older prime minister, and the enduring conservative threat all kept the two remarkably united throughout the 1930s. Phibun confined his political efforts to winning generous budgets for his army, and Pridi concentrated on establishing his own power base in the bureaucracy. Even after Phibun gained a significant advantage over Pridi with his accession to the prime ministership in 1938, Pridi remained in the cabinet as finance minister. Pridi tacitly supported Phibun's decision in 1939 to execute eighteen royalists and political opponents and imprison dozens of others on remote Tarutao Island. Having sworn in the 1932 coup never to do each other bodily harm, Phibun and Pridi still saw more reason in 1939 for partnership than enmity.

The outbreak of World War II abruptly ended the two men's alliance. Pridi had shown his sympathies, in the years leading up to the war, for the British, while Phibun had actively courted Japanese embassy officials. Once the war began, the split on foreign policy brought out all the latent differences between the two.[2] In November 1940, Phibun, against Pridi's objections, took the occasion of Axis military successes in Europe to recapture formerly Thai-held territories in Laos and Cambodia lost to the French at the turn of the century.[3] In December 1941 and January 1942, after the Japanese had occupied Thailand in conjunction with their attacks on Pearl Harbor and Southeast Asia, Phibun overrode Pridi's vehement protests and entered an alliance with Japan against Britain and the United States. Pridi feared the financial costs of a Japanese occupation, but Phibun saw important political and military benefits from the alliance.[4] With Japanese backing, Phibun seized additional territories, this time from the British in northern Malaya and the Shan States of Burma. Then, he kicked Pridi upstairs from the cabinet to the prestigious but powerless Regency. With Pridi gone, Phibun intensified his promotion of protofascist youth organizations, a "statist" ideology, and a personality cult praising Phibun as the "leader." Phibun acquired, during the war, a dictatorial hold over the country.[5]

Just as the Japanese occupation had boosted Phibun, however, Allied victories in the Pacific and Europe in 1943 and 1944 allowed Pridi and his civilian allies to turn the tables on Phibun and the army. By that point, Phibun and Pridi realized that Britain and the United States would determine who would rule Thailand, and a contest began between the two rivals for the Allies' affections. Both secretly sent representatives to China to make contact with Chiang Kai-shek, and both laid plans for armed resistance against Japan. His prewar friendship with the British and opposition to the declaration of war on the Allies, however, gave Pridi an insurmountable advantage, and, in August 1944, he convinced Parliament to replace Phibun with a civilian Promoter,

Khuang Aphaiwong, to appease the Allies.[6] Ironically, when the army then moved to stage a coup to put Phibun back in office, the Japanese ensured that Parliament's decision would stick. Concerned by Phibun's poorly concealed resistance plans, the Japanese commander in Thailand formally notified the Thais that Japan would not tolerate a coup.[7] From that point until the 1947 coup, civilian cabinets, led behind the scenes by Pridi, governed the country.

Over the next two years, Pridi and his civilian allies succeeded to a remarkable extent, given the trying circumstances of the war and its aftermath, in running a stable, effective government. In the area of foreign policy, Pridi's success was undeniable. Because of Phibun's alliance with Japan, Thailand faced the threat of severe Allied sanctions after the war, but the close cooperation in 1944 and 1945 of Pridi's anti-Japan, anti-Phibun Free Thai movement with Britain's Special Operations Executive and America's Office of Strategic Services (OSS) went far toward placating Allied resentment during the war, and Pridi's skillful diplomacy won Thailand a peace settlement more lenient than anyone had hoped for. In 1946, he returned the captured British territories and, under intense French military and diplomatic pressure, withdrew from the Indochinese provinces. Although these moves hurt him politically, they won him the Europeans' gratitude.[8] Then, his establishment of relations with China and the U.S.S.R. and repeal, on Soviet insistence, of the 1933 Anti-Communist Act guaranteed that the Security Council would admit Thailand to the U.N. Meanwhile, Pridi managed to reform the country's political system. In January 1946, he oversaw open, nonpartisan, partial elections and, that May, led Parliament in promulgating a new, more liberal constitution. This constitution was the most democratic that Thailand enjoyed before 1973. It opened the way for free and partisan by-elections that August to fill the remaining parliamentary seats.[9]

Before Pridi could bring the elections to fruition, however, matters began to slip from his grasp. In March 1946, his wartime ally, Khuang Aphaiwong, resigned from the prime ministership. Until Khuang's resignation, the various civilian elements of the anti-Phibun coalition—Pridi and his supporters in the bureaucracy, politicians from the northeast, and royalists—retained a fair amount of unity. All hoped to see constitutional government succeed, and all wanted to prevent a resurgence of military power. With his unexpected resignation, Khuang and his royalist supporters withdrew from the diverse and somewhat artificial Pridi-led coalition, and Thailand's first real political parties appeared.[10] Pridi supporters formed the Constitutional Front and Cooperative parties, and Khuang and other royalists established the Democrat Party. Although ideologically uninterested opportunists filled each party, real social differences divided the two sides. Aristocrats and royal family members hoping to restore the power and prestige of the monarchy dominated the Democrat Party. Khuang and party leaders Seni and Kukrit Pramoj all held large tracts of land and enjoyed ties with royalty. Commoners of often humble origins from the economically depressed northeast, on the other hand, held the most important positions in the Cooperative Party, the party closest to Pridi. Tiang Sirikhan, Chamlong Daoruang, Thawin Udom, and Thong-in Phuriphat, for example, all came from middle- or lower-class northeastern families.[11] For the moment, Khuang's departure posed little threat to Pridi. The August elections left the Cooperative Party with sixty-four seats and the Constitutional Front Party with thirty-one, giving Pridi's parties an absolute majority in the 178-seat Parliament and a ninety-five to sixty advantage over the Democrats.[12] But the long-term consequences for Pridi of the break with the royalist Democrats were serious. Although parliamentary divisions are natural, if not healthy, in developed democracies, in a country lacking both a tradition of a legal opposition and a housebroken military, the formation of any powerful opposition party posed dangers. An opposition party as irresponsible as the Democrats proved downright disastrous.

The split with Khuang also threatened Pridi personally. Until Khuang's resignation, Pridi had held only the position of special adviser to the government under the title of "senior statesman" *(ratthaburut awuso)*. In that capacity, he enjoyed the prestige of national leadership without having to involve himself in the dirty world of everyday politics. With his assumption of formal control of the government in March 1946, however, Pridi became personally identified with all the government's troubles, both small and large. Unfortunately for him, most turned out to be large.

The most immediate domestic difficulties facing Pridi were official corruption and inflation. Inflation had plagued Thailand since the war began, when financial demands from the Japanese occupation forces compelled the Thai treasury to print money recklessly. Having resisted the pressure in 1941 to lend money to the Japanese and increase the circulation of currency, Pridi bore no responsibility for the problem, but, in his more than two years in power after the war, he failed to control inflation.[13] His reputation for competence consequently suffered. Similarly, official corruption, though largely beyond his control, bedeviled Pridi's governments after the war. Partly the result of government efforts to sell rice below market value to Malaya, as demanded by the British, and partly due to the government's own ill-considered price controls and regulations, smuggling and illegal trafficking of rice proliferated. As profit-maximizing merchants and corrupt officials saw to it that grain found its way only to those buyers willing to pay more than the official rates, major towns suffered shortages. Worst of all for Pridi, Thongbleo Cholaphum, his close associate and head of the hopelessly corrupt and inefficient Food Distribution Organization, attracted most of the attention.[14] Corruption had long plagued Thailand, and the inflation that Pridi failed to curb was more the fault of Phibun and the Japanese than himself, but an increasingly vigorous press in a polarized political atmosphere ensured that these two problems weakened Pridi.

The mysterious death in June 1946 of King Ananda Mahidol added another weight for the unlucky Pridi to carry. Although the circumstances of the death, the result of a gunshot to the head suffered in the palace, have never been determined with certainty, from the beginning, the incident detracted from Pridi's reputation. Few believed the government's initial claim that the king had accidentally shot himself, and suspicions grew when a commission Pridi appointed ruled out accident as a cause of death. No credible evidence linking Pridi to the king's death exists, but the old assertion that Pridi held republican sympathies, because of his leadership in the 1932 coup, made him vulnerable on the issue. Khuang and the royalists blamed Pridi almost immediately. They spread rumors that Pridi was behind the tragedy, and the pro-Democrat newspaper, *Prachathipatai* (Democracy), criticized Pridi's handling of the investigation and the government's negligence in protecting the monarchy.[15] Seni and Kukrit Pramoj went to the U.S. embassy within hours of the incident to accuse Pridi of involvement.[16] In response, Pridi showed his own readiness to play political hardball. He declared a short state of emergency, censored the press attacks, and briefly arrested two editors and two opposition members of Parliament. In the end, though, the controversy forced Pridi to resign in favor of a supporter from the Constitutional Front Party, Thamrong Nawasawat (Rear Admiral *Luang* Thawan Thamrong-nawasawat).

As Pridi bungled this series of crises, a restless and bitter army confronted the civilian government with a more serious danger. The ouster of Phibun and his supporters in 1944 had brought the antimilitary forces only a respite. Though lacking a strong leader, the army remained powerful, and many soldiers were determined to regain their previous preeminence. Disgruntled officers resented troop cutbacks Pridi ordered in the postwar years and fumed over the humiliation of

Phibun, the man who had brought the army glory on the battlefield and massive budgets in the legislative chambers. Especially dangerous were those officers Pridi had forced into retirement along with Phibun in the last years of the war. Because the postwar inflation drastically reduced the purchasing power of their fixed pensions, these cashiered officers had special reason to dislike Pridi.[17] Throughout 1946 and the first months of 1947, their lack of organization and fear of a strong response from the Allies kept them quiet, but when the coup finally came in November 1947, the ex-officers would be the main instigators.

The first sign of trouble—and the first time since the war ended that the United States was called upon to block the military's return to power—came with Phibun's return to the political spotlight in March 1947. Although Phibun had vowed, after the government dropped war crimes charges against him in April 1946, to retire for good to private life, by the end of the year he and his supporters had begun to plot his comeback. On November 20, a newspaper he funded, *Si Krung,* called for a "savior" to lead Thailand from "impending catastrophe."[18] Two weeks later, *Liberty,* an English-language newspaper also associated with Phibun, quoted opposition members of Parliament returning from a Cambodian province Phibun had captured from the French as saying that the residents of the province sent their respects to Phibun and thanked him for giving them freedom. On December 21, *Si Krung* quoted a long-time Phibun underling, Mangkorn Phromyothi, as advocating a "coalition government."[19] The subject of his return thus broached indirectly, Phibun dropped his political bombshell in two statements given in March 1947. On March 19, in an interview with the Chinese-language newspaper *Kong Hor Por,* Phibun declared that he had to return to public life to clear his name of charges of treason and war crimes.[20] Then, five days later, he told five Thai-language newspapers that, to solve the country's economic problems, he planned to form a new political party, the Thammathipat Party.[21] Together, the two interviews created a sensation. While proarmy figures celebrated their hero's return, Pridi's forces organized a demonstration on April 7 to protest Phibun's plans.[22]

Phibun's announcements confronted the United States and Britain with a challenge. Phibun likely intended his statements as a trial balloon to determine not merely domestic but foreign attitudes toward his return to politics. A year and a half after the armistice, Thailand continued to be extremely vulnerable to outside pressure, and a resolute response from the powers, he realized, would have rendered a comeback difficult, if not impossible. The main body of twenty thousand British occupation forces had left Thailand four months earlier, but six hundred British troops remained to dispose of Japanese properties and repair damaged rail equipment.[23] The British could easily apply military pressure on the Burmese and Malayan borders. And allied economic sanctions, especially if involving an oil embargo, would put an immediate stranglehold on Thailand's economy. In the fluid and highly factious world of Thai politics, a mere word from the British or Americans, the foreign powers most capable of applying military pressure and economic sanctions, could quickly tip the balance of political power. All eyes, therefore, turned to the British and American embassies.

Phibun's interviews appalled the British and Americans. While in power, Phibun had entered an alliance with the Japanese, declared war on the Allies, and attacked British possessions. He had also expelled from the country the American-owned Standard Vacuum Oil Company (Standard Oil) and the partly British-owned Shell Oil Company and had initiated a program of economic nationalism that frightened Western businessmen almost as much as the Chinese it targeted.[24] Time had not healed old wounds. For the British and Americans, Phibun remained the militaristic dictator who had invaded neighboring countries. His return to power in 1947, the Americans and British believed, could only bring more of the same. Western businesses would once again be harassed, political dissent would be suppressed, and Thailand's neighbors would suffer renewed aggression. Under a second Phibun government, American Ambassador Edwin Stanton predicted in the immediate aftermath of the November coup, the ex-dictator's "old ultra-nationalist and anti-foreign policies [would] likely emerge."[25] The fragile structure of postwar agreements the British and Americans had worked so hard to build would thus collapse.

Both the United States and Great Britain, therefore, actively opposed Phibun's announced return to politics. The British were the first to respond, instructing their ambassador, Geoffrey Thompson, to tell Prime Minister Thamrong of the British government's displeasure with Phibun's plans. The Foreign Office hoped that Thamrong or Pridi would leak the contents of the conversation to the press, thus informing Phibun indirectly of British concerns. In the week following Phibun's announcement, Thompson warned Thamrong twice of the Foreign Office's continued hostility to Phibun.[26] The Americans acted more slowly, but, after Thompson's second visit, a State Department cable instructed Ambassador Stanton also to tell Pridi of U.S. opposition to a Phibun return.[27] The Thai press reported Thamrong's meetings with the westerners, showing that, as planned, either Pridi or Thamrong had told all to the press.[28]

Despite the similarity of the British and American démarches, the two allies had not coordinated closely. Ambassadors Thompson and Stanton approached Thamrong separately, with the United States moving only after Thompson had met the prime minister twice. And although the British Information Service announced on March 28 that "it is not forgotten . . . that it was under the leadership of the ex-dictator [Phibun] that Siam declared war on British and American democracies," the United States maintained a public silence.[29]

In the next three weeks, the cracks in the Anglo-American united front against Phibun widened. Because Pridi requested stronger measures from the Allies, the Foreign Office began a campaign to persuade the Americans to take "parallel action" to block Phibun's return. On April 5, Hubert Graves of the British embassy in Washington pressed Kenneth Landon and Abbot Low Moffat of the State Department's Southeast Asian Division either to help publicize surreptitiously British and American disapproval of Phibun or to agree to issue a joint official communication stating explicitly Anglo-American concerns. Landon and Moffat, however, refused, telling Graves that the meetings between Thamrong and the two ambassadors had already had the desired effect.[30] Ten days later, Graves approached Moffat and Landon a second time, but, once again, Landon and Moffat rebuffed him.[31] Only after the first secretary of the U.S. embassy in London, Everett Drumright, refused them a third time did the British realize the cause was lost.[32]

The divergence in the British and American responses to Phibun's return reflected fundamental differences in attitudes toward Thailand and Southeast Asia. For the British, the Southeast Asian mainland held critical economic importance. Before the war, Britain had relied on proceeds from the sale of rubber and tin from its colony, Malaya, to the United States to balance its dollar accounts. The British home islands consistently ran large trade deficits with the United States in the prewar years, but the sale of Malayan rubber and tin alone compensated for almost half of the metropolis' deficits.[33] Although the war disrupted production, the importance of the trade to Britain increased in the postwar years. With the so-called dollar gap—a shortage of dollars caused by trade imbalances with the United States—blocking efforts to rehabilitate Britain's postwar economy, London looked to revival of Malayan rubber and tin sales to solve the country's trade woes. "While the Labour government imposed austerity at home," historian Andrew Rotter explains, "the British lavished effort and money on their Southeast Asian colony of Malaya in an attempt to reconstruct triangular trade [with the United States]."[34]

Thailand—and Pridi—lay at the heart of these plans. Britain depended on Thai and Burmese rice to feed Malayan rubber and tin workers. The Foreign Office feared that, if Phibun came to power, he would disrupt the rice procurement scheme drawn up with such difficulty by Thamrong and the British in December 1946. More expensive Thai rice would then raise the cost of production of Malayan tin and rubber and possibly create unrest in the colony. British officials also worried about prospects of including Thailand in a general defense system London was contemplating for the region. Because of Phibun's history of militarism and aggression, the British feared that a Phibun government would thwart the scheme. They confronted the prospect of his return with the deepest concern.[35]

Because the United States maintained no such special interests in mainland Southeast Asia, the Americans could view the matter of Phibun's comeback with composure. The United States had never possessed colonies in mainland Southeast Asia, and it traded little with the countries of the region other than Malaya and the Philippines. The development of an artificial rubber industry in the United States during World War II reduced the importance of even the Malayan trade. In Thailand itself, the U.S. presence was small. Until the war, Washington paid meager attention to the country, and, through the 1940s, American missionaries and philanthropic workers outnumbered U.S. officials there.[36] Trade between the two countries remained modest. Both Singapore and Hong Kong accounted for larger shares of Thailand's foreign commerce than the United States, and trade with the British empire as a whole was more than three times that of Thailand's trade with the United States.[37] In 1947—before the fall of China, the Korean War, and the appearance of the domino theory—American interests and concerns were focused on other areas. Europe, Japan, China, Latin America, and the Middle East all attracted more attention from U.S. policymakers than Southeast Asia, and the resulting lack of direction from higher-ranking officials blocked all attempts to set a well-defined, coordinated Southeast Asia policy. Within Southeast Asia itself, Thailand ranked in importance below the Philippines and Indonesia and no higher than Indochina. The most that senior State Department officials such as Secretary of State George C. Marshall and Under Secretary of State Dean Acheson hoped for from Thailand was that it would stay as quiet as possible. They resisted any involvement in its internal affairs.

Senior officials' lack of interest in Thailand created a unique situation within the State Department. In making policy concerning the other countries of the region, the newly formed Division of Southeast

Asian Affairs had to contend with the Office of European Affairs' advocacy of the colonial interests of America's European allies. French specialists in the European office fought Southeast Asian Division officials sympathetic to Indochinese nationalists, and Dutch specialists resisted division recommendations to support Indonesian independence forces. But Southeast Asian Division officials involved with Thailand, the only country in the region the Europeans had never colonized, faced no such constraints. Neither closely supervised by their superiors nor challenged by the Europeanists, these officials set policy toward Thailand as they saw fit.[38]

Although their perspective differed from that of higher-ranking State Department officials, the officers of the Southeast Asia Division also opposed strong measures to block Phibun's return. The necessity, if the United States were to take a firm stand, to coordinate more closely with the British concerned them the most. During the war, President Roosevelt and officials from the Office of Far Eastern Affairs had considered promoting decolonization in Southeast Asia.[39] In Thailand, this policy resulted in a number of clashes with the British. The two secret services, the oss and the British Special Operations Executive, competed for influence with the Thai resistance, the State Department and the Foreign Office argued over whether to treat postwar Thailand as a defeated enemy or a Japanese conquest, and the British resisted American pressure to disavow any intention to take back more land after the war than Thailand had captured. Although the need to placate and strengthen the United States' noncommunist European allies led the State Department after the war to soften its anticolonial stance in other parts of the region, with regard to always-independent Thailand, the policy continued in force. During the peace settlement talks, the United States negotiated directly with the Thai prime minister behind the backs of the British.[40] After the settlement had been signed, the United States sided with the Thais in disputes over revision of the agreement. Then, in the year that followed, the United States rebuffed British proposals to set up a joint U.S.–Great Britain military mission in Bangkok.[41]

The refusal to have Ambassadors Stanton and Thompson meet Thamrong together, to issue a joint communique, or to deliver a joint letter arose from this long-standing policy. As long as high-ranking policymakers were unwilling to expand American influence in Thailand, cooperation with Great Britain could only help the British regain their position of prewar predominance in the country. By avoiding entanglements, the officials responsible for the United States' Southeast

Asia policy at once preserved the United States' reputation for anticolonialism and kept the door open for future American advances in Thailand. It is thus not surprising that, as one American official commented, "the Foreign Office takes a rather more serious view of the possibility of Pibul's [Phibun's] return to power than does the [State] Department."[42]

As it turned out, Phibun was thwarted despite American caution. The British had responded firmly, and, equally important, the domestic reaction disappointed him. While Phibun probably expected that Pridiites would oppose his return, he clearly hoped that Khuang's Democrat Party would line up behind him. Indeed, on March 22, Khuang publicly backed Phibun's attempt to clear his name.[43] But the party's royalists still resented Phibun for having jailed a number of them in the Tarutao Island prison after the 1939 crackdown on his political opponents. Party leaders Seni and Kukrit Pramoj and Sor Sethabut (author of a famous Thai-English dictionary and former Tarutao prisoner) thus strongly objected in press interviews to Phibun's intentions.[44] Khuang then had to retract his statement of support for Phibun.[45] Denied domestic support and taken aback by the swift British reprimand, Phibun returned to his previous obscurity. In a March 30 interview, he disavowed any desire for political office.[46]

Nonetheless, American disengagement from the dispute boosted Phibun's prospects. As helpful as Stanton may have considered his single meeting with Thamrong, American determination to act independently vitiated its effect. The U.S. refusal to warn Phibun publicly showed Phibun and dissident army officers that American opposition to him had limits. Then, the Americans' aloofness from their wartime ally gave Phibun and army officers the impression that they could profitably play the Americans off the British, as Pridi had done when negotiating the peace settlement. Although Stanton believed that Phibun's silence indicated that the two ambassadors' démarches had persuaded the field marshal to abandon politics, subsequent events proved him wrong. Phibun had made his announcement not so much to clear the path for the immediate formation of a political party as to test the waters and determine probable domestic and foreign responses to his return. The message the Americans sent soothed him. It signaled that they would resist, but not too much. The future consequences of this cautious policy were profound. One Foreign Office official ruefully commented after the November coup that, because of their foot-dragging during the March crisis, "the Americans (including Mr. Stanton) bear some responsibility for the Marshal's emergence now."[47]

In the months following Phibun's short return to the political limelight, Pridi reached out again to the Americans for help in his long-standing effort to tame the military and again was rejected. His strategy, unchanged since Phibun's ouster in 1944, centered on strengthening control over armed forces traditionally opposed to his main adversaries, Phibun and the army, and on increasing his influence in the army itself. He hoped that evidence of American support for his government would aid the processes.

Pridi struck his first alliance with the navy. With its emphasis on technical expertise, the navy had long attracted a more patrician officer corps than the army, and a deep-seated rivalry developed between the two services in the prewar years. When World War II divided the ranks of the ruling clique, the navy sided with Pridi against the army's champion, Phibun. In return, Pridi not only spared the navy from troop cutbacks in the postwar years but also funneled to the navy many of the modern arms the oss had provided for the fight against Japan. While the army's budget plummeted by 40 percent from 1944 to 1946, the navy's outlays increased by 50 percent.[48] Since the navy thus came to possess more advanced weaponry and better-trained forces than the army, the admirals' friendship with Pridi added considerably to his governments' stability. For several years, the navy helped check army ambitions to oust him.[49]

Pridi's other power base lay in the Free Thai. Although ostensibly an anti-Japanese organization, ever since its formation by students in England and the United States in early 1942, the Free Thai attracted those elements of Thai society most at odds with Phibun and the army. Aristocrats and princes angered by Phibun's execution and imprisonment of royalists in 1939, reformist northeastern politicians opposed to excessive military budgets, navy officers smarting over the army's recent ascendancy, and former students of Pridi from the university he founded and taught at, Thammasat University, all flocked to the Free Thai banner. Although he first lacked clear command of the Free Thai, by the end of the war Pridi had managed to use his intimacy with the former Thammasat students—many now in the bureaucracy—and his looser connections with the navy and northeastern politicians to assert his control over the organization. After the war, he continued to manipulate the Free Thai. Although he disbanded the forces, instead of distributing to the army the weapons the oss had provided, he held the arms in stockpiles under his command.[50] Stanton believed that Pridi hoped to broaden the Free Thai's political role. In a speech on Peace Proclamation Day in August, Stanton noted, Pridi "repeated five times that the Free Thai Party included not only those persons directly involved in the wartime underground but all sincere Siamese patriots as well." "In effect," Stanton commented, "he [Pridi] was opening the door for expansion" to all interested in supporting him politically. Although the Free Thai lacked the organization and discipline to threaten the army militarily, it represented a significant political force.[51]

But Pridi was playing a dangerous game, and he knew it. Though well-armed, the navy and Free Thai were dispersed and based largely upcountry. Thailand, at the time, functioned as a city-state. To a large extent, whoever controlled Bangkok, controlled the country. The army's First Division maintained—as it has up to this day—the largest number of troops in the city. By favoring so conspicuously the army's rivals, therefore, Pridi was antagonizing even further the most important military force in the country.

To neutralize the threat from the army, Pridi tried, in succession, two separate approaches. In his first effort, he tried to assume control of the army from within. He appointed Lt. Gen. Sinat Yotharak commander of the army in 1944 (Police General Adun Detcharat replaced Sinat in July 1946) and in 1945 named Rear Adm. Sangworn Suwannachip as police chief and adjutant general of the armed forces. Both belonged to the Free Thai. Forced retirements of Phibun supporters followed, and Pridi men were placed in midranking positions.[52] Although such measures kept the army in submission through 1946, in the long term they failed to win Pridi control of it. Officers resented the appointment of outsiders to leading positions, and the purge of Phibun supporters never reached deep enough to restructure the forces. Active as well as inactive officers remained restless and dangerous. In 1947, therefore, Pridi modified his tactics. Now, instead of merely hitting army officers with the stick, he also showed them the carrot. The navy and Free Thai, as before, supplied the stick. U.S. military aid would now provide the carrot.

The political impact of American aid almost certainly occupied most of Pridi's attention at this time. The Thai army, then as afterward, behaved as much more of a political institution than a fighting force. Recognizing this basic fact of Thai political life, Pridi never, up to that time, took an interest in improving the army's military effectiveness. Instead, he dealt with the army strictly on political terms, trying to assert his control over it with crippling purges of senior officers and budget cuts. Similarly, in the spring of 1947, just as the threat from the army was increasing, Pridi could never have considered American arms assistance as a purely military issue. The impact on his own standing with this powerful and eminently political institution would clearly out-

weigh any effect on the forces' military effectiveness. Indeed, exploitation of American military aid for personal political purposes would
remain one of the dominant themes of the U.S.-Thai relationship long
after Pridi's exit from the scene.

American military assistance offered Pridi clear and undeniable
political benefits. Much of the officers' dissatisfaction arose from the
army's international isolation and poor equipment. Accustomed to
close contacts with the armed forces of the great powers and possessing
the best weapons in the land, the army found itself after the war treated
with circumspection by the Allies and holding outdated, inadequate
weapons. Were Pridi able to secure military aid from the United States,
he could solve this morale problem and soothe disgruntled officers.
Contacts with American military officers administering the aid and training would reduce the army's feelings of isolation, and new weapons
would ease resentment of the navy. Pridi could then present himself to
the army as the man who delivered the Americans. A symbol of U.S.
support for Pridi personally, military aid would make officers who
hoped to rebuild the army think twice before mounting a coup. Thus,
in April 1947—just one month after Phibun had announced his plans
for a comeback—Pridi instructed Col. Khab Kunchorn, a Free Thai acting as military attaché to Washington, to ask the Americans about establishing a U.S. military training program in Thailand. Implicit in the
proposal was that the U.S. would also provide arms.[53]

The Americans never responded. Lower-ranking officials believed
the United States should accommodate Pridi, and, soon after Khab
presented Pridi's proposal, Southeast Asian Division Assistant Chief
Landon advised the State-War-Navy Coordinating Committee to send a
training mission to Thailand. Landon recognized the political importance of the request. If the training mission were sent, he argued in a
memorandum to the committee, "American influence would be increased in Siam and indeed in all Southeast Asia and the American
democratic point of view would be impressed on forces which have
been used in the past to support a totalitarian form of government."[54]
Rear Adm. Arthur Davis, senior member of the Joint Strategic Survey
Committee of the Joint Chiefs of Staff, agreed. While offering few military benefits, the establishment of a training mission, he commented,
might earn political returns. But, despite Davis' and Landon's interest
in Pridi's project, inertia higher up killed it. Concerned primarily with
the problem of protecting and rebuilding Europe, the Coordinating
Committee never discussed Landon's memorandum.[55]

Pridi once more appealed to the United States for aid, but again got nothing. In separate meetings in Washington in early October—just a month before the coup—Foreign Minister Atthakit Phanomyong, Pridi's half-brother, informed first the new under secretary of state, Robert Lovett, and then Secretary of State George Marshall that the Thai government wanted to reorganize the army according to American principles and reequip itself with American arms. Atthakit asked the United States to send an adviser to Bangkok to assist the Thais in the endeavor. As with the earlier proposal for a training mission, implicit in his request was that the United States would also help reequip the army. Marshall told Atthakit that the United States "would carefully consider" the matter but never acted.[56] Just a month later, Pridi was overthrown.

U.S. reluctance to send arms and a training mission, like the earlier refusal to strongly oppose Phibun's return, hurt Pridi. To be sure, the stand, by itself, did not determine the outcome of the political struggle. As matters stood in 1947, the United States would never have provided more than modest arms aid, and even that would have come slowly. The Thais, moreover, never pursued the matter with determination. An agreement to help train and equip the army, however, would have placed the country's military relations with the Allies, for the first time since the war, on a stable basis, a major consideration in a country as vulnerable to foreign pressure as postwar Thailand. The military wanted badly to replace its outdated arsenal with weapons provided by the world's premier military power. Had the United States provided a small measure of arms and training along with the promise of more to come pending good behavior on the part of the army, critically important, but young, wavering officers, such as the commander of the First Regiment of the army's powerful First Division, Sarit Thanarat, and Thanom Kittikachorn, commander of the Officers' School, might have chosen not to jeopardize their careers and the army's future in a risky coup attempt. An American commitment to provide arms aid and military training, therefore, could have rendered the coup-makers' task more difficult.

When the American response to Pridi's request for aid is viewed alongside the most important component of America's Thai policy in 1947—the courtship by the diplomats in the field of the Democrats, the major opposition party—the U.S. rebuff of Pridi acquires added significance. As with the Americans' mild response to Phibun's March announcements, this support for the Democrats arose out of the competition with Great Britain for influence in the country.

Britain, for years, had maintained close relations with Pridi. Before the war, British embassy officials displayed their favor for Pridi over the more pro-Japanese Phibun, and the British financial adviser to the Thai treasury, William Doll, developed an intimate friendship with Pridi, then minister of finance.[57] Under Doll's influence, Pridi resisted Phibun's attempts before the war to tie the Thai currency to the dollar instead of sterling.[58] During the war, Pridi cooperated extensively with the British Special Operations Executive in underground activities, and in the peace talks after the war, the British negotiated over the head of the nominal prime minister, Seni Pramoj, directly with their favorite, Pridi.[59] Doll returned to the Thai treasury after the Japanese departure, exerting, as before, considerable influence over both Thai and British officials.

The Americans, on the other hand, developed ties in the years leading up to 1947 with Khuang Aphaiwong and Seni, another future leader of the Democrats and the very man Pridi and the British had offended by bypassing in the peace negotiations. The Americans first got to know Seni, a relative of the royal family with a law degree from Oxford, when he was appointed minister to the United States in 1939. During the war, American officials and Seni cooperated closely. Seni told the Americans that Phibun's January 1942 declaration of war on the Allies was unconstitutional and, in the years that followed, helped the OSS organize Free Thai forces in the United States. After the war, Pridi brought Seni back to Thailand to serve as prime minister because of his connections with the Americans. Then, when the British began negotiating directly with Pridi during the peace talks, the United States encouraged Seni to take a harder line in negotiations with Lord Mountbatten than Pridi was. After Seni helped his brother, Kukrit Pramoj, and Khuang Aphaiwong establish the Democrat Party in 1946, the United States found him a useful friend.

Khuang, in the meantime, fell under the influence of Walter Kahn, American policy member of the Anglo-American Rice Commission, the body charged with regulating Thailand's postwar rice sales. Kahn quickly gained favor with the Thais for his efforts to loosen enforcement of the rice reparations agreements. Khuang, because of his position in 1946 as both prime minister and minister of commerce, worked especially closely with Kahn. Almost immediately, Kahn assumed the role of Khuang's most trusted foreign economic adviser, and, through Kahn, the Americans got to know and respect Khuang.[60]

American support for the Democrats, at first uncertain and based solely on such personal connections, deepened in 1946 and 1947 as commercial competition with Great Britain intensified. In 1947, Britain remained, as it had been for almost a century, the dominant economic power in Thailand. Although a much stronger currency and economy backed American businessmen, the British still enjoyed a number of advantages. The large British firms dwarfed all American operations in the country other than Standard Oil, and American entrepreneurs—most newcomers—lacked the experience, capital, and connections of well-established British companies. British colonies, moreover, were better placed geographically than the United States to provide the cheap consumer goods Thailand needed. Most important, the British empire's domination of the Thai export trade created a surplus of sterling and shortage of dollars that made it easy for the Thais to buy British but difficult to buy American goods. American businessmen in the postwar years, nonetheless, were making advances. In 1941, only one American firm other than oil company agents did business in Thailand; in the three years after the war, the number increased to thirty. The number of American businessmen in the country, in the meantime, mushroomed from several dozen to more than three hundred.[61] Although this burgeoning trade with Thailand remained too small to catch Washington's eye, U.S. officials in the field worked hard to promote it. British and Americans in Thailand, as a result, came to see each other as commercial rivals.

Troubles arose between the United States and Britain when their embassies began manipulating the domestic political process to their respective economic advantages. The Americans, represented, in effect, by Kahn, got the ball rolling. Kahn, in his capacity as Prime Minister Khuang's informal adviser, recommended that, as part of the process of freeing Thailand's trade, Khuang loosen government control over the country's foreign commerce and allow domestic demand, not the government's financial status, to determine Thailand's imports. At the time, the Finance Ministry carefully managed the country's trade. Keeping a close eye on the country's capital accounts, the ministry made sure to direct purchases toward those areas dealing in the currencies Thailand held. As most Thai exports went to the sterling bloc, the ministry's policy demanded that most imports likewise come from sterling countries. Kahn, however, recommended reversing the equation and making material needs determine financial policy. He suggested that Thailand purchase goods from whichever source provided the best deal and then direct rice, rubber, and tin sales to those source countries to acquire the necessary currency. This "economic budget," as Kahn and Khuang called the plan, coincided neatly with American policies and interests. If the Thais were to consider prices, delivery dates, and favorable credit arrangements instead of the treasury's foreign currency reserves, the nearly bankrupt British would find it hard to compete with well-financed American corporations in supplying major capital goods such as iron, steel, and railroad equipment, and American exports to Thailand would increase. Khuang, convinced by the force of Kahn's argument, embraced the plan.[62]

Khuang lasted in office only about a month, however, before Pridi assumed the prime ministership and the British had their turn at manipulating economic policy. With Pridi in command again, Finance Ministry adviser William Doll took over from Kahn as the dominant foreign economic and financial influence. Close to Foreign Office officials and dedicated to promoting trade with Britain, Doll acted as much as a British commercial officer as an employee of the Thai government. Throughout the late 1940s, he recommended to Pridi policies favorable to British interests. Doll antagonized the Americans most when he persuaded the Finance Ministry to ignore Kahn's plan and hold the country's meager dollar earnings in reserve instead of releasing them for public expenditure. Although one possible way to bolster the government's weakened financial position, the measure, as Doll and the Americans realized, further inhibited Thai purchases of American products. U.S. embassy officials urged the government to abandon the policy, but Doll's influence with Pridi and the Finance Ministry thwarted the Americans. Doll's daily intellectual exchanges with Pridi before the war and Britain's years of political support for the "senior statesman" thus paid dividends. The British adviser's ascendancy marked the beginning of the Americans' estrangement from Pridi.[63]

In frustration, the U.S. embassy turned to Khuang and the Democrats. Realizing that the shortage of American currency represented the main obstacle to increased U.S. exports, Stanton began pressing the Thais in 1947 to reverse Doll's policy of conserving dollars. Since Pridi continued to support the British position, Stanton moved closer to the Americans' old friends, Khuang and Seni Pramoj and their anti-Pridi party, the Democrats. As Britain's Ambassador Thompson put it, Stanton favored the Democrats because "it is believed here that the [D]emocrats would be more ready than the politicians at present in office to twist the lion's tail."[64]

Previous studies have failed to recognize American preference for the Democrat Party in 1947. Instead, scholars have emphasized America's admiration for Pridi. Arlene Becker Neher, author of the most detailed study of U.S.-Thai relations in the late 1940s, has argued that, largely because of the influence of former oss officers, U.S. policy stood solidly behind Pridi. Several ex-oss officers, Neher notes, opened businesses in Bangkok after the war, and others entered the Foreign Service. "Because so many of the Americans who were involved in Thai affairs—both the officials and the private citizens—had had associations with the Free Thai during the war," Neher comments, many American diplomats and policymakers were pro-Pridi and anti-Phibun.[65]

But Neher exaggerates the influence of former oss officers such as Alexander MacDonald, founder of the English-language newspaper the *Bangkok Post;* James Thompson, famed Thai silk manufacturer; and Willis Bird, owner of an import-export firm. They represented only one segment of a now three-hundred-strong American business community in Bangkok. The more numerous non-oss businessmen, such as William Davis and Ray Derrick, partners of Phibun's son-in-law, Rak Panyarachun, lacked, for the most part, personal ties to Pridi. The law firm of William Donovan, wartime chief of the oss, advised the Pridi governments on the postwar territorial dispute with France, but Donovan did not exert much influence at the time over U.S. Thai policy. The two officials alleged to have propagated oss attitudes toward Pridi in the State Department, Southeast Asia Division Assistant Chief Kenneth Landon and Dwight Bulkley, vice-consul in Bangkok, actually played ambiguous roles in developing American policy. Landon, stationed throughout the war in the Washington offices of the oss and State Department, admired Pridi but never stood up strongly for him. Bulkley, occupying a low-ranking position, also failed to support Pridi. The few surviving examples of Bulkley's thinking on the matter reveal that he preferred Phibun to Pridi by mid-1948.[66]

Most important, the men directly responsible for the conduct of day-to-day policy in Thailand, Stanton and senior embassy officials, began their involvement with Thailand only after the war. Although Stanton shared the oss officers' abhorrence of Phibun, the Pridi Stanton knew was the sponsor of several increasingly corrupt and inefficient governments, not the heroic wartime leader of the Free Thai. Stanton felt no sympathy, he said after the coup, for the many Pridi associates "who, by their public acts have done much to lessen the high esteem in which Pridi was held two years ago."[67] The liberal but strongly anticommunist Stanton also suspected that Pridi might seek communist support for his governments. Stanton especially distrusted the "admittedly socialist" Cooperative Party, Pridi's closest political ally, for its support for the communist-influenced Central Labor Union.[68] The Democrats, on the other hand, Stanton considered genuinely committed to free-market principles.[69]

Beginning in late 1946, Stanton began pushing for a more prominent political role for Seni, Khuang, and the Democrat Party. Although Stanton never explicitly mentioned his support for the Democrats in his dispatches, possibly indicating that he was acting without instructions from Washington, the subject appeared regularly in British correspondence. "It is the darling ambition of the Americans," Ambassador Thompson complained in April 1947, "that the Democrats headed by the latter [Khuang] and Seni Pramoj should form a Government."[70] "Ever since he [Stanton] arrived in Siam," Thompson later added, "he has made a point of cultivating the Democrats, who are the pro-American group here." In both telegrams, Thompson claimed that the Americans would welcome even a Phibun government if it included the Democrats. A. M. Turner of the Foreign Office's Southeast Asia Department worried that, since the United States "apparently would do almost anything to help them [Democrats] back into Government," the "pro-British" Thamrong government would fall.[71]

As long as Khuang and the Democrats remained committed to the parliamentary process, Stanton's involvement with the party caused little harm, but, as the year progressed, evidence accumulated that Phibun and Khuang had struck a deal. For almost a year, the Democrats and army supporters had cooperated in Parliament, and, as early as the spring of 1947, rumors appeared that Phibun and Khuang had decided to oust Pridi and Thamrong. In March, Khuang had given his support for Phibun's effort to explain his wartime policies.[72] Then, in the late summer, several months after a Democrat-sponsored no-confidence motion failed in Parliament, Khuang began to woo Phibun more openly. In an August 9 interview with *Thai Ratsadorn,* Khuang declared approvingly, "I think Field Marshal P. Phibunsongkhram [Phibun] will definitely return to politics."[73] From that point on, the two met frequently.[74] Although Phibun remained on the sidelines, it was clear to Thais and westerners alike that Khuang and Phibun were considering an alliance against Pridi.

The British—and Pridi—viewed American support for Khuang with consternation. Pridi worried, he told the British naval attaché, that the Americans were "so openly and strongly backing Kuang [Khuang] . . . [that they were] giving indirect support to Pibul [Phibun]." At a "Society Ball" in July, Pridi reminded the attaché, Ambassador and Mrs. Stanton had made a point of sitting on the dais next to Khuang and Madame Phibun.[75] The British agreed with Pridi that the situation was disturbing and noted in addition that American politicking was aimed not only at civilians. "The American Military Attaché," Thompson complained, "is working very hard and with considerable success in Siamese army circles, where there is not only a lot of sympathy for PIBUL [Phibun], but also appreciable hostility towards ourselves."[76] The British, like Pridi, smelled a conspiracy. When the coup finally came in November, they blamed the Americans.

In one sense, Pridi and the British overreacted. Events proved wrong the British belief that a Phibun government including Khuang and Seni would please the United States. Even though the November coup brought Khuang into the prime minister's office, the Americans protested the army's actions. The Americans' fondness for Khuang, it turned out, only went so far. No evidence indicates that any Americans ever announced public support for Khuang. Stanton apparently never went beyond displaying it informally, as he had at the Society Ball.

But, in a country where personal or political conflict is rarely expressed openly, gestures carry weight. Stanton's display of favoritism for the Democrats signaled to all concerned that the Americans would accept or even applaud Pridi's replacement by Khuang. Coming at the same time as the U.S. rejection of Pridi's request for military aid and refusal to take a stronger stand against Phibun's political resurrection, Stanton's involvement in Thai domestic politics impressed potential coup-makers with the lack of American resolve. The Americans would verbally oppose a military coup, the events of the past year taught Thais, but would shy away from the joint measures with the British required to thwart it. Although the United States would protest Phibun's return, it would welcome Pridi's fall. The message the Americans sent was ambiguous, but struck with force. In effect, they told potential coup-makers that they could overthrow Pridi's elected government with impunity.

Chapter Two

KHUANG AND THE COUP,

NOVEMBER 1947–APRIL 1948

The November 9, 1947, coup was a coup of the army. The Coup Group *(khana ratthaprahan),* as it came to be known, consisted of about forty junior army officers led by a small number of commanding officers.[1] Officers Pridi had forced into retirement after the war—men with little other than conspiracy to keep themselves occupied—were most prominent. Several had served during World War II in the Shan States of Burma, where they were left after the war largely to fend for themselves. The hardships they experienced in their retreat to Thailand left them embittered at the man they held responsible, Pridi Phanomyong.

The key figures in the Coup Group were Lt. Gen. Phin Chunhawan (*Luang* Chamnan Yutthasat), Col. Phao Siyanon, Col. Kat Katsongkhram (Thian Keng-radomying), and Col. Sarit Thanarat. Phin, a relatively obscure general until he appeared as chief of the Coup Group, had led the troops occupying the Shan States of Burma during World War II. He had never held political office. Col. Phao Siyanon, though not a senior member of the Coup Group, played a major role because of his personal connections. A long-time aide and close associate of Phibun and married to Phin's daughter, Phao was responsible for maintaining contacts with Phibun. Because of such ties—and American favor—Phao would later become one of the two or three most powerful men in the country. Kat Katsongkhram, unlike Phin, had a long history of political involvement, including participation in the 1932 "revolution" and service as Phibun's deputy minister of finance in 1942–1943. Kat was probably the primary instigator of the coup and, after its success, was the Coup Group's most politically active member. Col. Sarit Thanarat, on the other hand, preferred a low political profile but was possibly the only indispensable member of the Coup Group. Because Kat, Phin, Phao, and other cashiered Coup Group officers commanded no troops, the participation of Sarit's critically important, Bangkok-based First Regiment of the First Division was crucial to the coup's success. Like Phin, Sarit had served in the Shan States during the war. And, like Phao, he was a rising star.

Phibun's role in the coup was limited. When planning the coup, the Coup Group, represented by Phao, prodded Phibun to join them, promising him command of the army. Even three years after his ouster, Phibun—the man who had defeated the French and obtained ever larger budgets for the military—enjoyed the respect of both soldiers and a great many civilians. The coup-makers, lacking anyone of distinction within their own ranks, hoped that Phibun could attract the support of army elements outside of the Coup Group. Phibun, however, refused Phao's offers. Although Phao informed him of the plans for the coup, Phibun neither joined the Coup Group nor seems to have participated in the preparations for the coup. In the days leading up to Thamrong's overthrow, Phibun tried to block any use of force, and, once that failed, he withstood pressure to associate himself with the coup until after the Coup Group had already attained effective control of the capital. On November 6, two days before the conspirators acted, Phibun informed Prime Minister Thamrong that a coup was in the making and advised him to resign in favor of the present army commander, Gen. Adun Detcharat. Phibun, according to the proposal, would assume command of the army, and the coup would be rendered unnecessary.[2] But Thamrong ignored Phibun's warning. Although he told Phibun that the government planned to resign on November 11, Thamrong apparently hoped merely to form a new government himself. Not until 6:00 P.M. November 8 did Thamrong and Pridi agree to hand over the prime ministership to Adun, and, by then, it was too late. That night, the coup began. Although his efforts to forestall the coup had failed, Phibun continued to resist the Coup Group's overtures. Only on the morning of November 9, after the Coup Group's forces had routed the opposition, did Phibun agree to assume the position of commander-in-chief of the army.[3]

Whether Phibun opposed the coup so long out of respect for the constitution or a preference to come to power on his own, his aloofness had serious consequences for his political standing. Despite the importance of his support for the Coup Group, his status as an outsider left him after the coup in a position of dependence on the coup-makers, a weakness he struggled with long afterward. Indeed, in his nine subsequent years as prime minister, he never overcame the handicap.

The coup, when it finally came, did not proceed exactly as planned, but succeeded. Although Adun had earlier informed Maj. Chatchai Chunhawan, a tank commander in the cavalry and son of Phin Chunhawan, that he would support the coup, when he succeeded in convincing Thamrong the night of November 8 to resign in his favor, Adun decided to resist. Adun then sped about Bangkok urging troops and officers to remain loyal to the government, while Thamrong, police chief Sangworn, and Pridi eluded the Coup Group's attempts to capture them. Despite these hitches, the Coup Group attained its objectives without bloodshed. Adun failed to keep the troops in the barracks, and, by dawn the following morning, the Coup Group's troops and tanks had occupied all the strategic points in the city. Phibun agreed within hours to assume command of the army.[4]

Although the coup leaders had succeeded militarily, their alliance with Phibun increased the threat of a strong Western response to the coup. The country's new leaders would have feared trade sanctions most, but even a firm statement from the great powers condemning the new government and calling for Thamrong's return to office could have galvanized opposition to the Coup Group. The coup had succeeded not so much due to the strength of the Coup Group as from the failure of Pridi's traditional supporters to come to Thamrong's defense. Partly because of their disenchantment with the corruption and inefficiency of Pridi's governments, partly because of their own ambitions and sense of caution, Adun, Adm. Sin (Sinthu) Songkhramchai, head of the navy, and Rear Adm. Thahan Khamhiran, commander of the marines, refrained from using force to resist the coup. Had the British and Americans strongly backed the return of Pridi and Thamrong, Adun, the navy, and the marines might have joined the Free Thai in trying to oust the new government.

To strengthen this weak diplomatic position, Phin and Kat persuaded Khuang and several of his Democrat allies to form the new government. Because of his high standing with the U.S. embassy, Khuang could help blunt any opposition from Britain or France, Phin and Kat must have reasoned. London and Paris, as one Foreign Office official put it, "can do [nothing on their own] but await American views."[5] In the negotiations with Khuang, therefore, the Coup Group gave in to all of his demands. Although many considered him a buffoon for his penchant for telling inappropriate jokes on inopportune occasions, Khuang took uncompromising positions in his political dealings. In the negotiations with the Coup Group, he insisted on and received a free hand in all political matters and assembled a cabinet of his own making. Selecting a large number of princes and aristocrats—many were former officials of the ancien régime—he excluded all Coup Group members from the new government. Khuang clearly intended to be nobody's puppet. This being the case, all turned their attention to the Americans.

Lack of interest higher up left it to just two Americans, Ambassador Edwin Stanton and Southeast Asian Division Assistant Chief Kenneth Landon, to determine the U.S. response to the coup. Never much interested in Thailand, Marshall and high-ranking Office of Far Eastern Affairs officials were not about to start interfering in the Southeast Asian Division's business in late 1947, when more important problems in Japan, China, the Middle East, and Europe continued to demand their attention. After division Chief Abbot Low Moffat, the other officer familiar with Thailand, was transferred to Greece shortly before the coup, Landon found himself alone among Washington-based officials in developing a response to the upheaval in Thailand.[6] Landon, by extension, relied heavily on the advice and reporting of Stanton, the one other senior official involved in Thai affairs. Landon let Stanton decide several important policy issues.

Though working together closely, Landon and Stanton came to their jobs with quite different backgrounds. Landon, a State Department official but not a member of the Foreign Service, had studied Thai language and culture ever since he first went to the country as a missionary in 1927. In the late 1930s and early 1940s, after ten years of missionary work in Thailand, he returned to the United States to earn a doctoral degree in comparative religions and wrote two books on Thai politics and society.[7] Several months before Pearl Harbor, he took a position as an analyst for the oss. He then transferred in 1943 to the State Department, where he stayed after the war's conclusion. Landon remained the department's premier Thai specialist into the early 1950s. Stanton, on the other hand, had come to Thai affairs only recently. A career Foreign Service officer, Stanton started out as a sinologist, serving in China for twenty years. Until he arrived in Bangkok as minister in June 1946 (his status was upgraded to ambassador in March 1947), he had little knowledge of Thailand. His outlook differed from Landon's, but not as their vocations might suggest. Landon, the former missionary, took a pragmatic approach to Thai politics and U.S. foreign policy. He was quick to recognize the limits of American influence and based his decisions on hard political realities. On the other hand, Stanton, the career diplomat, viewed matters with a moralistic bent. He became emotionally involved with his work and took failures of his diplomacy as personal rebukes. A strong sense of right and wrong infused his dispatches. Possibly, his own upbringing in a missionary family influenced his approach. But, although Stanton's and Landon's dispositions differed, the two men shared a deep personal involvement with Thailand that extended to their wives. Landon's wife, Margaret, also a former missionary, wrote the book that inspired the hit Broadway musical about Thailand's King Mongkut, *The King and I*.[8] Stanton's wife, Josephine, learned Thai better than her husband and converted to Buddhism during her stay in the country.[9]

Despite their combined experience, misunderstanding and lack of preparation shaped Stanton's and Landon's response to the coup. Although the signs of army dissatisfaction and rumors of military action were legion in the preceding months, neither Stanton nor Landon had foreseen the events of November, and neither had suggested that the United States should prepare itself for such an eventuality. When the coup came, Landon and his Southeast Asian Division colleagues had no policy options to choose from. Stanton's dispatches, moreover, presented an inaccurate analysis of the coup. Stanton believed, despite the evidence that he himself had collected of Phibun's ambiguous relationship with the coup-makers, that Phibun was the Coup Group's dominant figure. As a result, American policy in the several months following the coup focused on Phibun personally instead of the Coup Group as a whole. Because Landon and Stanton had no policy options in hand when the army moved in, events quickly overcame them. In the first days after the coup, the embassy and State Department took no action other than issuing a short statement.

The accession of Khuang to the prime ministership, announced the day of the coup, persuaded Landon and Stanton to refrain from taking strong measures. Besides Khuang and the Americans' old friend Seni Pramoj, the new government boasted princes, aristocrats, and bureaucrats. Many had studied in the West, and most of the important figures had been born wealthy enough to have no interest in using their offices for financial gain. Compared with the rustic, northeastern politicians prominent in Pridi's cabinets, the bilingual cosmopolitans of Khuang's government held great appeal for westerners. From the beginning, therefore, the Americans never advocated a return to the status quo ante. They wanted this cabinet to stay. The State Department's November 10 statement, the United States' one announcement on the coup, claimed that, although the United States would object to a government headed by Phibun, if "moderate" figures (i.e., neither Pridi nor Phibun, but Khuang) were given control, the United States would view matters "differently."[10] In the months to come, this preference for Khuang over both Phibun and Pridi shaped every aspect of America's Thailand policy. At all times, U.S. policy would aim to strengthen the Khuang government.

The question of recognition of the new government posed the first challenge to America's pro-Khuang policy. For all the major players—Khuang, Pridi, Phibun, the Coup Group—the question of foreign, and especially American, recognition was of crucial importance. With Adun, Admiral Sin of the navy, and Rear Adm. Thahan Khamhiran of the marines still sitting on the sidelines considering which bandwagon to jump on, a clear statement of recognition or nonrecognition could tip the scales in favor of either side. Stanton believed that the "question [of] recognition [will] likely be [the] decisive factor" in deciding the outcome of the struggle.[11] The Coup Group, hoping to bluff the powers into recognizing Khuang, thus falsely announced on November 11 that the ambassadors of all the major powers except France—the United States, Great Britain, and China—had personally promised Phibun that they would recognize the new regime. The three embassies had to deny the claim publicly.[12] Representatives of both Pridi and the Coup Group, in the meantime, lobbied the British and Americans to support their respective positions on recognition. Pridi's side readily acknowledged that the Western response would determine his decision to resist the coup or not. Unprepared to answer definitively, Stanton could only say to Pridi's initial request for the United States to withhold recognition that there was "no question [of] recognition [of the] Phibun regime [sic] at present and [that the United States is] awaiting clarification [of the] situation."[13]

Although the uncertainty evident in this dispatch quickly disappeared, the substance of the position Stanton outlined to Pridi would not change. Over the coming month, Stanton and Landon developed a rationale for continuing the "wait and see" policy. Inaction on the important issue of recognition, Landon and Stanton came to believe, offered the United States its best hope for influencing events in Thailand. While an explicit statement of nonrecognition as requested by Pridi would encourage his followers to take action against Khuang—an unacceptable prospect—outright recognition would enable the Coup Group (Phibun, as the Americans saw it) to oust Khuang and take absolute control. As long as the Americans offered recognition as a reward for Phibun's good behavior, Stanton and Landon expected, the ex-dictator would think twice before interfering with Khuang's government.

Conversely, once they recognized the government, the Americans would lose their leverage over Phibun. Landon thus made "deferring recognition without comment" U.S. policy. The elections set for January 29, Landon decided, would serve as a convenient point to finally recognize the new government. Phibun would refrain from attacking Khuang before then, while an election victory, Landon and Stanton hoped, would strengthen Khuang's hand.[14] Although disputes later arose over its implementation, the policy, in essence, would remain unchanged. Until the State Department actually recognized the new government in March, one month after the elections, the United States remained silent on the question of recognition.

The British, somewhat surprisingly, ended up taking a similar position. The initial attitude of British officials toward Khuang and Phibun remained little changed from the spring. In the immediate aftermath of the takeover, one Foreign Office official complained that the new regime "will certainly be more right-wing and narrowly nationalistic, with probably a pro-American swing," while another worried that the United States would force Britain into quickly recognizing Khuang's government.[15] Pridi and Thamrong, the Foreign Office hoped, would be returned to power. But the British found that they could do little for Pridi. Without support from the United States, London felt, British action would lack force, and, if Britain antagonized the country's new leaders, British interests could suffer.[16] The British required rice, peace on the Malayan and Burmese borders, and a friendly business environment. British businessmen in Thailand pressed the embassy hard to accommodate the new government.[17] British officials, moreover, found Khuang's "good men," as Stanton frequently called the ministers in the new cabinet, as charming as the Americans did. Perhaps even more than their allies, the British preferred the company of Khuang's European-educated ministers to the farmers' and schoolteachers' sons of Pridi's governments. Khuang's less corruptible "good men," the British hoped, would fulfill their rice obligations with greater efficiency. Ambassador Thompson, closest and most vulnerable to the pleas of anxious British businessmen and the charms of urbane new cabinet members, quickly fell into Stanton's way of thinking. As early as November 10, Thompson commented that the new cabinet "would be generally rated high" and, by November 24, had recommended immediate "de facto" recognition of the government to strengthen Khuang versus Phibun.[18] The Foreign Office remained skeptical of Khuang and worried that, because "Mr Thompson is becoming increasingly favorable towards the new regime[,] . . . the impartiality of the picture he is presenting to us is suffering" but still envisioned no alternative to the United States' "wait and see" approach.[19]

The British and American inclination to support Khuang against Pridi grew more pronounced as fears increased that armed resistance against the new government would lead to civil war. Although the Coup Group had quickly captured Bangkok, it had yet to confront Pridi's many possible allies scattered throughout the country. Thailand in late 1947 served as home to no less than seven separate and potentially antagonistic armed groups. Besides the army, the police maintained substantial forces in Bangkok, and the navy occupied the east coast as its private preserve. Thousands of Vietminh and other Indochinese nationalist refugees, armed by Pridi governments since their arrival in the country at the start of the French-Indochinese War in 1946, roamed freely throughout the northeast. The Free Thai worked closely with the Vietminh. And the local Kuomintang, Stanton estimated, had arms and six thousand supporters and the Chinese Communists fifteen hundred members, primarily in Bangkok.[20] In September 1945, World War II victory celebrations in a Chinese neighborhood in Bangkok had turned into bloody riots involving armed street battles, Chinese snipers, and army machine-gun attacks. Extremist Kuomintang elements possibly supported the Chinese gunmen.[21] The British and Americans feared that, if violence erupted between Pridi and the Coup Group, these ethnic Chinese, the Vietminh, the navy, the Free Thai, and the police would enter the fray and civil war would ensue. The unrest would likely spread to neighboring countries, and hopes for a more stable Southeast Asia would be dashed. As one Foreign Office official argued, "it would almost be better for Siam to have an authoritarian but comparatively efficient and stable government under a man we dislike than a period of chaos while the more liberal elements are fighting the more reactionary ones."[22]

In the immediate aftermath of the coup, prospects for maintaining the peace looked good. Although Pridi sent an emissary to the British and American embassies on November 12 to inform Stanton and Thompson that he was considering measures to oust Khuang and the Coup Group, the emissary indicated that Pridi would not act without support from the powers, support that neither embassy was about to provide. To calm him, Thompson and Stanton assured Pridi that they had sought "definite assurance from Phibun" that he, Thamrong, and their families would not be harmed.[23] The next day, unbeknownst to the British and Americans, Pridi and a number of ministers from Thamrong's cabinet meeting at the east-coast Sattahip naval base decided against armed action.[24] On November 19, the British and American naval attachés succeeded in evacuating Pridi from Sattahip to a Shell Oil tanker steaming to Singapore.[25] Although the Allies conducted the secret operation out of a genuine desire to help the man who had risked his life to oppose the Japanese, they also believed that it would forestall any countercoup. Pridi's departure, Stanton commented, "would probably result in his followers giving up the idea of using force in an effort to regain control of the political situation."[26] Reassuring the Allies further, Pridi wrote the British privately that he would employ only peaceful methods. On November 27, he broadcast a statement from Singapore calling on his followers to abjure violence.[27]

But the Americans and British still had much to worry about. Within a week of the coup, reports appeared of a deal between Pridi forces and local Chinese Communists. Thamrong admitted to Thompson that the Communists had approached him, and, on November 14, twenty Free Thai leaders boasted to the French and Chinese ambassadors that the group had the support of Chinese Communists, the Vietminh, and Indonesian nationalists and would fight with or without Pridi's consent. Although Thamrong assured the British that he had spurned the Chinese Communist offer, the Western embassies knew that the threat of a Free Thai–Communist alliance was real.[28] Since Tiang Sirikhan, the leader of the Free Thai forces in the northeast, had aided, under Pridi's orders, the Indochinese nationalists during and since World War II, the Free Thai could expect help from the Vietminh. Also, because Pridi's Cooperative Party had welcomed Chinese Communists into its Central Labor Union while Pridi's governments loosened restrictions on Chinese schools and businesses, both Chinese Communists and Kuomintang supporters favored Pridi.

Developments in December intensified Western concerns. Apparently having reconsidered his position, Pridi now wanted to fight. In the immediate aftermath of the coup, Stanton had dissuaded him from establishing a government-in-exile, but, by mid-December, Pridi was promoting a new plan for a rival government in the north of the country. In a letter sent on December 19, Atthakit Phanomyong asked William Donovan, former oss chief and agent of the Pridi governments, to "continue to serve as counsel" to Pridi and Thamrong and to lobby the State Department to support the plan. Atthakit suggested that Washington also impose an oil embargo, seize Thai government and Bank of Siam assets, and demand return from the illegitimate regime of arms and ammunition given by the oss.[29] When informed of the letter by a representative of Donovan's law firm, Landon immediately disapproved. "It would be regrettable," Landon explained, "if a small country like Siam were physically split asunder by two governments." Donovan's representative replied that he had expected Landon's response and believed that "the General [Donovan] would do his best to avoid representing" any such government.[30]

Thamrong, in the meantime, began planning for a countercoup independently of Pridi and the Free Thai. Since the beginning of the new month, Thamrong had been warning the British that his patience was wearing thin, and, on December 18, he informed Capt. Stratford Dennis, the British naval attaché, that he would act later that month. Thamrong admitted that the army crackdown had crippled the Free Thai and that Pridi could not aid the countercoup from Singapore but was confident that his good friend, Admiral Sin of the navy, would provide the necessary forces. Thamrong asked the British and Americans to supply material aid and refrain from recognizing the Khuang government until January 1, the deadline for the coup. He expected to run out of money on that date. Not surprisingly, Captain Dennis stoutly refused Thamrong's request for material aid.[31]

The British reacted to these developments with their now usual sense of alarm. Thompson, from the beginning, recommended an energetic response. If the British and Americans could arrange a reconciliation of Khuang and Thamrong, he argued, the Allies would, at once, freeze Phibun out of the government and avert a violent countercoup. He thus suggested that the United States and Britain press Prince Rangsit, chairman of the Council of Regents, to broker a coalition government of Democrats and Pridi supporters with Thamrong and Khuang.[32] Although skeptical of its prospects, the Foreign Office approved the proposal.[33] While Rangsit reluctantly agreed to help Thompson, however, nothing ever came of the scheme. The rabidly anti-Pridi Khuang refused to meet Thamrong, and a subsequent plan to involve the king in negotiations never got off the ground.[34] American refusal to participate doomed the initiative—never promising—from the start. Neither Stanton nor Landon wished to risk America's standing with the new regime, especially if it meant bringing Thamrong and the northeasterners back into the government. "The State Department," A. M. Palliser of the Foreign Office's Siam desk complained, "are lying well back and leaving Mr. Thompson to make the pace. Obviously their liking for the good men in the new Govt. makes them anxious to avoid embarrassing them by any hasty action."[35] Luckily for the British, the negotiations' failure did not lead to civil war. Thamrong never convinced Admiral Sin that the risk was worthwhile, and the countercoup never came off.

More important than what the British did to effect a reconciliation between Thamrong and Khuang was what the Americans did not do to help Pridi's political supporters. While Thamrong and Pridi spent the month of December writing letters and holding meetings, the Coup Group was acting. After showing a great deal of tolerance in November, Khuang and the Coup Group began in early December a sustained crackdown on the Free Thai and the northeastern politicians prominent in Pridi's governments.[36] On November 9, Khuang had issued a decree providing Phibun, as head of the army, the mandate to suppress the opponents of the new regime. Then, once Bangkok had been secured and the diplomatic situation stabilized, the Coup Group began the crackdown in December. Over the following two months, the government arrested four former cabinet ministers, questioned or harassed other ministers, and jailed dozens of prominent members of Pridi's political parties. Wichit Lulitanon, ex-minister of finance, and Thongbleo Cholaphum, ex-deputy minister of finance, fled the country after their release from prison. The crackdown also targeted the pro-Pridi *Siang Thai* and *Krungthep Times* newspapers, and the new government quickly took over the Bank of Asia, then controlled by Pridi's Thammasat University. Perhaps most damaging to Pridi's political prospects, Thawin Udorn, leader of the Cooperative Party, was jailed. The Coup Group released Thawin on bail only after the registration deadline for candidates had passed. Clearly, Khuang and the coup-makers aimed at nothing less than the complete destruction of Pridi's political network and support base.[37]

Jim Thompson and Willis Bird, former oss officers then doing business in Thailand, did all they could for their old allies. "We have been suspected of any number of acts of comfort to the Free Thais," Bird wrote Donovan, "most of which are true." Thompson provided shelter to Free Thais fleeing arrest, and Bird guaranteed an $80,000 loan Atthakit took out before leaving the country. "What a hell of a time they will have getting $80,000 out of me," the strapped Bird joked.[38]

The embassy and Washington, however, showed no such concern for the Free Thai and former government officials. Not once did Stanton protest the crackdown, and never did he or Landon suggest opposing it. Atthakit's request in January for an American statement of concern for the Free Thais' safety met silence. Hoping to avoid at all costs a confrontation that could destabilize the Khuang regime, the Americans spurned their former allies. The British, though they pressed for the inclusion of Thamrong in the government, also acquiesced to the crackdown.[39]

The repression of Pridi's supporters had a profound impact on the political events of the coming months. Pridi's political network had been extensive. In the elections Khuang had scheduled for January 29, 1948, Pridi's parties, if allowed to participate, might have won, as they had in 1946. As late as January 1, Prince Siddhiphorn, Khuang's minister of agriculture, told Stanton that Pridi's forces would triumph.[40] The crackdown devastated Pridi's machine, however, and when the elections were over, few of his supporters had made it into the next parliament. Although American intervention might have only softened the crackdown, even that much could have helped. Pridi was down but not yet out. His supporters occupied a number of important positions in the bureaucracy. Were he still in Thailand to lead such officials, his members of Parliament, and sympathetic journalists, he could have remained a counterweight to the army. Later, immediately before and after the elections, when conflict between Khuang's cabinet and Kat and Phibun intensified, the Coup Group reached out to Pridi, Thamrong, and their followers for support. American protection for Pridi's political network, therefore, could have enabled Pridi to maintain a substantive role in the political life of the country. His later resort to violence and reliance on the People's Republic of China might have been averted.

By mid-January, as the elections approached, Khuang's and Phibun's diplomatic campaign brought the foreign powers closer to recognizing the new government. From the day they came to power, Khuang and the Coup Group devoted their closest attention to appeasing the powers. In some cases, Khuang granted material concessions; in others, he merely made promises, occasionally empty. At the same time, Khuang and the Coup Group exploited any opportunity to divide the foreigners. When meeting representatives of one power, Khuang and the Coup Group criticized the other powers. And, if Khuang and the Coup Group saw the chance to deal separately with a single power, they took it. Initially hoping only to buy time, Khuang and the Coup Group eventually grew confident enough to aim for outright recognition.

France was Khuang's and the Coup Group's first, and perhaps most challenging, objective. Although no fans of Pridi, the man who had given arms and refuge to Indochinese nationalists, the French feared even worse from Phibun and Khuang. Phibun, after all, had taken the territories that Pridi had returned, and Khuang's estates lay in the provinces returned to France's Cambodian protectorate. Guerrilla attacks across their western border the French could live with. An irredentist war they could not. The French, therefore, took the hardest line of any foreign power against Phibun's and Khuang's return. France resolutely resisted any suggestion of recognizing the new government and strongly urged the United States and Britain to impose economic sanctions. The Americans, always ready to dismiss French suggestions on Thailand, gave the proposal little thought. The British, though slightly more sympathetic, agreed that Paris took an "unnecessarily tragic view" of the situation.[41]

Despite their initial antagonism, over the next three months, the French moved to the forefront of those advocating an accommodation with Phibun and the Khuang government. Their diplomatic isolation made the French easy targets for Khuang and the Coup Group. Frightened by the new government's potential to create trouble, the French grew desperate as the Americans and British spurned their proposals to discipline the Thais. Not only did the two allies refuse to impose sanctions, but the Americans rebuffed even the suggestion that the three countries issue a mild statement "expressing concern in regard to the situation" and consult regularly.[42] Khuang's refusal to assure France, as he had the United States and Britain, that he would respect agreements previous governments had made heightened French apprehension.[43] Thus, when Khuang began touting his anticommunist credentials and the army arrested in December a number of Indochinese "bandits," the lamentably isolated French latched on to the developments as hopeful signs. By mid-December, the French were urging the Foreign Office to take a more optimistic view of the situation, and, by the beginning of February, they advocated immediate, outright recognition.[44]

The Americans and British now lagged behind Paris, but Khuang's blandishments hurried their pace as well. For the British, the critical issue was the new government's implementation of the various trade-related peace treaties, and, on that count, Khuang gave the British all they asked for. The new government tendered on the new year 750,000 pounds of tin ore promised in the peace treaty, cooperated fully on the work being performed on the Burma railway, and delivered rice with unusual promptness.[45] "The present Cabinet," Thompson commented in December, "ha[s] created an excellent impression, which ha[s] gone a long way towards effacing in many minds the disagreeable memory of how they [the cabinet] had come into office."[46] The United States lacked the extensive economic interests the British maintained in the country, but the Americans too found reason to approve of the new government. Although communism never appeared in these months as an important issue in American dispatches or memoranda, Stanton, at least, accepted as genuine to some degree the professions of anticommunism delivered with increasing regularity by Khuang and the Coup Group. The Foreign Office's Southeast Asia Department continued to oppose formalizing relations with the new regime, and Landon maintained a curious silence, but, by mid-January, Khuang's diplomatic campaign had persuaded Thompson and Stanton that the powers should recognize the government after the elections. Half the battle had been won.

The other half of the battle—the effort to convince the Foreign Office and Landon—would turn on the power struggle between Khuang and the Coup Group. Although their common opposition to Pridi had joined the two sides, tensions always underlay the partnership between Khuang and the Coup Group. Khuang and the Coup Group shared no interests beyond their desire to oust the old government, and, while Khuang wanted the full administrative control of the country his position as legitimate (as he saw it) head of government bestowed, the Coup Group demanded the rights and privileges they believed the coup had earned them. Thus, although their broad agreement in November and early December to present a united front against Pridi helped smooth over differences, once the threat from Pridi receded, cracks in the Democrat–Coup Group partnership appeared.

In January, a series of incidents almost brought the two sides to violence. In the first week of the year, Seni Pramoj, now minister of justice, publicly appealed to Phibun to step down as head of the army. Reportedly speaking on behalf of most cabinet members, he claimed that Phibun's resignation would hasten foreign recognition.[47] The Coup Group took the statement as a challenge to their power, and Kat, the British learned from "well-founded" sources, wrote the cabinet a letter threatening an unspecified response if the government pushed the matter. Khuang, it was reported, had to dissuade the cabinet from resigning on the spot.[48] Then, two weeks later, Col. Phao Siyanon, the Coup Group leader closely associated with Phibun and Phin, demanded that the interior minister, Sinat Yotharak, appoint Phao director-general of the Police Department. When Sinat refused, Phao challenged the minister to a duel. The crisis ended only when Phin, Phao's father-in-law, personally apologized to Sinat.[49]

Despite the Coup Group's strength within the army, Khuang showed every sign in December 1947 and early 1948 of increasing his control of government. While Kat had intended the provisional constitution he had drafted to facilitate Coup Group control of government, Khuang turned the tables on Kat. When the Coup Group suggested to Prince Rangsit, chairman of the Council of Regents, that Phibun head

the powerful new Supreme Council, the anti-Phibun Rangsit de-
murred. Instead, Rangsit, whom Phibun had imprisoned on Tarutao
island in 1939, packed the council with royalists.[50] Then, the council,
charged with appointing the one hundred members of the new Senate,
ignored all but twenty-one of the Coup Group's nominees and selected
instead a Senate of seventy elderly nobles, seven princes, no more than
ten conservative members of the 1932 Promoters, and a dozen or so
businessmen.[51] It was a Senate made to order for Khuang's Democrat
Party. With the Democrats and their allies capturing in the January 29
lower-house elections an overwhelming majority of sixty-five out of one
hundred seats, compared with a paltry five seats for Phibun's Thammathipat Party and six seats for Pridi's Cooperative and Constitutional
Front parties, the picture grew even grimmer for the Coup Group.[52]
Were Phibun and his allies to lose so badly any future skirmishes, the
Coup Group, not Khuang, would end up the puppets. Since the elections gave the Democrats a mandate to draft the new constitution, that
prospect looked increasingly likely.

Fearful that matters were getting out of hand, Phibun and the
Coup Group increased their pressure on Khuang in late January and
February and, ironically, though not surprisingly, given the topsy-turvy
nature of Thai politics, now turned to Pridi and Thamrong for help. In
many ways, Phibun had more of a natural affinity for Pridi than for
Khuang. Pridi and Phibun were the two key members of the 1932 Promoters, and, while Khuang belonged to the group, his friendship with
royal family members and relation by marriage with Prince Charun set
him apart in later years.[53] Indeed, Khuang's party, the Democrats, had
been founded with the primary aim of breaking the Promoters'
monopoly of power. The royalists prominent in the party abhorred
Pridi and Phibun alike for having overthrown the absolute monarchy
and denigrated the throne. Thus, when the run-up to the elections
made clear that the Democrats were the party to beat, the Coup Group
relented in its harassment of Pridi's political supporters. In mid-January, Phibun's Thammathipat Party formed an informal alliance with the
remnants of Pridi's parties.

In the week before and three weeks after the elections, Phibun and
other Promoters actively attempted to draw Pridi and Thamrong into
an explicitly anti-Democrat alliance. Phibun, a Pridi associate informed
Stanton, pressed Thamrong in these weeks to join the Coup Group in a
coup against Khuang. After the coup, Phibun promised a representative of the man he had earlier helped overthrow, the Coup Group
would return Thamrong to the prime minister's office.[54] Skeptical,

Thamrong at first rebuffed Phibun, but, on February 5, an emissary of Phibun informed Alexander MacDonald, the American editor of the *Bangkok Post,* that Phibun and Thamrong had agreed to oust Khuang, using force if necessary. As Phibun probably hoped, the editor informed Stanton of the meeting.[55] There is no evidence that Phibun intended the meeting at the *Post* as anything more than a trial balloon, but, three days later, his supporters staged a march of two thousand people on the house of a privy councillor to demand that Phibun be appointed prime minister and Pridi and Thamrong ministers. On February 14, fifty of the seventy-five 1932 Promoters plus Colonel Phao and several other junior Coup Group members met and called for the appointment of Promoters to the crucial Defense, Interior, Finance, and Foreign ministries.[56]

The Phibun-Pridi alliance never came off, but the Coup Group moved ahead anyway. Phao approached Khuang shortly before February 21 and insisted that Khuang give Coup Group members the finance, defense, interior, and foreign affairs portfolios. Khuang, in a bold move, informed the Supreme Council of State of the challenge and requested it to ask Phibun to assume the premiership in his stead. Phibun, as Khuang expected, realized that foreign opposition remained strong and declined, thus giving Khuang the mandate he needed to form a cabinet of his choosing.[57] The Coup Group then decided to rid themselves of Khuang once and for all. When the time for the coup came on February 27, however, Admiral Sin sent sailors into Bangkok, Admiral Thahan alerted the marines already in the capital, and Phibun urged restraint. The Coup Group called off the operation, and Khuang's government lived to see another day.[58]

These increasing Khuang–Coup Group tensions, along with the January 29 election results, induced the Americans finally to recognize Khuang's government. The elections, apart from the block-out of most of the Pridi forces, had been conducted cleanly and smoothly, and the Democrats' smashing victory gave Khuang's government a semblance of legitimacy it had never before enjoyed. Happy to have reason to praise the Democrats, Stanton claimed ten days after the elections that any new government Khuang formed would "have been elected by and can be said to be fairly representative of the people." He recommended that "consideration be given to fairly prompt recognition" once the cabinet was formed. Acutely aware of the dangers Khuang faced, Stanton argued that the establishment of formal relations was imperative. "Recognition," Stanton asserted, will "likely strengthen [the] position [of the] new government and possibly act as [a] deterrent to [the] constant political maneuvering."[59] Cables from Washington thanked Stanton for his "excellent estimate" of the situation, and the State Department instructed the embassies in London, Paris, and Nanking to inform American allies that the United States was "prepared [to] consider . . . prompt recognition" upon the formation of a government.[60] The British and French, also wanting to strengthen Khuang, welcomed Washington's decision.[61] On March 6, after the cabinet received Parliament's vote of confidence, the United States led Britain, France, and China in recognizing Khuang's government.[62]

Recognition represented Khuang's greatest victory. It effectively precluded the possibility of outside support for a countercoup and established not merely functional, but friendly, relations with the United States and Britain. For the first time since before the war, the government of the day enjoyed the full and united support of both powers. In any future conflict with the Coup Group, Khuang could cite the evident support of the British and Americans.

But recognition also opened Khuang to new threats. Once given, recognition would be hard to retract. Any leverage the powers had maintained over Phibun and the Coup Group was lost after the United States and Great Britain extended recognition. Recognition, moreover, set a dangerous precedent. In recognizing Khuang's cabinet, the United States and Britain embraced as legitimate a government that had won elections only by excluding its most formidable rivals from the competition. He violated the most fundamental principles of democracy, but, by upholding the mere form of free elections, Khuang had gained American and British approval. In the month to come, the Coup Group would take this precedent to heart.

Chapter Three

PHIBUN'S RETURN,

APRIL–JUNE 1948

The Coup Group allowed Khuang to enjoy his position as fully recognized prime minister for only a month. Throughout the winter, Khuang had annoyed the Coup Group, and, with votes of confidence from the powers and the Parliament, he threatened to prove more irritating in the spring. Reports that he planned to slash military spending in the next budget circulated freely in March. No longer worried about foreign recognition, the Coup Group therefore decided that Khuang had to go. On April 6, four high-ranking members of the Coup Group called on Khuang and demanded that he resign within twenty-four hours. Khuang quickly wrote Phibun, Phin, and Kat, asking for confirmation of the demand, but Phin and Kat informed him personally that the Coup Group had, in fact, voted to ask for his resignation. When Khuang requested support from Admiral Sin of the navy and the air force commander, they too told him that he must yield. Neither commander wanted to risk his forces at that time against the stronger army. Eager to avoid a confrontation he would lose, Khuang submitted his resignation to the Supreme Council of State. For most of April 7, Rangsit, head of the council, refused to accept Khuang's letter, but extensive talks, first with Khuang and later with Phibun and Kat, convinced Rangsit he had no choice. Kat declared that the Coup Group would accept no one but Phibun as leader of the government, and Khuang warned that continued resistance would lead to an outright coup. Phibun told Rangsit that the Coup Group had not consulted him but argued that events forced him to take office. Rangsit then yielded. That afternoon, he accepted the cabinet's collective resignation and appointed Phibun prime minister.[1] To make clear to the public the coercion he had faced,

Khuang released his letter of resignation—including an account of the "hold-up" (*ji*) that forced him to resign—to the press.[2]

Stanton exploded at the news of Khuang's ouster. The day he learned of it, Stanton telegraphed the State Department that the "action of Phibun and [the] military has shown the most blatant cynicism for constitutional processes and [an] exceedingly objectionable type of self-interest." "Not a single legitimate reason," Stanton complained, "can be adduced [to] support [the] action [of the] military group, which can only be attributed [to the] ambition [of] Phibun and his overweening subordinates and particularly [the] desire of [the] latter for more power and financial benefits." Worried that Washington would merely take events in stride, Stanton strongly urged the State Department to withhold recognition for an unspecified period and issue a statement expressing American objections. He acknowledged that nonrecognition unaccompanied by concrete sanctions would have no material effect but argued that immediate recognition would indicate to the Thais that the United States condoned "such irresponsible use of force for selfish ends." Employing words with strongly moralistic connotations, such as "conscience," "selfish," "irresponsible," and "legitimate," Stanton expressed his displeasure with righteous indignation. He took the "hold-up" as a personal affront and expected a strong U.S. response.[3]

Movements within the country and from abroad, in the meantime, boosted the chances of ousting Phibun. On April 9, a representative of Admiral Sin informed the British and American naval attachés that the navy was planning a countercoup.[4] Sin elaborated on the scheme four days later. On April 15 or 16, Phibun's cabinet was due to ask Parliament for a vote of confidence. Sin and Adun planned to persuade a majority of MPs—most still Democrats—to abstain from voting and then press the Supreme Council of State to refuse to appoint Phibun. Sin expected that enough army officers would side with the navy to force Phibun to hand control over the government to a coalition of Khuang, Thamrong, and Pridi.[5] Although Sin asked for nothing beyond a period of nonrecognition from the British and Americans, he had an ally in the French, who lobbied the United States and Britain to join in imposing "coercive sanctions."[6] The British and Americans, according to French proposals, would cut off oil supplies and refuse new loans, while the French would close the border with Indochina. Worried that Phibun would renew his irredentist policies, Paris was willing to take drastic action to force him to step down.[7]

Washington, however, opposed not only the forceful policy the

French proposed but the more moderate approach Stanton had advised. While Stanton had largely been left on his own in the winter and previous year, in the spring of 1948, Landon and officials in the Office of Far Eastern Affairs began to take a greater interest in the impact of America's Thailand policy on Southeast Asia as a whole. For these officials, the most important challenge facing the United States was not to encourage the formation of a government of honest civilians amenable to relatively minor American business interests but to stem the recent advances of Communists in the region. In February, the Malayan Communist Party mounted a Singapore Harbor Board strike, and an Asia Socialist Youth Conference in Calcutta excited fears that the Soviets were preparing a region-wide political offensive. In March, the Burmese "White Flag" Communists[8] rose in rebellion against the newly independent government of U Nu. The Vietminh gained ground against the French throughout 1947 and 1948. To halt these frightening reversals, the Office of Far Eastern Affairs decided that the United States had to promote the establishment of a friendly, stable, noncommunist government, whether composed of civilians or soldiers, in the one country free of fighting, yet surrounded by nations torn by communist insurrections. Acceptance of Phibun, therefore, appeared unavoidable. Landon noted optimistically that the field marshal's return to power would allow the United States to work with the country's real power, not a stooge. "In dealing with Phibun," Landon explained to the director of the Far Eastern Affairs Office, W. Walton Butterworth, "we will be dealing with substance."[9]

Eventually, Stanton and the State Department compromised. Upon receipt of his initial recommendations on April 9, the department sent Stanton a telegram sympathizing with his anger but expressing a desire to ignore the question of recognition and conduct business as usual with the new government. The cable asked him to "refrain from any action which might prejudice this position."[10] As much as the "hold-up" itself, the department's reply outraged Stanton. ("Like most Americans," Geoffrey Thompson believed, Stanton was too emotional.[11]) According to a British dispatch, he responded that, if the State Department insisted on giving in to Phibun so easily, he would ask to be recalled.[12] Not wanting to lose Stanton at a crucial moment, the State Department yielded on several points. In a dispatch sent April 12, it agreed to let him "discreetly" air American disapproval of the Coup Group's actions and promised to issue a statement that the United States was monitoring the new government's behavior with regard to Thailand's "international obligations."[13]

On the most important point, however, the State Department's next dispatch indicated that Washington held fast to its refusal to consider a prolonged period of nonrecognition. The communist threat made accommodation with Phibun imperative. In March, just before Khuang's "hold-up," the Soviets opened a legation in Bangkok, and, in April, local newspapers reported that the U.S.S.R. had suggested an exchange of military officers and offered to train Thai soldiers in the Soviet Union. Although the Thai minister of defense rejected the proposal, the Americans concluded that the Soviets planned a major push in Thailand.[14] Were the West to shun Phibun, the Soviet Union would be left alone among the great powers in maintaining formal relations with his government. Phibun would then embrace the U.S.S.R. as an ally. "It is highly undesirable," the department cable to Stanton explained, to "create [a] situation in which [the] Siamese Gov[ernmen]t [would be] thrown into [the] arms [of the] USSR as [the] only nation which recognizes it."[15] Thailand had a reputation for bending with the wind in its foreign relations, and Phibun, the man who had sided with the Japanese in 1941 only to turn his back on them in 1944, was notorious for his diplomatic turnabouts. Despite his numerous professions of anticommunism, Phibun still resisted taking any action that would offend the Soviet Union. He told the *New York Times* that, although he was "personally anti-communist," his government was "neither of the left nor the right."[16] Indeed, he appointed a leftist with communist connections, Sawet Piamphongsan, as assistant minister of finance.[17] Washington, therefore, rejected Stanton's advice and decided to continue formal relations as before. Once Phibun had formed a cabinet and received Parliament's vote of confidence, the United States would acknowledge the establishment of the new government, thus bestowing de facto recognition. Besides opening the door to friendly relations with Phibun, the decision was significant for what it portended for the future. Over the next two years, the United States supported Phibun primarily to maintain his loyalty to the West.

The British dithered and debated but, in the end, approached the recognition issue much the same way. Richard Whittington, acting ambassador while Thompson joined in consultations in London, agreed with Stanton's recommendation that the powers should apply a "dose of non-recognition" to Phibun's new government.[18] Officials in the Foreign Office's Southeast Asia Department firmly believed, though, that nonrecognition could serve no useful purpose. Thai rice was utmost in their minds, and they feared disrupting its flow to Malaya with provocative policies.[19] The Foreign Office wanted badly to issue some sort of critical statement to punish Phibun but feared acting alone. Uncertain and hesitant, the British thus drifted toward the U.S. position. From the beginning, London dismissed French proposals for sanctions, and, by the second half of April, the Foreign Office decided to follow the State Department in recognizing Phibun when he received a parliamentary vote of confidence. London disagreed with the United States only in wanting to seek from Phibun assurances of respect for international obligations before recognition, instead of afterward.[20]

Phibun's success in maintaining the appearance of constitutionality provided the British and Americans the excuse they needed for de facto recognition of his government. Although Khuang's "hold-up" differed little from a full-blown coup d'état, Phibun, Phin, and Kat painstakingly cultivated an image of legitimacy for the new government. The three first persuaded Khuang to resign and the Supreme Council of State to appoint Phibun prime minister, and, then, on April 13, Phibun applied for and received council approval of his cabinet list.[21] Because Phibun and the Coup Group had acted according to the letter of the constitution, the State Department took the position from the start that no break in relations occurred and no statement of recognition was needed. The change of government, a department cable to Stanton explained, had "ostensibly followed legal procedures."[22] Phibun's success in Parliament allowed the State Department to formalize this position. Because Khuang withheld his support for the scheme, Sin's plan for defeating Phibun on the April 21 vote of confidence failed. Instead, Parliament approved Phibun's presentation of government policy by a vote of seventy to twenty-six. Stanton optimistically considered the vote a less-than-convincing victory and recommended waiting two or three weeks to see if Phibun lost future votes, but Washington pushed ahead with plans to normalize relations.[23]

In the end, the ever-volatile French decided the issue. Piqued at their allies' refusal to cooperate and desperate to win favor with the Thais, the French ignored British suggestions first to seek assurances on Thailand's international obligations and then issue de facto recognition jointly. Instead, Paris unilaterally acknowledged formation of the new government only two days after the vote of confidence.[24] With the powers' united front thus broken, the British abandoned their efforts to obtain assurances in advance, and Stanton and Whittington formally acknowledged on April 30 receipt of Phibun's letter announcing formation of the new government.[25] The British and American embassies received written assurances from Phibun three days later.[26]

In the coming months, de facto recognition of Phibun's government forced Stanton and Southeast Asian Division officials to discard their prejudices and develop a new understanding of Phibun personally and politically. As late as the first half of 1948, the image of him created in the early years of the war continued to shape Western perceptions of Phibun. He remained, for the British and Americans, the turncoat dictator who had sold his country to the Japanese. Many Thais, however, took a different view. Rather than considering him a traitor, they applauded Phibun's wartime policies as having preserved the country from destruction and foreign subjugation. By first siding with the Japanese, he saved Thailand from a harsh occupation, while, by tolerating the Free Thai and relinquishing power, he allowed the country to claim the status after the war of a victim, not a collaborator, of the Japanese. Assuming that all westerners were prejudiced against him, such Thais, U.S. embassy Vice-Consul Bulkley claimed, avoided speaking about Phibun with Americans. "On the other hand," Bulkley explained, "if an American professes a sympathetic interest in the subject, he will find that an overwhelming majority of Siamese feel strongly that Phibun did the best thing for Siam as a real patriot." Although he probably exaggerated the extent of support for Phibun and failed to discuss the popularity of Phibun's rival, Pridi, Bulkley's point that Americans and Thais viewed Phibun's wartime record differently was sound. And his recognition of the disparity showed that a new approach toward the field marshal was taking hold in the embassy.[27]

As they opened their minds to alternative opinions, the Americans developed a new understanding of Phibun's political persona. At least since the summer of 1947, Phibun's supporters had been trying to persuade the Americans and British that Phibun now recognized the error of his ways. His wartime followers, not Phibun himself, these later Phibun supporters claimed, had been responsible for the excesses of his earlier period in power. The new Phibun, the explanation went, would dispense with the advisers who had led the old Phibun astray.[28] Even a Phibun enemy, Prince Rangsit, agreed with the portrayal, describing Phibun as prone to believe whatever his advisers told him.[29] At first, the Americans dismissed such contentions, believing "rogues" such as Wichit Wathakan, Prayoon Phamornmontri, and Mangkorn Phromyothi would be prominent in any Phibun government, but, by the spring of 1948, ample evidence had appeared that Phibun had disassociated himself from most of his earlier dependents. In December and February, he had publicly disavowed any connection with rallies of the semifascist Yuwachon youth league and the Thammathipat Party organized by Wichit and Prayoon.[30] Then, in forming his cabinet after

Khuang's ouster, Phibun included only one of the three "rogues," Mangkorn Phromyothi, and gave him only the education portfolio. Compared with Mangkorn's previous positions as minister of defense and of the interior, this appointment amounted to a demotion. Stanton was convinced of Phibun's transformation. "There is no evidence thus far," Stanton commented after Phibun announced the composition of his cabinet, "that Phibun is seeking to revive the influence of his former henchmen[,] and his full cooperation with Prince Rangsit in forming his Cabinet demonstrates an attempt to form a reputable government." Stanton noted with pleasure that Phibun had appointed Thailand's first American-educated cabinet ministers, Phot Sarasin, deputy minister of foreign affairs, and Thonnawanik Montri, minister of finance.[31] The new Phibun, the Americans had reason to hope, would behave more agreeably than the old.

This abandonment of long-standing prejudices led to a reevaluation of Phibun's relation to the Coup Group and the army. After the November 1947 coup, Kat and Phin had managed to so annoy the Western powers that the British and Americans almost forgot how offensive Phibun had been during the war. While Phibun had maintained a low profile in the months Khuang held office, Kat and Phin raided the Thai treasury. With their War Veterans Association as a front for several lucrative monopolies, Phin and Kat made themselves extremely wealthy men within a remarkably short time. "Their [Phin's and Kat's] avariciousness," Stanton complained, "has no limit."[32] Kat especially irritated the Americans and British. More given to public displays than the shy Phin or the wily Phibun, Kat appeared the most greedy and manipulative member of the Coup Group. Stanton called him "obnoxious."[33] What others told Stanton and his colleagues reinforced their contempt for Kat. Seni Pramoj referred to him as an "insane nincompoop," and Pierre Eugene Gilbert, the French minister in Bangkok, called Kat a "gangster" and "uneducated, ruthless and grasping."[34] At first, the Americans failed to differentiate between Kat and Phibun, but, by January 1948, Stanton and others were noting the possibility of disagreements between the two.[35] By March, Stanton had also concluded that Phibun had not, as earlier believed, taken part in the November coup.[36]

The reevaluation of Phibun's relationship with the Coup Group convinced Stanton and other Americans that the ex-dictator offered Thailand its best hope for maintaining a role in government for civilians. Vice-Consul Bulkley described most clearly the new American attitude toward Phibun in his extended memorandum of late April, "The

Question of Phibun Again." In the essay, Bulkley claimed that the
United States had been mistaken to have ever believed that a civilian
government opposed by the army could survive in Thailand. "Recognizing the role that the military has played in Siamese politics throughout
the last sixteen years," he argued, ". . . it seems unlikely that any government headed by anyone who does not receive support from the Army
could be stable for any appreciable length of time." Because of his
unique ability to command military loyalty while remaining outside the
Coup Group, Phibun, Bulkley believed, represented a happy compromise between shaky democracy and unyielding dictatorship. Although
he now relied on the army's firepower, Phibun would find it in his interests in the future to maintain counterbalances to the Coup Group.
"One might say," Bulkley reasoned, "that he [Phibun] is the only con-
necting link between statesmanship and the basic fact of the importance of the military in Siamese politics." Kat, Bulkley conjectured,
might already be planning Phibun's "liquidation." If that happened,
the result would prove disastrous. "Should Phibun be disposed of,"
Bulkley warned, "the likelihood of an extreme form of military dictatorship would be almost inescapable." Setting the pattern for all future
analyses of the field marshal's political role, Bulkley's memorandum
showed that the Americans had come to see Phibun, the former ally of
the Axis, as good government's best friend in Thailand.[37]

With this reassessment of his personality and policies, the U.S.
embrace of Phibun—and, by extension, acceptance of a politically
active military—was now a fact. Never again would any embassy official
suggest weakening or ousting Phibun. From viewing him in 1947 as a
fascist inimical to U.S. interests, the Americans had come to see him by
late spring 1948 as a friendly leader with an interest in maintaining
civilian participation in government. Although U.S. officials still disapproved of the army's political role, their backing for Phibun brought
them that much closer to outright support for military government in
Thailand. In tolerating the use of brute force to oust Khuang, the
Americans conceded the demise of civilian supremacy over the military. By endorsing Phibun, they accepted the extension of military
influence over the government.

An air of inevitability surrounded the series of events leading up to
the American decision to support Phibun. Civilian government in the
Thailand of the 1940s was weak. From 1945 to November 1947, five different civilian governments came and went, each one facing increased
military dissatisfaction. The United States would have found it extremely difficult to help Pridi's governments counter such unrelenting

opposition. The pressure to work with the Khuang government brought to power by the November 1947 coup was intense, and once the informal relationship had been established, formal recognition of the Khuang government was nearly impossible to withhold. Then, with recognition granted Khuang, the denial of recognition to the stronger and ostensibly constitutional Phibun government would have involved a large risk and an embarrassing admission of error. Throughout the period, policymakers found themselves with few options. No matter what the Americans might have done, democracy, as it existed in the West, was not going to flourish in Thailand.

The Americans had made decisions, however, and their decisions had had an impact. By refusing to strongly oppose Phibun's attempted comeback in March 1947, by rejecting Pridi's request for military aid, and by ingratiating themselves with Khuang and the Democrats, the United States encouraged the Coup Group to oust Pridi and Thamrong from power completely instead of merely applying oblique pressure from the sidelines as before. Had the United States not made it so easy to remove the two civilians, some sort of compromise involving changes in the cabinet and army leadership, but allowing Pridi and Thamrong a continued role in government, might have resulted. Then, in the months after the coup, by rebuffing pleas for protection from the Free Thai, the United States denied Pridi and his close followers their last chance to retain political influence. Had Pridi supporters been fairly represented in Parliament and the press, Thailand could have enjoyed a stronger, more vital civilian opposition to the Coup Group. The question here, as before, was not whether the Americans would intervene in Thai internal affairs. Their open and strongly expressed support for Khuang—both before and after the coup—had already brought them to the center of the Thai political struggle. Rather, the problem was that the United States intervened solely on behalf of the undemocratic Khuang government and against the leaders of the only freely elected government the country had had. The United States, therefore, helped push Thailand in 1947 and 1948 closer to out-and-out military dictatorship.

As important as the U.S. influence on Thai politics was in these two years, possibly more significant is what U.S. policy revealed about American attitudes toward democracy in Thailand. Stanton and others can be forgiven for disliking Pridi. Pridi tolerated corruption among his supporters, and his declaration of a state of emergency in July 1946 betrayed a willingness to use force when persuasion failed. But however flawed, democracy under Pridi was real. Other than the brief state of emergency, Pridi's regime allowed the press and opposition ample liberty, and his several governments came to power in free and honest elections. U.S. willingness to interfere in parliamentary politics and oppose these freely elected governments showed that, with regard to Thailand, the United States bore little respect for the most basic principle of democracy—a people's right to choose its country's rulers. The Americans in 1947 and 1948 considered it their duty to manage the Thai democratic process. Later, this belief led them to conclude that the United States could similarly lead a military government in saving the country. Even before it had entrenched itself, therefore, the Americans were ready to accept rule by the military in Thailand.

PART TWO

U.S. MILITARY AID AND THE TRANSFORMATION

OF THAI FOREIGN POLICY, 1948–1950

From the end of World War II to 1950, Thai foreign policy was based on the principle that one should make as many friends as possible, but get too cozy with no one. In the immediate postwar years, the Thais worked intimately with Britain in the commercial sphere but resisted London's proposals for closer military cooperation. They courted French favor but played host to thousands of Indochinese insurgents. And though the Thais sought out American aid and diplomatic support, they maintained proper relations with the Soviet Union. Thai policy toward the Western attempt to contain communism in Southeast Asia, as Stanton described it in 1949, was to "run with the hare and hunt with the hounds."[1] As adept as Phibun was in joining both ends of the chase, however, he saw much to be gained by helping the dogs catch the rabbit. Throughout 1948 and 1949, Phibun moved Thailand closer to the West. Then, in 1950, he decisively broke with the middle-of-the-road policies of the previous five years. With two substantively insignificant but symbolically momentous decisions, he not only aligned Thailand firmly with the United States but also set the country in defiant opposition to the Soviets and the new People's Republic of China. The moves represented the most significant Thai policy initiative since the country allied itself with Japan in 1941. They revolutionized Thailand's postwar foreign policy.

What brought Phibun over to the American side was the prospect of military aid. Of all the things the Thais wanted from the United States—economic assistance, trade concessions, a security commitment—none shone with the glitter of new arms. Within six months of assuming the prime ministership, Phibun made it his top policy priority to obtain foreign weapons. Within twenty months, he had subordinated all aspects of his foreign policy to the quest for arms. The Americans were slow to respond to his overtures, but, by the last quarter of 1949, increased American interest in the region ensured that Thailand would get at least some military assistance. Once Phibun had effected his policy shift in 1950, the country was placed near the head of the list of aid recipients in Southeast Asia. The international situation in no way made his decision to side with the United States inevitable, but American military assistance was of crucial importance to Phibun and the domestic politics of the time. Once he began receiving it, many considered it vital to his political survival.

The U.S. decision to grant Thailand military aid and Phibun's consequent alignment with the United States spurred long-lasting changes in Thailand's military government. Until that point, civilians retained a significant voice in the making of Thai foreign policy. Phibun's decision in 1950 to unreservedly embrace the United States immediately diminished their influence. At the same time, alignment with the United States forced the Thai government to reassess its attitude toward internal dissent. In the wake of the policy shift, Phibun and the Coup Group found it possible—and desirable—to tighten controls over dissidents. Paying closer attention than ever now to the newly aroused left, the Phibun regime for the first time assumed the role of ideological watchdog. The Thai government, as a result, began at this point to promote the intolerance and authoritarianism that would later lead it to outright dictatorship.

And now the United States was along for the ride. The initiation of arms aid wedded American interests to the fate of the military government receiving it. Only because generals eager to receive new weapons controlled the government could Phibun's policy revolution occur. Once the arms shipments began, therefore, even the most ardent American supporters of democracy welcomed authoritarian Thailand into the camp of the Free World.

Chapter Four

MAKING THE CASE FOR MILITARY AID,

APRIL 1948–JUNE 1949

Almost from the moment Phibun returned to the Thai political scene with the November 1947 coup, he made the acquisition of foreign military assistance one of his primary foreign-policy goals. Over the previous several months, the United States had initiated large arms-assistance programs for Greece and Turkey and had begun planning for even more substantial Marshall Plan aid for western Europe. In the wake of these decisions, Phibun—like many Americans—believed that the United States would be willing to provide assistance to countries elsewhere, such as Thailand. At the same time, Phibun had compelling political reasons, as had Pridi, for seeking U.S. aid. The army still hungered for modern weaponry, and Phibun, needing to bolster his position within the Coup Group, badly wanted to please his subordinates. His authority had always derived from his ability to provide for the nation's leading military institution, and only the foreign powers could supply what the army wanted. Because most in the army preferred American weaponry, Phibun turned first to the United States.

Phibun took his case to the Americans immediately. In the second week of December 1947, only a month after the coup, Phibun sent a young American businessman friend, William Davis, to sound out the American military attaché about purchasing arms. Davis told the attaché that Phibun wanted to reequip the army with American weapons and reorganize it along American lines. Phibun also hoped, Davis reported, that American pilots could be sent to train Thai airmen. At the time, the army and air force were largely British armed and designed. Well aware of the rivalry that simmered just below the placid surface of U.S.-British friendship, Phibun had Davis warn the attaché that the army, if the United States refused, would buy arms from the British. The Americans, Phibun expected, would jump at the opportunity to gain influence in the army at their allies' expense.[1]

But Phibun had timed his request poorly. U.S. policy still aimed at strengthening Khuang against Phibun and the Coup Group, and the Americans wanted to do nothing to help the field marshal. Phibun's "prestige in military circles [before his ouster in 1944]," Stanton cabled Washington, "was largely predicated on building up the strength of the armed forces." U.S. aid, Stanton argued, would augment Phibun's control of the army. "If Field Marshall [sic] Phibun is successful in actually obtaining new weapons and equipment for the Army, his prestige in Army eyes will naturally be enhanced and his grip over the military appreciably strengthened." His position would then be unassailable. "The result of this," Stanton explained, "would likely be that it would be virtually impossible for the Khuang government or its successor to get rid of the Field Marshall." Stanton strongly urged that Washington reject Phibun's request.[2] The State Department never gave it a moment's thought.

The United States maintained its opposition to Thai arms acquisitions through the spring of 1948. In March 1948, Prince Wan Waithayakorn (Narathip Phongpraphan), Thai ambassador to the United States, asked Secretary of State Marshall in a letter to approve the sale of machine guns and ammunition for forty-two training planes the Thai government had contracted from the North American Company.[3] After the new Southeast Asian Division head, Charles Reed, opposed the sale in a memorandum four months later, Marshall signed a letter to Wan diplomatically refusing the request on the grounds that supplies for the planes were short.[4] Similarly, the United States rebuffed a third military assistance request in April. This time, Phibun sent a special delegation to present the petition. Headed by Phibun's associates, Maj. Gen. *Luang* Suranarong and Maj. Chatchai Chunhawan (Phin's son), the delegation went straight to Landon and Office of Far Eastern Affairs Director Butterworth on April 1 to ask that the United States provide arms and establish a military mission in Bangkok to train Thais in the use of the new weapons. Suranarong and Chatchai did not specify whether the arms would come in the form of sales, loans, or grants, but Landon and Butterworth so lacked interest in the proposal that they did not ask. They merely reminded Chatchai and Suranarong that the United States had already refused such a request. The State Department saw no reason, they coldly added, to reconsider it. Bringing the unpleasant meeting to an uncomfortable end, Butterworth advised the

Thais to present any other matters they wished to discuss with the relevant American army officials.[5] Chatchai and Suranarong returned to the State Department six days later with a new, more detailed plan, but Landon proved no more receptive now than before. Again, he fobbed the Thais off on his military colleagues, and, for the third time in five months, Phibun had to shelve his plans to reequip the army.[6]

In the summer and fall of 1948, however, the domestic political pressures that had prompted Phibun to make these aid requests intensified. Although Khuang had relinquished the prime minister's office without a fight, the Democrats remained a force to be reckoned with. In the "hold-up" of Khuang, the Coup Group and Phibun had not dissolved Parliament. The Democrats maintained their strong majorities in both houses, and, because Parliament on July 7 appointed Democrats and their sympathizers to about 80 percent of the seats in an assembly charged with drafting a new constitution, the royally appointed Senate was certain to retain its considerable powers.[7] So strong was his position in the legislature that several days later Khuang dropped plans to scuttle Phibun's budget only when faced with an intimidating army alert.[8] Realizing the precariousness of his position in Parliament, Phibun had tried in April to draw Khuang and Seni into the cabinet, but the two refused, preferring to take pot shots at Phibun from the sidelines.[9] Although Khuang never succeeded in toppling the government, his confidence was such that he reportedly predicted in July that he would be premier again within a month.[10]

Problems with the military also continued to trouble Phibun. The navy remained hostile to him, Pridi supporters still held important posts in the police force, and army officers not belonging to the Coup Group could not be trusted. Within the Coup Group itself, Phibun enjoyed less than full support. In forming his cabinet in April, he had excluded all but two relatively low-ranking members of the Coup Group. Phin and Kat responded by writing Phibun a letter pledging their backing but ominously requesting that they or their representatives be allowed to "sit beside" Phibun during every session of Parliament. The letter provoked a furor in Thai political circles, the U.S. embassy reported, when released to the press on April 19.[11] Kat, more than anyone else in this period, proved a nettle in Phibun's newly regained crown. His peculations greatly embarrassed the field marshal.

In October, a coup plot in the Army General Staff presented a new threat. The officers involved, including Lt. Gen. Sinat Yotharak, Pridi's former army commander-in-chief, and Maj. Gen. Net Khemayothin, Phibun's aide during the war and later a Free Thai, objected to the army's corrupt and inefficient leadership. Planning to arrest Phibun, top government officials, and leading army officers during a birthday party for Sarit Thanarat scheduled for the evening of October 1, these officers hoped to reorganize the military and professionalize its staff.[12] They received financial and moral backing, one of them told the British ambassador the night before the scheduled start of the coup, from a number of Pridi's allies, including Thamrong, Atthakit Phanomyong, and Direk Jayanama.[13] Although the officers enjoyed widespread support within the General Staff, the Coup Group apparently received advance notice of their plans. On September 21, Phin wrote the minister of the interior to suggest that the Ministry of Defense and other ministries carry out a purge of government officials. Phin claimed that the operation would eliminate "Communists" who had infiltrated the government, but, clearly, he was referring not to real Communists but to the rebellious officers.[14] On October 1, the cabinet approved Phin's recommendation, and that day, the arrests of the coup plotters began.[15] Before the week was over, more than fifty army and reserve army officers and several prominent Pridi supporters were arrested, and the government was crowing that it had thwarted a "communist" coup. The arrests, reassignments, and purges removed almost every high-ranking Army General Staff officer.[16] Although the plotters targeted not so much Phibun as Kat, Phin, and Phao, any such coup launched without the field marshal's support could only have undermined his authority. U.S. Chargé d'Affaires Barry Benson commented that the crisis "goes far to illustrate . . . that the greatest danger to Phibun's regime lies within the Army and those who originally established him."[17]

Faced with such threats, and especially the challenge from within the army, Phibun again asked the British and Americans in the first week of October—just days after the arrests of the coup plotters—for military assistance. His request, as with his April proposals, was substantial. Though he again failed to mention whether he wanted sales, loans, or grants, Phibun asked for enough automatic weapons, radios, trucks, and jeeps for five infantry battalions. To win over the westerners, he claimed that the army needed the equipment to suppress Malayan Communists taking refuge in southern Thai jungles. But clearly Phibun cared less about these ethnic Chinese Communists with no particular grudge against the Thai government than the political benefits he hoped to gain.[18] As he knew from experience, in Thailand, well-equipped soldiers tended to be happy soldiers.

Phibun's first three requests had gotten nowhere, but this one won a sympathetic reply. Although the United States had stood firmly opposed throughout the summer to Phibun's April aid request, the worsening situation in the region had already begun to affect the Americans' thinking. The communist insurrections in Burma and Indochina had gained ground throughout the spring, and, in June, the British declared a state of emergency in their economically vital Malayan colony. In the wake of the February Czechoslovakian communist coup and Red Army advances in China, such developments alarmed American policymakers. Many in Washington believed by that summer that a region-wide, Soviet-led, communist offensive anticipated in the spring had begun.

The State Department's response to these challenges, a conference in Bangkok from June 21 to June 26 of Office of Far Eastern Affairs officials and leading American diplomats from the Southeast Asian nations, defined the new American approach to Thailand. The State Department called such ambassadors' conferences merely to encourage the exchange of information and draft recommendations for Washington, not to set policy, but this conference merits examination. It forced Stanton and embassy officials for the first time since the November coup to examine in depth Thai politics, regional developments, and the implications for U.S. policy. The ideas Stanton and others presented there would guide America's Thailand policy for the next two years.

Thailand itself, the conferees agreed, had to worry little about communist subversion. The Communist Party of Thailand counted an "extremely small" membership, commanded little popular support, and enjoyed few prospects of expanding.[19] Although the party published a weekly newspaper, *Mahachon* (The Masses), the group's leaders had failed to widen the membership beyond a limited, primarily urban constituency. The conservative, religious, largely landowning Thai peasantry showed little interest in radical ideologies. Even the party's one MP, Prasert Sapsunthorn, understood little of Marxist principles. "The fear of exposing his ignorance of communist doctrine," the conference report speculated, "might well explain his [Prasert's] general reluctance to give interviews."[20] Though influential in the Chinese community, Communists were capable of mounting only an occasional strike or demonstration.[21]

The conference concluded, however, that, despite their relative weakness, Communists in Thailand threatened the region as a whole. The Soviets planned their new legation in Bangkok as a base of operations for Southeast Asia, Rolland Bushner, second secretary of the Bangkok embassy, told the conference.[22] The Vietminh in the northeast had long provided lines of communication for their comrades in Indochina. Now that the new U.S.S.R. legation had started operations, the Soviets would similarly employ Chinese Communists to transmit instructions to Malaya and Burma. Chinese Communists, the conference summary claimed, were well-organized and eager to perform the Kremlin's bidding.[23] The Soviets, moreover, were not limiting their activities to harassing noncommunist governments militarily. The U.S.S.R., Stanton explained to the conference delegates, had initiated a plan to sell underpriced goods through Chinese firms in Thailand to drive the British and Americans from the marketplace in Southeast Asia.[24] John Paton Davies of the State Department's Policy Planning Staff commented that "the whole problem sounded very ominous."[25]

Such conclusions, though resulting in no immediate policy changes, forced U.S. officials to view Phibun's aid requests in a new light. The conference had directed the Americans' thoughts to the problem of communism in Thailand and the country's significance for the fight against the ideology's spread in the region. As a result, Cold War concerns moved to the forefront of America's Thai policy after June. With the communist threat to Asia growing, this new focus meant that Thailand's importance to America's Southeast Asia policy would increase daily. Although Stanton betrayed no sympathy for Phibun's aid requests at the conference, for the first time, Thailand's crucial role within the region had grabbed the Americans' attention. Now, a material investment in the country in the form of military assistance might seem worthwhile.

Understanding the new American concerns, Phibun pressed forward with a plan to remake his image in the West. Since early 1947, Phibun had placed his hopes for winning over the West on an effort to portray himself as a hardline anti-Communist. While emphasizing other issues when speaking with Thais, he always mentioned in interviews with the foreign press or meetings with Western diplomats his abhorrence of Communists. He engaged his old friend, M. Siviram, the Reuter correspondent in Bangkok, as an unofficial publicist in the campaign. Siviram published a stream of articles in 1948 trumpeting the field marshal's anticommunist credentials.[26] Although Phibun occasionally delivered his message clumsily, he took care in scheduling and targeting his statements. He issued one important statement, a claim that the Thai people would stand firm against communism despite the infiltration of insurgents into the country from Indochina and Malaya, to the American-owned *Bangkok Post*. Though a poor instrument for warning his countrymen of the communist threat, the English-language

Post offered Phibun the ideal medium for impressing foreigners with his opposition to communism. As usual, he timed his statement to the *Post* impeccably. He gave the interview on June 25, as the diplomats and State Department officials met in Bangkok at the regional conference.[27]

Phibun's publicity campaign had its effect on the Americans. Embassy First Secretary James Scott told the conference in June that, "if his [Phibun's] government were threatened with Communism[,] he would deal effectively with it," and, in a September 10 telegram to the Nanking embassy, the State Department referred to Phibun's government as "anti-communist" and urged the Nationalist Chinese government to support him on that basis. No one at the June conference suggested doing anything to weaken Phibun.[28]

Phibun's publicity campaign succeeded not because it thoroughly convinced the Americans, but because the ambiguities in his stance troubled them. Although Phibun had suppressed the few leftists in Thailand during his first term as prime minister, his opposition to communism after the war proved far from unyielding. Ideology maintained only a minor role in the Thai political system of the late 1940s. Phibun, having championed democracy in the 1932 coup only to abandon it in the late 1930s for semifascism before finally embracing the military dictatorship–parliamentary hybrid of the post-April 1948 regime, adopted new political philosophies readily. At the very least, his economic policies did not conflict strongly with communist ideals. Since Chinese controlled the country's domestic commerce, Phibun favored state-owned industry over private enterprise.

Indeed, Phibun's policy toward local Chinese highlighted his indifference to ideology. Because of Thai suspicions that the Kuomintang had incited the 1945 riots, at no point in 1948 or 1949 did Phibun selectively target Chinese Communists for repression. Instead, he intentionally maintained a balance between Communists and local Kuomintang partisans. Although his government perpetually harassed Chinese schools, newspapers, and secret societies, he repressed Communist and Kuomintang activists equally. The repeated arrests hit the Kuomintang so hard that the government in Nanking asked the United States in September (without success) to help it topple Phibun.[29] That same month, conservatives in Parliament criticized Phibun's minister of the interior, Liang Chayakan, for the government's lackadaisical attitude toward Chinese Communists. Liang responded bluntly that Thailand had no communist problem.[30] Later, in December, when another MP attacked the government's tolerance of Communists, Phibun similarly replied that, "at present, as you must know, there is not at all any unrest in Thailand created by admitted Communists."[31] Phibun genuinely opposed communism, but his emotions on the subject did not run deep. Communists were just one of several foreign and domestic groups, along with Muslim separatists in the south, Pridi supporters, Burmese, and Chinese, that he disliked or feared. And Communists almost certainly did not appear at the top of Phibun's most-wanted list. Communism raised fears in Thailand largely because of its association with the Chinese. Since foreigners accounted for almost all of the prewar Communists in Thailand, Phibun's early arrests of Communists had, in fact, amounted to a suppression of Chinese. The only consistent elements of his political thought were his nationalism and ethnic chauvinism.

The Coup Group held similar views. Phin, Kat, and Phao espoused a fervent anticommunism when meeting westerners, but nationalism and anti-Sinicism figured most prominently in their political thinking. During Khuang's last weeks in office, though Coup Group members never advocated stricter anticommunist measures, they loudly criticized Khuang for not acting against the Chinese. An article in *Thahan Ma* (Cavalry) monthly magazine in March 1948, "Jek Teun Fai kap Jek Prathad" (Panicky People and Firecracker Chinese), typified the military viewpoint. Employing the derogatory term for Chinese, *jek,* the article ridiculed Chinese personal habits and lashed out at their disloyalty, refusal to assimilate, and formation of communal societies that acted as "governments."[32] Kat was the most vocal member of the Coup Group in denouncing the Chinese. Ever since the 1947 coup, he had spread rumors or publicly warned of Chinese plots to take over the country.[33]

A speech Phibun delivered over the radio in February 1949 revealed clearly his own views of communism. Beginning his talk with a lengthy description of the international situation, Phibun explained that most of the world was at war and that some of the fiercest conflicts were close to Thailand. Political "ideologies" or "doctrines" *(latthi),* Phibun claimed, had created these disputes. Political doctrines pitted people of the same nation against each other and tore countries apart. Citing not merely the struggle of the West against the communist nations but also the Palestine war, a conflict not involving communism, Phibun warned Thais to shun political doctrines of any kind. Communism appeared in his paradigm as merely a secondary danger. Only once the spread of political doctrines had already riven Thai society would Communists take over the country. Phibun displayed here a distrust of any set of political principles other than ethnic Thai national-ism. Communism, Chinese Nationalist (Kuomintang) ideology, Muslim religious and cultural revivalism, and even democratic liberalism—all distracted Thais, in Phibun's eyes, from the task of building the state and nation. The announcement betrayed Phibun's awareness that any political doctrine could threaten the very basis of the nonideological political system he and the Coup Group thrived in. Were ideology to replace the dispensation of patronage and use of force as the main props of Thai political groupings, Phibun and the Coup Group would be left without a leg to stand on. Although he aimed his February announcement primarily at the threat of a Pridi countercoup, the ideas Phibun expressed in the speech revealed the failure not only of him-self, but of much of the military as well, to identify communism as uniquely evil or dangerous.[34]

Phibun's treatment of the Indochinese problem typified the Thai government's two-track approach to communism. On the one hand, Phibun and the Coup Group continually emphasized to France their opposition to the Indochinese rebels. The Coup Group branded as communist the anti-French Southeast Asia League Pridi had founded in mid-1947 and disavowed any intention to aid the Vietminh or the Laotian and Cambodian independence groups, the Lao Issara and Khmer Issarak. In May 1948, Phibun renounced unequivocally any claim to the retroceded Cambodian and Laotian territories.[35] During a trip to Saigon in September, Kat signed an agreement allowing France to pursue Indochinese guerrillas into Thai territory and committing the Thai government to suppressing the lucrative cross-border arms trade. While Phibun and the Coup Group said all the right things, how-ever, they backed their words with few actions. Although Phibun pro-vided the Indochinese rebels in the northeast of Thailand with no material assistance as Pridi had, he allowed them to operate relatively freely. Each of the Indochinese groups maintained a purchasing mis-sion in Bangkok, and arms smuggling continued unabated. The Thai government never implemented Kat's agreement with the French. Phibun simply claimed that Kat's mission lacked official sanction.[36] Phibun may not have approved of the Vietminh's communist connec-tions, and the Thais never bore an excessive fondness for Cambodians and Vietnamese, their traditional rivals, but Phibun had no desire to offend the Vietminh, the possible future masters of Indochina. Thai animosity for the French remained intense. Thais from all points of the political spectrum resented France for bullying Pridi into returning the Laotian and Cambodian territories, and, in their franker moments,

Thai officials expressed openly their desire to see the French leave Indochina. An article from the cavalry journal, *Thahan Ma*, even praised the Communists for aiding Indochinese nationalists fighting the French.[37]

Phibun's treatment of Indochinese represented only one aspect of a broader decision, linked to the government's political weakness, to tolerate domestic Communists. With the navy, the Free Thai, the Democrats, and anti-Coup Group army officers all waiting for any chance to overthrow his regime, Phibun could not afford to make new enemies. Although no domestic Communists—Thai, Chinese, or Vietnamese—considered Phibun their friend, none did anything tangible to oppose him. While Chinese Communists protested the occasional harassment the party suffered, they cared much more about overturning the government in China than about fighting a regime in what many considered a temporary home. Likewise, the other two groups of domestic Communists never took up arms against the government. As long as Phibun only talked about anticommunism, ethnic-Thai Communists limited their attacks to verbal criticism. The Vietnamese, eager to retain their refuge and base of operations, did not go even that far. Through the end of the decade, they spoke of Phibun—as they spoke of all Thais—only in terms of friendship. While these domestic Communists posed little threat to his government as long as he left them alone, had Phibun launched an all-out offensive against them, the outcome would have been uncertain. Pridi's purges had weakened the government's principal investigative body, the police's Santiban division (then known in English as the Criminal Investigation Department and later as the Special Branch Division), and intelligence on leftists was poor.[38] A crackdown on domestic Communists might only have driven them into insurgency.

The Thai government's vulnerability internationally convinced Phibun that caution was the order of the day regarding domestic communism. The Southeast Asia of the late 1940s presented numerous dangers to Phibun and the Coup Group. Communists were on the march in Malaya, Burma, and Indochina, and, most alarmingly, appeared on the verge of victory in the potential superpower of East Asia, China. In the meantime, the West, and America in particular, showed little interest in protecting Thailand. The United States and Britain continued to begrudge Thailand even a token of their commitment to the country's safety, much less something of substance like a concerted aid program or a pledge to defend the country against attack. Phibun and the Coup Group perceived a threat, moreover, not merely from the communist powers. Few forgot the support that Britain and the United States had given Pridi and Khuang in the immediate postwar years, and, even after the West's assent to Phibun's resumption of power, Britain maintained its friendship with the navy, while the community of oss-officers-turned-businessmen continued to call for Pridi's return. Fears of U.S. or British support for a countercoup kept Phibun and the Coup Group on pins and needles throughout 1948 and 1949. During the October General Staff crisis, Phao placed police guards inside the British and American embassy compounds to prevent the coup plotters from contacting the westerners.[39] Although the move clearly violated the compounds' sovereign status, the Coup Group's continued distrust of the Western powers overwhelmed any regard Phibun and the generals held for diplomatic protocol.

By allowing Communists to operate relatively unimpeded within the country, Phibun maintained his maneuverability within this uncertain and dangerous international environment. His soft-pedaling of the communist question from the beginning won him unexpected foreign friends. Like the Vietminh, the Soviets refrained from criticizing Phibun in any way in 1948 and 1949.[40] Although Mao's forces objected to Phibun's anti-Chinese policies, a focused attack on local Chinese Communists would surely have antagonized Mao further. Thus surrounded by fickle friends and appeasable adversaries, Phibun may even have planned to co-opt leftists into a coalition government if communist victory in the region appeared inevitable. With leftists in his government providing political cover, he possibly reasoned, he could hope to survive either Thailand's passage to the communist sphere of influence— as he had survived and prospered from the Japanese occupation—or renewed hostility toward his regime from the West. With no hard evidence to support it, such an explanation must remain speculative, but the Americans, at least, believed it.

An entirely incoherent interview Phibun gave Tillman Durdin of the *New York Times* in July 1948 revealed clearly the competing international pressures the field marshal was confronting. Phibun claimed in the interview that he resolutely opposed the spread of communism. He was planning to introduce legislation soon to outlaw the pernicious ideology, he boasted, and explained that he had recently placed troops at strategic points in Bangkok to protect against communist attack. In the same breath, however, he denied that conservative, religious Thailand had to worry about communism and described himself as "not left, but not too right." He noted that the police had charged sixty-one Chinese recently arrested with membership in secret societies, not communist activities, and affirmed that Thailand would maintain friendly relations and continue to trade with the Soviet Union. He denied that the fall of any of Thailand's neighbors to communism would threaten the country. He had called the military alert that he cited, moreover, actually in response to the ever-present rumors of coups by anti-Coup Group army and navy officers. Though evident to all who read the interview, these contradictions in no way reflected muddled thinking on the field marshal's part. Phibun spoke lucidly when willing, but he was talking here to two audiences at once. On the one hand, he was trying to win over the West with pledges of good anti-communist intentions. On the other hand, however, he wanted to reassure foreign and domestic Communists that he in no way planned to act on those intentions.[41]

In this early period, therefore, Phibun never initiated the suppression of Communists the Americans wanted. As he promised Durdin, Phibun ordered the Juridical Council (Kritsadika) to draft an anticommunist bill the day after the *New York Times* interview, but the law bore little resemblance to the specifically anticommunist measure he had described earlier. The bill, never presented to Parliament or made public, would have increased penalties for the commission of a variety of serious criminal offenses if done with the aim of "spreading a political or economic doctrine [*latthi*]." Titled "A Draft Act to Set Punishments for Offenses Threatening the Security of the Realm," the broadly defined bill targeted Pridi, Muslims, and the Kuomintang as much as any communist organization. Indeed, the timing of Phibun's message to the Juridical Council—a day after his meeting with Durdin—raises suspicions that he granted the interview primarily to impress the westerners with his plan. Or, possibly, given his propensity to oversell himself in press encounters, he sent the order to the Juridical Council only after having spoken more boldly to Durdin than he had originally intended. In any case, Phibun ordered the matter dropped in December.[42] Communism remained legal, and Communists stayed active. The party newspaper, *Mahachon*, continued to publish.

These ambiguities in Phibun's policy toward communism abroad and at home provoked a restless anxiety in the Americans. Although Phibun's campaign to portray himself as anticommunist had convinced many that he carried sound instincts, his equivocation also induced fears that he lacked the decisiveness to take effective action. In the months following the June 1948 ambassadors' conference in Bangkok, therefore, the United States held up Phibun's willingness to crack down on local Communists as a test of his good faith. In a meeting with

Phibun on June 30, Stanton told the field marshal in so many words what the United States wanted. After Phibun apologized for not capturing major communist figures in the arrests of the Chinese that Phibun had discussed with Durdin, Stanton described to Phibun "the increase in the activities of communists in Southeast Asia and [noted] that these activities appeared to be well-coordinated and had been intensified in recent weeks." Understanding completely the suggestion implicit in Stanton's statement of "concern," Phibun pledged that the government would "take steps against the communists in Bangkok."[43] In Washington in late August, Landon similarly lobbied the Thai ambassador, Prince Wan. When Wan told Landon that the government planned no action against Chinese Communists in the provinces, Landon cited the danger presented by communist advances in Burma, Malaya, and Indochina. Wan calmly replied that Thailand would maintain friendly relations with its neighbors, no matter who governed them. Thoroughly annoyed with Wan's insouciance, Landon tried to gain the prince's support for strong anticommunist measures with a crude appeal to traditional Thai prejudices. "I reminded him," Landon recounted, "of the centuries of perennial warfare which had gone on among the Burmese, Annamese [Vietnamese] and Siamese." Wan, though, stood his ground, and Phibun maintained his tolerance of Communists within the country and proper relations with the U.S.S.R.[44]

Whether he had intended it, the anxieties Phibun's equivocation provoked helped him in the fall with his most recent aid request. Col. Elliot Thorpe, the embassy's military attaché, almost immediately recommended that Washington accede to the request, and, on October 27, Stanton added his approval.[45] Britain's Ambassador Thompson, at the same time, advised the Foreign Office to provide the weapons, and in Washington, the State and Defense departments began actively reviewing the matter.[46]

Although Stanton and Colonel Thorpe couched their recommendations in terms of military expediency, no one believed that more weapons would increase Thai military potency. The various branches of the Thai military functioned much more as political instruments than defense forces, and military effectiveness was minimal. The Americans considered discipline within the army poor, while, perversely, an excess of generals and officers rendered it unwieldy. The army maintained eleven regional commands, one American observer noted, partly because "such a number would take care of all the generals which they [the Thai army] now have."[47] Interservice cooperation was nonexistent. The suppression of the October 1948 coup plot had paralyzed the

Army General Staff, already something of a retirement home for old generals, and the navy, air force, and army commanders operated their services like self-governing fiefs. The minister of defense administered the army, the deputy minister of defense oversaw the navy minister, and the assistant minister of defense supervised the air force. Because individual commanders designated the ministers overseeing their respective services, they retained complete control over their branches. One American complained, "It is unfortunate that . . . the three Commanders in Chief are able to play their own individual games unhindered by any regard of a unified service. Combined exercises are unheard of, and combined action in combat would be impossible."[48] Interservice rivalries added to the confusion. The navy, the army, and, to a lesser extent, the police remained blood enemies throughout the late 1940s. The army positioned the bulk of its forces not on the borders to protect against foreign attacks and incursions, but in the Bangkok area to counter navy and police forces. Indeed, until 1950, the military had no plans for the defense of the country. Even then, Phibun ordered one drafted merely in response to a Foreign Ministry memorandum indicating that its presentation to the United States would strengthen Thailand's case for receiving aid.[49] In such circumstances, military aid would less likely help the armed forces defend the country than it would increase the intensity of the internecine clash both Thais and westerners believed probable in the near future.

The extracurricular activities of the irrepressible Kat Katsongkhram widened these divisions. The October 1948 coup plot had been aimed primarily at ousting Kat and ending his raid on the Thai treasury and military budget. Then, a mere month later, the story broke that Kat had expropriated for his own use much of 9.5 million *baht* (about $475,000) procured from the treasury for purchase of clothing and army supplies. The finance minister's revelation of the embezzlement on November 9 enraged the public, the navy, and non-Coup Group army officers. The scandal led to a cabinet reshuffle on November 30, and high-ranking army officers reportedly demanded Kat's resignation. Stanton considered the event a serious blow to the country's defenses. Prince Dhani, a member of the Supreme Council of State, Stanton approvingly reported, claimed that, because of Kat's unpopularity in the ranks, the "army [was] split, demoralized and could not be depended upon [to] act as [a] bulwark against [the] Communist threat."[50]

In February 1949, the so-called Palace Rebellion proved the near impossibility of building the Thai military into an effective fighting force. In the immediate aftermath of the November 1947 coup, Pridi

disavowed violence, but, by the beginning of 1949, his frustrations overcame him. While in exile in China, he had maintained contacts with his
supporters in Thailand and, with their help, laid plans for a countercoup. In the first week of February 1949, he secretly returned to Thailand. Phibun, learning of Pridi's intentions, announced over the radio
that he considered Pridi his "friend" and was willing to do anything to
"bring union to the Siamese nation" and later offered Pridi a position
in the government, but Pridi rebuffed Phibun's overtures.[51] He went
ahead with his plans, and, on February 16, the government voted to
declare a state of emergency, issued a week later.[52] On February 26, the
countercoup began. That morning, an army officer loyal to Pridi and a
group of supporters seized a radio station, and Free Thai elements and
Thammasat University teachers and students occupied the Royal
Palace. The group at the radio station announced over the air the formation of a new government headed by Pridi's friend, Direk Jayanama.
Sarit then moved the army to the palace to crush the coup, while the
navy and marines, whether they had participated in the planning for
the coup or merely came in after the fact to protect their allies, took
defensive positions in the city. Although Sarit managed to oust Pridi
from the palace grounds fairly quickly the following morning, the
rebels escaped in navy vessels across the river, and naval forces engaged
the army in fierce battles in the city. A cease-fire was declared that afternoon, but tensions remained high for another week as the navy and the
Coup Group negotiated a resolution to the crisis. Finally, on March 3,
the two sides agreed to a simultaneous withdrawal of forces from
Bangkok.[53]

   The Palace Rebellion demonstrated most tellingly the inability of
the Thai government, as it then stood, to defend the country. Politically, the coup attempt intensified already fierce personal and institutional disputes. It brought the most intense fighting the capital had
ever seen, and hundreds of bystanders and an unknown number of par-
ticipants died in the struggle. On the day of the force-withdrawal agreement, in the crackdown accompanying the suppression of the coup,
Phao's police murdered six Pridi supporters they had arrested, including four northeastern MPs. The violence left Pridi supporters seething
at the government's brutality and Phibun and the Coup Group outraged by Pridi's treachery. Although it turned out that the coup
attempt ended Pridi's ability to influence the course of events in Thailand, the Coup Group remained terrified of the possibility of a Pridi
return to Thailand for years.

   The disunity the attempted coup had uncovered within the armed forces showed just how incapable the government was of protecting Thailand from foreign aggressors and how little military assistance would strengthen defenses. As Thailand's neighbors descended into chaos, the watchmen of Thailand's independence, the army and navy, had left their posts to settle old scores. A foreign aggressor could easily have exploited the fighting to its advantage. The danger the fighting had raised, moreover, could only increase in the future. The coup attempt transformed the latent mistrust between the army and navy into an active enmity while it also left both forces almost entirely intact. Renewed conflict was nearly inevitable. Amid such tensions, any argument for military assistance claiming that the Thais would put the weapons to good use was laughable. No American would raise it for some time.

Rather than for military purposes, therefore, Stanton, Colonel Thorpe, and Southeast Asian Division officials now supported aid out of the purely political desire to strengthen Phibun's shaky anticommunism. In a November 1948 report, Stanton claimed that aid was needed to maintain Thailand's pro-Western policies. If the West refused Phibun, he commented, Thais would lose faith in the West and soften their opposition to the Communists. "We cannot expect the Siamese to remain on our side and combat the growing strength of Communism in Asia," the ambassador concluded, "if we refuse to give them material military support in at least token quantities."[54] Stanton's argument quickly won adherents. Malcolm MacDonald, Britain's commissioner-general for Southeast Asia, told Stanton at the end of the month that "the psychological effect of giving some assistance would be great and that on the other hand a refusal to give any assistance would be interpreted as an abandonment of Siam to the menace of Communism."[55] Southeast Asian Division chief Charles Reed repeated Stanton's concerns when reporting to Butterworth. Thailand, Reed noted to his superior, "has traditionally guaranteed her security by taking on the political coloration of her strong neighbors." Reed feared that the Thais would "assume the political pattern of Communism out of expediency" after the fall of China.[56] Although he did not address the question of aid here, his statement carried the implication that only tangible evidence of Western interest in Thailand could stiffen Thai resolve. Otherwise, the weak Thai reed would inevitably bend with the communist wind.

From November 1948 to January 1949, Phibun's failure to repress Communists within the country convinced these officials of the political urgency of an assistance program. In separate meetings in November and December, Stanton and MacDonald expressed their concerns to Phibun about communist activities in Thailand. Although Phibun promised both men that he would capture the Chinese Communist leaders the police had failed to arrest in the summer sweep, he never acted on the pledge.[57] British and American worries, as a result, multiplied. Indeed, the Thais' propensity to speak loudly but carry a small stick continually rankled the Americans. In mid-November, the government announced formation of a high-ranking, interministerial Central Peace Maintenance Committee charged with preventing internal disturbances by communist elements. U.S. Military Attaché Thorpe complained that "the composition of the Committee affords good opportunity for establishment of an actual Gestapo," but Stanton retorted that, "in fact, however, it seems to be merely another top-heavy grouping of which the Siamese are so fond[,] and it is doubtful that any concrete results in the way of good order will be achieved."[58] When his prediction proved correct in the coming weeks, Stanton's frustration increased. The problem, he believed, derived from Thais' heightened concern, in the wake of communist advances in mainland China, over a communist takeover of Southeast Asia. "Fears of Communist domination and control of Siam," Stanton claimed, "have reached serious proportions and there is a tendency among Siamese of a particularly fatalistic turn of mind to accept such domination as inevitable."[59] Certain that Thai officials' insecurity prevented them from dealing properly with the internal communist menace, Stanton urged that the United States supply military aid to bolster their anticommunist resolve. A "concrete manifestation" of U.S. support, such as an arms program, he contended, "would provide definite stimulus [to] counteract and possibly dispel this feeling of fatalism and insure more active opposition both mental and physical to [the] spread [of] Communism [in] this country."[60] Military aid, in other words, would encourage the Thais to crack down on communist dissidents.

The British agreed that aid was needed. While sharing Stanton's concern over Communists within the country, London had special reason to want to arm the five battalions in the south. The Malayan Communists' ability to freely cross the border to Thai territory was hampering British efforts to quell the insurgency in Malaya, and London badly wanted Thai cooperation in suppressing the insurgents but, during the summer of 1948, was getting little. Although Phibun agreed to send additional troops to the south and speed the extradition of captured Malayan Communists, the Thais resisted British pressure to fight the rebels.[61] "The Siamese authorities on the spot," one British official

complained, "are clearly intimidated by the Communists and are unwilling to take any firm action against them."[62] More important, the
Thais possibly sympathized with the insurgents' desire to drive the
British out of Malaya. Phibun and the Coup Group knew that Muslim
separatists in the south received moral and material support from
Malays in the Malayan state of Kelantan and suspected that the British
were aiding the separatists' political leader, Mahyidden, then residing
in the Kelantan capital of Kota Bahru.[63] Indeed, Phibun had every
reason to distrust lower-ranking British officials in Malaya. As the Thais
may have learned, one British colonial official actually proposed that
Britain annex the four Thai southern provinces.[64] Certainly, Phibun
resented pressure the British had applied on him in June to cease operations against the southern Muslim separatists.[65]

London, therefore, now supported military aid to Thailand both to
soothe Thai anxieties over British intentions in the south and to enable
the Thai army to tackle the communist border problem. In late November, the Defense Ministry, on Foreign Office recommendation, approved
selling the arms requested.[66] Since the British felt capable of providing
only the small arms, ammunition, and radio equipment Thompson
had discussed with Stanton in November, they wanted the United States
to supply the necessary jeeps and armored vehicles. The British thus
added their voices to the Thais' in urging the Americans to carry their
heavier half of the aid burden.

But progress came more slowly in Washington. Concern in the
embassy and Division of Southeast Asian Affairs over the spread of communism in Thailand and Southeast Asia had increased since 1947, but
the rest of official Washington did not yet consider the issue urgent.
State Department officials and General Staff officers met on November
5 to determine a response to the Thai aid request. Deciding that the
United States maintained little strategic interest in Thailand, they set
aside the matter of aid to Thailand for possible inclusion in any future
assistance program for Southeast Asia.[67]

That decision ensured that the Thais would have a long wait before
receiving any aid. Without special legislation authorizing aid for Thailand, a Thai program could only come under a worldwide, omnibus
foreign assistance bill the administration planned to present to Congress in the summer of 1949. Even then, inclusion of Thailand in the
bill faced obstacles. While the 1947 and 1948 aid programs for Greece,
Turkey, and western Europe had earlier raised hopes that the United
States would soon assist other parts of the world, programs for non-
European nations, with a few exceptions, failed to materialize. Through

1948 and 1949, the only aid to mainland Southeast Asia remained the indirect assistance to the French war effort in Indochina offered by Marshall Plan aid for France. Thailand could receive aid only if the administration included the country in the omnibus bill set for the summer, and if Congress passed it.

As the summer 1949 presentation of this bill approached, Stanton and supporters of aid in the Southeast Asian Division grew more insistent that it provide for Thailand. By the late spring of 1949, the need for the United States to provide assistance appeared to these officials urgent. Under the weight of price disputes and Thai gripes over London's insistence on selling, not giving, the arms promised, the British aid program had, by then, nearly collapsed. The Thais decided in May to purchase only a fraction of the arms the British offered, and even those weapons were delivered late.[68] Deputy Under Secretary of State for Political Affairs Dean Rusk, worried over the failure of the British program, suggested prodding London to provide the arms immediately and talk price later, but the embassy and Division of Southeast Asian Affairs argued that the United States had to produce its own assistance package.[69] During the spring, Stanton and Thorpe sent five dispatches encouraging Washington to provide military aid. Thorpe claimed in early June that, because of communist advances in China and the region, "the potential threat to Thailand's political integrity is much more serious than three months ago." Underlining his final prophecy of doom to add a sense of urgency to the appeal, Thorpe concluded that "the Army, fully aware of the Communist threat, is counting heavily on foreign aid. If such aid is not forthcoming the Army will, along with the Field Marshal, reorient its position towards Communism."[70]

Such arguments failed to convince senior officials in Washington. Stanton, Reed, and Thorpe had asserted that aid was needed to strengthen Thailand's "will to resist," but, in an April telegram to the embassy, Dean Acheson, now secretary of state, turned the political argument for aid on its head. The Thais, Acheson explained, needed to clean their house before, not after, they received any arms. Otherwise, they would waste the aid, as the Chinese had. Were the United States to provide assistance before the Thai government had strengthened itself, "the Siamese might be led to the erroneous conclusion that the struggle against communism in Siam is primarily an American one to which the Siamese may contribute some help, if they see fit, rather than primarily a Siamese responsibility."[71] Then escaping one sinking ship in China, Acheson was in no mood to climb aboard another in Southeast

Asia. Acheson, moreover, still accorded little attention to Thailand and Southeast Asia. The comprehensive foreign military assistance bill the State Department was then drafting focused on Europe. In Asia, only Nationalist China, South Korea, and the United States' former colony, the Philippines, seemed likely to receive grants of weapons. The draft contemplated allowing Thailand, like India, Pakistan, and Latin America, only the right to purchase arms.[72] Although Stanton recommended that, such being the case, the United States should sell the Thais weapons at bargain-basement prices, he received no response.[73] Washington was prepared to offer only the same package the Thais had already rejected when proposed by the British.

But a transformation in American attitudes had occurred over the fourteen months from April 1948 to June 1949 that laid the basis for later profound changes. From opposing military aid as politically undesirable in late 1947 and early 1948, many American officials came to support aid in the fall of 1948 and first half of 1949 as a crucial diplomatic tool in the fight against communism. Assistance would reinforce the Thai government's oft-proclaimed but weak pro-Western policies and encourage Phibun to establish the anticommunist internal order the United States accorded such importance. This rationale rapidly won over official Washington. When developments in the State Department and Congress finally took a turn for the better over the coming months, it provided the intellectual foundation that made military assistance—and a revolution in postwar Thai foreign policy—possible.

Chapter Five

U.S. MILITARY AID AND THAILAND'S

COMMITMENT TO THE WEST,

JUNE 1949–DECEMBER 1950

As late as July 1949, Phibun's foreign and domestic policies toward communism remained unchanged. He still proclaimed his commitment to fighting communism, but when the subject turned to actions, he equivocated. When a member of Parliament asked in February what he was doing to protect against communism, he responded that "there is now no communist unrest in Thailand," and, in June, he told a British newsman that Thailand would support a Western-led security pact in Southeast Asia but dismissed the need for the government to take any defensive measures. He explained in the interview that, "for our country, there is not much to be feared from communism." "The Premier," the reporter recounted, "did not consider that there existed in Siam any 'extreme left' party in its true sense, though it is known that there are two or three communists. To keep the balance, the Premier is holding a middle course between the leftists and the rightists."[1] In early July, when an MP griped that the field marshal's aggressive criticism of the communist powers was endangering the country, Phibun replied that "I will consider... toning down [criticism of Communists] in interviews with foreign newspapers."[2] Phibun again promised Stanton in late June that the government would issue an anti-communist law but, as before, failed to act.[3] The Thai government continued to wink at Vietminh activities in Bangkok and the northeast, the police still tolerated communist as much as other local Chinese organizations, and, in January 1949, Phibun broached the possibility of establishing relations with any future communist government in China.[4] Caution, prudence, and inaction remained the defining features of Thai foreign policy.

Phibun's desire for American military assistance, however, induced him to harden his policy stance. Over the preceding year, military pressure on Phibun to win foreign arms shipments had intensified. Coup rumors increased following the Palace Rebellion, and the navy, non-Coup Group army officers, and the Coup Group itself all threatened his position. American aid, Phibun hoped, would placate dissident military elements. In an August 2 speech to senior officers of the three branches, he explained that the foreign powers were refusing to supply arms because they "fear that we will fight each other." To help gain the aid they all desired, he urged the officers to support "His Majesty's government," that is, Phibun.[5] As the speech clearly shows, Phibun at the time was facing serious military criticism of his failure to extract any weapons from the United States. Equally clearly, it demonstrates that Phibun was counting on American aid to enhance his tenuous standing with the military.

TAKING A FIRMER STANCE

Just as Phibun's need for U.S. military aid increased, his hopes of receiving it brightened. Stung by criticism from congressional Republicans over the administration's "loss" of China and frustrated by the West's seeming inability to stem the communist advance in Asia, Acheson began to reconsider his attitude toward military aid for Southeast Asia in the summer of 1949. A paper the State Department prepared in July calling for the United States to retake the initiative in the East convinced him that he should adopt a more positive policy for East and Southeast Asia.[6] Therefore, when the administration submitted to Congress its omnibus aid bill on July 28, Acheson threw his weight behind Southeast Asia. Congressmen immediately attacked the draft for designating none of the recipient countries—in effect, the administration was asking for a $1.4 billion blank check—but Acheson defended the bill. Testifying before the Senate Foreign Relations Committee the first week of August, he explained that "there was a desire also to have a certain amount of flexibility with Southeast Asia. There will be problems with regard to the Philippines and Siam and places of that sort that would make some flexibility necessary." Although the administration quickly abandoned its dream of a billion-dollar-plus slush fund, Acheson and the State Department continued to fight for some sort of contingency reserve for East and Southeast Asia. On August 8, Acheson told an open session of the Senate committee that he supported appropriating a small sum of money to be used in the Far East at Truman's discretion. Three days later, he testified to a closed House session that he favored a contingency fund of $75 million to $100 million for China or elsewhere in Asia.[7]

In the weeks that followed, the domestic politics of foreign policy, more than his growing interest in containing communism in Southeast Asia, led Acheson into supporting even more strongly an aid program for the region. Congress, sensitive to the influence of the China Lobby, pushed for continued high levels of aid for Chiang Kai-shek's Nationalist government, but Acheson, now viewing China as a lost cause, opposed providing large amounts of military assistance to the Chinese Nationalists, assistance he feared would fail to save China while shoving the Chinese Communists into Stalin's embrace. To thwart the China Lobby, he decided to shift funds intended for the Nationalists to other parts of Asia. The United States could then begin extracting itself from the morass in China, and the administration would be able to use the money in places that needed it. Acheson had not yet resolved to provide aid to Southeast Asia, but his congressional strategy inexorably pushed him in that direction. Thus, although he continued to reject proposals from the embassy and the Office of Philippine and Southeast Asian Affairs (the reorganized Division of Southeast Asian Affairs) for aid for Thailand in July, he began in August a concerted campaign to divert aid for China to a generalized fund for the Far East.[8] He engaged in active horse-trading with Congress over the contours of the Asian aid program in the first two weeks of the month, and, on August 24, the chairman of the Senate Foreign Relations Committee, Tom Connally, announced that he and Acheson had agreed on a $100 million contingency fund for the Far East.[9] Congress and the administration remained far from a resolution of the dispute, but, for the first time, chances appeared good that the United States would have a substantial military assistance program for Southeast Asia in 1950.

It is not clear how closely Phibun followed developments in Washington in July and August, but he had easy access to information on the progress there. The local press gave prominent coverage to reports (unsubstantiated) that Truman now favored providing material assistance to anticommunist Asian nations, and Prince Wan in Washington cabled the Foreign Ministry on July 31 that, as he understood it, the United States would provide aid to its formal allies and to "other nations whose increased ability to defend themselves against aggression is important to the national interests in the U.S.A."[10] Phibun, therefore, probably understood that Thailand had a good shot at getting a slice of the $1.4 billion pie.

To further improve his prospects—now brighter than ever— Phibun made his first tentative steps that summer and fall away from the cautious policies of the past. As before, Phibun offered the Americans more style than substance and never carried his policy initiatives beyond the public relations arena, but even his merely rhetorical hardening of policy mattered. Although this change of tone itself was limited, Phibun's firmer public stance helped put in motion a new policy dialectic that continually pushed the Thais and Americans closer together. Once Phibun had begun reshaping Thai foreign relations in these months, American and Thai policies reinforced each other. Progress on the aid issue in Washington, on the one hand, consistently emboldened Phibun to denounce communism more loudly, while, on the other hand, the harsher anticommunist rhetoric that progress on aid inspired further improved Thailand's prospects for receiving assistance. As the two sides gained confidence in each other, barriers to closer relations fell.

An excellent opportunity for Phibun to distance himself from the cautious policies of the past and prove his anticommunist mettle arose with the renewed movement in July and August toward an anticommunist pact of East and Southeast Asian nations. Philippine President Elpidio Quirino had first proposed a "Pacific Pact" of noncommunist Asian governments in March 1949. Because the United States, wary of overextending itself, demonstrated no interest in sponsoring a defensive alliance, Quirino had replaced the suggested pact's military aspects with provisions for economic cooperation and later abandoned the project altogether, but a meeting of Quirino and Chiang Kai-shek in mid-July in the Philippine city of Baguio breathed new life into the plan. As Quirino had done in March, the two leaders called on noncommunist Asian nations to join in fighting the communist menace.[11]

This latest initiative proved useful to Phibun because of the confusion it provoked. Chiang and Quirino reiterated at Baguio their desire to establish a military-oriented, explicitly anticommunist Pacific Union, but domestic opposition and other Asian states' reluctance to associate themselves with the discredited Chinese Nationalists quickly forced Quirino to backpedal again. He once more dropped the pact's military provisions and proposed instead an economic, political, and cultural Southeast Asia Union excluding Chiang. Chiang, in the meantime, continued to lobby for the anticommunist Pacific Union, enrolling South Korea's Syngman Rhee in the effort. By August, therefore, two separate plans to promote noncommunist Asian unity were on the table, and no one knew which plan Quirino genuinely favored. The United States' equivocal policy on the issue reflected the confusion. The United States refused to support a Pacific NATO, and the State Department believed that Quirino and Chiang intended the proposal primarily to attract U.S. military and economic assistance, but Washington favored closer Asian economic and political cooperation. Therefore, although the State Department instructed embassies overseas to avoid public statements of support for the plan, it authorized officials to privately express their personal belief that increased economic cooperation would be desirable.[12]

The Thais, at first, matched Quirino's diplomacy misstep by misstep. When the Philippine ambassador to the United States first approached his Thai counterpart about the proposed conference immediately after Quirino's meeting with Chiang, for some reason he ignored the Baguio meeting's military focus and emphasized that the Pacific Union Quirino envisaged would involve no formal commitments. Deputy Foreign Minister Phot Sarasin, reporting on the Philippine ambassador's message, urged Phibun to accept any invitation Quirino issued. Phot noted that, although Thailand had refrained from participating in a January conference on Indonesia in New Delhi to avoid association with criticism of the Netherlands,[13] the Philippine conference would attack no country in particular. Wanting to cement ties with the emerging nations of the region, Phot argued that "there may be more conferences of Eastern countries [in the future] since they are just getting independence and reestablishing themselves. It is thus necessary and important that we participate from the beginning." Phibun approved in principle Phot's recommendation.[14] But as uncertainty increased as to Quirino's real intentions, the Thai position in turn grew confused. Prince Wan told Reed on August 17 that the Thai government had decided to accept any invitation to a conference Quirino would issue, but, the following day, Phibun told newsmen that he had not yet made up his mind.[15] Then, the day after this press statement, Phot asked Phibun to have the cabinet consider the matter. Worried about the direction the conference proposal had taken since the Quirino-Chiang meeting, Phot warned Phibun that participation in an anticommunist organization not receiving full Western support would endanger Thailand's security. "If the Thai government," Phot recommended, "will be committed to participating in some activity, including military cooperation, that will antagonize any country, the Thai government should consider carefully whether . . . the Union will receive support from those countries [i.e., the United States or Britain] in a position to give real assistance."[16] Phibun noted his approval of the advice, indicating again his preference for the tried and true in foreign affairs. It seemed that, as before, caution, reinforced in times of crisis by equivocation, would characterize Phibun's foreign policy in the latter half of 1949.

But his gnawing desire for aid forced Phibun to reconsider his stance. Like Quirino, Chiang, and much of the Asian press, Phibun believed that a Pacific pact would attract U.S. military assistance to its signatories. In his August 18 interview, he explained that "the establishment of a Pacific Union would depend on a question of funds and on who would supply the necessary armaments." "Should the Western Powers support the proposed union," he claimed, "beneficial results would be rapidly forthcoming."[17] While he expected the Americans to reward the members of a Pacific Pact, however, foreign press reports of his ambiguous stance cast doubt on his support for it. In the week following his August 18 interview, Philippine and Hong Kong papers claimed that Phibun's statement that the West should aid any Pacific or Southeast Asian union showed that he would join no alliance actively opposed to communism. Just as he had succumbed to the Japanese, a *Manila Times* editorial explained, Phibun would yield to the Communists. "Pibul hated communism," the article commented, "but recent achievements of the Chinese Communists have impressed him in about the same way the success of the Japs impressed him."[18] The editorial, reprinted by the Hong Kong press, dealt an apparently significant setback to Phibun's campaign to convince the United States of his anticommunism. Were he to receive any aid, he decided, he had to correct the misunderstanding.

Phibun seized on Quirino's plans for an anticommunist conference to make his point. On August 27, about a week after announcing that he had yet to decide whether to attend Quirino's conference, Phibun called a press conference specifically to discuss the communist problem. Citing the advance of Mao's forces toward the Laotian border, the supposed switch to the communist side of the Kuomintang's Yunnan-based 93rd Army, and the advance of Karen insurgents around the northern Burmese town of Kengtung, Phibun claimed that the threat to Thailand had increased dramatically in recent weeks. To protect against the menace, he called for an urgent conference in Bangkok of noncommunist Asian nations. Ignoring entirely the diplomatic discussions of the previous six weeks, Phibun made no mention of the Quirino-Chiang plans. The initiative was all his own. As he had hoped, it immediately grabbed both the headlines and Western attention.[19]

Substantively, Phibun's initiative counted for less than nothing. Despite the bravado, Phibun showed no real increased concern over the communist threat and no intention to lead the fight against communism. When meeting Stanton two days before making the announcement, he made no mention of the conference. The following day, the Foreign Ministry notified the embassy that the government had decided to sponsor a conference but indicated that, as no pressing danger existed, the ministry would sound out the Western powers before publicizing the plan.[20] Prince Wan, now back from Washington, told *Kiattisak* weekly that communism posed no immediate threat to the country.[21] Despite the reports of communist offensives he had alluded to, Phibun asked Thai intelligence officials to report on the communist situation in neighboring countries only after giving the press conference.[22] No one ever explained his bizarre claim that the Kuomintang 93rd Army had turned communist. The Karen insurgents Phibun cited were also noncommunist.

Most important, Phibun's plan to hold the anticommunist conference in Bangkok outraged Quirino. The proposal immediately established Thailand as a rival of the Philippines within the noncommunist camp and threw the diplomatic community into turmoil. All movement toward a conference to discuss greater Asian cooperation came to a screeching halt. Had he tried, Mao Zedong himself could not have devised a better vehicle than Phibun's announcement for dividing the noncommunist nations of Southeast Asia and scuttling the incipient anticommunist alliance. Phibun virtually admitted as much. A mere three days after the press conference, he told Stanton he was willing to drop the proposal if Quirino preferred.[23] When the Philippines issued formal invitations to its own conference on September 14, Phibun did just that.

While Phibun's plan did little to enhance cooperation with his weak, developing neighbors, it succeeded magnificently in improving his image in the world's great aid-giving nations. Although he had contributed nothing of substance to the anticommunist struggle, the mere announcement of his unlikely proposal hardened Phibun's declared opposition to communism. Before, he had excoriated communism in general but denied that the country needed to protect itself against any immediate external danger. Now he proclaimed the threat imminent and demanded action. The plan delighted the Americans. "My impression," Stanton reported to the State Department, is that the "Prime Minister [is] really seriously concerned over [the] threat [of] Communism [to] Thailand and [is] increasingly anxious [to] do something about this threat."[24] An Acheson telegram drafted by Landon gushed that, if genuine, the proposal is "probably [the] first occasion on which any Thai GOVT in recent history has taken [a] strong position in [an] international political issue which might jeopardize [the] future status [of] Thailand."[25] Rhetorically, at least, Phibun had distanced himself from the cautious policies of the past four years. The Americans were grateful.

In the following weeks, Phibun impressed the United States further. On September 12, in an interview with United Press' Richard Applegate, he declared that Thailand was ready to go to war and, if attacked, would welcome British and American troops.[26] As government sources later revealed to the press and Applegate told friends, Phibun had not issued this statement enthusiastically. Through most of the interview, Phibun evaded Applegate's more pointed questions, prompting the newsman to exclaim, according to Stanton, "You and I are just wasting our time!" Then, when Applegate asked about the attitude of the Thai government to entry of British and American troops in case of communist invasion, Stanton recounted, Phibun "noticeably hesitated before replying to the question, which he [Applegate] said he realized rather put Phibun on the spot, but finally replied that Thailand would welcome British and American troops who were combating Communism in other parts of the world."[27] But though he had responded halfheartedly, Phibun's statement was significant. Leftist newspapers attacked him for compromising Thai sovereignty, and, in Parliament, Suwat Phunlop, an opposition member, claimed he had needlessly antagonized the communist powers, but Phibun stood his ground.[28] In response to Suwat's interrogatory, he explained that Thailand would try to defend itself without foreign aid but reaffirmed that Thailand would accept British and American troops if the country could not withstand the invaders alone.[29] In another interview with *Near and Far East News* in October, he repeated the essence of what he had told Suwat.[30]

His latest statements won Phibun much of the respect in Washington he had sought so long. Although grudging expressions of conditional willingness to welcome a hypothetical expeditionary force in case of an unlikely invasion hardly amounted to a firm commitment, Phibun's declarations on the issue of foreign troops marked a significant shift in his public stance. For the first time since his return to power, he had defied local opinion and risked his political position to improve relations with the United States. Stanton noted with pleasure that, "despite the criticism he has received on account of his recent statements, in essence, the Prime Minister did not modify in the least his previous commitment of Thailand to the West. In fact, by reiteration of the general policy of opposition to Communism and cooperation with the West, Phibun appears to have given increased emphasis to his earlier statement."[31]

Again, as with the conference proposal, the need to impress American aid planners had dictated Phibun's stance. On September 12, a joint House-Senate committee in Washington voted to include in the aid bill $75 million for the "general area of China," and Congress passed the full bill on September 28. As Wan reported to Bangkok in early September, the $75 million was intended for East and Southeast Asian nations "such as Thailand."[32] The stakes, therefore, had become too high for Phibun not to cultivate his anticommunist reputation among the Americans. He made his statement to Applegate the day of the House-Senate committee vote.

While change was in the air in Bangkok in the summer and fall of 1949, however, the time was not yet ripe for substantive modifications to the Thai-U.S. relationship. Washington's consideration of the aid question stalled in October, and, with the pause, Phibun halted movement toward a firmer pro-U.S. policy. Despite State Department interest in Southeast Asia, the Defense Department insisted on applying most of the $75 million to covert activities in China. Defense-State conflict blocked final agreement in Washington over an assistance program for the region through the remainder of the year. Despite his growing support for Southeast Asian aid in general, moreover, Acheson still resisted assuming a burden in Thailand traditionally carried by the British. In a discussion with the British ambassador in late December, Acheson explained that the United States would "bear the major responsibility" in Japan and the Philippines and would "give a helping hand in Indonesia" but that in Malaya, Burma, and "in a lesser degree in Thailand," "the physical location of power points, custom, knowledge and circumstance made this area of primary United Kingdom and Empire concern."[33]

The lack of evident progress in Washington in the months following the aid bill's passage dissipated the initial high hopes for aid and raised troubling doubts among Thais about American interest in Thailand. Phibun had declared his optimism regarding Thailand's chances of receiving aid in his October *Near and Far East News* interview, but

British embassy dispatches and press accounts show that expectations in Bangkok dropped over the next two months. Thompson expressed his view in December that "there is small prospect of United States cooperation in assistance to the Siamese army unless or until the conference of American representatives to be held here in February recommends a change of the present rather negative United States policy towards South East Asia."[34] The British embassy's first secretary reported that Thai faith in the United States had plummeted in November.[35] In December, the *New York Times* claimed that "several [Thai] political leaders have shown distrust of the ability of the United States and Britain to provide military aid sufficient to bolster Thailand's ill-equipped border forces."[36] The longer Washington remained deadlocked over the aid issue, the less confidence Phibun placed in his would-be benefactors.

Had this uncertainty arisen at a time of relative stability abroad, Phibun could have continued his anticommunist publicity offensive as before, but the slowdown in the aid process in Washington occurred just as the communist takeover of China posed several important political and diplomatic challenges to Thailand. Although Chiang Kai-shek's defeat had appeared inevitable since the beginning of the year, only in the fall did the matter become urgent. Then, the formal establishment of a communist government in Beijing on October 1 forced Phibun and the Foreign Ministry to consider in earnest how to respond to the alarming events. The Chinese colossus now had a united and possibly aggressive government, and Phibun could overlook it only at the risk of losing everything. Though he would succeed in postponing the painful decisions for a short while, for the first time since his return to power, Phibun encountered serious policy dilemmas that could not be ignored indefinitely.

Above all, Phibun had to decide whether to recognize the new communist government in Beijing. Although Phibun had expressed an interest in January in possibly forming ties with the Communists in China, no one in the Thai government viewed the prospect of full relations with the "New China" with equanimity. As always, Phibun and others feared that a legation backed by an assertive and powerful government in Beijing would incite local Chinese to violence. Phot later told Malcolm MacDonald that, as long as the Chinese lacked a legation in Bangkok, the government and local Chinese had negotiated their problems in peace, but, once China opened its embassy in 1946, there was "shooting in the streets."[37] Mao's government was already displaying that fall a special hostility toward Phibun. In September, a New China News Agency release charged the field marshal with depriving local Chinese of their property to clear the way for the take-over by American capital of the Thai economy.[38] Despite his strong inclination to reject all ties with the Chinese Communists, however, the possibility that the foreign powers would recognize the new govern-ment demanded that Phibun consider establishing formal relations with Beijing. Given the pressures, the Foreign Ministry's Political De-partment recommended that Thailand merely grant China de facto recognition, meaning apparently that no diplomatic personnel would be exchanged. On the assumption that the powers would, in fact, end up recognizing Mao's regime, the memorandum concluded that Phibun should "wait and see what the [Chinese] government's position towards Thailand will be" before deciding on de jure recognition.[39] Phibun, realizing that he might have no choice in the matter, told a press con-ference a few days later that he would await the decision of the "United Nations."[40]

In the end, the competing demands they faced again confounded Phibun and the Foreign Ministry. In early November, Phibun asked the Foreign Ministry to present him policy recommendations regarding the various foreign problems he was then assessing. The memorandum Phot sent Phibun in response on November 15 advised that Thailand should "wait and see" before making any decision concerning recogni-tion of China. Phot noted that the continued fighting on the continent gave Thailand good reason to postpone action. The following day, the cabinet approved Phot's memorandum.[41] Two weeks later, the Thai ambassador to the former Nationalist government cabled from Hong Kong that the new government planned to incite unrest in Thailand. He strongly urged that Thailand await the response of Britain and America before recognizing the Beijing regime. The cabinet approved the ambassador's recommendation, in effect reaffirming its earlier res-olution.[42] Into the new year, therefore, Phibun's China policy remained uncertain.

Meanwhile, a related issue of importance to both Thailand's do-mestic and foreign policies, the treatment of local Communists, espe-cially Chinese Communists, also confronted Phibun. As the Red Army advanced on the mainland, the rough balance of power between the Kuomintang and Chinese Communists in Thailand swung in favor of the Communists. Mao's victories had enhanced the Communists' pres-tige in local Chinese eyes, and, by the end of the year, Communists and their sympathizers had taken control of the Chinese Chamber of Com-merce, the most important local Chinese institution.[43] The Americans and British, as before, pressed Phibun to repress Communists, and the prospect that a revitalized China would provide moral and possibly material support to a hated ethnic group adhering to a subversive ideology clearly frightened Phibun. As long as he doubted both the West's commitment to containing any expansion of Chinese influence in Southeast Asia and his own ability to effectively control them, however, he could act against the local Chinese only at his own peril.

Phibun's reaction to local Communists' political gains, therefore, sorely disappointed the United States. He publicly warned Chinese against political activities and ordered the police to raid a communist newspaper in anticipation of the October 1 formation of the Beijing regime, and the government pushed a bill through Parliament in November blocking Chinese business expansion in the country, but little came of such modest measures. The business bill proved largely unenforceable, and, as before, Phibun never followed up on a pledge he gave Stanton in the fall to outlaw communism.[44] Stanton complained bitterly over the release in October of twenty-two Chinese merchants arrested on charges of price-gouging. "In a recent conversation with an officer of this Embassy," Stanton sarcastically related to the State Department, "a C.I.D. [Police Criminal Investigation Department] source expressed touching sentiment in describing the plight of these 'poor unfortunates' who had been convicted of profiteering 'to the extent of only a few pennies worth.' However, it is of interest to note that some of the men were convicted for illegally raising subscriptions, and that subscription is one of the ways in which Communists obtain their funds."[45] A report prepared by the State Department's intelligence division concluded that Phibun had no plan to suppress Chinese Communists. "To date ... the effectiveness of action against Chinese Communists appears negligible. No important Chinese Communists have been arrested; Communist press propaganda in Chinese and Thai newspapers continues to grow with little opposition or counterpropaganda from the government; there has been no interference with Chinese Communist political organizations; and the Communist-tainted Central Labor Union remains the only effective labor organization in spite of the formation by the government of its own labor union." Phibun's recent anticommunist statements, the report decided, reflected only his desire for military assistance. "It appears that Thailand, under Premier Phibun," the report lamented, "hopes to receive military assistance with minimum commitments on its part in return for voicing opposition to Communism."[46]

In these months of political and diplomatic uncertainty, Phibun pinned his hopes for controlling local Chinese on a curious institution called the Combined Thai-Chinese Committee (Kammakan Phasom Thai-Jin). A September police account of plans by Chinese merchants to raise funds to build an embassy for the new Chinese government gave Phibun the idea for the committee. After reading the report, he ordered the Interior Ministry to form a committee of prominent Chinese and high-level ministry officials to deal with Chinese problems. His plan combined an unusual mixture of old and new. The impetus for the committee clearly came from the Red Army's takeover of the mainland and his anxiety over the communist political advances within the local community. But Phibun conceived of the Combined Thai-Chinese Committee in traditional terms unrelated to any contemporary ideological conflict. Under the ancien régime, Thai monarchs controlled local Chinese through a government department called the Krom Tha Sai. In the absence of a Chinese embassy or a Chamber of Commerce, the Krom Tha Sai transmitted both official orders to the Chinese community and Chinese leaders' desires to the government. Though uncertain about the prospects for a new embassy, Phibun believed that an organization similar to the Krom Tha Sai could manage Thai-Chinese relations. He even suggested that the committee be named Krom Tha Sai.[47]

Such a committee worked better with the compliant, easily assimilated Chinese merchants of the ancien régime than with the ideologically aroused Chinese community of 1949. In the meeting called to form the committee, Interior Minister Mangkorn Phromyothi told the businessmen he had summoned that the government was establishing the organization in response to the events in China. The government wanted local Chinese, he explained, to avoid involvement in the mainland's politics. Another official described the government's desire for the Chinese to present any problems the community had to the committee, and Mangkorn claimed that any "respected" Chinese could join the group, but the minister pointedly asked the Chinese present of their political views and affiliations. Although the Chinese answered that they were merchants and thus not sympathetic to communism, Mangkorn knew that many, in fact, maintained communist affiliations. The merchants themselves were far from pleased with the composition of the committee. The presence of the police chief and the deputy commander of the Criminal Investigation Department clearly intimidated them.[48]

The Thais, therefore, quickly developed second thoughts about the committee. A November 7 Foreign Ministry report predicted that the committee would fail to control the Chinese community. If fully assimilated Chinese were recruited as members, they would lack community support, the memorandum claimed, but recently arrived Chinese would prove recalcitrant. The report thus recommended that Phibun refrain from associating himself personally with the project so that it could easily be dropped.[49] Phibun abandoned the committee the next month.[50]

Coming at a critical moment in government-Chinese relations, the dissolution of the Combined Committee highlighted Phibun's inability, within the prevailing climate of diplomatic and political uncertainty, to develop a coherent policy for dealing with domestic dissidents. His traditional remedy had failed to cure the country's modern ailment. As Thailand confronted the most serious threat to its security since the war, government policy remained mired in the difficult transition from the outdated methods of co-optation to the relatively novel procedures of the modern police state.

BAO DAI

The French-supported Bao Dai regime in Vietnam confronted Phibun with his final, and, for Thai-U.S. relations, most important, dilemma. The Bao Dai government—if it could accurately be called a government—had existed for less than a year. In early 1947, the French, searching for a conservative Vietnamese leader who could attract popular support from Ho Chi Minh, began negotiations with former Emperor Bao Dai to take over a new, nominally independent Vietnamese government. Bao Dai, a puppet of the French in the 1930s, a Japanese collaborator during the war, and an ally of the Vietminh in the immediate postwar years, reached accord with the French in March 1949, but the government he established offered little hope of achieving French aims. Despite the lengthy negotiations, the French granted Bao Dai none of the powers he needed to present himself to the people as a nationalist leader, and he had no plan of action to win the war with the Vietminh. Personally, Bao Dai inspired faith among neither Vietnamese nor westerners. Dissolute, lazy, and lacking charisma, Bao Dai enjoyed a "loyal following," a British diplomat quipped, probably consisting only of "some half-dozen Hong Kong concubines."[51]

As long as France stood alone behind Bao Dai, Phibun could ignore the feeble experiment, but, as the Americans and British slowly increased their backing for the playboy-emperor, pressure on the Thais to act intensified. Although most officials in the Bureau of Far Eastern

Affairs (the office became a bureau in the spring) at first stoutly opposed associating American prestige with such a weak leader, the State
Department's more influential Europeanists pushed for the United
States to support its French ally's effort, and, by the second half of the
year, increased fears of a Vietminh takeover of Indochina led even the
Asianists to promote Bao Dai. In June, the State Department released a
statement pronouncing the March agreement "gratifying." By December, Acheson and other high-ranking officials favored formally recognizing the Bao Dai government when the French legislature finally
ratified the March accord.[52] From early on, this shift in American opinion translated to pressure on the Thais. In anticipation of the June
State Department statement praising Bao Dai, Landon urged Prince
Wan on June 21 to advise his government to issue its own declaration of
support for the new regime.[53] When Prince Wiwatthanachai Chaiyan,
the minister of finance, visited Washington in September, Landon
again exhorted the Thais to support the new government. "I under-
lined," Landon said of his conversation with Wiwatthanachai, "the
importance of the success of Bao Dai to Thailand and reminded the
Prince again of the unfortunate results which might occur if Ho Chi
Minh should achieve control of Indochina."[54]

The Thais, though, felt no sympathy for Bao Dai. They recognized
his lack of popular appeal and, because of their hatred of France, did
not want to see him perpetuate colonialism in Indochina. A July memorandum prepared by the Foreign Ministry's American adviser, Kenneth
Patton,[55] captured neatly the contempt the ministry held for the Bao
Dai experiment. The former emperor, Patton commented, was a puppet doomed to failure, and Thailand had no reason to support him.
"There is no positive action," Patton wrote, "which Thailand can take to
support the Bao Dai regime, the failure or success of which will not, in
the slightest degree, depend upon the attitude of this Kingdom." More
than just unwise, Patton argued, support for Bao Dai was immoral.
"Any sign of approval of the B[ao].D[ai]. government," he explained,
"would be a deviation from the principle of the right of self-determina-
tion." Reflecting the mood of caution at the ministry, Patton contended
that Thai policy should aim no higher than the small country itself
could reach. The government should base its foreign policy, he recommended, "on the realization that this country cannot make any effective contribution, military, financial, or otherwise towards the defeat of
the Chinese communists or to the maintenance of the Bao Dai
regime."[56] Phibun and the Foreign Ministry seem to have agreed with
Patton's recommendations, and the Thais refused to declare their sup-

port for Bao Dai. When Butterworth lectured Prince Wiwatthanachai on Ho's aggressive plans during the prince's trip to Washington, Wiwatthanachai tartly replied, "Ho Chi Minh is your problem not ours."[57]

While they rejected the Bao Dai experiment on its own merits, however, the Thais saw a clear linkage of the issue and U.S. military aid. Prince Wiwatthanachai had made his September trip to Washington to seek American support for a World Bank loan. Butterworth's exploitation of the occasion to lecture the prince on Bao Dai communicated clearly to the Thais that the United States expected diplomatic performance in return for any material assistance. After Congress passed the omnibus assistance act the last week of September, Prince Wan approached Deputy Under Secretary of State Rusk to ask again for a share of the money. Rusk replied that Thailand would have to enter a "common defense arrangement" and that he would need to talk to Wan about Thai foreign policy in general. Wan explained to Phot that, as he understood the intent of the aid bill, "the American government probably wants to receive a definite confirmation regarding the policy of the Thai government in defending against communist aggression"[58] in return for any military assistance. More important, the Americans would likely also ask about Thailand's stance on the matter of recognition of the People's Republic of China and "whether or not the Thai government will also support [the Bao Dai government] and . . . exchange diplomatic representatives with Vietnam."[59] Stanton, skeptical of Bao Dai's prospects from the beginning, seems to have refrained from joining the State Department's arm-twisting of the Thais, and, in December, the department instructed Stanton to bring up the subject only at his own discretion. No evidence exists, moreover, that the Americans ever explicitly linked the aid and Bao Dai issues when speaking with the Thais. As the United States committed itself more firmly to the new Vietnamese government, however, the Thais' interest in receiving aid without providing anything in return increasingly frustrated American officials. In January 1950, Acheson telegraphed Stanton that Thai reluctance to recognize Bao Dai's government "raises doubts in the Dep[artmen]t of the desirability of strengthening the Thai against Commie aggression."[60]

U.S. lobbying on behalf of Bao Dai gave the Thais pause—for the first time—over whether arms aid came with too high a political price tag. As far back as May, disagreements had arisen within the government over the Foreign Ministry's apparent lack of zeal in seeking assistance from the United States. Some cabinet ministers accused Prince Wan of dragging his feet on the matter, and Phot had to angrily defend his ambassador to Phibun.[61] Although the complaints about Wan may have lacked substance, it would not be surprising if, even as early as the spring, Wan and other Foreign Ministry officials had indeed pursued this matter of primarily political, not security-related, concern with reluctance. Then, when the United States began associating military assistance with a bolder Thai foreign policy in the fall, Thai doubts multiplied. When describing to Phibun in October Wan's encounter with Rusk, Phot noted with some alarm that the United States expected not merely stricter control of domestic Communists, but also a more assertive anticommunism abroad, including support for Bao Dai's puppet regime. The implicit American demands, Phot claimed, struck at "important policy principles." He recommended that the cabinet give them urgent consideration.[62]

For the time, Phot and the Foreign Ministry got their way. In the second week of November, Phibun called a cabinet meeting to consider, in light of the possibility that strings would be attached to any U.S. aid program, the proper stance toward the China and Bao Dai questions. In anticipation of the meeting, Phot and the ministry prepared a memorandum presenting their recommendations. As described earlier, Phot advised Phibun in this paper to adopt a "wait and see" attitude toward China. Regarding the Bao Dai government, Phot urged even more strongly that Phibun withhold any recognition or support. Bao Dai, Phot believed, commanded negligible popular backing, and eventual French withdrawal from Indochina was inevitable. Were the Thais to rush into recognizing Bao Dai's doomed regime, they would "make an enemy of a neighbor" once Ho assumed control of Vietnam.[63] Phibun agreed, and, on November 16, the cabinet accepted Phot's recommendations.[64] Phibun maintained his public silence on Bao Dai, and, a month later, Wan informed Reed of the impossibility of any recognition in the immediate future.[65] The heavy-handed American pressure seems even to have dampened the enthusiasm of the proudly nationalistic Phibun for American military assistance. In early December, he instructed Phot to take his time in submitting the weapons request lists. "We should not rush" in asking for the arms, Phibun explained. "We should behave with some dignity."[66]

By the new year, however, events were leading Phibun to reconsider his rebuff of the Americans on Bao Dai—and the cautious policies of the past four years. Before then, foreign concerns and his political weakness had prevented Phibun from implementing significant policy changes. But 1950 saw the fog of international uncertainties that had clouded his path disappear, and domestic political triumphs opened the way for him to pursue new foreign-policy initiatives. Not all of these developments pleased Phibun, but each contributed to his decision to align Thailand with the United States and the new French-controlled regime. Within a remarkably short span of time, he reversed course completely on Bao Dai and altered the basic thrust of his foreign policy.

On the American side, renewed movement toward a military assistance package for Thailand gave Phibun reason to hope that a policy shift would be rewarded. On December 10, Stanton sent the State Department a $15 million request drafted by the Thais and the American military attachés.[67] Three weeks later, the acceptance by Truman and the National Security Council (NSC) of the State Department's version of the policy paper NSC 48/2 guaranteed that Southeast Asia would receive a large portion of the $75 million for the "general area of China." By mid-January, the Defense Department was working in tandem with the State Department to develop country programs. Truman first approved $5 million for the Indonesian constabulary on January 9.[68] Then, surprisingly, although the Bureau of Far Eastern Affairs recommended in December only $5 million for Thailand, the Joint Chiefs of Staff (JCS) proposed to Secretary of Defense Louis A. Johnson on January 20 that the Thais be granted $10 million. On February 1, Johnson forwarded the proposal to Acheson with his approval.[69] The Thais were not privy to the details of the American decision-making process, but, on February 7, Landon informed Wan that the Thai aid "request is receiving consideration from high-ranking officials." "They view the request in a positive light," Wan telegraphed Phot, "because the Sec[retary] of State and Sec[retary] of Defense are well aware of Thailand's needs."[70] Phibun, therefore, knew that matters were again reaching a critical point in Washington and that, once more, his own diplomacy could tip the balance in Thailand's favor. A revised request list he had Wan present the Americans in January provided clear evidence of his high hopes. The U.S. Joint Chiefs of Staff calculated the cost of the weapons cited at $660 million![71]

While Phibun's expectations of U.S. aid soared in January, any ambition he might have entertained of establishing proper relations with the Chinese communist regime, along with any reason to placate China's new government, vanished. Although the British, fearful for their Hong Kong colony, formally recognized Mao's government on January 6, Beijing maintained its resolutely anti-Western policy. Chinese authorities harassed American diplomats, and official and press sources issued a stream of denunciations of the United States and its allies. With the new year, Beijing extended its attacks to Thailand, and

Phibun in particular. On January 26, the Chinese Ministry of Foreign Affairs formally protested Phibun's treatment of local Chinese. Claiming that the police had jailed or deported in excess of a thousand Chinese and that "more than ten persons have been beaten or poisoned to death," the ministry demanded that the Thai government cease its repression of Chinese and "bear full responsibility for such atrocities." Two days later, the Shanghai newspaper *Ta Kung Pao* launched a more fearsome assault, aimed this time more forcefully at Phibun. The Chinese government broadcast the article over the radio. "Following the resurgence to power of the war criminal, Phibun Songgram," the editorial exclaimed, "the fascist government of Thailand has again only changed from an enemy satellite into an imperialist lackey. . . . However, in selling out the interests of the Thai race and people, in looking on New China with scorn, in humiliating Chinese nationals, and in depending upon American imperialism to oppose the people of Southeast Asia, these Thai fascists shall ultimately end up in being buried in the graves of their own digging." Ominously, the newspaper warned that "the voice of the Fatherland shall further reach the ears of all overseas Chinese, telling them that they shall no longer be defenceless for their Fatherland is now behind them."[72] With Beijing thus implicitly threatening to incite local Chinese to overthrow him, Phibun could no longer even contemplate allowing a new Chinese embassy to open in Bangkok. Fortunately for him, by then the United States had similarly decided not to recognize Beijing. On January 14, the United States removed all its remaining diplomats from China, closing the door on recognition.[73] Taking a pro-U.S. stance on Bao Dai and other questions, therefore, would now cost Phibun little. Any attempt to placate Beijing would likely prove futile, and, with the United States already shunning relations with China, he felt no pressure from the West to do so.

The strengthening of his political position provided the decisive impetus for Phibun's bolder foreign policy. In legislative matters, Phibun finally enjoyed by 1950 an uneasy but relatively secure control of Parliament. The Parliament he had inherited from Khuang in April 1948 contained an intractable, heavy Democrat majority, but, in the year and a half following Khuang's "hold-up," Phibun managed to tame the unruly institution's lower house. Suasion, patronage, and bribery lured a steady stream of Democrats to the government side, and partial elections in June 1949 increased government seats further. By then, although his own Thammathipat Party remained weak, Phibun was able to form a coalition of smaller, more easily manipulated civilian parties excluding the Democrats. His promises of material and political rewards continued to attract opportunistic Democrat legislators the remainder of the year. Where sweetness failed Phibun, moreover, coercion always succeeded. When the government faced a possible Democrat-sponsored no-confidence debate in July 1949, police strongman Phao Siyanon entered the legislative chambers as a blunt reminder to recalcitrant MPs of the fates of their four colleagues after the Palace Rebellion in February. The cowed House voted its approval of the new government sixty-three to thirty-one. After that, Parliament never again threatened to force Phibun's resignation.[74]

The removal of Kat Katsongkhram, in the meantime, reduced the threat to Phibun from within the military. Throughout 1948 and most of 1949, Kat remained influential, but, by 1950, he had managed to offend just about everybody with any say in public affairs in Thailand. The press hated him for his corruption, cabinet ministers resented his interference in government enterprises, and Phin and Phao considered him a rival. Only Sarit supported Kat in 1949, and, when the showdown finally occurred, even he turned his back on Kat. By the new year, Kat had only his sizeable ego to sustain him. On January 27, Phao lured the now isolated Kat to Phibun's office and arrested him at gunpoint on charges of rebellion and treason. The Coup Group then whisked Kat off to Hong Kong, and his tempestuous political career came to an end.[75] Although in the long term, Kat's removal strengthened Phin and Phao more than anyone else, Phibun's prestige benefited enormously from the departure of this nuisance. For the time being, at least, Phibun could approach the foreign-policy challenges facing him with greater confidence of his domestic political position.

As events in Bangkok, Beijing, and Washington thus at once created possibilities for and provided incentives to Phibun in early 1950, the Bao Dai soap opera also reached a climax. Despite their sympathy for French efforts, the United States and Britain withheld recognition of Bao Dai's government throughout 1949 as they waited for the French parliament to ratify the March agreement formally establishing the new Vietnamese government. In mid-January 1950, however, Britain rushed a declaration of de facto recognition, and, on January 29, almost a full year after the signing of the accord, the French assembly ratified the March agreement. Five days later, Truman approved Acheson's recommendation to recognize Bao Dai, and, on February 7, the United States publicly announced its recognition. China and the U.S.S.R., in the meantime, declared their acceptance of Ho Chi Minh as the legitimate leader of a united Vietnam.[76] Phibun, therefore, confronted in February an issue of clearly demarcated East-

West conflict. Any decision—or lack of decision—on his part would profoundly affect his and Thailand's standing with the world powers.

Phibun's desire to nail down an American aid package settled the issue. Although most in the country knew that a U.S. military-assistance program was probably already certain, Thais remained convinced that American arms aid and Thai diplomatic support for Bao Dai were intimately related. Rumors swept the Thai capital in February that the United States had proposed an aid program as an explicit quid pro quo for recognition of Bao Dai, and Thais inside and outside the government came to believe that, though the country was certain to receive some sort of aid, the size and speed of arms shipments depended on Phibun's stance toward Bao Dai. The lessons they drew from their own political upbringing confirmed Thais in this assessment. Since they operated every day in a patronage political system based on the dispensation of material and political rewards from powerful figures to their underlings in exchange for political support, the Thais quite naturally viewed U.S. policy in similarly Machiavellian terms. The Americans, it seemed, were pursuing the same strategy that any successful Thai leader would follow in his own rise to the top. They were recruiting supporters. By February 1950, Phibun was ready to sign on.

As with his past grand gestures of support for the West, the arrival of another delegation of American dignitaries determined the timing of Phibun's decision on Bao Dai. On December 15, Acheson's trusted adviser, Philip C. Jessup, left Washington for a three-month fact-finding tour of the Far East culminating in a conference of high-ranking Bureau of Far Eastern Affairs officials and regional ambassadors in Bangkok February 13–15. Washington trumpeted the tour and the Bangkok conference as crucial elements in the development of a comprehensive plan to contain communism in Asia. In Thailand, the conference received headline coverage.[77] Phibun decided to implement his foreign-policy initiative as the conference met.

Phibun prepared the way with a decision of importance, his public rejection of Beijing. The local press reported in early January that the cabinet remained divided over the question of whether to recognize the Chinese Communists, and Phot announced soon afterward that the government was still awaiting the reaction of other Asian nations to the new regime, but Phibun declared outright to UP's Applegate in the first week of February—several days before Jessup's arrival—that Thailand "has no intention" of recognizing Mao's government. Phibun added that he was even considering curtailing the activities of the Soviet embassy in Bangkok.[78]

Three days after his UP interview, Phibun decided on Bao Dai. Although he had again rebuffed a Stanton appeal on February 8 to recognize Bao Dai and told a CBS reporter the same day that Thailand would establish relations with Vietnam only after the French-supported regime had attracted popular support, on February 9, Phibun told a reporter for the English-language *Bangkok Post* that he would ask the cabinet on February 13, the first day of the ambassadors' conference, to approve the recognition of Bao Dai.[79] Diplomats and some cabinet ministers expressed doubts that he had actually made the surprising comment, but Phibun confirmed to the *Post* the next day his intention to recognize the new regime.[80] In two days, therefore, Phibun had discarded six months of Foreign Ministry recommendations and overturned recent cabinet directives he himself had supported. The statements commenced his most important policy initiative since his return to power.

Phibun, however, still had several obstacles to overcome before he could fully implement the initiative. Opinion in Parliament, the press, and much of the government strongly opposed recognizing Bao Dai. Although the Democrats patriotically spared Phibun from a divisive parliamentary debate on the matter, Khuang had made clear in a January press interview that he favored a more neutral international stance pending a Western commitment to defend Thailand.[81] The conservative newspaper, *Prachathipatai*, publicly opposed recognition, and, after Phibun's declaration of support for Bao Dai, Khuang privately urged him to reconsider. Khuang argued that any recognition of the pro-French Cambodian and Laotian governments along with Bao Dai would preclude return of the retroceded provinces (i.e., Khuang's ancestral lands).[82] Seni opposed recognition publicly.[83] Likewise, an unnamed cabinet member griped to the *New York Times*, "The day we see Western moral support and sympathetic interest towards independent Asian governments translated into action will be the day when we hazard our chances of national survival by recognizing Western-sponsored regimes, such as Vietnam, which the Communist world has pledged to destroy, along with all nations supporting them."[84] The strength and prevalence of such sentiments forced Phibun to tell Jessup on February 10 that the cabinet might reject recognition.[85]

The strongest protests against Phibun's Bao Dai proposal came from the Foreign Ministry. Despite Phibun's declaration of support for the French-backed regime, Phot—now foreign minister—continued to oppose recognition. Phot told the *New York Times* after Phibun's announcement that he doubted Bao Dai could succeed and, when meeting Jessup, complained that, "if they [the Thais] backed Bao Dai and he failed, the animosity of the people of the country [Vietnam] would be turned against the Siamese."[86] Phot's subordinates agreed. On February 11, Konthi Suphamongkhon, chief of the Foreign Ministry's Western Department, presented Phot an eight-page memorandum Phot had ordered Konthi to draft. Konthi strongly opposed recognition. Bao Dai was unpopular, lacked real power, and enjoyed scant chance of success, Konthi contended. Recognition would help prolong French domination of Indochina and set back the cause of decolonization. No one particularly liked Bao Dai, Konthi noted, and even the Americans and British supported him only for lack of a better alternative. Although the great powers could take chances, Thailand could not afford to gamble away its friends in the region. "Thailand is a small Asian country and a close neighbor of Vietnam," Konthi explained. "Thailand risks more than the United States or England, both of which are great powers." The government should hold out for a Western commitment to defend Thailand before acting, Konthi believed. He recommended that Phibun recognize Bao Dai only after receiving "firmer assurances of the help the two countries [the United States and Britain] will give us." Konthi concluded that Thailand should withhold recognition of any of the French-sponsored Indochinese governments but noted that, if a gesture of support for France was absolutely necessary, the government should recognize only the more credible royal governments in Laos and Cambodia.[87] The chief of the ministry's Eastern Department agreed with Konthi, and a meeting of high-ranking ministry officials approved the memorandum. Phot supported its conclusions to Phibun and the cabinet.[88]

The military, however, backed Phibun completely. No less than the press and the public, the military believed that the size and speed of an American assistance program depended on Phibun's recognition of Bao Dai. Stanton denied publicly that any linkage existed, but the unbecoming rumor gained currency in the ranks after Phibun's initial declaration of support for Bao Dai. Stanton reported to the State Department that "representatives [of the] Thai armed forces [are] convinced [that the] recognition issue [is] linked with aid to Thai[land]." "I have confidentially informed [the] Prime Minister some military aid [is] likely," Stanton complained, "but [the] expectations [of] Thai Army chiefs [are] fantastic."[89] From the beginning, such hopes won military backing for Bao Dai. Phao and another high-ranking officer expressed their support in public.[90]

The disagreement between the civilian and military elements of government over Bao Dai in no way reflected differences in attitudes toward communism. Although leftists sympathized with the Vietminh, and others, such as Konthi, doubted that Ho was a Communist, the most prominent critics of Bao Dai in Thailand were staunch anti-Communists. Indeed, the groups opposing recognition represented possibly the only ideologically committed anti-Communists in the country. While Phibun and most in the military bore little more than a gut-level dislike of communism, the social elites of the Democrat Party and Foreign Ministry shared a solid economic and social interest in opposing any radical ideology. Aristocrats, royalty, and old wealth dominated the Foreign Ministry as well as the Democrat Party. Atypical, in fact, was the high-ranking diplomat who lacked a title. Phot, though not a career diplomat, enjoyed all the economic privileges of the model Thai foreign minister. Scion of one of Bangkok's oldest and wealthiest assimilated Chinese families, he maintained substantial interests in real estate, farmland, and rice trading. Among all the losers in any communist takeover of Thailand, Phot and the other opponents of Bao Dai in the Foreign Ministry and Democrat Party would be the biggest. Not growing fat, like the Coup Group, off the excesses of government monopolies, these conservatives could maintain their economic position only by upholding the sanctity of private property. None of them expressed any sympathy for communism when criticizing Bao Dai. They protested recognition precisely because they so feared provoking the Communists without getting a corresponding commitment from the West to defend Thailand.

With the opposition to Bao Dai so strong within the government and politically active public, Phibun secured cabinet approval of recognition only with great difficulty. The first cabinet meeting on the issue on February 13 ended in a deadlock. Although Phibun won majority support for his position, he fell far short of the unanimity he wanted. Suasion and arm-twisting won over most of the skeptics, but the civilian ministers holding the communications, industry, health, and justice portfolios defiantly joined Phot in opposing the measure.[91] When Phibun ordered another meeting a week later, he intensified the pressure on the recalcitrant ministers. This time, he called together not only the cabinet but also the Central Peace Maintenance Committee and the National Defense Council.[92] The cabinet, because of a constitutional provision banning active military officers from holding ministerial portfolios, remained largely in civilian hands as late as 1950, but Coup Group members dominated the internal security-oriented Peace Maintenance Committee and external defense-oriented National Defense Council. Arguing that the issue touched on national security and thus fell within the purview of these two military-controlled organizations, Phibun stacked the deck in favor of Bao Dai. Phot and his sympathizers, however, stood firm. The same civilian cabinet members again voted against recognition, and, once more, the tally came five votes short of the unanimity Phibun desired.[93] Finally, after several more inconclusive combined sessions, he had to settle for a less-than-convincing victory.[94] On February 28, without having broken the opposition but with authorization from a majority of those voting at the meetings, Phibun issued formal recognition of the French-controlled Vietnamese, Laotian, and Cambodian governments. He drafted the announcement personally.[95]

Phibun's final victory had not turned out exactly as he or the United States had hoped. Phibun's promotion of recognition had provoked a divisive public debate, and his eventual decision to abandon the search for consensus embittered Bao Dai's critics. After Phibun announced recognition, Phot resigned. The two were close friends, with Phibun appointing Phot foreign minister in return for the financial help Phot had provided after Phibun's release from prison in 1946 on charges of war crimes,[96] but Phot considered the recognition issue too important to ignore. It was the first and last time a Thai foreign minister would quit on a matter of principle. Although Phot dissuaded other ministers from also resigning and accepted the position of ambassador to Washington as a sign of his continued support for the field marshal, Phibun regretted his old friend's departure. Phot's replacement, a wealthy businessman named Worakan Bancha, had nothing to commend himself to the job other than the financial support he had provided the Coup Group in November 1947. These developments worried Stanton. The loss of Phot would be deeply felt, and Phibun's heavy-handed methods had partially defeated the measure's secondary aim of mobilizing anticommunist sentiments in the country. The widespread belief that recognition had involved a quid pro quo on aid hampered American efforts to portray the assistance program as an act of disinterested generosity. "It was obvious," Stanton commented, "that if left to themselves to judge the question of recognition on its own merits, a large majority of the Cabinet and perhaps even of the military councils would have opposed recognition."[97]

Nonetheless, the United States greeted Phibun's Bao Dai decision as a major triumph. Thai recognition was crucial to the Western effort to portray Bao Dai as a genuine nationalist accepted by independent governments in the region. Phibun's declaration made Thailand the first and, along with South Korea, one of only two Asian countries to recognize Bao Dai.[98] America's former colony, the Philippines, ignored U.S. pleas on the matter. Phibun's volte-face on the issue, moreover, permanently changed the course of Thai foreign policy. After years of diplomatic caution, Phibun had dared to antagonize Ho, Mao, and Stalin to win points with the United States. This single political decision, backed as yet by no real efforts to fight communism in the country or the region, hardly committed Thailand irrevocably to the West, but, by closing the door to the East that he had until then held open, Phibun laid the path for his final commitment later that year. Even Seni told the press a week after Phibun's formal announcement of recognition that, though he considered the decision unwise, now that the field marshal had exposed the country to communist retaliation, he should "follow through with a strong policy."[99] No one in the West considered the price paid for Thai recognition too high. Britain's Ambassador Thompson described the outcome as "a great success for my United States colleague."[100] Phibun's decision had set the wheels turning in Thailand's foreign-policy revolution of 1950.

KOREA

Phibun's policy revolution gained the momentum that would carry it to completion soon after his Bao Dai decision when Washington finally approved aid for the country. On March 9, after receiving the recommendation of the Bangkok ambassadors' conference for a Southeast Asian aid program, Acheson delivered a letter to Truman urging that the president authorize $15 million of military assistance for Indochina and $10 million for Thailand. Citing the political argument for aid he had rejected the year before, Acheson claimed that U.S. assistance was absolutely necessary to maintain and strengthen Thailand's anticommunist policies. "Some Thai political elements," he wrote, "are showing evidence of preparing to swing over to the communist side if the pressure should become too great." Overstating his case as he often did when trying to get something out of Truman, Acheson warned that "unless Thailand is given military assistance it cannot hold out against communist pressure."[101] The following day, Truman approved the proposal "in principle."[102]

Somewhat unexpectedly, economic assistance also came Phibun's way in the spring of 1950. Although the Defense Department resisted any transfer of funds from military programs throughout 1949, by the end of January 1950, Acheson had decided to push for economic aid for Southeast Asia.[103] Phibun, apparently getting wind of developments, asked Stanton in early February for a portion of the aid.[104] Then, at the beginning of March, Acheson sent a mission headed by R. Allen Griffin, a Republican publisher, on a tour of the nations of the region to present recommendations for programming the economic and technical assistance. Conducting its survey of Thai needs from April 4 to April 12, the Griffin mission suggested a prompt and highly visible package. Although the relatively good health of the Thai economy argued against an assistance program, Griffin noted, political necessity demanded that something be done. "There is hardly any important economic urgency in Thailand," the mission report commented. "There is a political urgency." The United States, Griffin advised, should plan its aid program accordingly: "If we are to sustain the present line of Thai orientation, prompt concrete evidence of our appreciation of its partnership should be produced. The speed and nature of U.S. economic and technical aid should be planned with this in mind."[105] Griffin recommended providing Thailand $11.4 million in economic and technical assistance. Aid officials in the State Department agreed, and, in September, several months after Congress actually authorized the assistance, the United States and Thailand signed an accord initiating economic and technical aid.[106]

The American decisions to provide military and economic aid elated Phibun—and inspired him to bolder acts of political and diplomatic derring-do. Because of the need to decide on the specifics of the Thai program and aid packages for other countries, the Americans had not intended to inform Phibun of official approval of aid, but, on April 1, American press reports citing unnamed sources described Truman's decision. A week later, Deputy Assistant Secretary of State Livingston T. Merchant confirmed to Wan the accuracy of the reports. Although Merchant emphasized that the United States wanted the matter kept secret, Phibun could not restrain himself. When Worakan reported Wan's meeting with Merchant to him on April 11, Phibun straightaway called in reporters to announce the U.S. decision.[107] Phibun thus was able to claim that his diplomacy and recognition of Bao Dai had won the aid package. While it embarrassed the United States, Phibun had every reason to promote the notion that the Americans had bought Thai diplomatic support. He had made the aid request, after all, for political reasons, and he was not about to forgo its political payoff.

Having benefited handsomely from this one initiative, Phibun could not help but jump at the chance to further please the Americans

—and complete his postwar foreign-policy revolution—when war came to Korea in June. As with the Bao Dai question, the Korean War brought immediate pressure from the United States on Phibun. Within twenty-four hours of the North Korean invasion of the south on June 24, the United States had pushed through the U.N. Security Council a resolution condemning northern aggression, and, on June 27, the Security Council called on all U.N. members to "render every assistance" to the effort to stop the invasion. Two days later, the U.N. cabled the Thai Foreign Ministry to request material aid. The United States strongly urged Phibun to comply.

Again, arms assistance and military politics determined the issue for Phibun. By July, the generals were desperate to loosen the U.S. aid purse strings. Although Truman had approved a $10 million assistance package in principle, Acheson's anger over Thai inability to stem arms smuggling to Indochina and disputes in Washington over the specifics of the program delayed shipments.[108] And more was involved by then than just the $10 million. On June 1, the administration submitted to Congress a request for an additional $75 million for the "general area of China" for use in 1951, and Congress, on June 5, reprogrammed $40 million originally earmarked for China in 1948 for distribution instead in Southeast and East Asia. On July 28, Congress passed the $75 million aid bill. Excited over the prospect of receiving these additional monies and frustrated by the delay in the original aid program, the military pressed Phibun hard to get Thailand its share. The same day that Congress passed the new aid bill, Defense Ministry heads met to discuss Thailand's armament needs. They pleaded with Phibun to expedite U.S. military assistance.[109]

Phibun got the message. In response to the U.N. request for food assistance, Phibun not only agreed to deliver rice but suggested publicly that he would send troops if the U.N. asked. On the morning of July 3, even before the U.N. had made any request, he had the cabinet approve in principle the dispatch of military forces. Eleven days later, after the U.N. formally requested troops, the National Defense Council and the cabinet unanimously voted to issue final approval.[110]

Phibun's decision again drew sharp criticism from civilians inside and outside the government. The press opposed the move, and the Foreign Ministry, Konthi has recounted, considered the dispatch of material aid provocative.[111] New Foreign Minister Worakan Bancha told the press: "Thailand is a small country. If Thailand [tries to] provide aid in the form of armed forces, it would be most difficult and we would be at our wit's end [in attempting it]."[112] When Phibun presented his policy on the war to Parliament on the afternoon of the cabinet meeting, Khuang attacked the stance as too bold. Other MPs expressed concern over the effects of the rice shipments on local grain prices. When considering the measure on July 22, MPs and senators criticized the deployment as unconstitutional, hasty, and dangerous. Thongdi Isarachiwin, who a year and a half earlier had faulted Phibun for tolerating internal Communists,[113] argued that the dispatch of troops would weaken domestic defenses. Sen. Pridithephaphong Thewakun (Pridi Debyabongse), Phibun's foreign minister in 1948, pleaded with the field marshal not to divert the nation's already inadequate defense forces from the more important home front. All in all, parliamentary opinion was overwhelmingly skeptical or outright hostile to the expeditionary force.[114]

But Phibun made clear to his critics—and the military—what he expected to gain from the dispatch of troops. In Parliament, Phibun defended his position not by citing the justice of the cause or the danger the invasion posed, but by pointing to the windfall that would come Thailand's way from participation in the U.N. effort. In return for sending troops to aid France and England in World War I, Thailand had gained concessions at Versailles regarding the two countries' extraterritoriality privileges. Similarly, Phibun claimed, Thailand could expect a payoff from Korea. In the July 3 session, he told MPs that, "by sending just a small number of troops as a token of our friendship, we will get various things in return."[115] On July 22, he made the connection explicit. "If we invest just a little [in this undertaking]," he predicted, "we might get aid from these countries [the West]." He hoped at the least, he said, that the United States would transfer aircraft and equipment to the Thais for use in Korea and, afterward, in Thailand.[116]

With this promise of additional weapons uniting the military behind him, Phibun overcame the civilian opposition easily. When push came to shove, Worakan acceded to the measure, and Parliament approved Phibun's decision despite the qualms of a probable majority of members. The cabinet ministers who had fought the recognition of Bao Dai yielded instantly. Phibun's ruthlessly executed implementation of that decision in February had taught them the futility of opposing him.

This second triumph over the civilians pleased the Americans even more than the first and secured the payoff in military assistance that Phibun had promised the generals. Thailand's pledge of four thousand troops made it the first Asian country to commit forces to the U.N. cause in Korea. Although the troops actually proved more of a financial burden than a military asset for the United States, Washington was grateful. Desperate to portray the intervention on South Korea's behalf as a truly international effort, the United States hailed the Thai decision as evidence of regional backing for the U.N. Privately, American officials had nothing but praise for the Thais. Echoing Landon's commendation of Phibun's proposal for a conference of anticommunist Asian nations a year earlier, Lacy opined that "never before in Thailand's history has it so forthrightly committed itself politically in an international situation which might jeopardize its own future sovereign status."[117] Richard R. Ely of the Office of Philippine and Southeast Asian Affairs noted that the prompt offer of troops "is unique among Asian countries."[118]

Aid programmers' lethargy and Acheson's petulance over the arms-smuggling problem, therefore, quickly dissipated. On July 14, Truman finally allocated the $10 million approved in principle in March.[119] In the first week of August, the World Bank, with U.S. backing, approved a $25 million development loan for Thailand, the first funding it authorized an Asian country.[120] Then, in the second half of the month, the United States sent the first arms shipment to Thailand. Before Korea, Washington had assigned Thailand low priority on the list of countries to receive armaments, and, in the immediate aftermath of the invasion, arms exports were halted worldwide, but Phibun's dispatch of troops raised his status in Washington. Acheson wrote his Defense Department colleagues that "Thai[land]'s determination [to] support U.N. action [in] opposition [to] communism represents [a] political decision [of the] most profound importance in Thai-U.S. relations [and an] indication [of] confidence [in] our promises of mil[itary] aid to those who aid themselves." "It would be most destructive to [the] morale [of the] Thai," Acheson concluded, "if their nation[,] which has supported U.S.-U.N. objectives more forthrightly than other SEA nations[,] should receive mil[itary] aid more slowly than those nations."[121] In late August, a State Department representative informed the Thai chargé of the delivery of the weapons just sent. He explained that, "because the [Thai] government has taken a clear stance in recognizing Bao Dai and supporting the United Nations in Korea, on August 24 the State Department was able to arrange the release of the first set of weapons to be sent to Thailand. The reason for doing so is that the arrival of the weapons will have a profound impact on political feelings in Thailand."[122] Despite American denials, Phibun and Washington had engaged in a clear quid pro quo exchanging Thai diplomatic support for U.S. material assistance.

Phibun's final acquisition of American arms with the dispatch of troops to Korea marked a watershed in modern Thai political history. Until then, foreign policy had remained much as it had been since the end of the war, and Phibun pursued a domestic agenda little changed from the time he returned to power in November 1947. In both arenas, Phibun favored caution and moderation. But arms aid and the Bao Dai and Korea decisions set Thailand on a new course. To secure American military assistance, Phibun had steered the ship of state sharply to the right, and, in its wake, the government grew increasingly oppressive and foreign policy turned much more anticommunist. Repression internally and adventurism abroad steadily replaced the circumspect policies of the past five years. These changes were crucial. They helped make Thailand the authoritarian, staunchly pro-Western U.S. ally that it would remain for the next two decades.

COMPLETING THE REVOLUTION

The initiation of American arms aid and Phibun's consequent decision to send troops to Korea completed the revolution in the Thai government's postwar international relations begun in the fall of 1949. The dispatch of the expeditionary force aligned Thailand firmly with the West and decisively against the Communists. No longer merely talking about doing something about Communists, Thais would now actually be killing them. Phibun's decision made him a declared enemy of Stalin's and Mao's North Korean allies. It ended the field marshal's policy of maintaining friendly relations with the communist powers. Demonstrating the depth of his commitment to the West after the dispatch of troops, Phibun had Thailand vote in the u.n. in February 1951 to censure the Chinese intervention in Korea, and, in May 1951, Thailand voted in favor of a strategic embargo of China. Before 1950, such boldness was unthinkable. The recognition of Bao Dai and the dispatch of troops, however, had brought Thailand to the heart of the Western camp, and there was no going back.

Just as military aid, by inspiring the Bao Dai and Korea decisions, revolutionized postwar Thai foreign policy, it also contributed to changes in Thai domestic politics, changes that would increase the government's authoritarianism. Arms assistance helped transform the country's foreign-policymaking process in a way that strengthened military control of government. Since the war, the Foreign Ministry and the politically active public had opposed any policy that would either limit

Thai maneuverability or antagonize a neighbor or foreign power. Partly out of agreement, partly due to his political weakness, Phibun heeded such opinions throughout 1948 and 1949. Whether regarding participation in a Pacific military pact, recognition of the People's Republic of China, or Indochina policy, Phibun followed the recommendations of the Foreign Ministry on all important foreign-affairs issues. Although he ran ahead of public opinion with his anticommunist rhetoric, he never in this period entirely left the public behind. He always took care to lead opinion, not abandon it. In 1950, however, Phibun rejected compromise and caution. By manhandling the opponents of Bao Dai, he humbled the civilian end of the foreign-policymaking apparatus. And by defining this supremely political matter as an issue of national security, he ensured that military concerns would determine the outcome of future foreign policy disputes. Phibun had to pay civilians' concerns only scant attention with regard to his Korea decision. After that, public opinion and the parliamentary opposition exerted negligible influence over Thai foreign-policymaking. The Foreign Ministry was reduced after July 1950 to executing, not shaping, policy. With American encouragement, therefore, the military had, by the spring of 1950, extended its hegemony over one more element of the Thai government.

American military assistance also strengthened Phibun and the military regime he led. After the Americans agreed to provide assistance, Phibun argued, with good reason, that the decision was his personal victory, and when the first arms shipments arrived in the summer of 1950, his prestige within the military rose to new heights. For the moment, at least, this triumph rallied the army behind Phibun and provided the military regime a greater sense of unity than it had ever enjoyed. By helping to prevent the Coup Group from imploding, therefore, American military assistance gave the regime the stability it needed to fight its internal enemies—and further limit civilian control of government.

U.S. military assistance, moreover, energized the government's lethargic policy toward leftists in the country. Before 1950, the United States, in some ways, fought communism in Thailand more than Phibun himself did. Stanton had taken an interest in manipulation of the press from the first, and, in 1949, he initiated an extensive anticommunist propaganda campaign. Beginning that spring, Stanton had the United States Information Service (USIS) representative distribute supposedly incriminating clippings from *Soviet Affairs* to local newspapers and hired a "fairly prominent Thai" to translate anticommunist literature from the Buddhist Society of London. Stanton also arranged for "one of the better known Thai newspaper editors" to translate and publish a series of anticommunist articles by a local American the embassy had engaged.[123] Later, Stanton made plans for a program aimed at Chinese-language newspapers.[124] In 1949, USIS began publishing an illustrated magazine portraying American rural life and a political circular purporting to expose the "weak points, lies and contradictions on the Soviet record." The embassy distributed the circular to "opinion-making leaders in politics, education, [and] military affairs."[125] While the Americans took an active interest in winning the hearts and minds of the Thai people, however, Phibun had no concerted plan in this period to promote anticommunism among the populace. Stanton complained that "the Thai government has taken no action through the press or the radio to counteract this [Soviet and communist] propaganda or to expose the dangers of Communism."[126] The police chief told Stanton in October that the Thais felt too insecure internationally to increase repression of Communists.[127]

The events of 1950, however, enlivened Phibun and the Thai government. Inspired by the developments on the mainland, Communists had by then almost entirely supplanted Kuomintang supporters as leaders of the Chinese community, and leftists grew more outspoken in condemning the United States in 1950. In May of that year, the leftist Thammasat Student Committee staged a walkout of a Kenneth Landon lecture.[128] And in late 1949 and 1950, a small but vocal left wing, led at this point by Phethai Chotinuchit, appeared in Parliament. None of these developments threatened Phibun or the Coup Group, but the field marshal's policy shift—inspired by the promise and subsequent reality of American military assistance—increased the nuisance value of leftist dissidents. Phethai and his allies concentrated their attacks on Phibun's pro-Western policies and refusal to recognize the People's Republic of China, and the leftist press repeated Phethai's arguments.[129] At the same time, Phibun's rebuff of Mao and Ho angered Vietnamese in the northeast and ethnic Chinese. Beijing's January threat over the radio to incite local Chinese against the Thai government brought this worst nightmare of Phibun closer to reality. In such an atmosphere, a policy of repression gained appeal.

When the arms shipments actually started, the argument for repression grew even stronger. As long as aid remained merely a possibility, Phibun could sidestep American moves to pin him down on domestic Communists, but once arms entered the pipeline, he could defy his benefactors only at the risk of seeing the flow stopped. Until Phibun's dispatch of troops to Korea, Acheson explicitly linked Phibun's policy toward Indochinese arms smuggling to the initiation of weapons shipments.[130] After Korea, Phibun could not expect the Americans to let him off the hook so easily. Even as American aid applied pressures, moreover, it created possibilities for Phibun. As long as Thailand remained vulnerable to Vietminh or Red Chinese invasion and subversion, suppression of Communists within the country would merely increase the likelihood of aggression. But the American aid agreement committed the United States more firmly to Thailand's security. Intentionally symbolic of U.S. resolve, the arms shipments, along with Truman's quick response to the Korean War, went far in convincing Phibun that the United States was in Southeast Asia and Thailand to stay. After the shipments began, Phibun felt freer to follow his instincts, inclined as ever toward repression, and deal more forcefully with troublemakers on the left.

Phibun's harder stance manifested itself first in the form of a more active anticommunist publicity campaign. On January 30, the National Defense Council was reported to have resolved to expand its program to counter communist influence in Thailand.[131] Immediately afterward, Sang Phatthanothai, a close friend and long-time Phibun publicist, began organizing an anticommunist press grouping to supplant the leftist Press Association of Thailand.[132] In March, the government distributed leaflets to factory workers warning of communist plans to incite labor unrest, and Phibun had the Buddhist priests' council publicly denounce communist pamphlets supposedly aimed at exploiting divisions between the two orders of Thai monks. Phin, in the same month, called together one hundred fifty merchants to urge their cooperation in the government's fight against communism, and the government-appointed head of Thammasat University lectured students on the dangers of the ideology.[133] In July, the government's Publicity Department took over Sang's semiofficial Allied Freedom League (Sannibat Seriphap) and began its own anticommunist broadcasts.[134] The government transformed the nation's military journals, in the meantime, into anticommunist mouthpieces. Before 1950, the veterans' monthly, *Khao Thahan Phan Seuk*, and the army organ, *Yuthakot*, published only articles of strictly military interest, but, in the wake of Phibun's Bao Dai decision, the two journals began printing anticommunist propaganda regularly. The harshly anticommunist "The Great Danger of Communism" appearing in the May 12 issue of *Yuthakot* typified the new military propaganda.[135] The article's passionate polemics contrasted sharply with the dry, scholarly pieces of previous years.

More slowly, the government also intensified its repressive activities in 1950. On February 28, Phibun again ordered the Juridical Council to study the possibility of enacting an anticommunist law.[136] In March, he ordered the police to find ways to close leftist newspapers, and a month later, the Central Peace Maintenance Committee appointed a group to curb communist publications. Immediately after the Bao Dai decision, Phibun ordered the Interior Ministry to intensify surveillance of Vietnamese in the northeast and forced the Vietminh mission in Bangkok to move to Rangoon.[137] Over the summer, Phibun began taking forceful action. In June, the government announced that it would prosecute any journalist who "reports news aimed at provoking unrest in the country in accordance with communist principles."[138] The police prohibited the import of twenty-one Marxist Chinese-language books and one English-language book about the "New China," and, in July, the government banned all press comments damaging Thailand's foreign relations.[139] That November, the police confiscated all issues of the Thai Communist Party organ, *Mahachon*, and, in early January 1951, arrested the editor of *Santiphap* and impounded copies of *Maitrisan* quarterly.[140] At the same time, the last half of 1950 saw increased harassment of Chinese Communists.[141] The government deported a number of Chinese Communists in October.[142] That same month, the Interior Ministry initiated a plan to move Vietnamese refugees to the border provinces.[143]

Phibun was still far from the all-encompassing anticommunist crackdown the Americans wanted. The measures taken against the Chinese remained tentative. U.S. Chargé d'Affaires William Turner complained that "the Thai Police are still only picking at the fringes of Chinese Communist activity in Thailand."[144] Phin and Phao, in fact, were beginning to develop lucrative associations with procommunist Chinese businessmen, associations that would grow closer as the years passed.[145] And even when sincerely attempting to repress Communists, the Thai government, at this early point, still seemed to be learning the rules of the tricky game of Communist-fighting. In March, the Interior Ministry ordered teachers and government officials around the country to watch for communist leaflets or leftist literature sent through the mail. Many officials, unfamiliar with their new duties as ideological watchmen, actually opened personal letters delivered to their offices. The ministry had to issue a new order in response for officials to act more discreetly.[146] The Thailand of 1950 was still no police state.

But a pattern had been set. Communist advances in Asia, Beijing's belligerence, and the new relationship with the United States had set the Thai government on a path toward decreased tolerance of dissent. Once the government had determined that leftists were troublesome enough to need to be eliminated, it was just a matter of time before it gave the Americans the all-out crackdown they wanted. Phibun's political conversion to domestic anticommunism, lagging just behind his foreign-policy commitment to the United States, was nearly complete.

Because most Thai official documents on local Communists in the period are closed, it remains uncertain just how much the Americans influenced the government's repression of dissidents, but the limited evidence available indicates that U.S. policy had a significant effect. Although none of the papers open to researchers reveals Phibun's views of press censorship, he had banned criticism of the government's foreign policy and allies (i.e., the United States) in late July clearly in response to the protests against his dispatch of troops to Korea, a decision made because of American military aid. Similarly, the government almost certainly took measures against the Vietminh and Vietnamese refugees partly as a result of fear that recognition of Bao Dai had antagonized them. An Interior Ministry document ordering the surveillance of Vietnamese says so explicitly.[147] Although the effectiveness of American efforts to persuade the Thais to tighten repression is hard to measure, documents and events from later years show that the Thais heeded American advice on the matter. While the consequences of the increased sense of security a more prominent American presence in Thailand fostered are equally difficult to trace, the available evidence demonstrates that the Thais did consider the international situation when setting policy toward domestic Communists. In October 1949, the police chief admitted to Stanton that Thai anxiety over the spread of communism in the region prevented the government from taking stronger measures against domestic Communists, and a Juridical Council memorandum of 1951 states that the Foreign Ministry opposed a law specifically outlawing communism on the grounds that the act would damage relations with the Soviet Union.[148] The conviction of Stanton and other westerners that Phibun's apprehension of the foreign communist powers debilitated his opposition to domestic Communists is, at the least, revealing. The Americans certainly had not created the impulse toward repression, which had already arisen in the minds of Phibun and other leading Thais, but U.S. policy strongly reinforced it. U.S. military assistance speeded and intensified the implementation of repressive measures.

Most important politically, U.S. military aid transformed America's relationship with Thailand's military government. Thailand's security requirements had not made alignment with the United States inevitable. Civilians concerned with the country's security, such as Phot, Foreign Ministry officials, and both progovernment and opposition politicians, resisted abandonment of the policy of flexibility. Rather, military politics—and the lure of military assistance—made alignment with the United States compelling. The mere prospect of military aid had sparked a revolution in postwar Thai foreign policy amenable to American interests, and, once actually begun, the weapons flow secured Thai diplomatic support on nearly every issue of importance to the United States. Because this military assistance mattered much more to the generals than to civilians, the United States found reason after the arrival of the first arms shipments to view Thailand's military government more favorably. Many American officials retained democratic ideals with respect to Thailand, and the United States over the next several years resisted the military's most aggressive power grabs, but the initiation of military assistance created shared interests between the United States and the Thai military. Now, the American position in Thailand depended on military control of the budgetary process, security programs, and foreign policy. After 1950, therefore, advancing authoritarianism and expanding American influence marched in lock step.

PART THREE

FORMING THE ALLIANCE,

1950–1954

Despite Phibun's Bao Dai and Korea decisions and the initiation of U.S. military assistance, Thailand remained in 1950 a distant place in Washington policymakers' minds. Washington had yet to accord Southeast Asia the geopolitical importance it later gave the region, and even policymakers concerned directly with Southeast Asia did not know what role they should assign Thailand in their regional strategy. As late as 1952, John M. Allison, assistant secretary of state for Far Eastern affairs, claimed after a trip to Southeast Asia that Burma mattered more to the United States than Thailand. "I came away with the general feeling after I had been to Bangkok and Rangoon," he wrote, "that in many ways Rangoon was by far the more important place to concentrate our efforts."[1] But Thailand soon rose in American estimations. As communist forces advanced on several fronts in Asia from 1950 to 1954, Americans increasingly focused their attentions on Southeast Asia. As U.S. policymakers found new, more important roles for the country to play in the region, Thailand in particular attracted greatly heightened American interest. Policymakers devoted much more time to Thailand, and U.S. material and political investment in the country soared. By 1954, American policymakers had based their entire strategy in Southeast Asia on Thai support and committed the United States, for the first time, to defend Thailand's security. The fate of America's position in the region, by then, depended on the relationship with Thailand. No one after 1954 claimed that Burma mattered more.

Basic changes in both Thai internal politics and the relationship with the United States made possible this new U.S. reliance on Thailand. In 1950, the Thai-U.S. relationship remained primarily political in nature, involving the exchange of relatively small amounts of U.S. military assistance for Thai diplomatic support, but, after 1950, the partnership between the United States and Thailand became more purely military. As a result, the country's usefulness to the United States increased. At the same time, domestic political developments from 1950 to 1954 made Thailand a more reliable and effective military partner. After 1950, the Thai military government acquired new strength, and by 1954, the threat of a coup directed at the ruling clique had diminished. This political stabilization effectively precluded the possibility that political upheaval would bring to power a government unwilling to cooperate with the United States. Then, once the military government had gained its political footing, it also toughened its stance toward dissidents. This new policy of repression ensured that the United States could implement its various programs in Thailand in a congenial atmosphere. By 1954, the United States found reason to expect more from Thailand. Secure, dedicated, and willing, the Thai military regime now seemed to be America's best friend in Southeast Asia.

As with the earlier movement toward closer relations between the two countries, this most recent strengthening of ties contributed to the extension of military domination of government in Thailand. The impetus for the newly restrictive policy toward dissidents had arisen primarily from domestic political forces, but American pressure ensured that the policy culminated in a harsh crackdown aimed especially at leftists. While civilians had already largely withdrawn to the sidelines of the policymaking process, the American emphasis on military cooperation enhanced the generals' control over foreign policy. Although far-right elements achieved prominence in these years largely as a result of their own unrelenting ambitions, the Americans' direction of a disproportionately large share of the military aid to them guaranteed their ascendancy. In 1954, American influence and authoritarianism were again advancing in unison in Thailand.

The bonds that had been forged by then between the two demanded even more closely connected progress in the future. The importance to the United States of Thailand's pro-American policies peaked in 1954. As dependence on those policies escalated, reliance on the military government that implemented them soared just as high. Therefore, while the initiation of military assistance in 1950 had earlier bound American interests within Thailand itself to Phibun and the generals, by 1954 America's entire Southeast Asia policy rode on the backs of Thailand's small military elite. With that change, the Americans could not help but view more favorably the prospect of outright military dictatorship in Thailand.

Chapter Six

THE ESTABLISHMENT OF AN AMERICAN

MILITARY PRESENCE, JUNE 1950–DECEMBER 1951

Despite the initiation of military assistance to Phibun's regime, U.S. military involvement in Thailand in 1950 remained limited and uncertain. The $10 million the United States granted the Thais was significant but modest, and little heavy equipment was involved. At the time Truman approved it, most considered the program a one-shot deal.[1] The three service attachés maintained the only U.S. military presence in the country, and no one was sure whether a permanent military advisory mission would be established to administer the aid. This being the case, the Americans at that time never hoped for more from the Thai government than modest backing for the West in the international arena and simple survival domestically. The United States was in no position to lay heavier burdens than these on the Thais.

But the Korean War set the United States on a new path in Thailand. A watershed in the Cold War, the Korean War provoked a rapid increase in U.S. defense spending, hardened the American stance toward communism in general, and inspired a more active foreign policy.[2] It emphatically changed policy toward Thailand. After Korea, Southeast Asia got a larger slice of an expanded worldwide military assistance pie, and assistance for Thailand in particular skyrocketed.

The United States broadened its plans for military assistance to Thailand almost immediately after the North Korean invasion. Following Truman's spring approval in principle of the various Southeast Asian arms programs, Acheson and the Joint Chiefs of Staff (JCS) drafted plans for a joint survey mission to tour the region and present detailed proposals for implementation of the assistance. When this mission, headed by John Melby of the State Department and Maj. Gen.

Graves Erskine of the Defense Department, left, it had instructions to recommend allocation only of the $10 million the president had approved in March for Thailand. Melby and Erskine were to consider this aid as political in purpose, in line with the rationale for assistance developed since mid-1948. The commission was told upon departure, one member later wrote, "that the Thai could not be relied upon and our purpose should be to give them something, for political reasons, but as little as necessary." By the time the mission arrived in Bangkok on August 26, however, Washington had widened its aims. Ignoring the inefficiency and disunity of the Thai military, the State and Defense departments now instructed Melby and Erskine to suggest a multiyear assistance package designed to "produce a well-equipped and well-trained force" capable of defending the country against outside attack or subversion.[3]

The size and duration of the aid program the mission drafted exceeded anything the Americans had considered before. Melby and Erskine recommended both a massive increase in yearly expenditures and extension of the program at least through 1954. They proposed expanding the army from thirty-five to fifty thousand men at a total cost of $40 million and strongly urged that the United States provide the other two services, the air force and the navy, equipment and training. The mission members told Washington that Thailand was of primary importance to the fight against communism in the region. They proclaimed in their final report that "we are convinced that Thailand possesses the required conditions which could make it an impregnable nucleus in Southeast Asia" and advised assigning Thailand's assistance program the highest priority in Southeast Asia after Indochina.[4]

Though several times more ambitious than anything previously suggested, these proposals failed to shock officials back in the United States. Indeed, Washington soon set even grander goals. In 1951 alone, the United States programmed $44.8 million in military aid, and policymakers foresaw additional large shipments for later years.[5] Eventually, Washington settled on sixty, not fifty, thousand men as the army's force objective. At the same time, the Defense Department sent a permanent Military Assistance Advisory Group (MAAG) to Bangkok in 1950, thus establishing the first American military presence in Thailand beyond the three service attachés. By mid-1953, MAAG-Thailand had ninety-seven American advisers, and, for the first time, U.S. government officials outnumbered American missionaries in the country.[6]

The United States also initiated a wide-ranging covert aid program in late 1950. Although planning for it got started much later than for the long-developing overt program, covert assistance suffered from fewer bureaucratic delays and had more immediate military impact. Its political influence, moreover, would be just as profound as that of the conventional assistance. For years to come, the changes in the balance of power covert aid produced would affect Thai politics.

The moving force behind the American covert assistance program was none other than Willis Bird, the former OSS officer who had backed an $80,000 loan for Pridi's brother after the 1947 coup. Although Bird had not served in Thailand during the war, he opened an importing firm there after leaving the OSS in late 1946. As with so many American officials serving in Thailand at the time and since, Bird rapidly sank roots in the country. He soon made friends with former Free Thais who had worked with the OSS in 1948 and married the sister of one Free Thai he met, Air Force Colonel Sitthi (Siddhi) Savetsila (Thailand's foreign minister from 1980 to 1990). By 1950, Bird's business was thriving. His firm by then was importing food containers, fruit and dairy products, beer, whiskey, fertilizers, insecticides, and tear gas for the military and police.[7] Like Claire Chennault, famed World War II airman and the original owner of CIA-associated Civil Air Transport, Bird combined money-making with anticommunism.[8] Using the connections he had acquired in his three years in the country, Bird organized in 1950 a secret committee of leading military and political figures to develop an anticommunist strategy and, more important, lobby the United States for increased military assistance. The group, dubbed the Naresuan Committee, included police strongman Phao Siyanon, Sarit Thanarat, Phin, air force chief Fuen Ronnaphakat, and Bird's brother-in-law, Sitthi. As a result of his participation, Sitthi, who later saw another sister marry CIA operative William Lair, began his long service as one of Phao's closest aides-de-camp and translator. Phao, in the meantime, effectively took control of matters from the Thai end.[9]

Bird's reasoning in establishing the Naresuan Committee was compelling. As Bird well understood, the Coup Group had long viewed Stanton with suspicion. The ambassador's clear preference for civilians annoyed the generals, and they believed that he was blocking increased assistance to the military government. For the most part, in fact, Stanton was an outspoken supporter of augmented aid for Thailand, but, temporarily overwhelmed by pessimism over the prospects of Thailand's survival in the wake of the North Korean invasion, he had strenuously objected to any aid increase during the Melby-Erskine visit, and this momentary opposition may have turned the Thais against him.[10] In any case, the Coup Group considered Stanton as well as the State Department untrustworthy, and Bird and the generals established their committee to bypass the ambassador and conventional diplomatic channels. Instead, Bird decided to work through his old oss buddies now employed by the CIA.[11]

Bird's strategy succeeded magnificently. His CIA contacts sent an observer to meet the committee and, impressed with the resolve the Thais manifested, got Washington to agree to a large covert assistance program. Because they considered the matter urgent, planners on both the Thai and American sides decided to forgo a formal agreement on terms of the aid. Instead, Paul Helliwell, an oss friend of Bird now practicing law in Florida, incorporated a dummy firm in Miami named the Sea (i.e., South-East Asia) Supply Company as a cover for the operation. The CIA, the agency on the American end responsible for the assistance, opened a Sea Supply office in Bangkok. Tangible progress then came quickly. By the beginning of 1951, Sea Supply was receiving arms shipments for distribution, and in April, the company opened a paratroopers' camp in Lopburi province north of Bangkok to train fifty policemen per year in airborne and guerrilla warfare. The Americans intended these new special forces to engage in harassing, stay-behind tactics in case the Chinese overran the country. Besides practicing sky-diving, the trainees learned sabotage and jungle survival techniques and use of advanced weaponry. Bird, the Pridi supporter turned Coup Group champion, in the meantime, profited from the new military assistance no less than the Thais. The CIA appointed Bird's firm general agent for Sea Supply in Bangkok.[12]

The biggest winner, however, was Bird's friend, Phao Siyanon. Cunning, ruthless, and ambitious, Phao had begun a rapid climb to the top of the Thai political heap even before the Americans stepped in. Although just an army colonel with no fighting or administrative experience at the time of the November 1947 coup, Phao used his years of service to Phibun and marriage to Phin's daughter to get himself appointed deputy secretary-general of the police department. Ignoring the nominal chief, *Luang* Chattrakankoson, Phao exercised, in his position as second in command, effective control over this nationwide force of tens of thousands. Quickly, he made the police a political instrument. The police's assassination of the four MPs after the Palace Rebellion sent a clear signal to Phao's potential enemies not to cross him. Although the police at first could not match the more powerful army and navy, Phibun helped Phao strengthen the department. Phibun expanded the size of the police force dramatically in 1949 and 1950 and bought it substantial quantities of heavy weaponry. Throughout, the British aided Phibun and Phao. Working more closely with the police than the army on the Malayan border, the British admired Phao for his forceful leadership and administrative capabilities. They sold the police not only the same small arms, radio equipment, and ammunition they had agreed to supply the army in late 1948, but also armored cars.[13] As well, the British enhanced the police's investigative and intelligence-gathering capabilities. They trained Phao's closest lieutenants—including Phut Buranasomphop, one of the killers of the four MPs—in England.[14]

Phao used the aid he received to transform the police department into an additional army. In 1949, the police formed a mounted division, a mechanized division, a tank division, a mobile division, and even a speedboat division. A southern MP sarcastically predicted in 1949 that the police would soon inaugurate a submarine division.[15] By the last half of 1950, the police possessed better weaponry than their military rivals and had achieved a rough numerical parity with the army at about thirty-five thousand men.[16]

Despite Phao's repellent political activities, the Americans, like the British, developed a deep respect for him and the police. Although the Melby mission had split over the question of aid to the police, most Americans valued the police more than the three military branches. Military advisers considered the police the most competent force in the country and more open to new methods and thinking than the army. Phao himself the Americans admired, if at times grudgingly. His leadership was forceful and his drive undeniable. Stanton, a Phao critic, admitted that, despite being "ruthless," Phao "is capable . . . and has brought [the] police force to [a] high state of military efficiency."[17] Washington, therefore, decided on a large and speedily expedited covert assistance package and directed it all to Phao's police. Through Sea Supply, the CIA provided the police mortars, bazookas, grenades, and medical supplies, and, later, ships, planes, artillery, tanks, and helicopters. The CIA also began at this time its assistance to the police's primary anticommunist unit, the Criminal Investigation Department. And, of course, the Lopburi camp provided Phao a new, modernly equipped, elite paratrooper force. By 1953, two hundred CIA advisers had arrived to train and supply the police.[18]

All this covert American assistance—much more generous than the aid the British provided—helped Phao tremendously in his struggles with the army and navy. The CIA furnished the police more modern and powerful weapons than those MAAG supplied the military, and they arrived earlier. While army generals were still complaining about delivery delays, in March 1951 Phao was able to tell his police that they would all get new weapons and vehicles.[19] The elite Lopburi camp especially benefited Phao. Although in its second and third years the camp trained paratroopers for the army, air force, and navy as well as the police, Phao's forces always figured most prominently in the program, and, after 1953, Sea Supply reverted to teaching police alone. From the beginning, the Lopburi camp was identified with Phao.[20] Soldiers strongly resented its bias in favor of the police.[21] Perhaps most irksome to Phao's rivals, the police department's American contacts, Bird and CIA operatives such as Sea Supply chief Sherman Joost, worked—and socialized—more closely with Phao and the police than MAAG did with the army or navy. Unlike MAAG advisers, Sea Supply trainers ate, slept, washed, and marched with their Thai students, often in isolated jungle surroundings. The rapport that developed between the police and the Americans gave Thais the not wholly incorrect impression that Phao was the Americans' favorite. Most effective in boosting Phao's aura was his association with the CIA. Secret and thus seemingly important while also heir to the heroic image of the OSS, the CIA possessed a mystique in Thailand in those years that it would never entirely lose. Not yet suffering from its later negative association with interventionism, the agency at that time had the power to turn to political gold anyone it touched. Since the CIA worked almost exclusively through the police, Phao reaped all the benefits of association with it. The figure Seni once branded "the worst man in the whole history of modern Thailand" was now making his political ascent with a big boost from the Americans.[22]

Together, the expanded overt and the new covert military assistance programs dramatically increased American influence in Thailand. The aid packages gave the United States added leverage in convincing the military to adopt pro-American policies and enhanced American prestige in Thailand. Most of all, they enabled the Americans to forge intimate relationships with the country's top leaders. While the considerable political benefits Phibun derived from U.S. assistance earned his profound gratitude, the generosity of police aid also brought Bird and the CIA into close cooperation with Phao. Because Thailand's political system was so highly personalized, American intimacy with these leaders added weight to U.S. pronouncements and requests.

In effect, the assistance programs initiated in 1950 and 1951 created a series of multilevel patron-client relationships between the Thais and the Americans. On one level, the United States acted as patron of the state as a whole. American economic aid benefited the entire state apparatus, including the civilian bureaucracy. On another level, the United States took on the military in particular as American clients. In this respect, aid strengthened the military versus its civilian opponents by increasing its firepower and wealth. On yet another level, the United States functioned as patron of individual leaders. Here, the United States took Phibun, the leader whose diplomacy had won the aid, and Phao, the direct beneficiary of the largest share of assistance, as individual clients. From this domestic perspective, the United States was now working within the Thai political system and assuming the top positions in the patronage networks of Phao and Phibun.

The United States exploited its new influence to gain Thai participation in the first U.S. military intervention in Southeast Asia since the war—the arming of Chinese Nationalist insurgents in Burma for an invasion of southern China. Ever since the final days of the Chiang Kai-shek regime on the mainland in 1949, American policymakers had contemplated assisting the scattered remnants of anticommunist forces in China. As late as 1951, proponents of such schemes asserted that up to a million anticommunist fighters remained on the mainland and that they could seriously weaken the communist government if activated.[23] In April 1950, the Joint Chiefs of Staff argued that a "program of special covert operations" could mobilize these fighters.[24] The JCS did not mention where it would direct the operations, but, by that time, fifteen hundred to two thousand Nationalist troops who had recently fled southern China's Yunnan province for the Shan states of northern Burma presented a promising possibility. Sometime shortly after the writing of the JCS memorandum, the United States began supplying arms and matériel to the troops.[25] In the fall, the CIA's Office of Policy Coordination (OPC) drafted a daring plan for them to invade Yunnan. The CIA's director, Walter Bedell Smith, opposed the risky scheme, but Truman rejected his warning. Desperate following the Chinese intervention in Korea in November to divert the Red Army's attentions from American forces, Truman approved the proposal at the end of the year. In January 1951, the CIA initiated its project, code-named Operation Paper. It aimed to prepare the Kuomintang (KMT) forces in Burma for an invasion of Yunnan.[26]

The CIA's plans depended on Thai support. Without official Thai acquiescence, the United States could not transport the necessary supplies through northern Thailand, the only feasible route to the Shan States. Without Thai diplomatic cover, the United States could not plausibly disassociate itself from the KMT's activities. Without Thai assistance, the Americans could not conduct the sensitive operation with any modicum of secrecy.

Because the project would advance fundamental Thai interests, the United States had little trouble convincing Phibun to help. Since World War II, the security policies of almost every Thai government have involved covert assistance to political dissidents from neighboring countries. Immediately after the war, Pridi armed Indochinese nationalist groups, and, after the November 1947 coup, Phibun continued to provide safe haven to anti-French insurgents. After 1954, when the Indochinese states achieved independence, the Thais backed a succession of political dissidents fighting the new regimes. In the south, it even seems that the Thais connived in the Malayan Communists' use of southern Thailand as a base of operations. The British and Malayans long complained of Thai reluctance to fight the Malayan Communists, and surrendered guerrillas have claimed that the Thais, in effect, left them alone.[27] The Thais have supported such dissidents because they perceived the various groups as both buffers against potential threats and tools in the country's drive to expand its influence in the region. As historian Alfred McCoy has astutely recognized, this policy derives from traditional Southeast Asian political methods and centuries-old international realities in the region.[28] In precolonial Southeast Asia, national borders—never well defined—mattered much less to a ruler's might than his relationships with local powers. Traditional rulers thus often extended their authority not by occupying land, but by influencing regional notables.

In Burma in the early 1950s, such a strategy appealed to the Thais. Although they recognized greater immediate threats elsewhere, Thais still disliked the Burmese more than any of their other ancient enemies. Burma's sacking of the former Thai capital, Ayutthaya, in 1767 and the two countries' endless wars provided the backdrop for numerous Thai movies in the 1950s. Thais still feared a resurgence of Burmese power. At the same time, Burma's present weakness offered tempting opportunities. After Pearl Harbor, the Thais temporarily annexed the region of Burma that the Chinese Nationalists now occupied, the Shan States. Because of their close ethnic and linguistic ties to the Shans (called *Thai Yai* in Thai), this region carried sentimental importance for Thais. The Coup Group, with its contingent of veterans, including Phin and Sarit, from the Shan States campaign, likely attached special significance to the region. Thus, the Thai government favored arming the Chinese Nationalists both to weaken the traditional

Burmese enemy and to increase Thai influence in northern Burma. With Burma fragmented and the government in Rangoon, like the Southeast Asian rulers of old, enjoying only nominal control over the region, the traditional strategy of befriending local powers made sense. Indeed, once Operation Paper started, the Thais aided not only the Nationalists, but indigenous rebel minorities in northern Burma as well.[29]

Also important in convincing Phibun to participate in Operation Paper, the Thais wanted to please their American patrons. Phibun had initiated his anticommunist publicity campaign of the summer of 1949, recognized Bao Dai, and sent troops to Korea all to win American military assistance. Likewise, Phibun and the Coup Group almost certainly perceived a link between Thai participation in Operation Paper and the military assistance packages. The important decisions on overt aid to the military came over the summer of 1950, just as the United States was starting to assist the Nationalists. General Erskine met Li Mi, commander of the KMT forces in Burma, in August while the Melby-Erskine mission was in Bangkok drafting the military aid recommendations. The coincidence was surely not lost on the Thais. Similarly, Phibun and Phao would have noted that the same people pushing for Operation Paper, Bird and the CIA, also initiated the covert police program. Whether the Americans in fact predicated their aid programs on Thai support for the Nationalists is unclear, but the Thais likely believed— with good reason—that the degree of Thai cooperation would affect the aid programs.

Phibun and the Coup Group, therefore, fully supported Operation Paper. Over the summer of 1950, as the United States was making initial contacts with the KMT remnants in Burma, the Thais began allowing the Nationalists to buy foodstuffs and supplies in northern Thailand. The Burmese ambassador formally protested official Thai complicity in the Nationalists' illegal movements in both July and August.[30] In October, the Thais permitted the United States to open a consulate—probably planned, in part, to aid the operation—in Chiang Mai, Thailand, near the northern border with Burma.[31] Toward the end of the year, the Thais helped Li Mi set up a KMT office in Mae Sai district on the Burmese border.[32] By that point, the U.S. embassy described Li Mi's previously ill-equipped and ragtag forces as "organized [and] well-armed."[33]

Then, as the CIA began planning in earnest for an invasion in early 1951, the Thais provided the United States crucial diplomatic cover against the most immediate obstacle to the project, Great Britain. The

British, as the Americans knew, were certain to object to Operation Paper. Largely out of regard for their Hong Kong colony, the British since 1949 had opened up to Mao's regime much more than the United States had. London recognized the new People's Republic of China (PRC) government and initially objected to the U.N.'s American-inspired condemnation in February 1951 of Chinese intervention in Korea.[34] The British feared provoking Beijing. London, moreover, was energetically working to improve relations with Britain's former colony, Burma, and to strengthen the control over the country of the shaky democratic government of Prime Minister U Nu. Because they occupied a portion of Burma already dominated by rebellious minorities, the KMT forces in northern Burma posed an especially worrisome threat to the country. Support for the KMT could only weaken further U Nu's government and poison Western—including British—relations with the Burmese. Were the Americans to pursue Operation Paper, they would have to do so behind their British allies' backs.

To maintain a veneer of plausible deniability with Britain, the Americans engaged Phibun in a simple, but effective, deceit. In March 1951, an officer from the Thai General Staff approached the British ambassador about arming Li Mi's forces. As the ambassador reported, the officer reported that Phibun had advised Thailand's "Central Security Council"[35] that the Nationalists in Burma represented Thailand's "first line of defence" against China and that the government should assist them. Phibun wanted to know what the British and, the officer claimed, the Americans thought about this plan.[36] As expected, the British firmly rejected it. And, as Washington had clearly planned, someone—possibly an American—told the British that Stanton had similarly dismissed the plan.[37] Even before Li Mi began marching, therefore, London focused its suspicions on the Thais instead of the Americans.

With the diplomatic cover set, the CIA initiated Operation Paper in earnest in early 1951. In February, the CIA's Civil Air Transport, recently acquired from Claire Chennault, transported to Bangkok a consignment of mortars, radio sets, and hundreds of rifles and carbines, and, in March, as Phibun and the State Department performed their diplomatic charade for the British, the CIA flew the consignment to Burma. At the same time, Civil Air Transport began making direct parachute drops to the KMT forces five times a week. Trainers from Taiwan arrived separately.[38]

Thai help was crucial here. When Civil Air Transport began the parachute drops in early 1951, Phibun allowed some of the planes to refuel in Bangkok. He arranged for the other flights to unload their stores in Bangkok for Sea Supply and the Thais to transport overland. Phao aided Phibun and the United States tremendously. Accompanied by two American military officers, he personally delivered the first arms shipment, the February consignment of radio sets, carbines, rifles, and mortars, and he met Li Mi frequently.[39] In March, Phao arranged for police maneuvers in the north to provide a cover for the operation and in September secretly traveled to New York, where the CIA's purchasing mission was located.[40] He almost certainly discussed there CIA plans for expansion of the KMT aid program. Eventually, it seems even that Phao's police assumed some of the heaviest burdens in the operation. In June of 1952, the embassy reported that one hundred graduates from the Lopburi camp were in Burma training the Nationalists in jungle warfare.[41] At some point, Phao established a police "Special Operations Unit" in Burma under the command of Phut Buranasomphop, one of the killers of the four pro-Pridi MPs in 1949. Phao charged Phut with facilitating the transfer of American arms to Li Mi's troops.[42]

Now in possession of modern weapons and receiving American and Thai advice, Li Mi initiated his long-awaited invasion. With only two thousand troops, he marched sixty miles north into Yunnan in June 1951 and captured an airfield without resistance. When a Red Army counterattack pushed him back to Burma after less than a month, he regrouped and invaded a second time. Again, the Red Army easily repulsed him, but his forces remained intact and ready for further action.[43]

The Li Mi forces' dramatically improved effectiveness now began to arouse British suspicions, but the Thai cover held. Even as reports of American overflights, sightings of westerners in northern Burma, and increased KMT activities made clear that *someone* was arming the Nationalists, Foreign Office officials refused to blame Washington. At times they speculated that only private American citizens, including Bird, were involved, or that the Nationalists had hired Western mercenaries, but all in the Foreign Office and the Bangkok embassy agreed that the Thais were the principal players. As late as September—three months after Li Mi's first incursion into Yunnan—the new British ambassador in Bangkok, G. A. Wallinger, believed that the Thais alone were responsible for the operation.[44]

But the Americans told one too many tall tales, and, over the fall, the fabrication collapsed. The Foreign Office, still wanting to believe Washington's indignant denials of involvement with the Nationalists, suggested to the State Department in September that Wallinger and the American chargé d'affaires in Bangkok jointly protest to Phibun over Thai aid for the Nationalists. The State Department, apparently trusting Phibun to continue playing the game, agreed, and instructions were sent to Wallinger and U.S. Chargé Turner to present the démarche. But the U.S. plan miscarried. A few days before the scheduled protest, Wallinger broached the subject of Thai aid for the Nationalists while golfing with Phibun. Phibun, either because he assumed the British already knew the truth, or out of irritation at having to accept the blame for an American-led operation, told all to the ambassador. He was helping to arm the Nationalists, Phibun peevishly explained, merely because the CIA had requested it. All decisions on the program lay with the Americans, and he could end the operation, he claimed, only on American instructions. When Wallinger then lifted his eyebrows in displeasure, Phibun caustically remarked, "Why are you surprised? Aren't you just as interested in killing Communists as I am, or as the Americans are?"[45]

From that point on, Washington's efforts to preserve its cover descended into absurdity. Before proceeding with the joint protest, Wallinger related his encounter with Phibun to Turner. The State Department had never informed Turner of official U.S. involvement with the Nationalist operation, but Wallinger presented irrefutable evidence. Turner could only respond that "all circumstances must have been considered in Washington before instructions were issued."[46] By then, the presentation of the démarche had lost all purpose, but, because Washington felt forced to maintain the deception and because Foreign Office instructions to drop the protest, sent by air, not cable, arrived in Bangkok too late, Turner and Wallinger delivered the démarche as planned.[47] In a comic-opera ending to a diplomatic performance that all involved knew to be a fraud but felt too embarrassed to expose, the two westerners sternly presented their protest to Worakan, and Worakan dutifully informed the two that he would bring it to Phibun's attention.[48] From then on, the game was up as far as the British were concerned.

Operationally as well, the Yunnan invasion project had nearly reached its end. Working for one final push, the CIA accelerated its aid to the Nationalist forces dramatically. At the end of 1951, the KMT, with U.S. help, opened a runway at Mong Hsat in northern Burma to accommodate large two- and four-engine planes. Quickly, the United States began transporting more powerful weapons, including .50-caliber machine guns, bazookas, and antiaircraft artillery. In early 1952, seven hundred regular KMT soldiers from Taiwan landed at the Mong

Hsat airstrip. Thus fully equipped, Li Mi attempted one more desperate invasion in August 1952. As before, however, his offensive went nowhere. His forces made it only sixty miles into Yunnan, and the Red Army easily repulsed him. Never again would Li Mi—or the CIA—attempt a large-scale invasion of southern China. Operation Paper had ended.[49]

In almost every respect, Operation Paper had proven a miserable failure. Militarily, it accomplished nothing. Li Mi invaded Yunnan three times between June 1951 and August 1952 and each time was easily repelled. Very few in southern China rallied to his cause, and huge numbers died in the attacks.[50] Diplomatically, the operation cost the United States friends and embarrassed the American government. The Burmese, badly troubled by Nationalist depredations, lost faith in the United States. British confidence in American policy in the region plummeted. Perhaps most painfully, the Americans' refusal to acknowledge responsibility for the operation badly damaged U.S. credibility. Despite the State Department's vehement denials of involvement in the invasions and its elaborate schemes to back American claims, by the end of 1951, all knew that the United States was sponsoring the Nationalists. The Soviets and Chinese accused the United States publicly, Thai politicians openly discussed the U.S. role, and diplomats regularly debated the operation's merits at social functions.[51] The wife of U.S. embassy Second Secretary Norman Hannah had to answer questions about American involvement with the Nationalists from her Thai hairdresser.[52]

Adding insult to injury, when these various losses forced the Americans to try to end the operation in 1952 and 1953, they found that they had created too many vested interests to terminate it easily. At some point in the first half of 1952, the United States decided that the invasions were futile and ceased its aid to the Nationalists, and, in early 1953, when the Burmese threatened to appeal to the U.N., the Americans forged an agreement among the Thais, Taiwanese, and Burmese to evacuate Li Mi's troops to Taiwan via Thailand.[53] Despite giving formal assent to evacuation, however, the United States' partners in the operation saw few reasons to end the project. The Taiwanese had established Burma as an important base of operation against the mainland, the Nationalist troops had settled down with their wives and children in their new Burmese homes, and Li Mi had begun growing rich off the opium trade. Later comments by Thai army generals show that most Thai military leaders continued to view the Nationalists as crucial to Thailand's defenses. As late as 1954, the chief of the Ministry of Defense's Intelligence Section openly informed a U.S. embassy official that he considered the Nationalist troops "a buffer" against possible aggression.[54]

Phao especially benefited from the KMT's presence in this infamous poppy-growing region. For several years, the Coup Group had profited from the illicit traffic of opium from Burma. Until the early 1950s, Phao and Sarit shared control of the trade, but the various CIA programs helped shift the commerce toward Phao. CIA arms and training increased the police's firepower in northern provinces important to the trade, and Phao's involvement in Operation Paper gave him contacts on the producing side. By the mid-1950s, such connections allowed him to monopolize the opium trade from the Thai end. Because profits from this illicit commerce financed many of Phao's political activities, he resisted all pressure to remove his KMT suppliers from Burma.

The American effort to evacuate Li Mi's forces, therefore, collapsed as quickly as their invasions. The Thais dragged their feet in implementing the evacuation accord, and Li Mi refused to turn over his best weapons or send off all of his troops. Although the United States airlifted some five thousand Nationalist soldiers to Taiwan by March 1954, thousands more stayed in Burma.[55] They remained a nuisance for Burma for decades to come, and the Thai military continued to deal with them well into the 1960s.[56]

Despite its complete failure militarily and diplomatically, Operation Paper, along with the expanded aid programs, had important consequences for Thailand and its relations with the United States. Politically, the operation further marginalized civilians in foreign-policymaking. A full year after the Bao Dai and Korea decisions, Foreign Ministry officials and opposition politicians still opposed any policy that would antagonize the communist powers or Thailand's neighbors. These civilians criticized the KMT project privately whenever given the chance. Each time the Burmese delivered one of their several démarches over Thai support for the Nationalists to the Thai Foreign Ministry, Worakan or another ministry official protested strongly to Phibun. Worakan told the field marshal that Thai aid to the Nationalists "may lead to troubles with the Burmese."[57] Khuang also opposed the operation, and the press warned of diplomatic repercussions from Thai involvement.[58] As with the Bao Dai and Korea decisions, however, Phibun disregarded civilians' opinions and met all the Americans' requests. Each time Worakan complained of Thai participation in Operation Paper, Phibun had the cabinet formally ban aid to the Nationalists, but the prohibitions were only for show.[59] Phibun and

Phao continued to conduct policy on the operation in secret and without official sanction. Whereas the Bao Dai and Korea decisions, therefore, had reduced the cabinet to a rubber-stamp body and the Foreign Ministry to the executor of policies Phibun and the military had already determined, Operation Paper removed even these limited foreign-policy tasks from civilian hands. Now civilian politicians and officials would have no say at all in the most important areas of Thai-U.S. cooperation.

The expanded arms aid programs, moreover, made the military regime dependent on the United States. Within three years of the initiation of American aid in 1950, the United States provided $72 million in military assistance, and, in 1953 alone, it gave $56 million. Even excluding the large covert programs, for which figures are not available, the 1953 aid accounted for more than 70 percent of all the money reported spent—Thai and American—on Thai defenses that year.[60] The Thai military likely would have collapsed had the United States halted this assistance. Once it began in force in 1951, therefore, Phibun and the Coup Group could not afford to refuse U.S. requests and risk losing it.

Together, Operation Paper and the expanded military assistance programs of 1950 and 1951 reshaped the triangular relations among the United States, Thailand, and Britain—to the Americans' advantage. Up through 1950, the United States and Britain shared the spotlight in Thailand fairly equally. Acheson's December 1949 comment that Thailand remained primarily a British responsibility demonstrated that, as late as that point, Washington still deferred to Britain on Thailand. Even after Truman approved the initial $10 million military aid package in the spring of 1950, the British, with their longer history in the country, more advanced commercial penetration, and greater interest in the region, retained almost as much influence in Thailand as the United States. Until late 1950, the British remained Phao's most important arms supplier. But the expanded U.S. aid programs of the end of that year gave the Americans an insuperable advantage over their allies. The sheer size of the U.S. programs dwarfed the British projects, and American arms, unlike British weapons, came without a price tag. This generosity turned Thais' attentions to the United States exclusively. In 1950, Phibun began a reorganization of the army to fit it to American standards. Discarding its past reliance on British methods and practices, the army borrowed the West Point curriculum for its academy, adopted American training techniques, and restructured the general staff according to the U.S. pattern.[61] The reorganization both prepared the army for future cooperation with its U.S. counterpart and made collaboration with the British more difficult. Then, when the United States asked the Thais to stand with it and against Britain in Operation Paper, the Thais agreed without flinching. In the face of strong British opposition, the Thais provided full logistical support and lied to the British on the Americans' behalf. The operation represented the first instance since the war in which Thailand risked serious conflict with Britain on an important foreign-policy issue.

Thai willingness to join in the project left Thailand less an ally of the West as a whole than a client of the United States in particular. Now, the Thais would back the United States against its European allies as well as against the Communists. Later, when heated disputes arose between the United States and its European allies over political and military strategy in Indochina, this willingness to support the United States helped make Thailand the Americans' one crucial ally in the region.

Most important, the expanded aid programs and Operation Paper laid the groundwork for much closer relations between the United States and Thailand. With the precedent and the institutional framework the KMT project provided, and with the Thai forces and American military presence the aid programs established, the United States was, by late 1951, in a position to plan for even more extensive covert and overt military operations in Thailand. For the moment, the military regime was too unstable and the political atmosphere too unfavorable to implement any such plans, but if those obstacles were eliminated, the United States could move forward quickly. Then, the Americans would be ready to stake their entire Southeast Asian strategy on Thailand.

Chapter Seven

THE UNITED STATES AND THE MILITARY'S

CONSOLIDATION OF POWER,

JUNE 1951–DECEMBER 1952

Although military aid and Operation Paper had increased U.S. interest in Thailand, the Americans still felt too uncertain about the military government's stability to risk a much greater investment in the country. While Phibun had come a long way toward taming conservatives in Parliament and the bureaucracy, the military government's fundamental political problems remained unsolved. Opposition to the Coup Group within the military itself stayed strong, and official corruption seemed to be eating away whatever popular support the government enjoyed. Even the conservative politicians Phibun had largely subdued retained enough influence to inflict political damage on the government. Most worrisome to the United States, the military government seemed unwilling to stem a small leftist resurgence in the country. American officials feared that pressure from this new force might weaken the military government's pro-U.S. policy. Only if the government stabilized its position and eliminated the left would they be able to assign Thailand a larger role in their regional strategy.

In June 1951, the consolidation of power that U.S. policymakers needed began with the failure of the so-called Manhattan Rebellion, the navy's long-expected attempt to take power. In April of that year, Phao initiated a campaign to transfer the navy's coastal patrol duties to his police. Wanting to secure control over the endpoint of the opium trade, he pushed the issue despite strong navy opposition. High-ranking naval figures, U.S. embassy dispatches reported, may have begun plotting with Khuang and Kat (now back in Thailand) to overthrow the government.[1] Before the admirals could implement their plan, however, less senior officers acted. On June 29, during a ceremony transferring the American dredge *Manhattan* to the Thai navy as part of the U.S. military assistance program, a small group of junior naval officers kidnapped Phibun at gunpoint and took him to the nearby flagship *Si Ayutthaya*. Naval guards loyal to the officers also seized fleet headquarters, and a small group of naval and marine officers captured the navy radio station. Although the rebels appear to have taken no part in any plotting by higher-ranking naval figures, they possibly expected the navy to rally to the rebel cause. In this, the young officers made their first crucial mistake in the badly arranged operation. Khuang and the navy leadership stood still, leaving the rebels to fight the government alone. Because of the rebels' second fatal error, their assumption that the Coup Group would accede to their demands in order to save Phibun's life, the young officers faced an extremely difficult fight. Instead of bargaining with the rebels, the military began a fierce counterattack. The army and police besieged naval bases throughout the city, and the air force and police even bombed and shelled the ship holding Phibun. Within thirty-six hours, the rebellion had ended. The Coup Group, by then, controlled the city, and the plotters had fled the scene. Casualties were extremely high. Shooting wildly and acting without discipline, government soldiers and police killed twelve hundred—mostly civilians—and injured an additional eighteen hundred. Ironically, despite the bloodshed, the rebels' primary target, Phibun, survived unscathed. After the *Si Ayutthaya* was hit, he swam to the shore and safety.[2]

The navy, of course, lost the most in the Manhattan Rebellion. During the fighting, the police and the army overran navy positions in the city, and, once they had quashed the rebellion, Phao, Sarit, and Phin dismantled the navy. The Coup Group replaced most leading admirals, assigned the central and eastern provinces previously occupied by the navy to army command, and disbanded entire battalions. The air force assumed control over the navy's air section, and navy headquarters were moved from Bangkok to the eastern seaboard.[3] Nothing remained of the navy's political power.

Phibun, however, also suffered from the navy's defeat. The Coup Group's evident willingness to sacrifice him belied his supporters' contention that Phibun was the government's indispensable prop. Moreover, the dismemberment of the navy—over Phibun's protests[4]—rendered it more difficult for him to play one service branch against another as he had done earlier to great effect. After the rebellion, Phibun lacked much of his previous authority.

Phibun's and the navy's loss was Phao's gain. Sarit's Bangkok-based First Division, as in the Palace Rebellion, and Phao's police had figured most prominently in the defeat of the Manhattan rebels, and both generals reaped the consequent benefits in prestige and power, but Phao especially profited. Although Sarit still had to share control of the army with Phao's father-in-law, Phin, Phao enjoyed unquestioned command of the police, without doubt one of the nation's two most powerful armed forces now that the navy was broken. Phao moved quickly after the Manhattan Rebellion to take key offices. Symbolically important, he assumed formal command of the police days after the fighting ended with his promotion to director-general of the department. Phao also had the government issue an order empowering provincial police commissioners, rather than deputy provincial governors, to act for provincial governors in their absence and got himself appointed assistant to the permanent secretary of the Interior Ministry.[5] These changes gave Phao extensive influence in provincial administration. The navy's defeat, moreover, enhanced Phao's moneymaking ability, a critical attribute in the country's patronage politics. Before the rebellion, the navy, in exchange for coast guard connivance in outbound shipments, had demanded a cut of the opium trade. The dismantling of the navy after the rebellion enabled Phao finally to transfer the coast guard to the police and complete his capture of the trade.[6] While it became common in the upcoming months and years, therefore, to refer to a triumvirate of Phibun, Phao, and Sarit, many observers considered Phao the most powerful man in the country. From then on, Phibun viewed Phao not as a supporter, but as a rival, and for several years Phao posed the greatest immediate threat to Phibun's power.

In important ways, these developments damaged U.S. interests in Thailand. The violence accompanying the Manhattan Rebellion highlighted the government's instability and disregard for public safety, and the undeniable, though largely unwitting, U.S. role in the events soiled the United States' reputation within the country. The presentation of the *Manhattan,* a much-heralded element of the American military-assistance package, had provided the occasion for the rebellion, and American-supplied weapons had figured in much of the fighting. One high-ranking policeman has claimed that a CIA-supplied mortar fired by a Sea Supply–trained policeman, not an air force bomb as commonly reported, sunk the *Si Ayutthaya.*[7] Many Thais, as a result, blamed the United States for the bloodshed accompanying the conflict. Several days after the rebellion, the *New York Times* reported that "already anti-U.S. reports are sweeping Bangkok. . . . The rumor-spreaders are saying 'American guns killed our people.' "[8]

The U.S. embassy, moreover, regretted the rise of Phao and the weakening of Phibun. As long as the police backed Phibun, Stanton and his assistants accepted Phao as a necessary evil. They had long considered Phao a dangerous, thoroughly corrupt political gangster, but no one questioned U.S. support for him. The embassy personnel considered Phibun the most competent, pro-Western, statesmanlike leader in Thailand and applauded almost anything or anyone strengthening him. But once Phao's power grew to the extent that he threatened, not protected, Phibun, the embassy turned on him. Post-rebellion embassy dispatches warned about Phao's ambitions, and officials predicted serious damage to U.S. interests were he to overthrow Phibun. In September, embassy Second Secretary Rolland Bushner expressed his hope that Phibun and Sarit would combine forces to oust Phao and the following month recommended to the State Department that the United States stop dealing with him.[9]

Stanton and his assistants resented covert aid to Phao and Operation Paper as CIA intrusions on embassy turf. Of the embassy personnel, only Stanton received information from Washington on CIA dealings with the police, and even he exerted little control over Sea Supply, with its offices on Chitlom Lane, several blocks from the embassy. The embassy's exclusion from the police and KMT aid programs continually embarrassed U.S. diplomats. Khuang's criticism of American aid to the Nationalists at a party mortified Second Secretary Norman Hannah.[10] Similarly, Turner's presentation of the disingenuous British-American démarche on Thai assistance to the Nationalists seems to have humiliated him. He complained to Washington about aid to the police and Bird's semiofficial work with Phao. "Why is this man Bird," the exasperated Turner protested, "allowed to deal with the Police Chief?"[11]

The embassy believed that U.S. interests lay with Phibun. Stanton and his assistants still supported the related ideals of constitutionalism and civilian participation in government. The embassy considered Phibun both the legitimate head of government and the leader best placed to maintain a role in the military regime for "conservative" politicians. Stanton later described Phibun as "the only personality able, in the circumstances, to maintain an effective balance among the contending factions of the military clique and at the same time restrain their excesses."[12] Phao, the occupant of a relatively low-ranking, nonpolitical office whose power derived solely from coercion and terror, conversely represented extralegality and dictatorship. His peculations especially irked the embassy. Although Phibun had had his own corruption scandals in the 1930s, by the 1950s, the Phao-Phin clique's activities had clearly eclipsed Phibun's. Involved in the opium trade, gold-selling, rail, transport, banking, and trucking, Phao-Phin enterprises had, by the early 1950s, penetrated almost every commercial sector in the country, legal or otherwise. An embassy report of 1952 claimed that a popular backlash against such venality could throw the country to the Communists. Official corruption, the report warned, "can no longer be viewed simply in moralistic terms, and it now constitutes a threat to the internal political and economic stability of the country."[13]

The embassy, therefore, fiercely resisted Phao's ascendancy. In the spring of 1951, Stanton pressed Phibun to include Khuang and anti-communist Free Thai in the cabinet, in part to lessen the field marshal's dependence on Phao.[14] In January 1953, he recommended that Washington support Phibun fully against Phao.[15] While Stanton was in the United States at the end of 1951, Hannah, Bushner, and two other political officers, Gerald Stryker and Robert Anderson, sent Rusk a memorandum under Turner's signature detailing the CIA's dealings with Phao and the Nationalists and asking Washington to halt the activities. Aid to Phao, the memorandum contended, was upsetting the balance of power in the country.[16]

Despite embassy displeasure with Phao and the damage the use of American weapons had inflicted on U.S. prestige, however, the Americans in no way regretted the government victory in the Manhattan Rebellion. On the contrary, the suppression of the rebels greatly relieved American officials. Although the British had long maintained close ties with leading admirals, the United States viewed the navy as, at best, an unknown quantity, and, at worst, a destabilizing force. Thus, whereas the British vehemently protested the government's violent methods in suppressing the rebellion and angrily demanded recompense for collateral damage to British embassy property, the United States voiced no objections to government actions. Indeed, the State Department congratulated Phibun on his escape.[17]

Furthermore, although Phao's ascendancy upset the embassy, the CIA had no complaints. Before the rebellion, the CIA's extensive covert assistance to the police communicated its tacit approval of Phao's political activities. During the rebellion itself, the evidence suggests that Bird and the CIA directly aided the government forces. Bird stayed at Phao's side through much of the fighting and seems to have provided emergency assistance to the police effort.[18] Turner, in his dispatch protesting Bird's activities, commented that Bird "featured somewhat prominently in the June 29th incident as the character who handed over a lot of military equipment to the Police."[19] No hard evidence exists that American help for Phao during the rebellion extended beyond Bird,[20] but, clearly, many Americans outside the embassy still considered Phao the most promising Thai military leader. His conduct during the rebellion had demonstrated his determination and leadership, and his harsh rhetoric was distinguishing him as the most hardline anti-Communist among the Sarit-Phin-Phao triumvirate. In the months and years after the rebellion, CIA assistance to the police accelerated.

While the Americans debated the consequences of the navy's latest defeat, the Coup Group turned its attentions toward the next enemy on its list, the remaining civilians in government. Although the Coup Group now enjoyed complete control over the country militarily, politicians and legislators continued to annoy the generals. Phibun had reduced Democrat MPs, through elections, bribery, and clever distribution of patronage, to fewer than forty in the 109-seat lower house, but his small Thammathipat Party and the Coup Group's newly formed Chat Sangkhom Party remained several dozen seats short of a majority. To form his cabinets and pass legislation, Phibun had to rely on civilian politicians grouped in three parties, Issara, Ratsadorn, and Prachachon. Controlling more than a third of the parliamentary seats, these parties conflicted sharply with the Coup Group. Throughout 1950 and 1951, the civilian and military progovernment parties fought over spoils and offices, and, despite its monopoly on use of force, the Coup Group lost some political battles. In January 1951, the civilian parties succeeded in forcing Phibun to replace two military ministers with civilian politicians. Similarly, though the Democrats had withered in the lower house, the Senate remained a royalist stronghold. In a late-October session, senators sharply attacked the government for the violent suppression of the Manhattan Rebellion. In early November, the upper house blocked a bill designed to increase the military voice in elections.[21]

The Coup Group decided soon after the Manhattan Rebellion that, to eliminate these irritants, it had to amend or rewrite the constitution. Besides granting the royally appointed Senate considerable powers, the constitution drafted in 1949 by the Democrat-controlled assembly barred active government officials from the cabinet. Because this provision extended to military and police officers, Phao, Sarit, and Air Marshal Fuen Ronnaphakat found the 1949 constitution entirely objectionable. Phao, therefore, traveled twice to Switzerland in August and

October 1951 to persuade the young King Bhumibol Adulyadej, then studying in Lausanne, to accept a constitution more amenable to the Coup Group. On the first trip, the king apparently failed to object to the plan, but Phao returned to Thailand from the second journey empty-handed. In November, the Coup Group decided to proceed without the king's approval.[22]

By then, only Phibun blocked the new constitution. Phibun's strength since 1948 lay in the multiplicity of political groups in the country and his ability to play one off the other. As the number of such groups increased and their individual powers decreased, so Phibun found it easier to maintain a balance of power among them. Conversely, with fewer and individually stronger political forces, Phibun's ability to uphold his supremacy diminished. Thus, he opposed the dismemberment of the navy in July, and in late 1951, when the Coup Group acted to remove civilians from their remaining positions in the administration, he resisted.

In the end, the Coup Group disregarded Phibun as well as the king. On November 26, several weeks following the failure of Phao's second trip, the Coup Group sent a representative to Phibun to suggest reverting from the Democrat-written 1949 constitution to the antiroyalist, but less democratic, constitution of 1932. Phibun rejected the proposal out of hand, but, three days later, nine leading Coup Group members pressed him in person. Although he angrily rebuffed them a second time, the nine demanded that Phibun agree to dissolve Parliament and abrogate the present constitution. By then, the Coup Group was desperate. The king planned to return from Switzerland in two days to resume his royal duties, and, after that, the generals risked a dangerous confrontation with the popular monarch. That evening, therefore, the same nine Coup Group members, led by Phao, Phin, Fuen, and Sarit, announced over the radio the dissolution of Parliament, reinstatement of the 1932 constitution, and formation of a provisional cabinet. Phibun initially refused to join the new government but, after lengthy bargaining, accepted the fait accompli. The next morning, he signed on again as prime minister.[23]

This so-called Radio, or Silent, Coup consolidated the Coup Group's hold on the country. The reinstated 1932 constitution eliminated the Senate and established a unicameral legislature composed equally of elected and government-appointed members. The government thus was guaranteed control of at least half the seats, and, because a prohibition on parties made it easy to manipulate elections, the opposition's share of even the elected seats was certain to be small. Facing such restrictions, the Democrats refused to contest the subsequent February 1952 elections. Because the 1932 constitution allowed serving government officials into the cabinet, leading Coup Group members could now supplement their military commands with important minis- terial portfolios. The generals exploited their new rights to the utmost. Coup Group representation in the government increased from six to ten after the coup, and, as a whole, military men grabbed nineteen of the twenty-five cabinet-level offices.

As with the Manhattan Rebellion, Phao gained the most from the coup. His visits to the king indicate that he probably led the coup, and, most likely because of this role, he was able to take advantage of the civilians' defeat more readily than other Coup Group members. Thus, while Phao's rival, Sarit, entered the cabinet as deputy minister of defense unaccompanied by close supporters, the Phin-Phao clique cap- tured five cabinet slots.[24] Phao's own appointment as deputy minister of interior gave him effective control over this politically powerful minis- try. The elimination of the parliamentary opposition enabled Phao to replace Phibun as chief manipulator of Parliament. Several months after the elections, Phao organized a de facto party, the so-called Legis- lative Study Committee, as the government's and his own personal political tool. He exerted nearly complete control over this powerful group, the first progovernment party to hold a majority of parliamen- tary seats since the military had ousted Khuang in 1948. Phao's ability to wield actual political power, as a result, increased substantially after the Silent Coup.

The United States reacted to the Silent Coup with surprising anger. In contrast to their mild response to the suppression of the navy in June, the Americans, this time, forcefully criticized the government. Stanton, then in Washington for consultations and health care, opposed any further movement toward dictatorship and, along with Landon, decided to protest the coup. He and Landon drafted a cable to Turner instructing the embassy to deliver the Thais a mildly worded, but potentially explosive, démarche. Pointing out that "frequent exhi- bitions of mil[itary] interference in politics, twice within five months, creates [*sic*] [an] impression of instability and polit[ical] immaturity," the dispatch directed the embassy to explain to the Thais that every time there is a coup in Thailand, "agencies engaged in mil[itary] and econ[omic] aid . . . [ask about the] desirability [of] continu[ing] their various ventures."[25] Turner delivered this implicit threat to suspend the aid programs to Phibun on December 6, and the U.S. military attaché similarly criticized the coup to his counterparts in the Thai army.

According to the British ambassador, the attaché "expressed himself in colourful language."[26] When Stanton returned to Bangkok in January, he released a public statement echoing Turner's démarche.[27] It created an uproar in the Thai press and government circles. In response, the Defense Ministry withheld for a year intelligence reports it had previously shared with the embassy.[28]

Despite the United States' evident anger, however, the Americans had, in fact, unwittingly contributed to the Silent Coup. With its covert aid programs, the CIA continually signaled to Phao that he could get away with just about anything as far as the United States was concerned. Providing arms and training, possibly aiding his suppression of the navy, and cooperating closely with him on Operation Paper, the CIA let Phao know in no uncertain terms that its strategy in Thailand depended on him. Phao's secret late-August trip to New York, the location of a Sea Supply purchasing mission, must have particularly impressed him. Apparently called on short notice to confer on preparations for Li Mi's third invasion of Yunnan, Phao unexpectedly cut short a scheduled visit in England to make the surprise ten-day trip.[29] Significantly, the CIA called the meeting on the return leg of Phao's trip to Switzerland to win the king's approval for constitutional changes. At this crucial point in Thai internal politics, the urgent meeting in New York sent Phao the clear message that the CIA relied on him. Whether the Silent Coup, in fact, pleased his CIA friends is unclear, but Phao could be sure, as Operation Paper moved into high gear in late November, that the agency would never allow Washington to damage its relationship with him. He moved ahead with the Silent Coup, confident that aid to his police would continue.

The Americans, moreover, had let it be known in the year leading up to the Silent Coup that they would tolerate increased military interference in Thailand's government if neutralist politicians were eliminated from the cabinet. Among the civilian politicians the Coup Group resented most were Deputy Minister of Commerce Thep Chotinuchit, Education Minister Liang Chayakan, and Minister of Communications Pathom Phokaew, two of whom, Pathom and Liang, had replaced the two Coup Group ministers in the January 1951 tussle. Pathom, Liang, and Thep worried the United States as well as the Coup Group. Phibun's underling, Sang Phatthanothai, told Hannah in early February that the three—all from the northeast—were pressing Phibun to adopt a neutralist foreign policy but that Phibun could not dismiss them from the cabinet for fear of losing their support in Parliament.[30] Other reports alleged (improbably) that they passed state secrets to the

Vietminh via their followers in the northeast. Turner believed that the three planned to increase their leverage with Phibun "in preparation for the day when it may be necessary to make a fast shift to accommodate a Communist-oriented regime."[31] Thep especially frightened the Americans. Although he had served in Phibun cabinets since defecting from the Democrat Party in 1948 and himself advocated nothing more radical than democratic socialism, his brother Phethai had clear leftist connections. Cofounder of Thep's Ratsadorn Party, Phethai Chotinu-chit had formerly edited the leftist *Kanmeuang* (Politics) weekly and had helped found the procommunist Thailand Peace Committee.[32] Largely because of U.S. opposition to Thep and his two neutralist ministerial colleagues, Stanton urged Phibun that spring to bring Khuang and "conservative" Free Thai such as the pro-American Tiang Sirikhan into the government. Stanton hoped that Phibun could then dispense with Thep, Liang, and Pathom as well as Phao.[33] In early February, the press reported that Phibun, apparently referring to Stanton's pressure, had told the cabinet that "diplomats of some countries in the democratic camp made the observation that some of our ministers are inclined toward communism."[34]

The Coup Group made the ouster of the three politicians a cornerstone of their justification of the coup. The very first communique the Coup Group's provisional ruling council issued after the coup announced that the government had had to dismiss the cabinet since "the present Council of Ministers as well as Parliament is largely infiltrated by communist elements [i.e., neutralists]."[35] To please the United States as well as to serve its own interests, the Coup Group excluded Thep, Liang, and Pathom from all postcoup cabinets.

The United States sent additional signals to the Coup Group that it would welcome increased repression. As before, the Americans made clear in the months leading up to the Silent Coup that they wanted a total crackdown on Communists. Official support for a rival labor union had weakened the communist-affiliated Central Labor Union Pridi had founded, and a more hostile environment had driven cadres underground since 1948, but the Communist Party of Thailand stayed active and possibly grew in 1951. Although it still confined itself to nonviolent recruitment and propaganda activities and remained small, Mao's victory on the mainland had won the party widespread support among local Chinese. Community support may not have translated into membership gains, but it certainly increased donations to the party and created new connections with sympathetic Chinese businessmen. Thus, although the embassy dismissed Phao's contention that Communists led the Manhattan coup, the Americans exploited the atmosphere of repression following the rebellion to again press for a crackdown.[36] Hannah, in a meeting with Phao two weeks after the rebellion, "referred to rumors that the Communists had been closely involved in the attempted coup d'etat and told General Phao that if they were actually involved I would expect that a number of them would be arrested."[37]

As well, the Americans wanted the group Phethai Chotinuchit had recently helped found, the Thailand Peace Committee, suppressed. Closely aligned with the Communist Party, the Peace Committee acted as the Thailand chapter of the World Peace Movement organization.[38] Although European peace activists had founded the Peace Movement in 1948 with genuinely neutralist intentions, the Cominform managed within two years to turn the group into a Soviet mouthpiece.[39] The Thailand chapter, as elsewhere, combined praise for the "peace-loving" Soviet and Chinese peoples with harsh criticism of supposed U.S. war-mongering and imperialism. The committee's leaders, Jaroen Seub-saeng and Kulab Saipradit, were knowledgeable, if idiosyncratic, Marx-ists. An influential writer and long-time social critic, Kulab translated a number of Marx's works into Thai and published a book titled *The Philosophy of Marxism.*[40] Under Kulab and Jaroen, the Thailand Peace Committee publicized its cause, collected signatures for the so-called Stockholm Peace Appeal, and, in April 1951, sent a delegate to the World Student Confederation conference in Beijing.[41] The committee attracted a great deal of attention from both the local press and the embassy. The United States Information Service worked with royalist Kukrit Pramoj, now owner and editor of the conservative *Sayam Rath* newspaper, to publicize links between the world movement and Mos-cow, and, probably on U.S. urging, the government sponsored its own anticommunist peace petition.[42]

The burgeoning leftist press also worried the United States. Al-though most Thais remained ignorant of or hostile to leftist ideologies, Marxism was gaining adherents among some sectors of literate, urban society, and journalists in particular. By 1951, leftists dominated many independent Thai newspapers, which still greatly outnumbered and outsold government publications. Journalism, a low-prestige profession in Thailand in the 1950s, attracted many young Thais unable to get government jobs and, as a result, alienated from the country's political and economic establishment. Some leftist newspapers and journals maintained personal or financial connections with the Thai Commu-nist Party, among them *Mahachon, Kanmeuang, Thammajak, Sangkhom Niyom, Maitrisan, Puangchon, Thang Mai, Yuk Mai,* and *Satjatham.* Other more independent publications, such as *Sayam Nikorn, Phim Thai, Aksornsan,* and *Sayam Samai,* offered leftist critiques of the government and occasionally published Marxist writings.[43] These newspapers regularly attacked the United States and praised the "New China." Most worrisome for the United States, the leftist press exerted much more than a merely marginal influence. The Thai Phanitchayakan Company chain owned by pro-China Ari Liwira was the most successful newspaper organization in the country.[44] Ari's leftist *Sayam Nikorn* was reported to control the market in every town in the militarily strategic northeast,[45] and his *Phim Thai* possibly enjoyed the largest circulation in the country.[46] The United States badly wanted independent publications like Ari's as well as the Communist-affiliated press muzzled. As Bushner told Air Marshal Fuen soon after the Silent Coup, the United States believed that "the propaganda of pro-Communist [i.e., independent leftist] newspapers is much more effective and dangerous than that contained in Communist news organs."[47]

American officials in Thailand felt strongly about all these groups —the neutralist politicians, the Communists, the Peace Committee, and the leftist press. The public criticism by the press and the Peace Committee embarrassed the United States, and the neutralist cabinet members threatened American aims in the country. The United States worried that, together, the neutralist politicians, the leftists, and the Communists would affect the government's foreign policy. Their activities fed the Americans' already exaggerated fears about Thailand's security. The outbreak of war in Korea in June 1950 had induced a siege mentality among Americans in Asia, and U.S. officials in Thailand viewed the future with foreboding. After the North Korean attack, Stanton believed, a colleague wrote, "that no matter what we [the United States] do now in Southeast Asia the game is lost."[48] In February 1951, Stanton wrote a report described as "excellent" by William Lacy of the Office of Philippine and Southeast Asian Affairs predicting imminent Chinese aggression against Thailand. Within two or three months, Stanton forecast, the PRC would launch guerrilla attacks in the north, northeast, and south, intensify "communist activities within the country including sabotage, terrorism and propaganda designed to confuse and terrify the Thai people," and mount a "coup d'etat using Thai political outs."[49] The Americans viewed even the nonviolent, purely political activities of the Communists, the Peace Committee, and leftist journalists as a real threat to the nation. Given Phibun's own collaboration with the Japanese, U.S. officials naturally believed that neutralist Liang and Pathom and leftist Thep similarly planned to hop on the advancing communist bandwagon for personal political benefit.

The Americans' well-known fears and their pressure on the government to crack down on Communists and leftists provided the Coup Group the excuse it needed to mount the Silent Coup. When pushed by the United States to take action, Phao and other Thais argued, with good reason, that, without legislation specifically aimed at Communists, a crackdown would prove ineffective and that, without constitutional change, the government could not enact an anti-Communist law. After mounting the Silent Coup, therefore, the Coup Group proclaimed that it had abrogated the constitution not only to purge the government of Thep and his neutralist colleagues, but also to enact an anti-Communist law. Similarly, the Coup Group's second postcoup communique claimed that the government acted because the fight against communism "is obstructed by the present Constitution under which not even an anti-Communist law may be passed."[50] Given the pressure from the Americans to repress leftists and Communists, even the antimilitary Stanton could accept the Silent Coup, Phao and the Coup Group seem to have figured, if the government finally took a hard line. Bushner confirmed the accuracy of this expectation just two weeks after the coup. When Air Marshal Fuen asked him in a meeting after the coup what course of action the government should follow, Bushner sternly replied that it should fulfill "its promises to eradicate corruption and act against Communists."[51]

The Coup Group's claim that the pre-Silent Coup legal structure blocked effective suppression of Communists was accurate. Ever since the dispatch of troops to Korea in July 1950, the military leadership had sought to tighten restrictions on the left, but the lack of satisfactory anti-Communist legislation hindered its efforts. Although articles 104 and 105 of the Amended Criminal Act of 1935, with their broad language outlawing activities posing a threat to the peace and well being of the nation, provided some grounds for arresting Communists,[52] Phao and the police felt, with good basis, that, to obtain convictions, the government needed stronger legislation. In September 1950, less than two months after dispatching troops to Korea, the cabinet therefore asked the Juridical Council to consider whether the constitution implicitly outlawed communism for opposing religion and the monarchy.[53] If so, the government hoped that an anti-Communist act could be passed. Over the next several months, little happened, but, in February 1951, the Interior Ministry wrote Phibun that the lack of supporting legislation was badly hampering police operations against Communists.[54] The cabinet, in response, again asked the Juridical Council to address the problem, and the council finally began active consideration of an anti-Communist act.[55] But the council's findings did not please the government. René G. Guyon, the French adviser to the council, recommended in April that any prohibition of the Communist Party would probably "not come without serious inconveniences from the . . . provisions of the Constitution" guaranteeing freedom of speech and freedom to form political parties, and, in August, the Juridical Council's secretary, Serm Winitchaikun, reported that the Communist Party platform did not ban religion and thus did not conflict with the constitution.[56] Therefore, although the cabinet instructed the council in September—less than three months before the Silent Coup—to prepare an anti-Communist law for presentation to Parliament in October, nothing came of the order.[57]

But the Silent Coup got the ball rolling again. The reinstatement of the less liberal 1932 constitution eliminated the legal obstacles to passage of an anti-Communist act, and the further weakening of the civilian opposition allowed the government to enact the law without real debate. Bushner's postcoup encounter with Fuen, moreover, had reminded the Coup Group that the United States expected it to keep its promises to repress Communists. By strengthening Phao, the leader most eager to suppress the opposition, the Silent Coup ensured that pressure within the government to act would be intense. Soon after the Manhattan Rebellion gave him a political boost, Phao had managed to have his deputy, Col. Jamrat Manthukanon of the c.i.d., assigned responsibility for drafting an anti-Communist bill in place of Phibun supporter Khab Kunchorn. Then, on December 1, two days after the coup, the Coup Group's provisional government instructed Worakan, at that time in the Phao camp, to study analogous foreign laws to aid the Juridical Council's consideration of the bill. The Coup Group hoped to enact the law within two months.[58]

Triumvirate politics, however, stymied progress on the bill. Phao wanted an anti-Communist law to aid police repression not only of Communists, but moderate opposition groups as well. Indicative of his intentions, he warned darkly in early January that the government planned to establish a new prison for political prisoners along the lines of the notorious Tarutao Island prison of World War II, and, on January 15, Worakan announced that the Foreign Ministry favored a bill outlawing not only Communists, but anyone "in general who plans to do harm to the democratic system and the peace of the nation."[59] The anti-Communist bill Colonel Jamrat and the Juridical Council finally presented the cabinet on January 18, titled a "Draft Act on Control of Subversive Activities," expressed its prohibitions as broadly as possible. The bill would have outlawed all forms of association with organizations seeking "to promote economic transformations, by which private ownership of property and means of production shall be abolished entirely or partly and shall be transferred to the State by way of confiscation or otherwise."[60] Any contacts with such groups, even if limited to attendance of a single meeting or providing lodging to a member, invited arrest. Under this law, many Pridi-ites and social democrats like Thep, as well as pro-Communists such as the Peace Committee activists, could have been jailed. Phao thus would have been able to eliminate much of the civilian opposition, save the remnants of the badly weakened Democrat Party.

Phibun, though, would have none of this. The Silent Coup had already removed most of the civilian political forces he used to counter the Coup Group, and he was not about to let Phao get rid of the few civilian politicians remaining. In mid-January, Phibun publicly rejected Phao's plans for a Tarutao-style prison, saying that the government merely would separate political prisoners from violent criminals.[61] Then, just a few days before Worakan's call for a broad antisubversives act, Phibun announced that the new constitution would specifically outlaw the Communist Party but made no mention of the more sweeping act Phao and the Juridical Council were promoting.[62] Implicitly, Phibun seems to have been expressing his preference for a constitutional provision aimed specifically at Communists over a broader law giving Phao scope to harass the noncommunist opposition. On January 18, the cabinet rejected Phao's bill—almost certainly at Phibun's behest—and sent it back to the Ministry of the Interior and the Juridical Council for revision.[63] Apparently, Phibun relied on an old trick, the threat of resignation, to defeat Phao on the measure. Rumor had it that the field marshal was threatening to quit after the elections.[64]

Phibun, nonetheless, still had a fight ahead of him. Given the mandate to rewrite the anti-Communist bill, Phao had his police subordinates on the drafting committee broaden, not weaken, the law. The new bill, submitted to the cabinet on March 13, specifically included the production and distribution of "subversive" propaganda as an offense.[65] Phao, it seems, then provoked a serious confrontation with Phibun regarding the revised law. On March 7, at the height of a high-level struggle over the date for formal promulgation of the constitution, Phao told Phibun, as recounted by Sang, that "for four years the Premier has had a free hand to apply his policy of pacification of the Government's enemies in an effort to bring about a coalition" but had failed. Phao thus proclaimed, Sang said, "that it is now time to try the Phao method[,] which is 'to dispose of one's enemies.' "[66] As before, however, Phibun thwarted Phao. That same night, the U.S. embassy learned, Phibun offered Phao the prime ministership. This likely elated Phao but frightened Sarit. Sarit, it was reported to the embassy, asked the field marshal to reconsider, and, with that, Phibun agreed to stay on.[67] Phibun emerged from the conflict with somewhat greater political leverage, and the cabinet dropped Phao's subversive activities bill.

Phibun could not ignore the political and diplomatic pressures to increase government repression, however, especially in view of his own political agenda at the time. During the war, Phibun had established a National Council on Culture to encourage nationalism and adherence to "modern" customs, such as wearing pants and hats and kissing one's wife before leaving for work. After the Silent Coup, he revived this "cultural" campaign. To enhance the legitimacy of his position as national leader after the coup had reduced much of his actual power, he elevated the cultural council in the spring of 1952 to ministry level. Taking personal command of the agency, he mounted a public-relations offensive to promote traditional Thai values such as filial piety. Above all, his campaign emphasized the need for Thais to oppose communism.[68] Having thus staked his reputation on anticommunism, Phibun found it much harder by mid-1952 to tolerate leftists. He began to press Phao sometime over the summer, or possibly earlier, to drop the antisubversives legislation and crack down on leftists using existing laws.

Now, though, Phao was the one to oppose repressing Communists.[69] Phao told the Americans that the police were holding back to further develop sources within the communist movement, but it seems likely that other considerations mattered more to him. Since failing to get cabinet approval for a comprehensive program of repression in the spring, Phao had acquired a number of useful business contacts with leftists and opposition forces. In addition to gaining the parliamentary support of the centrist Pridi-ite Tiang Sirikhan, Phao in 1952 began expanding his commercial dealings with procommunist Chinese merchants. That spring, he wooed Ari Liwira, owner of the pro-Chinese newspapers, *Siam Nikorn* and *Phim Thai*.[70] Had the government initiated a general sweep of the country's leftists, Phao would have had to either include these potential political and economic allies or damage his anticommunist reputation with the West by exempting them from arrest. Despite his secret contacts with leftists, moreover, opposition MPs and the press were already focusing their antigovernment attacks on Phao because of his position as government censor.[71] He had no desire to take responsibility for a sweep of leftists and further serve as a lightning rod for such antigovernment criticism.

Most important, without strong antisubversive legislation, Phao could mount a successful anti-Communist crackdown only with great difficulty. Police intelligence on the country's leftists was shockingly scanty, a fact Phao tacitly admitted when informing the Americans he needed to develop his sources, and the police lacked reliable information on the leadership of the Thai Communist Party. Phao possessed little of the evidence needed to convict leftists in Thailand's relatively independent courts. Any attempted sweep of leftists, he realized, would miss important figures, while most of those actually caught would escape punishment. Because that outcome would have seriously embarrassed him, Phao demanded that the government pass all-encompassing antisubversive legislation in support of any repression of leftists. He could then deal with Communists with confidence, while also eliminating the remaining noncommunist civilian opposition. Phibun, on the other hand, had much to gain from forcing Phao to mount an anti-Communist crackdown without supporting legislation. At best, the leftist nuisances, so troubling to Phibun, the architect of the country's pro-U.S. foreign policy, would be eliminated without further weakening the noncommunist opposition. At worst, Phao, Phibun's arch-rival, would be taken down a notch or two. Phibun and Phao, therefore, again found themselves at odds in the summer over anticommunist legislation.

The Thailand Peace Committee's announcement at the end of August that it would send a delegation to the World Peace Conference in Beijing in October seems to have finally decided the matter.[72] Because the Americans were so sensitive to this organization devoted almost exclusively to criticizing the United States, and because the presence of Thai citizens in the enemy capital would embarrass the entire government, the announcement must have deeply worried Phibun, and probably even Phao. Phibun, therefore, finally agreed to support enactment of an anti-Communist law, and, on September 1, the cabinet voted to order the Juridical Council to draft a new bill.[73]

The dispute between Phao and Phibun did not end there, however. Although he held no truck for Communists or "peace" activists, Phibun still opposed Phao's plans to crack down on the noncommunist opposition. He therefore personally drafted a bill for presentation to the Juridical Council of much narrower scope than the subversive activities laws Phao had earlier proposed. Besides eliminating the Phao bill's more sweeping provisions, Phibun replaced references to "subversive activities" with prohibitions specifically of "communist activities." He did so, Phibun's representative told the Juridical Council, "because such provisions [in the Phao bill] may be an instrument of the Government to suppress the [noncommunist] opposition." Although the abridged bill contained broad language of its own, the inspiration was pure Phibun. In line with his cultural campaign promoting filial piety, Phibun wedged in a provision to outlaw "instigating children not to respect their parents."[74] Not one to give in easily, Phao, however, managed to have the cabinet reject Phibun's draft in mid-October and gained appointment as head of a committee charged with writing a new law. The bill Phao submitted to the cabinet on October 31 was the toughest yet presented. In addition to Phibun's own prohibition on seeking to nationalize private property, it banned any nonofficial political action "posing danger to the military, the economy, or the governance of Thailand" and any "expression of oneself as if one were a supporter or representative of a foreign government or organization" from a country having a form of government conflicting with Thailand's. With that mandate, Phao could have jailed just about anyone. The provision on association with foreign governments or organizations would have especially helped repression of the Peace Committee. Phao, therefore, warned the public on October 27 that he had ordered the police to "clamp down sternly on all persons, including those producing or distributing propaganda, who are suspected of aiding the Communist cause."[75]

But the crackdown did not come off as Phao had planned. Throughout October 1952, reports of agitation among junior army officers increased tensions between Phao and Sarit. Each thought the other was inciting the junior officers, and coup rumors spread. The army went on alert October 11–12.[76] On October 31, the U.S. embassy received a "reliable report" that Phao planned to move against Sarit's supporters soon on the pretext of purging the army of Communists.[77] Several days after Phao submitted his bill, therefore, Phibun got the cabinet to declare Phao's bill too broad and began drafting one more to his own liking.[78] Then, on November 8, Phao initiated the police action that unwittingly led to the antileftist crackdown the Americans wanted. That night, the police arrested an air force officer linked to the National Liberation Committee (Khabuankan Ku Chat), an obscure Marxist-influenced group with vague plans for a revolution, and the following day, police detained two army officers allegedly implicated by papers found in the airman's possession. Phibun and Sarit believed that Phao intended these initial arrests as a springboard for a more general attack on Sarit supporters in the army. Upon learning the night of November 9 of the arrests, Phibun, the press and the embassy reported, drove immediately to Sarit's and Phin's headquarters, and only then to Phao's office in Parusakawan Palace. The army, navy, and air force went on alert, and Phibun, Phao, Phin, and, later, Sarit met at the Criminal Investigation Department. According to a source close to him, Phibun got the meeting to approve a general crackdown on Communists and leftists. He hoped to divert Phao from the purge of Sarit supporters while also forcing the police to move against Communists. Yielding to the pressure, Phao ordered the police to begin the crackdown immediately. At 5:00 A.M. on November 10, the police initiated their sweep.[79] By November 14, one hundred forty-five leftist journalists, students, and members of the Peace Committee and the National Liberation Committee had been detained, and arrests of politicians, other leftists, and, above all, Chinese, continued for three more months. Close to a thousand had been caught before the crackdown, later known as the Peace Rebellion *(Kabot Santiphap),* ended.[80]

Phao liked none of this. To his chagrin, he had to conduct all the arrests without benefit of the broad subversive activities act he had promoted. The government presented its communist activities bill to Parliament only on November 13, and even this law did little to satisfy his demands. Although broadly prohibiting the nationalization of private property, the law the legislature passed that day was the narrowest yet considered.[81] In all of the trials of the suspects arrested over the next three months, the police had to rely on articles 104 and 105 of the criminal code, not the new anti-Communist act, and, because of the police's inability to acquire the incriminating evidence required by these relatively restrictive provisions, Phao had to release quickly all but a handful of the detainees. Only thirty-seven Thais were ever convicted.[82] The crackdown on the Communist Party itself, coming several weeks after the arrests began, concluded much as Phao feared. The police apprehended only one relatively important figure, a party leader in the south caught by accident on a train several days before the other arrests began.[83] Phao exaggeratedly claimed he had nipped in the bud a plot by the Peace Committee, the National Liberation Committee, and the Communist Party to kill the king and overthrow the government, but his braggadocio fooled few.[84] Despite the arrest of seven hundred Chinese, an embassy officer later noted, "the majority of important Chinese Communists in Thailand had not yet been apprehended."[85] Embarrassed by the arrests, Phao told a meeting of progovernment MPs that he had initiated the crackdown only because of U.S. and British pressure. His newspaper, *Chao Thai,* published the remarks the following day.[86] When asked by a reporter on the first day of the arrests why the government was conducting the sweep, he disassociated himself completely from the operation. "I don't know about it," was his reply.[87]

Despite the poor cards Phibun had dealt him, however, Phao made the most of a bad hand. At first, Phao tried to include centrist Pridi-ites in the sweep. On November 11, he claimed that Pridi had masterminded the conspiracy the police had allegedly uncovered, and, in the second and third weeks of the sweep, he focused police attention on Pridi associates such as Maj. Gen. Net Khemayothin and Pridi's wife and son.[88] Probably on Phibun's orders, Phao dropped his investigation of Net and Pridi's family, but he quickly found new personal enemies to target. In December, former Free Thai Tiang Sirikhan fell victim to Phao. While Tiang had cooperated with Phao through much of the year, in October, the two fell out. Tiang accused Phao to his face of unfairly harassing Tiang's supporters, and the always-uncomfortable allies engaged in a heated quarrel.[89] After the arrests began, Phao exploited the atmosphere of repression and fear to settle this old score. In mid-December, Tiang and four associates disappeared. Phao's police had killed them.[90] Similarly, after trying unsuccessfully for months to persuade leftist newspaper magnate Ari Liwira to move his considerable journalistic forces behind the Phao political banner, the police arrested Ari along with the other leftist journalists on November 10. Phao released Ari on February 7, apparently with the understanding that he would sell Phao shares of his newspaper chain, but Ari reneged. Phao's police killed him a month later, while he was at the beach on his honeymoon.[91]

Presented with a mandate to repress, Phao had again shifted government policy toward the civilian opposition away from compromise and suasion and toward intimidation and murder, always an advantage for a police general with a knack for political terrorism. After the arrests, disappearances, and assassinations, Phao's political opponents might criticize the police department's inefficiency and his own ruthlessness, but they would never complain openly. That would invite arrest or even death. Indeed, police killed at least a dozen opposition figures and Phao enemies from 1952 to 1957.[92] Such murders stifled almost all open opposition speech in the country.

But for all that Phao gained from the arrests, the Americans benefited more. Although party leaders escaped Phao's dragnet, the crackdown drove Communists further underground and made propagandizing more difficult. "While this new, positive action may not succeed in eliminating entirely the Communist threat to Thailand's security," Stanton commented, "it has undoubtedly disrupted the present Communist strategy."[93] The crackdown sharply reduced public criticism of the United States. Phao having demonstrated that critics of Thailand's foreign friends would receive severe punishment, no one dared, in the coming years, to strongly oppose Thai or American foreign policy. The United States thus found new opportunities to disseminate propaganda of its own. "The arrests," the embassy counselor explained, "have created a more favorable atmosphere for the activities of USIS [United States Information Service]."[94]

Most important, the crackdown cut Thailand's few remaining bridges to the East. Since the end of World War II, official treatment of leftists had derived as much from foreign as domestic policy considerations. In 1946, the Soviet Union demanded repeal of the Anti-Communist Act of 1933 in return for Thai admission to the U.N. After 1949, the heat of PRC criticism of Phibun varied in direct proportion to the harshness of official Thai policy toward communist Chinese. From 1948, the United States took government treatment of leftists as a litmus test of Thai loyalty. The crackdown of 1952, therefore, had a profound impact on Thai-U.S. relations. It further antagonized the Chinese and Soviets, and Beijing lost no time in denouncing it.[95] Accommodation with China became less feasible, and Thai commitment to an anticommunist, pro-U.S. foreign policy necessarily increased. The arrests, the embassy predicted, "will probably . . . estrange Thailand from Communist China and the Soviet Union" and "may strengthen Thailand's pro-Western orientation."[96] Again, Thailand's military government had thrown itself headlong into the Americans' warm embrace.

Given the American role in encouraging the crackdown, it is not surprising that the United States gained so much from the arrests. Thai military leaders felt the weight of American pressure both directly through U.S. lobbying and indirectly through the government's need to defend its pro-U.S. policies from leftist criticism. Although the crackdown arose primarily from domestic political concerns, this direct and indirect U.S. pressure sparked the sweep. As would be the case several years later, tensions within the triumvirate had prevented the Thai government throughout most of 1952 from firmly dealing with Communists and leftists. While both Phibun and Phao wanted to remove the leftist nuisances, disagreements over methods blocked effective action. These disputes allowed the Americans to play a central role in the events. With the Thai government close to moving on leftists, but unable, because of its disunity, to take the crucial first step, the heavy American pressure on the Thais dislodged the government from its political gridlock. Indeed, the timing of the arrests—within several weeks of the Beijing Peace Conference—and the specific ban in Phao's October bill on contacts with communist governments indicate that the need to end public criticism of the United States was the single most important factor in the decision to repress.

The anticommunist crackdown was the last of several events in the second half of 1951 and 1952 that eliminated the internal political obstacles to growth of American-Thai relations. Although Phao, Phibun, and Sarit continued to maneuver for advantage over each other after 1951, the Manhattan Rebellion and the Silent Coup imparted a new permanence to the country's foreign policy. The crippling of non-Coup Group political forces ensured that any future coup would restructure, not overthrow, the ruling military clique and that the government's pro-U.S. policies would remain in force. As Stanton said in early 1953, a change of leadership would not "materially affect Thailand's present alignment with the United States and the United Nations or adversely affect United States policies and objectives in Thailand."[97] Once the coups of 1951 had stabilized the political situation, the arrests of late 1952 and early 1953 opened the way to intensified U.S.-Thai military and political cooperation. The country emerged from the crackdown more committed than ever to following the American lead. By 1953, therefore, Thailand's military government was ready to carry any burden the United States laid on it.

Chapter Eight

BUILDING THE BASTION,

JANUARY 1953–SEPTEMBER 1954

In 1953, American policy toward Thailand changed fundamentally. Until then, the United States viewed Thailand as just another Southeast Asian domino, more stable than the others, but ready to topple at any moment due to internal strife or willingness to compromise with Communists. Policymakers primarily hoped up to that time to protect Thailand itself from communism. No one considered more than a limited projection of Thai military power beyond its own borders possible. But the Americans felt new confidence in Thailand after 1952. Operation Paper had provided the framework for more extensive covert activities, the Manhattan Rebellion and Silent Coup had strengthened the government, and the 1952 crackdown had created a friendly political environment. Thailand now offered tempting possibilities.

Changes in America's Indochina policy in 1953 induced the United States to exploit those possibilities. When Dwight Eisenhower assumed the presidency in January of that year, he and his fiercely anticommunist secretary of state, John Foster Dulles, confronted a troubling situation in Southeast Asia. By early 1953, the Vietminh had overrun vast areas of the Vietnamese countryside. Ho's forces at that point controlled more than two-thirds of northern Vietnam and had driven the French from most of the coastal regions of the center and south. On the offensive in most areas throughout the year, the Vietminh had limited the French by the spring of 1953 primarily to urban conclaves.[1] Most important for America's Thailand policy, in 1953 the Vietminh took their war against the French into Thailand's northern neighbor, the French colony of Laos. In an offensive in March and April, the Vietminh reached striking distance of Luang Prabang, the Laotian royal capital. The campaign nearly divided the French forces in Indochina in two and excited new concern in Washington over the West's prospects in Southeast Asia. Although the Americans recognized that, in a guerrilla war such as the Indochina conflict, the Vietminh would hold on to these latest territorial gains only briefly, policymakers understood correctly that the Laotian offensive spelled the defeat of current French military and political strategy in Indochina.

The offensive convinced the United States that only major changes in American and French policies could hold Indochina. After the offensive began, the United States initiated a diplomatic campaign to persuade France to finally grant Vietnam genuine independence and to develop a more assertive military strategy. The Americans urged the French, as a Joint Chiefs of Staff memorandum in April put it, to adopt "aggressive guerrilla warfare" tactics and turn over conduct of the war to native commanders. At this time, the Americans began demanding a greater say in French military planning. They wanted France, one U.S. military memorandum explained, to "devise ways and means of promoting closer and continuing French-U.S. Military Assistance Advisory Group (MAAG) contact on the plans and operations level."[2] The French, however, fiercely resisted.

To aid their struggles with their French allies and communist foes, the Americans turned for help in the spring of 1953 to Thailand. The Thai military government, at that point, was the best friend the United States had in Southeast Asia. Burma was neutralist, the British held sway in Malaya, and France still jealously guarded its Indochinese colonies from outside (i.e., American) interference. None of these states enjoyed a modicum of political stability. The Thais, on the other hand, had demonstrated in Operation Paper their commitment to the United States in any disagreement among the Western powers, and the country faced no short-term internal threat. Thailand's military regime had given its American patrons everything they had asked for. It presented itself as the perfect instrument to apply pressure on the Communists and French alike.

American plans for employment of Thailand as an anticommunist, anti-French bastion took shape at the height of the Laotian crisis of the spring of 1953. On May 6, during the National Security Council (NSC) meeting discussing the crisis, C. D. Jackson, a deputy chief of Eisenhower's Psychological Warfare Division during World War II then acting as special assistant to the president for international affairs, suggested that the NSC "look into what could be done by way of psychological warfare with Thailand as a base." Eisenhower approved the idea, and, after Jackson, a firm believer in the efficacy of psychological warfare, delivered his recommendations the following week, the NSC ordered the Psychological Strategy Board (PSB) to draft detailed plans for psychological warfare based in Thailand.[3] The board, an interagency body operating since 1951, presented its report, titled "U.S. Psychological Strategy with Respect to the Thai Peoples of Southeast Asia," on July 2.[4] With some alterations, the report served as the blueprint for America's Thai policy of the next year and a half.

The PSB's report, designated PSB D-23, took as its premise that the French needed to change their policy and strategy drastically, and that the United States had to increase its involvement in Indochina. The PSB believed that the secret of Vietminh success lay in Ho's ability to win the war at the psychological level. Because of French refusal to grant Vietnam genuine independence, the Vietminh had acquired a reputation as defenders of Vietnamese nationhood, and the Vietminh's ability to always maintain the military initiative created an impression of invincibility. Vietnamese, therefore, flocked to the Vietminh banner. To reverse the trend, the PSB contended, the United States needed to augment its influence in Indochina. It could then force the French to adopt an offensive, guerrilla-warfare strategy and to grant the Vietnamese government more control over its army. More dynamic guerrilla action by the French would "create an atmosphere of victory."[5] A more active U.S. leadership in Southeast Asia, the report added, would give Indochinese hope of receiving genuine independence. U.S. intervention, the PSB commented, will "raise the morale of non-communist indigenous nationalist elements in Indochina—particularly in Laos and Cambodia—because it will suggest the possibility of greater U.S. pressure on the French to accelerate reform."[6]

China's formation of a Thai Autonomous Zone in the Sipsongpanna region of Yunnan province in March 1953 convinced the authors of PSB D-23 that a psychological-warfare strategy centered on Thailand would enable the United States to achieve its goals. Because Beijing proclaimed that the zone, which gave political form to Yunnan's Thai-related minority, would provide a model for Thai-speaking peoples wanting freedom from American imperialism, Thais and westerners feared that China planned subversive activities in Laos, Burma, and Thailand. As some in the United States noted, the initiative was consistent with Chinese administrative policy, and Beijing never employed the zone as a base of operations against Thailand or other countries,[7] but concerns over Chinese intentions excited a new interest among policymakers in the ethnic and linguistic bonds among the speakers of Thai and Thai-related languages in Thailand and its neighbors.[8]

PSB D-23 represented the culmination of this new fascination with Thai ethnology. Based on a variety of truths, half-truths, misconceptions, and outright falsehoods, the thirty-eight-page report drew heavily on "impression" and, apparently, anthropological theories in vogue at the time describing Thailand as a "loosely structured society."[9] The report began its analysis of Thai ethnography with a set of sweeping generalizations of the Thai "national character." Thais, the PSB explained, are "incorrigible individualists." "Gentle and light-minded," the document continued, Thais are "not given to ponderous philosophic thought nor to great warlike and military ambitions."[10] Because of such attributes, "Thai character and cultural institutions are better suited to guerrilla activities than to the development on a large-scale of conventional military forces."[11] Thailand's ethnic makeup, PSB D-23 emphasized, made it ideal for psychological warfare against the Vietminh. Lao, a dialect of Thai, was spoken, the PSB noted, in northeastern and northern Thailand as well as in Laos, and indeed, Thailand has several times more ethnic Lao than lightly populated Laos.[12] Shans in northern Burma and tribesmen in northern and central Laos and in Yunnan's new Thai Autonomous Zone also speak Thai dialects. Significant numbers of Lao, the PSB added, live in Cambodia.[13]

In fact, the PSB sorely misunderstood the relationships among the various Thai-related groups. Just as the board misinterpreted the Chinese government's intentions in establishing the autonomous zone, it also presumed a greater affinity than actually existed between central Thais and Thai-related groups in China who had never had close contacts with modern Thailand. Relations between the highland Thai-related tribes in Laos and Vietnam and lowland Thais and Lao, moreover, would prove more of an obstacle than an advantage. As anthropologist Guy Morechand says of the Thai-related groups of Laos, "in the past all have been at war with one another, and the Tai [Thai-related] language groups should not be seen as a harmonious social or political unit."[14] Indeed, the Laotian communist party, the Pathet Lao, probably drew so successfully from Thai-related tribes because of their hostility to lowland Lao.[15]

However inaccurate, the PSB's ethnographic findings convinced the board that the United States should concentrate its attentions on Thailand. Thailand, "the central core of the Thai ethnic group," PSB D-23 explained, ". . . is the logical—in fact the only possible—focus of the integrated, offensively-defensive U.S. strategy needed to defeat the communists in Southeast Asia."[16] Ideally situated, economically and politically stable, and ethnically inviting, Thailand offered itself as a wonderful instrument for turning the tables on the Communists and the French. A wide-ranging set of psychological operations in the country, the PSB suggested, could build Thailand into an "anti-communist bastion."[17] Because the operations would increase American involvement in the Indochina war, a psychological-warfare strategy based on Thailand would create "a possibility of exerting greatly increased U.S. influence over the French conduct of their struggle against communism in Indochina."[18] The war against the Communists would be won, and in the way the United States—not France—wanted. Best of all, Thailand's role as an American proxy answered the demands of Eisenhower's "New Look" defense policy. Eisenhower wanted not American but local allies' ground forces to fight regional conflicts.

Eisenhower once described psychological warfare as encompassing anything "from the singing of a beautiful hymn up to the most extraordinary kind of physical sabotage."[19] In Thailand, PSB's psychological-warfare strategy involved all this and more. The board suggested a two-stage plan. In the first phase, the United States would implement psychological-warfare operations to strengthen Thailand itself. These operations involved many mundane matters—increased propaganda activities, appointment of diplomats and advisers sensitive to Thai cultural peculiarities, intensified efforts to convince the Thai people and leadership of America's commitment to the country, and aiding development—but the key to the program lay in its military goals. The United States, PSB D-23 recommended, should "develop, expand, and accelerate to the greatest extent sound programs for the creation and employment of indigenous guerrilla and para-military forces" in Thailand.[20] Initially, such forces would be used for self-defense, but, once the United States had decided, after consultation with the French and British, that the program had strengthened Thailand sufficiently, phase two would "extend programs for guerrilla and para-military forces composed of Thai and related groups" into Indochina.[21] Thailand's ethnic bonds with its neighbors, the PSB believed, would enable Thai paramilitary fighters to defeat the Vietminh on the village level. Then, as the success of the United States' Thailand-based guerrilla warfare became apparent, the French would change their own strategy. As a result, the Americans could beat the Communists at their own game and "extend U.S. influence—and local acceptance of it—throughout the whole of Southeast Asia."[22]

THE U.N. APPEAL ON LAOS

The United States first implemented its anticommunist/anti-French policy on a political, not a military, issue—a proposed protest to the U.N. over the Vietminh incursion into Laos. Although discussions on a U.N. appeal began before PSB D-23 had been completed, the two initiatives were intimately related. Decisions crucial to both were made with the same goal and at the same National Security Council meeting. Identical strategies underlay them.

Thailand did not, at first, figure in the U.S. plans for a U.N. appeal. Initially, it appeared that the Laotians themselves would protest the Vietminh incursion to the U.N. Soon after Ho's offensive, the Laotian government appealed in general for assistance from the great powers, and, on April 22, the Laotian foreign minister informed the United States that he would petition the U.N. directly. The United States approved the proposal wholeheartedly.[23]

France, however, still exercising great influence over the nominally independent Laotian government, vetoed the plan.[24] The French feared that a U.N. appeal would invite Third World attacks on French colonialism in Indochina and North Africa and, above all, opposed any internationalization of the Indochina conflict. The French considered the struggle an internal affair, and, beyond themselves, they wanted no outsiders—including the United States—interfering. Growing American military and economic influence in East Asia was threatening to overwhelm French Indochina. A U.N. appeal, the French feared, would internationalize the war and facilitate the American advances.

The United States favored a U.N. appeal precisely because it would pry Indochina from the French. Since the U.N. handled only disputes between sovereign nations, not domestic concerns, a U.N. appeal would both add to the pressure on the French to treat the Indochinese states as sovereign nations and legitimize increased U.S. involvement. The appeal, in addition, offered Dulles and Eisenhower domestic political benefits. Republicans in Congress were demanding that the administration stop the Vietminh advance, and, in the first week of May, Sen. William F. Knowland publicly urged Eisenhower to consider "the use of air or naval power" in the crisis.[25] Promotion of a U.N. appeal, Dulles believed, would satisfy these congressional hawks that the administration was taking action. On April 26, Dulles asked French Prime Minister René Mayer to have the Laotians make the appeal.[26] The French, however, refused.[27]

Facing French opposition, Dulles turned to the Thais for help. On

May 5—just two days after receiving the French rebuff—Dulles asked Ambassador Phot to have the Thai government make the appeal in the Laotians' stead. Dulles personally instructed Phot on how to lodge the protest the next day. In return for their cooperation, Dulles offered the Thais a political windfall. In the first meeting, he agreed immediately to praise Thailand in a subsequent public speech. Delivered May 7, the speech lauded Thailand as "one of the nations which, showing its faith in collective security, has gallantly and substantially contributed to the U.N. effort in Korea." Dulles promised in the statement that, "by performing this act for others, it [Thailand] has won the right to help from others."[28] Then, several hours before the second meeting between Dulles and Phot and during the same session in which it ordered Jackson to report on its psychological warfare strategy, the NSC agreed to a long-standing Thai request for a general to head MAAG-Thailand and a recent petition for urgent delivery of badly needed ammunition.[29] Dulles told Phot the good news that afternoon when presenting the instructions on the appeal. The ammunition, Dulles told a surprised Phot, "was already enroute."[30] Coming with a speed and decisiveness never before seen in American consideration of Thai aid proposals, U.S. approval of the two requests impressed the Thais. The day after Dulles' second meeting with Phot, Bangkok cabled its approval of the U.N. appeal. Dulles publicly announced the arms shipments to further reward Phibun and send the Communists a message about American resolve.[31]

In the following weeks, the Thais—in the face of strong opposition from the Europeans—did literally everything the Americans asked. On May 9, the French Foreign Ministry pressed the Thai ambassador to drop the appeal, and the following day, the French asked the United States to similarly lobby the Thais.[32] The British, in the meantime, responded unenthusiastically to Thai requests for support for the measure. Wan, foreign minister since March 1952, thus ordered Phot on May 11 to postpone submission of the appeal. The Vietminh, Wan noted, had mostly withdrawn from Laos, and any military urgency had disappeared.[33] The Americans were nonetheless determined to push the appeal to the end. When Phot told him that day of Wan's decision, Assistant Secretary of State Walter Robertson warned the ambassador that "the United States government, and especially the secretary of state, will be very disappointed" if the Thais abandon the appeal. After Phot asked whether the United States would support the measure even if Britain and France opposed it, Robertson again linked Thai diplomatic performance with American military aid. "Certainly," the United

States would support the appeal, Robertson explained. "When it [the Vietminh incursion] becomes an issue for the United Nations, the United States will be in a better position to provide in strength assistance that is needed."[34] The Foreign Ministry, as a result, informed Phibun that a delay of the appeal would affect the ammunition shipments.[35] Wan noted that the American press was devoting great attention to the appeal and that Dulles had already stated his support for the measure publicly.[36] Phibun ordered the cabinet to consider the appeal "urgently," and, on his return to Bangkok from a tour of the northeast on May 19, he and the cabinet instructed the Foreign Ministry to proceed with the appeal immediately. Phibun directed the embassy in Washington to tell the Americans that he had "no intention of disappointing the American government or secretary of state."[37] The French ambassador pleaded with Wan three days later to drop the appeal, but the Thais held to the U.S. line.[38]

Then, when the Americans themselves paused, the Thais too slowed their pace. On May 21, the Mayer cabinet fell, exciting fears in the State Department that further provocation of the French would damage even further their capacity to intensify the war effort. The next day, the French Foreign Ministry began an all-out campaign against the appeal. French Ambassador Henri Bonnet told the State Department that France was "very upset" that the United States had pushed the Thais to proceed with the appeal only a day after France had asked the United States to dissuade them.[39] The French embassy formally notified the State Department that same day that Paris now considered the dispute "the most serious problem in relations between our two countries."[40] By May 27, the French had gone so far as to persuade four other Security Council members to vote against the appeal.[41] Realizing that the appeal would embarrass the United States if openly opposed by France, Dulles arranged a meeting with Phot on June 1. Facing implacable French "hysteria," as he put it, Dulles told Phot that the United States still supported the appeal but favored postponement of it pending formation of a new French government. Phot immediately replied that he would withhold the appeal, and the Thai government formally agreed to the delay soon afterward.[42]

The Americans renewed their attempts to force the appeal on the French in June, but, again, the French faced them down, and, once more, the Thais backtracked as instructed by Dulles. On June 14, King Norodom Sihanouk of Cambodia fled to Thailand in protest against French refusal to grant his country independence and asked the Thai government to lodge a complaint against France with the U.N. on his behalf. When Bonnet asked Dulles on June 16 to block any such appeal, Dulles replied that the United States had already had the Thais delay their own appeal and was reluctant to press them any further on France's behalf. Dulles coyly suggested that the United States would discourage the Thais from presenting Sihanouk's petition if the French supported the Thai appeal.[43] At the same time, Dulles presented Phot a draft of a toned-down appeal with all specific references to Indochina deleted.[44] Such American backtracking had already left Phot, Phibun, and Wan hanging several times, but, again, the Thais quickly decided to follow the American lead and agreed to water down the appeal. Alteration of the petition, however, failed to persuade the French. France rejected both the milder appeal and the proposed trade-off on the Sihanouk protest, forcing Dulles once more to yield. On June 22, Dulles asked Phot to again postpone the appeal until after a conference of the Western powers in Bermuda in July.[45] Phot reluctantly, but immediately, agreed.

After that, little could be done to save the appeal. Although the Bermuda conference was postponed for several months, by July, all reason for a protest had disappeared. In the second week of the month, the French finally presented the United States their proposal for a more aggressive military strategy, the so-called Navarre Plan, and the new prime minister promised to "perfect" Vietnamese independence.[46] Having thus gotten what they wanted, the Americans ceased their pressure on the Thais. The appeal was quietly dropped.

Dulles' U.N. campaign had proven a complete fiasco. After two months of public reports on U.S. and Thai plans to lodge an appeal against the Vietminh incursion, his efforts had come to nothing. The French had blocked the appeal in every form offered, and Dulles had had to go back on his word several times. The episode embarrassed the Thais.

But the events of those two months showed clearly Thailand's potential for pressuring the French and the Communists—and the country's appropriateness as the centerpiece of American strategy in the region. No matter how strongly the French protested or how much the British cautioned, the Thais heeded American requests in every regard. As he had with Operation Paper, Phibun maintained full support for the United States against the Europeans. Although the initiative failed in the end, the Thais carried no blame. Dulles, not Phibun, had yielded to European pressure. By mid-1953, Thailand was functioning, as C. D. Jackson and the PSB had planned it, as an anticommunist, anti-French U.S. bastion—in this case, a diplomatic one—in Southeast Asia.

IMPLEMENTING PSB D-23

The Eisenhower administration's new Thailand policy sounded the death knell of Stanton's diplomatic career. A liberal Democrat, Stanton had little in common with the Republicans of the new administration. Stanton shared Dulles' predilection for mixing moralism and politics, but his represented a gentler, less stern, brand of righteousness. He opposed communism as forthrightly as Dulles but argued that the United States needed to support indigenous Indochinese nationalism to win the fight.[47] He could never play Dulles' role of anticommunist hell-fire preacher. Stanton, moreover, carried heavy political baggage. Because of his history as a China specialist in the 1940s, he had come under the scrutiny of Sen. Joseph R. McCarthy in the early 1950s. McCarthy's committee almost called Stanton to Washington as a witness.[48] Dulles would have risked additional criticism from the Republican right had he reappointed this object of McCarthyite suspicion. Most of all, Dulles wanted a representative in Bangkok who would more aggressively intensify military programs in Thailand and eliminate the infighting between the embassy and the CIA. Dulles wanted action. Therefore, when Stanton submitted his letter of resignation according to custom upon Eisenhower's inauguration, the State Department never responded. Stanton, expecting, at the least, appointment to another posting, took this "inexcusable" treatment, as he put it, as an insult. He retired from the State Department after more than twenty years of service.[49]

The choice for Stanton's replacement—William "Wild Bill" Donovan—demonstrated the new administration's determination to break with the past. Tapped for the job only two days after the NSC ordered the PSB to draft a psychological-warfare strategy for Thailand, Donovan was exactly the kind of high-stakes operator Stanton was not.[50] Stanton, the lifetime Foreign Service officer with no powerful friends and little experience in Washington, had functioned well in the late 1940s, but, as the aid programs transformed Bangkok into America's military, political, and covert-action hub in the region, he failed to adapt. Quickly, the non–State Department operations in the country fell from his grasp. Donovan, the former OSS chief, cofounder of the CIA, Wall Street lawyer, and lobbyist for foreign governments, on the other hand, had all the connections and breadth of experience needed to administer the myriad operations being planned for Thailand. Having worked during the war with Eisenhower, CIA chief Allen Dulles, former CIA director and now Under Secretary of State Walter Bedell Smith, and

C. D. Jackson, Donovan had the attention of the most powerful men in the American foreign-policy establishment. As well, his long-time association with the intelligence community ensured a smooth relationship with the new CIA station chief in Bangkok, Vernet Gresham.[51]

For its part, the State Department strongly resisted Donovan's appointment. Because of Donovan's work with Pridi as OSS chief during the war and in 1946 and 1947 as an agent of Pridi's governments, the present Thai leadership strongly disliked Donovan, and, in deference to Thai sensibilities, the State Department suggested appointing someone less controversial.[52]

But the new administration had no need for old-style diplomats capable merely of making friends. Eisenhower and Dulles wanted an ambassador who would perform much more than diplomacy. Before Donovan left for Bangkok in August, Smith instructed him "to gather together quietly under his personal direction and coordination the activities and money spending by FOA [Foreign Operations Administration], USIS [United States Information Service], and CIA." Donovan's primary mission, Smith explained, was to implement PSB D-23. After he had "insure[d] that these three agencies operate in close covert coordination with the stepped-up Military Mission," Smith explained, Donovan was "to prepare a plan for the intensification and increased efficiency of the [psychological warfare] activities . . . for the purpose of building a bastion in Thailand from which various operations can be initiated into adjoining areas."[53] The directive Donovan requested from Eisenhower before departing for Bangkok reflected how broadly Dulles and the president conceived the ambassador's new role. Donovan asked for a personal staff of twelve, unlimited funding, the right to travel anywhere in the region, a direct line of communication with Eisenhower, and "in case of necessity the resumption of military in addition to diplomatic status."[54] The fighting never got close enough to Thailand for Eisenhower to grant him this extraordinary military authority, but Donovan did assume the broad control he desired over operations in Thailand.

Donovan emerged as one of the strongest proponents of PSB D-23. Because the OSS had worked with Ho Chi Minh, Donovan felt that he understood Vietnam and the Vietminh. Only a guerrilla strategy mirroring Ho's aimed at winning over the Indochinese peasantry such as PSB D-23, he contended, could defeat the Communists. Although JCS preference for direct aid to French forces forced the NSC in September to authorize implementation of only phase one, postponing indefinitely execution of the provisions in phase two taking the psychological war to neighboring countries, Donovan stood firm.[55] Even before his arrival in Bangkok, he requested immediate dispatch of advance parties from the army's Radio Broadcasting and Leaflet Group and the 10th Special Forces Group to implement PSB D-23 "with the minimum delay."[56] In the months that followed, he fought vigorously for adherence to both the letter and spirit of the report.

Easiest to implement, because of the small costs and risks involved, was the intensification of anticommunist propaganda. Building on USIS's substantial presence in Bangkok, Donovan laid plans soon after his arrival for extension of the agency's propaganda activities to the rest of the country. In December, he convinced Phibun to establish a high-ranking U.S.-Thai psychological warfare committee. The body, chaired by Phibun and including Donovan, aimed to "disclose [the] aims and techniques of Communism through press, church [sic], universities, youth groups, radio, military indoctrination and cultural groups."[57] Donovan also asked the Thais to allow USIS to open three branch offices in the provinces. Although the cabinet refused out of fear that other countries would demand similar privileges, the Thai Public Relations Department agreed to open its own branch offices and act as USIS's representative. With USIS aid, the new offices opened libraries, broadcast radio programs, exhibited photographs, and showed movies, all with an anticommunist message.[58] Eventually, Donovan extended the propaganda campaign, originally aimed at the peasantry, to the Thai bureaucracy. This later program involved "indoctrination of the Thai government officials at national, provincial, and local levels." USIS sponsored the first of a series of anticommunist lectures to government officials in May 1954.[59] Although such programs likely had little immediate effect, their long-term impact was significant. The United States and Thailand maintained and intensified the propaganda programs begun in this period for two more decades.[60]

Also receiving early attention were programs aimed at solving the economic and military problems of northeastern Thailand. Dry, impoverished, and lacking, for the most part, secure natural barriers on its borders with Cambodia and Laos, this region was the most susceptible to communist attack and subversion. Neglect from Bangkok had long made the northeast a breeding ground for political mavericks, and, by the 1950s, leftist politicians such as Thep Chotinuchit found it a hospitable home. In 1965, it gave birth to the country's first communist insurgency. Until 1953, the United States devoted no more time to the northeast than the Thai government itself did, but the Vietminh incursion into Laos awoke the PSB to the region's vulnerability. PSB D-23 advocated augmented economic aid and intensified propaganda activities for the northeast.[61] Two of the three public relations offices USIS helped the Thais establish—in Udorn Thani and Ubon Ratchathani—were in this strategically important region. The third the United States wanted in the northeast as well, though the Thais set it up in northern Lampang province, also close to the Laotian border.[62] Most important, the United States initiated, after PSB D-23, construction of a highway from Saraburi to Nakhorn Ratchasima. This so-called Friendship Highway linked the central region with the northeast by paved road for the first time. Of limited economic importance, the project attracted no World Bank support, but the JCS considered the highway crucial to possible military operations in the region. The United States ended up funding $13 million of the road's $20 million price tag.[63] Later, the United States extended the highway up to the Laotian border, and, for the next several years, the Americans focused their economic aid efforts on the northeast. In 1954, although the region contained 34 percent of the country's population, 40 percent of all American economic aid for Thailand went there.[64]

While the propaganda and economic aid were important in the long term, Donovan's intimacy with the CIA ensured that increased aid to the police would form the core of PSB D-23 activities. Bringing in his own personal assistant, William vanden Heuvel, from his law firm, Donovan relied little on embassy personnel, but he needed no introduction to many of the CIA and Sea Supply advisers. He cabled Bird news of his appointment before anyone else and, once in Bangkok, quickly picked up with the numerous former OSS officers then with the CIA. Donovan spent many of his weekends at the Lopburi paratrooper camp, not so much to oversee Sea Supply's work as to relive old times with his buddies.[65] Partly because of these connections, Donovan became a major supporter of Phao. The two worked together closely during Donovan's short stay in Thailand, and Phao impressed the new ambassador with his unsurprising acceptance of all proposals to expand police capabilities and activities.[66] Like Bird and the CIA, Donovan considered the police the most flexible and effective fighting force in the country. He centered PSB D-23's guerrilla-warfare program on Phao's department.

The new police programs associated with PSB D-23 took a variety of forms. In the last half of 1953, the CIA helped the Thais establish a new intelligence organization, the Krom Pramuan Ratchakan Phaen-din.[67] This agency followed communist (and noncommunist) dissident activities in Thailand and neighboring countries. Although the body was formally subordinate to the Office of the Prime Minister, Phao acted as director-general and exercised complete control over it. The agency cooperated closely with the CIA.[68] Also formed during Donovan's tenure with U.S. help was the Border Patrol Police (BPP). In the wake of the Vietminh spring 1953 offensive, the Thais asked the United States to train policemen for military-style patrol of the border with Laos and Cambodia. In response, the United States established a new police drill camp in Nakhorn Ratchasima in July, and, in the second half of 1954, formed camp graduates into the core of the new five-thousand-man-strong BPP.[69] The unit implemented most of the guerrilla-warfare aspects of PSB D-23.

Most important, Donovan helped Phao found in 1953 the elite of the police paramilitary units, the Police Aerial Reconnaissance (Resupply) Unit (PARU). As any threat of Chinese invasion had substantially receded, Washington decided by that year to discontinue the Lopburi training program, but the CIA head of the Lopburi camp, William Lair, resisted. Lair proposed moving the camp south to Hua Hin and forming a new Thai unit to operate covertly in neighboring countries. Because the plan answered the demands of PSB D-23, Donovan and Washington readily approved Lair's recommendations. PARU was the result. Over 1953 and 1954, PARU developed into a small, yet effective, guerrilla and antiguerrilla force. Airdropping leaflets advertising the unit over the Thai side of bilingual border regions to recruit trainees, PARU enlisted primarily high school graduates—a distinct minority in upcountry Thailand—proficient in the languages of neighboring countries. The CIA trained the recruits in parachuting, jungle warfare and survival, and sabotage. Starting with fifty recruits, at its height, PARU numbered almost four hundred.[70] The CIA paid the salaries of PARU, as well as BPP, troops.[71]

Besides developing these purely military forces, Phao and the Americans employed PARU and BPP in establishing civilian-based unconventional forces. The first civilian program, the Volunteer Defense Corps (VDC), took its inspiration from British civil defense projects in Malaya. Concerned, like the British programs, with warfare at the village level, the VDC set the ambitious goal of arming 120,000 Thai peasants.[72] Apparently at Donovan's urging, Phibun passed legislation authorizing the VDC in February 1954, and in July, the government formally established the unit.[73] The United States immediately granted the VDC an initial installment of $950,000 and in December allocated another $3 million.[74] The BPP, receiving funding, advice, and equipment from the CIA, formed and administered this new national guard. Assigning schoolteachers, the only government presence in many Thai villages, command of individual units, the BPP distributed light weapons and trained villagers to fight communist guerrillas and propaganda agents. If faced with overwhelming force, the VDC units were to disperse and request help from PARU troops.[75]

The CIA's second civilian-based guerrilla-warfare program, also administered by the BPP, focused specifically on Thailand's northern provinces. In a twist on PSB D-23's emphasis on "*Thai* Peoples of Southeast Asia," this second program targeted the roughly two hundred thousand non-Thai hill tribesmen, belonging to some twenty different ethnic groups, in the northern mountains. These peoples ignored national boundaries. Most living a seminomadic existence based on slash-and-burn agriculture, they roamed freely across the poorly defined and almost entirely undefended borders of northern Thailand, Burma, Laos, and Vietnam and often maintained close relations with kinsmen in neighboring countries. After PSB D-23, the Americans recognized the political and military potential of the hill tribes. In early 1954, the NSC discussed plans for a guerrilla campaign against the Vietminh in case of French defeat in Indochina, and, in January, CIA director Allen Dulles sent famed operative Edward Lansdale to Vietnam to prepare Thai-related and other hill tribesmen for the campaign.[76] After the partition of Vietnam in July, Lansdale initiated the hill-tribe attacks on North Vietnam.[77] Beginning at about the same time, the Thai hill-tribe program seems to have complemented this Vietnam project.[78] The BPP, again with CIA funding and equipment, began establishing sometime after the summer of 1954 a permanent presence in hill-tribe villages in the north. Openly, the BPP set up schools and clinics and improved village infrastructure. Secretly, it armed and trained tribesmen in guerrilla warfare. The United States hoped eventually to deploy these roving tribesmen, with their ethnic connections in neighboring countries, in Laos. Although providing no uniforms and little organization to the new fighters, the CIA devoted a large proportion—possibly most—of its resources to the program.[79]

While these various guerrilla-warfare programs took several years to get off the ground, in time they played important roles in U.S. military strategy in Indochina. Around 1958, the CIA, with Thai help, began forming an anticommunist army of Hmong hill tribesmen—the largest such group in Laos—under the command of Hmong leader Vang Pao.[80] In the mid-1960s, the United States fought, through these Hmong proxies, America's so-called Secret War in Laos.[81] Because the Thai hill-tribe program has, until this time, remained unknown to scholars, no research has been conducted on the effect of the Thai Hmong on the Secret War, but, clearly, the experience gained from the earlier Thai program aided the Thais and the CIA in the later Laotian operations. Indeed, in the early 1960s, PARU fought alongside Vang Pao's army. Lansdale praised the performance of the ninety-nine PARU fighters helping Vang Pao as "outstanding."[82]

THAILAND'S INDOCHINA THRUST

The Eisenhower administration's policy of projecting American—and Thai—power throughout Indochina at French expense suited the Thais perfectly. Thai dislike of the French had not dissipated following recognition of Bao Dai, and the French continued to distrust the Thais. Relations remained tense throughout 1953 and 1954. At their low point during the dispute over the U.N. appeal, the Thai government formally protested French flights over Thai border provinces and arrested a number of Laotian soldiers who had entered Thai territory.[83] The French had nothing but disdain for the Thais. The French commissioner for Laos called Thailand in early 1953 the "Italy of this part of the world."[84] Throughout this period, the Thais wanted the United States to replace France in Indochina. When Dulles asked Phot in June 1953 what Thailand wanted the United States to do in Laos, Vietnam, and Cambodia, the cabinet voted to reply that the United States should send increased military assistance directly to the three Indochinese governments, bypassing the French. The cabinet wanted the United States to force France to give the states genuine independence.[85] For most of the period since the late 1930s, the Thais had been trying, first by outright invasion in 1940 and then by support for dissident groups after the war, to expand their influence in Laos and Cambodia. American ouster of the French from Indochina, the Thais hoped, would enable them to fulfill these dreams. They expected—correctly, as PSB D-23 demonstrated—that their American patrons would bring them in as proxies. As long as France retained its grip on Indochina, the Thais avoided involvement in Laos and Cambodia, but, once French withdrawal appeared likely after the spring 1953 Vietminh offensive, Thai policy grew bolder.

Thai strategy took shape in the fall of 1953, within several months of Donovan's initiation of PSB D-23 operations. In September, the Thai minister in Laos, Samai Waewprasert, wrote a memorandum explaining that French troubles in Indochina provided Thailand with an excellent opportunity to advance its interests in Laos. Despite French withdrawal, Samai wrote, "Laos must be under the influence of another country." "Because of this necessity to depend on a foreign country," the minister continued, "Thailand has a good chance to increase its influence in this neighboring country." Samai recommended reopening the border, facilitating trade, and augmenting economic cooperation.[86] The Laotians, hoping to reduce their dependence in a post-French Indochina on Vietnam, welcomed such proposals. On October 6, the Laotian minister in Bangkok told the *Bangkok Post* that Laos hoped to use Bangkok as a seaport "when no longer bound by economic and financial union with Vietnam and Cambodia."[87] The Thai cabinet approved Samai's recommendations a week later, and, the week after that, the Foreign Ministry began arranging talks with Laos on commercial and economic cooperation.[88]

In December, the government intensified its diplomatic campaign in Indochina. That month, the Thais gave, behind the backs of the French, ammunition and two thousand rifles to Prince Sihanouk's Cambodian government. Because France still jealously guarded its influence in Cambodia even after having granted it a large degree of independence in November, the French reacted angrily, but the arms won the Thais points with Phnom Penh.[89] In January 1954, the Thais advanced more ambitious plans. That month, the Thai minister in Phnom Penh publicly proposed a scheme for union of Laos, Cambodia, Thailand, and eventually Burma. Although stressing the importance of commercial ties, he alluded to the possibility of a political and military alliance. The press, noting the common Theravada Buddhist heritage of the four suggested members, dubbed the proposed bloc the "Buddhist Union."[90] Because it subverted their own plans for a semicolonial French Union in Indochina, the French strongly opposed the Thai initiative, forcing the Cambodians and Laotians, despite reported interest, to reject the plan, but the Thai diplomatic campaign did not cease.[91] In March, the government sent a mission to Phnom Penh to arrange railroad connections between the two countries and announced it was considering plans for joint development of the Mekong River basin. In April, the government eliminated transit fees on goods to Laos and Cambodia passing through Thailand. And that same month, the first Thai bank opened in Phnom Penh.[92] Many French, in view of such efforts, pessimistically considered eventual Thai hegemony over Laos and Cambodia inevitable.[93]

The Thai government's efforts to extend its influence in Indochina reached their peak with the assassination of the Laotian defense minister, Kou Voravong, in September 1954. Because the investigation into the assassination was never officially completed, most scholars consider it a mystery as to who was behind the crime.[94] The few who express an opinion assert that Phoui Sananikone, then foreign and interior minister, ordered the killing. Several months after the crime, the Thai police arrested the admitted assassin, Udom Luksurin, and, after interrogation, Udom confessed that Phoui had hired him. Kou's family has ever since blamed Phoui and his brother Oun for Kou's death. "The Voravongs," scholar of Laotian politics Charles Stevenson relates, "have never forgiven the Sananikones for their presumed involvement in the 1954 assassination of Defense Minister Kou Voravong."[95] Similarly, one writer critical of the U.S. intervention in Indochina implied that the CIA conspired with the Sananikones to eliminate the neutralist Kou and put the pro-U.S. Phoui in power. "Phoui Sananikone," this reporter noted, "has remained one of the most trusted U.S. assistants in Laos until the present time [1970]."[96]

The evidence, however, strongly implicates another Laotian leader, Prince Phetsarath Ratanavongsa—and the Thai government. Phetsarath had good reason for wanting to create turmoil in Vientiane, the Laotian administrative capital. Leader of the Japanese-created substate of Luang Prabang in northern Laos during the war, he had lived in exile in Thailand since the French return to Indochina in 1946. Although at first aligned with other anti-French Free Lao based in Bangkok, he had been unable, because of his antagonism with the Laotian king, to go back to Laos with his half-brothers, Souvanna Phouma and Souphanouvong, when the French allowed Free Lao activists to return in 1949.[97] For the next five years, Phetsarath remained in Bangkok and awaited the chance to regain power.

The Thai government badly wanted him to succeed. Fluent in central Thai and married to a Thai, Phetsarath maintained a sentimental attachment to Thailand held by many other southern Laotians. Because the Thais, while predominant in Laos during the previous century, had established Phetsarath's family in the viceregal line, he enjoyed close social, cultural, and kinship ties with the Thai elite.[98] Gen. Sawai Sawaisaenyakorn, Sarit's assistant and later successor to Phao as police chief, was Phetsarath's cousin.[99] The Thais considered Phetsarath their closest Laotian ally in these years, and Phao funded and housed him.[100] Phetsarath, in return, promoted Thai interests in Laos. Later, in 1955 and 1956, he helped the Thais conduct secret negotiations with the Laotian government over a possible union of the two countries.[101] Thai strategy in Laos depended on him.

By the summer of 1954, Phetsarath—and apparently the Thais—had decided to act. By then, the French position in Indochina had weakened considerably, and prospects for disengagement of Laos from France and alignment with Thailand appeared brighter than ever. Foreign press reports that the Thai foreign office collected even claimed that the United States was considering supporting a union of Laos, Cambodia, and Thailand.[102] Only the Laotian government, still clinging to the French Union, blocked Thai plans. The Thai acting foreign minister, Khemchat Bunyarataphan, gave Phibun the translation of an article on possible union with Thailand from *Siang Lao,* the newspaper of the Laotian defense minister, the soon to be assassinated Kou Voravong. Khemchat informed Phibun that the article, strongly critical of union with Thailand, typified Laotian government thinking.[103] The Thais, therefore, had good reason to want to see Phetsarath supplant his pro-French half-brother, Souvanna Phouma, as prime minister and to want to remove Kou from the scene. Phao's underling and head of the Criminal Investigation Department, Rattana Watthanamahat, later branded Kou and, significantly, Phoui, "the most extremely pro-French sympathizers" in Laos.[104]

In June, Phetsarath, with Thai knowledge, and likely with official Thai support, made his move. On May 26, U-thong Suwannawong, the acting Laotian foreign minister, informed Thai Ambassador Samai in Vientiane that Phetsarath was planning a coup. U-thong asked Samai to have the Thai government prevent Phetsarath from acting.[105] Ten days later, U-thong again called on Samai, warning the ambassador that Phetsarath planned his attack for June 7. As before, U-thong appealed to Samai to stop Phetsarath.[106] The Thais ignored U-thong's pleas, however, and on the evening of June 12, a group of Laotian cadets at Kinaimo Officers School seven miles south of Vientiane attacked a police and customs post with the aim, apparently, of capturing important government officials and overthrowing the government. Contacts were made during the raid with the Thai side of the Mekong.[107] Although the operation failed and the rebels were never found, few doubted that Phetsarath was the instigator. As well, Laotian, French, British, and American diplomats all believed that Phetsarath's Thai benefactors had supported him.[108] Given the Thai government's advance notice of the coup and close contacts with Phetsarath, the diplomats were almost certainly correct.

Several months later came Kou's assassination. On September 18, Phoui held a dinner party for a number of high-ranking government officials, including Kou. While the guests were eating, Udom Luksurin and an accomplice, Bunkong Wongphaibun, attacked the house. The assailants lobbed a grenade into the dining area and fired shots at the guests, hitting Kou, who died soon afterward. Udom and Bunkong fled to Thailand, and Vientiane was thrown into confusion.[109]

The evidence strongly indicates that Phetsarath and his Thai patrons, not Phoui, were behind Kou's death. Clearly, the attack was aimed at the government as a whole, not Kou alone, and Phoui was as much a target as Kou. The strike, of course, occurred at Phoui's home, and the grenade the assassins threw injured four people other than Kou, including the treasury minister and Phoui himself.[110] As the commander of the BPP at the time subtly, but tellingly, commented in a recent interview, the assassination resulted from "a plan that failed."[111] The plan, almost certainly, was to overthrow the Laotian government. Phetsarath, having intrigued for months against his brother's regime, and having traveled to northeastern provinces bordering Laos in July,[112] immediately fell under the suspicion of the Laotians and Western diplomats.

Because he was in a position of nearly complete dependence on Phao and the Thai government, observers also assumed, with good reason, that the Thais had backed the plot.[113] The implausibility of the official Thai explanation of events itself casts suspicion on the government. The Interior Ministry report on the assassination perversely claimed that the French ordered the attack. Allegedly, they considered the French-aligned Souvanna Phouma government pro-Thai. Significantly, while the ministry probably drafted this unlikely report to whitewash Phetsarath's and the Thais' involvement, even the author of the memorandum presumed that the attack targeted the government as a whole, not Kou alone, as Udom, Phetsarath, and the Thais later claimed.[114] The circumstances of Udom's arrest and implication of Phoui in January 1955 add to the reasons to suspect the Thais. As early as October 1, the Laotian government had informed the Thais that Udom and Bunkong were in Thailand, but the police arrested Udom, allegedly for a crime committed in Bangkok, only after four months of pressure from the French, British, Americans, and Laotians.[115] Although the Laotian Foreign Ministry asked the Thais to extradite Udom, they refused, arguing that he was a Thai citizen.[116] The Laotians refuted that assertion.[117] Udom gave his account of the assassination—that Phoui, one of the victims, had ordered the attack—while in the custody of Phao's police. Judging by their refusal to give up Udom, the police likely extracted the implausible story either by coercing him or by promising to protect him from the Laotian government. Phao released Udom in November.[118] In any case, the confession implicating Phoui fooled few diplomats, and foreign observers continued to believe Phetsarath and the Thais responsible.[119]

Phao's own behavior shows that he felt he had something to hide. In a meeting with Dulles in Washington two months after Kou's death, Phao exclaimed to a perplexed Dulles, without anyone present even hinting at Thai misconduct, that Phetsarath probably was involved in the attack, but that "our [the Thai] side did not know or have any fore-knowledge" of the assassination.[120] As Hannah, the U.S. embassy's primary contact with Phao, wrote two years earlier, "General Phao has always been inclined to tell more [when meeting Americans] than he means to tell as a result of his extreme sensitivity regarding his own weak points. He tends to plunge in and defend himself on his weak points before they have even been called into question."[121] When meeting Dulles, at least, Phao certainly considered Kou's death the Thais' weak point.

Kou's assassination achieved, to a large extent, Thai aims in Laos. Within a few weeks of the attack, the political turmoil the murder had provoked forced Prime Minister Souvanna Phouma's resignation. Katay (Sasorith Don Katay), a southern Lao with close social and political connections to Thailand, succeeded Souvanna,[122] and conditions within the country looked favorable enough for one Phao lieutenant to predict in November that Phetsarath would win elections planned for the coming year.[123] Phoui and Souvanna, whom Thai Ambassador Samai termed "dangerous," remained in the government but could not challenge Katay.[124] In January 1955—at the same time that the police arrested Udom—Phao broached to the Americans a plan, unspecified in the available documents, to bring Phetsarath to power immediately. Phao abandoned the scheme, described by an American official as "startling," only under U.S. pressure.[125] The Thais, nonetheless, continued to fund Katay on into 1956.[126]

Because of the Thais' plans for extension of their influence in Indochina—aid for Phetsarath, the Buddhist Union, the supply of arms to Cambodia—the government fully supported PSB D-23. Already well disposed toward all American offers of military or economic assistance, Phibun, Phao, and military leaders favored any program, such as PSB D-23, projecting Thai (and U.S.) military power into Indochina. Although PSB D-23 posed the danger of a confrontation with the Viet-minh—and the French—the clear boost to the government's Indochina policy outweighed any risk. The Thais, therefore, took readily to the U.S. effort to make their country America's military bastion in Southeast Asia.

GENEVA AND SEATO

The Thais again eagerly assumed the role of American political bastion in the spring of 1954 when Dulles laid plans for a new Southeast Asia policy. By April 1954, events in Indochina had taken a frightening turn for the United States. In late 1953, the French, tired of the "Dirty War" and eager to sign an armistice, began to consider making peace, and, in February 1954, Paris agreed with the Communists to include discussion of Indochina at the conference on Korea planned for the late spring in Geneva. Dulles and Eisenhower vigorously opposed this decision to meet face to face with Vietminh and Red Chinese representatives. Meanwhile, the French continued to lose ground militarily. Ho's forces again drove into Laos in December 1953, this time reaching the Thai border at Thakaek, and, in early 1954, Vietminh advances forced the French to concentrate at a base in the remote northern Vietnamese village of Dien Bien Phu, near Laos.[127] In early March, the Vietminh succeeded, against all odds, in moving enough heavy weaponry to the surrounding hills to initiate a sustained siege of the stronghold. As the French position deteriorated, Dulles and Eisenhower began planning seriously, for the first time, for direct American military intervention. At the end of March, the administration commenced talks with the French on possible American air strikes on the Vietminh.[128]

The political success of the U.S. plans depended on Thailand. Both to strengthen the West's bargaining position at Geneva in May and to justify to Congress and the world any intervention Eisenhower might approve, Dulles began promoting in late March and April an ad hoc coalition of anticommunist nations. Dulles proposed that the coalition, called United Action, consist of the United States, France, Britain, Australia, New Zealand, the three Indochinese "Associated States," the Philippines, and Thailand.[129] Dulles asked the British and French ambassadors on April 2 and 3 for their countries' support and, on April 5, discussed the plan with the Philippine and Thai ambassadors, but the allies' response was not encouraging.[130] The British worried that the initiative might jeopardize the Geneva talks, and the French, despite their pleas for an American air strike, continued to oppose internationalization of the war. Even the Americans' Philippine protégés agreed to participate reluctantly, and only after a delay of two weeks.[131] But, again, Thailand came to Dulles' rescue. A mere two days after Dulles broached the topic to Phot, Phibun gave his hearty approval of United Action. Dulles promptly announced publicly Phibun's decision, and, to ensure continued Thai support for United Action, Smith told Phot that the United States might help Thailand expand the size of its army from sixty to ninety thousand men.[132] British and French opposition, in the end, killed the proposed anticommunist pact, but the Thais had again proven their willingness to support American plans in Southeast Asia. Thailand alone among the countries Dulles approached gave unconditional approval to United Action.[133]

Eisenhower and Dulles decided in May to base their diplomatic strategy for Indochina on Thai support. By the second week of May, the Western diplomatic and military position in Vietnam had nearly collapsed. On May 7, Dien Bien Phu fell, and, in a piece of horrendous luck, the Geneva talks turned to Indochina the very next day. Dulles and Eisenhower feared that, in the aftermath of the humiliating defeat at Dien Bien Phu, the war-weary French would stop fighting and accede to Communist demands at Geneva. To forestall a French collapse and provide the Communists pause at the bargaining tables, an alarmed U.S. administration quickly renewed consideration of direct military intervention under the guise of United Action. British Prime Minister Winston Churchill again opposed the plan, but, by that point, Thai backing for United Action had helped convince Eisenhower and Dulles that the United States could go ahead without Britain.[134] In the second week of May, the United States revived planning, premised largely on Thai support, for possible air strikes and an anticommunist pact.[135]

Dulles wasted no time in mounting his Thai-based political offensive. In a meeting with JCS Chairman Adm. Arthur W. Radford on May 9, just two days after Dien Bien Phu's surrender, Dulles suggested that the United States provide the Thais a definite security commitment. Dulles envisioned, he said, a " 'chip on the shoulder' mutual defense treaty with Thailand which might be open-ended to permit other adherents and which might provide for the stationing of a detachment of U.S. troops in Thailand." Radford, opposing any dispersal of precious American military resources, objected, but Dulles, with Donovan's help, pressed the matter.[136] The following day, the Thai army's chief of staff, Lt. Gen. *Luang* Det Detpradityud, publicly announced, probably on Donovan's advice, that Thailand was willing to accept American air bases, and Donovan cabled recommendations for establishment of leased air bases in Nakhorn Ratchasima in the northeast and at the Isthmus of Kra in the south.[137] The Operations Coordinating Board (the successor to the PSB), Smith, and then Dulles approved Donovan's air base plan, and work began on a draft mutual security treaty.[138] Smith broached the air base proposal to Wan on May 14.[139] Within two weeks of Dulles' initial consideration of the idea, the Bureau of Far Eastern Affairs presented him with a draft mutual defense treaty.[140] Dulles also now agreed to a proposal for increased military assistance that Donovan had recommended in December 1953 and told the Thai embassy's chargé, Thuaithep Thewakun, that the United States "wants to see the strength of the Thai army increased as fast as possible." He pressed for the Thais to present a formal aid request immediately.[141] On May 13, Dulles revived plans for a second appeal to the U.N. to send observers to Indochina and Thailand. He ordered Smith to ask the Thais to issue the appeal, as before, despite British and French opposition.[142]

Though appearing at first glance unconnected, these various initiatives formed a coordinated campaign to advance prospects for a Southeast Asian collective defense pact and justify possible American military intervention in Indochina. As his reference to "other adherents" to the "open-ended" mutual security treaty with Thailand shows, Dulles intended the bilateral defense pact as the starting point for a larger Southeast Asian collective military agreement. The U.N. appeal, he hoped, would encourage such an agreement. Even if other nations remained aloof, the mutual security treaty, the dispatch of troops, increased military aid, and the U.N. appeal would have bolstered American claims that Vietminh victories threatened the Thais as well as the French. The United States would then be able to bomb Vietminh positions in the name of protecting Thailand. Were the initiatives never to lead to actual U.S. military intervention, they would still show the Communists that the United States was preparing for it. The mere specter of American air strikes would provide the West an added bargaining chip in Geneva and give Vietminh commanders pause.[143] To make sure the Communists knew of U.S. plans, the Americans leaked news in early June that the Thais had requested increased assistance and that the United States would probably comply.[144] The JCS opposed the plan, but the State Department argued that increased aid was needed "to obtain full Thai cooperation with respect to a Southeast Asian treaty."[145] Eisenhower agreed. Telling his advisers that "we should not lose any asset we don't have to lose," he suggested in late May stationing a small number of troops in the country "to keep Thailand friendly."[146]

The Thais, as usual, strongly supported all these initiatives. Dulles never actually approached Phibun about a bilateral treaty, but the Thais, not surprisingly, greeted the offer of increased military assistance enthusiastically. Only a disagreement between them and MAAG over the contours of the program prevented speedy implementation. To resolve the dispute, the JCS proposed high-level staff talks in Washington, much to the delight of the Thais.[147] Phibun assented to the air bases a week after Smith broached the subject to Wan on May 14. On Wan's recommendation, he rejected the idea of leasing the bases as unacceptable to Thai public opinion but agreed to the proposal if linked to a security pact or U.N. resolution.[148] The Thais fully supported Dulles' latest U.N. initiative. Wan, apparently agreeing with Phot's characterization of U.S. policy as "very uncertain and subject to change with each crisis," worried that Dulles would again abandon Thailand in the U.N., but, after consulting Phibun, he agreed on May 25 to present the appeal.[149] Five days later, the Thais formally requested the U.N. to dispatch a Peace Observation Subcommission to "the general area of Thailand."[150] Caught by surprise, Britain and France pleaded with Phibun to delay or narrow the appeal, but he stuck with Dulles.[151] The Security Council placed the Thai appeal on its agenda.[152]

Over the summer, Dulles had to scale back his plans for Thailand. Facing continued opposition from the JCS to any dispersal of U.S. forces, he abandoned proposals for U.S. air bases in Thailand. Instead, the United States agreed to help build bases at Nakhorn Ratchasima and Takli in the north for the Thais' own—and possible future U.S.—use.[153] Dulles also cut the proposed military assistance increase. Sarit, leading the staff talks in Washington, had requested assistance in elevating force levels from sixty thousand to one hundred fifty thousand men.[154] Although all on the American side considered this excessive, Donovan, Smith, and Dulles suggested that the Thais draft plans for raising levels to ninety thousand.[155] The JCS and MAAG, however, opposed any increase. They believed that more officer training was needed first.[156] MAAG estimated that it would take two years to school the officers the Thai army already required.[157] Dulles and the Thais, therefore, had to accept an aid increase that was significant, but less than either had hoped for. While the United States added $25 million to Thailand's military assistance package, no force expansion was planned.[158] Though not as effective politically as Dulles had wanted, this aid package, the JCS persuasively argued, made military sense.

Dulles also left the Thais hanging, yet again, in the U.N. Immediately after the Thais lodged their appeal on May 29, the British and French began pressing Wan and Dulles to soften it. British Foreign

Minister Anthony Eden suggested dispatching observers to Thailand alone.[159] As long as the British were refusing to follow the Americans' hard line at Geneva, Dulles readily discounted such recommendations, but, by the second week of June, London was coming around to the U.S. viewpoint. On June 9, Eden told the U.S. delegation in Geneva that he had concluded that the Communists' intransigence would make a Western walkout necessary. He proposed having Laos and Cambodia present their own appeals after the conference's failure but in the meantime having the Thais drop their current petition.[160] Although Dulles did not forgo the Thai appeal completely, the British change of heart induced him to urge the Thais to limit the appeal to Thailand.[161] Phot angrily protested, but the Thais had little choice in the matter. They presented the appeal to the Security Council on June 16, altered to British and French specifications.[162]

Over the next two weeks, the Thais' worst nightmare came true. After the Soviets vetoed the appeal, as expected, the Thais and the United States prepared to take it to the General Assembly, but again the Europeans intervened.[163] The British and French now asked the United States to delay the General Assembly session on the appeal until after the scheduled conclusion of the Geneva conference on July 20.[164] Eden feared, as before, that the appeal would disrupt the conference. While Churchill and Eden were still blocking United Action, Dulles resisted such pressure, but, in the last week of June, they endorsed plans for a Southeast Asian defense pact.[165] On June 28, following a visit to Washington to patch up American-British differences, Churchill agreed to issue a joint communique promising a defense pact regardless of Geneva's outcome.[166] With that, Dulles felt obliged to placate the British on the U.N. appeal. The urgency of the appeal, meanwhile, had dissipated. By mid-June, Dulles, concluding that the French wanted only the threat of U.S. intervention, not actual U.S. military action, for negotiating purposes, decided firmly against air or naval strikes.[167] He therefore no longer needed a pretext for intervention. Two days after the Churchill-Eisenhower communique, he and Wan agreed to postpone the General Assembly session until after the Geneva conference.[168] After that, no one raised the matter again.

Despite Dulles' decision to scale back his May plans for Thailand, the initiatives had scored points for the West—and Thailand—at Geneva. Dulles' saber rattling and Thailand's publicized willingness to accept American bases raised Chinese fears that the United States would station troops in Thailand or Indochina. Zhou Enlai therefore subordinated Vietminh interests at Geneva to China's desire to prevent the establishment of a large American military presence in Southeast Asia.[169] Similarly, the Soviets showed much greater interest in convincing France to oppose the U.S. proposal to rearm Germany than in advancing the communist cause in faraway Indochina. Like the Chinese, they urged Ho to settle for less at Geneva than the Vietminh position on the ground justified. Because of such pressure, the Vietminh agreed to withdraw from all of Cambodia and Laos except two Laotian provinces on the Vietnamese border and accepted a "temporary" partition of Vietnam into northern and southern halves. The conference drew the dividing line in Vietnam several degrees north of Vietminh-controlled areas. In return for such concessions, the West agreed to ban foreign military bases in Vietnam, thus preventing establishment of a large American presence on China's borders.[170] Although the accords left northern Vietnam completely in Ho's hands and scheduled for 1956 nationwide elections that Ho was likely to win, the West also had gained much. France escaped with its honor and much of its position in Indochina other than North Vietnam intact, and, while the United States refused to sign the Geneva accord, instead "taking note" of it, senior American officials considered the conference's results "the best obtainable by negotiation."[171] Thailand too had cause for relief. Although Wan and Phot, fearing the establishment of a precedent that could be applied to Thailand, had protested the partition of Vietnam, the mandated French and Vietminh pullbacks from Laos and Cambodia opened those countries to Thai influence.[172]

Furthermore, Dulles' earliest proposal—a mutual defense treaty centered on Thailand—actually was implemented in altered form. Soon after Churchill's acceptance of U.S. plans for a pact, negotiations between the British and Americans began, and by mid July, the State Department was circulating a draft treaty among the proposed members. Foreign Ministers from the United States, Britain, France, New Zealand, Australia, Pakistan, the Philippines, and Thailand met in Manila on September 6 to discuss the pact. Two days later, they signed the treaty forming the Southeast Asia Treaty Organization (SEATO).[173]

This so-called Manila Pact produced a grouping, in the words of Phot, much more prone to United Inaction than United Action.[174] Opinions on the purpose of the pact nearly outnumbered signatories. Pakistan sought protection against India, the British wanted to emphasize economic development, and the Philippines expected increased U.S. assistance. France joined simply not to be left out. Although the threat of Chinese or Vietminh aggression ostensibly prompted the pact, only Thailand of the eight signatories was on the Southeast Asian mainland. While Dulles had pushed hard for a collective defense treaty over the previous six months, once the Geneva accord ended planning for U.S. military intervention, he grew wary of increased military commitments.[175] Bowing to pressure from Congress, he inserted into the treaty a stipulation that each signatory would act, in case of aggression against one of the member states, "in accordance with its constitutional processes."[176] In this, SEATO resembled the loosely structured ANZUS (Australia–New Zealand–United States) grouping, not the stronger NATO with its automatic response clause. Also like ANZUS, and unlike NATO, SEATO, on Dulles' insistence, lacked a unified command or joint forces. In case of communist subversion, as opposed to open attack, the Manila Pact provided only for the signatories to "consult" on defense measures.[177] Since the majority of observers believed that Chinese and Vietminh subversion posed the only possible immediate threat to Thailand and Indochina, this vaguely worded clause diluted the treaty's strength.

The Thais regretted SEATO's weakness. Phibun had hoped for a U.S. security commitment since 1950, and, by the fall of 1954, his reasons for wanting to formalize the alliance had increased significantly. The Chinese had shown, through their military assistance to the Vietminh in the last years of the war, that they could project their power into Southeast Asia, and now they had an ally practically on Thailand's doorstep in North Vietnam. China made clear after Geneva its continued hostility toward Phibun. On July 30, Beijing broadcast an article Pridi had that day published in *People's Daily*. After criticizing "U.S. imperialists" and "the Thai reactionary government," Pridi urged the Thai people to "wage a struggle against the rulers [of Thailand]— American imperialism and its puppets, the government of Thailand."[178] Again, the Chinese were threatening to overthrow Phibun, this time through Pridi. The broadcast frightened the Thai military leadership and made Pridi anathema to the United States. Although China probably publicized Pridi's statement to warn Phibun against joining Dulles' collective defense treaty, the threat seems only to have encouraged the Thais to seek the strongest pact possible. During the negotiations over the treaty in the late summer of 1954, Wan pushed continually for the tightest, most restrictive language the Americans would accept. He sought to limit the pact's membership to maintain unity of purpose among the signatories and, to maximize the treaty's deterrent effect, fought for establishment of joint forces under a unified command.[179] Wan made clear that the Thais wanted an Asian NATO.[180] The lack of NATO-like certainty in SEATO's provisions disappointed them.

Nevertheless the Thais embraced the Manila Pact wholeheartedly. Like the Filipinos, they expected that the treaty would lead to increased U.S. aid. And like the Americans, Thai leaders believed that the pact would make their anticommunist foreign policy more appealing to the public. Just as Dulles counted on SEATO to satisfy congressional preconditions for allied assistance in any U.S. military intervention in Southeast Asia, Phibun afterward justified his essentially bilateral, U.S.-based foreign policy on the need to support the multilateral Manila Pact. He thus was able to counter leftist criticism that the United States controlled him, while the American pledge to defend Thailand also answered conservatives, such as Khuang and Seni, who faulted him for committing the country to the West without getting an American security guarantee in return. SEATO, moreover, covered nonmembers Laos, Cambodia, and South Vietnam. Although the Geneva accord prohibited their participation in collective defense organizations, the Manila Pact, at Thai and American insistence, unilaterally extended its security guarantee to the three noncommunist Indochinese states. The Thais considered this provision crucial to their national security.

Most important, the Manila Pact put down on paper the U.S. commitment to fight for Thailand. Though multilateralism had its political benefits, the Thais viewed the European and Asian signatories as superfluous. British insistence on including faraway Pakistan in a "Southeast Asian" treaty and French opposition to the security guarantee to Indochina did not bother Phibun so long as the United States promised to defend Thailand and its Cambodian and Laotian buffer states. At all times, the Thais chose to interpret the multilateral Manila Pact as encompassing a bilateral U.S. security commitment to Thailand. Although Phibun would have liked greater automaticity of U.S. action than SEATO provided, the Thais accepted Dulles' word that the United States would not let Thailand fall. The new administration had worked hard to win the Thais' confidence over the past year. Both in implementing PSB D-23 and in the increased military assistance and offer of air bases, the Americans had shown the importance they now attached to Thailand. In July 1954, Dulles emphasized this point by supporting Wan's bid for the U.N. presidency. Dulles took the unprecedented step of publicly announcing his support for Wan in advance, despite angry Dutch opposition. The Dutch, then promoting their own candidate, pointed out that an Asian, Madame Nehru, had just held the presidency and that it was now a European's turn.[181] Wan, impressed by this and the other displays of American interest in his country, set aside his reservations about SEATO and called on his Thai colleagues to have faith in American intentions. "We must trust," Wan wrote Phot, "that, if something happens, the United States of America will give full support [to Thailand], including the sending of troops with congressional approval."[182] A mere two weeks after its conclusion, the Thais ratified the Manila Pact. They were the first to do so.

The Manila Pact symbolized the importance the United States now attached to Thailand. The Americans had shown little interest in committing themselves militarily to this weak, distant country in 1950, but Thailand's military government proved its mettle to the United States in subsequent years. In 1951, the Thai leadership established itself as a loyal client willing to follow the United States into conflict with European powers and Communists alike, and, in the following year, the government swept aside the critics of its pro-U.S. policies. The military regime acquired, at the same time, a new stability. As the Americans increased their involvement with the Indochina war in 1953 and 1954, they also, by necessity, relied more heavily on their one client state on the Southeast Asian mainland. Once they decided in those years to predicate their strategy in Indochina on Thai political and military support, the Americans had little choice but to guarantee the country's security. The Manila Pact, though also intended to protect noncommunist Indochina, had Thailand as its main beneficiary, its principal Asian signatory, and the primary object of its attentions. Without its Southeast Asian bastion, the United States would not—and could not—have gone through with the treaty. To demonstrate Thailand's importance, the SEATO foreign ministers agreed to hold their first meeting in Bangkok. After four years of loyal diplomatic and political service, Phibun and the Thai government had moved to the center of American regional strategy and entered the select club of formal American allies.

America's new dependence on Thai diplomatic and military support bound U.S. policy more firmly to the fate of military government in Thailand. In 1950, most Thais, other than leftists, considered the United States a distant, but friendly, power. Despite the pressure exerted on the government to recognize Bao Dai, few Thais at the time perceived any American designs on Thailand, and U.S. support for the country in the war settlement negotiations with Britain in 1945 and 1946 continued to win sympathy for the Americans. Public criticism of the United States rarely appeared, and most Thais wanted the United States to take a greater interest in Thai affairs. Today, some older Thais describe the period between the war and 1950 as the golden age of Thai-U.S. relations.[183] But America's cooperation with the country's increasingly corrupt and authoritarian military rulers, especially the brutal Phao, eroded the American image in Thailand from 1950 to 1954. As the United States identified itself more closely with the increasingly unpopular military leadership, Thai doubts about the Americans' professed disinterest in political and economic gain grew. Popular anti-Americanism emerged ready—if political restrictions were ever loosened—to disrupt relations. Thailand now was too important to the United States for the Americans to let that happen. By 1954, therefore, conditions were ripe for the United States to reject emphatically even partial democracy in Thailand.

PART FOUR

DEMOCRACY, DICTATORSHIP, AND

THE NEW ALLIANCE, 1955–1958

As much as the United States had contributed to the extension of military rule in Thailand, many policymakers remained committed in 1954 to encouraging democratic institutions there. Despite the CIA's cooperation with the right-wing Phao Siyanon and the moral and material support supplied the military, Americans in Bangkok and Washington continued to try to temper the military's excesses in the first half of the decade. The State Department and MAAG strongly protested the Silent Coup in 1951, Stanton sought until his departure in mid-1953 to restrain Phao and strengthen the more moderate Phibun, and the embassy maintained close contacts with conservative opposition figures throughout the period. Most American policymakers retained a hard-headed idealism that democratic institutions and civilian participation in administration offered the country its best hope for efficient and honest—and thus stable and durable—government. In 1955, the Americans most closely involved with Thailand still believed that the country's fight against communism depended on civilian checks on the military. When the Thais instituted serious democratic reforms that year, therefore, Americans greeted the changes with hearty approval. As restrictions on the press and free speech were lifted, parties formed, and plans for free elections proceeded, important U.S. officials concluded that the country had set out on a more promising and prosperous political path. Democratic reforms, many policymakers believed, would make Thailand a stronger partner of the United States.

The Americans found, however, that the democracy they had imagined bore little resemblance to the reality of Thai democratic institutions in action. While the Americans conceived of democracy as a game with strict rules against criticism of the United States and limited to gentlemanly players who respected established anticommunist etiquette, the Thais envisioned a much more raucous match. The reforms of 1955 opened the political process to almost all Thais—including leftists—and the government now permitted open advocacy of neutralism. Anti-Americanism emerged as a staple of the new political dialogue. For three years, the United States took hits from all sides, and official policy, partly as a result, veered toward neutralism. The reforms weakened the alliance and hampered the United States' Thailand-based regional military strategy. They threatened all that mattered most to the United States in Thailand.

The Americans learned from this experience. Although policymakers retained faith in the ability of civilian political institutions to enhance governmental efficiency and stability, Americans recognized by 1958 the danger Thai democracy posed to U.S. global strategy. Democratic institutions and the full diplomatic, political, and military support the United States had come to expect from Thailand, Americans now realized, were incompatible. When the military ended the country's latest experiment with democratic reform in 1958, therefore, the Americans shed no tears. By then, after a decade of ambiguity and indecisiveness, they were ready to embrace military dictatorship in Thailand enthusiastically.

Chapter Nine

DEMOCRATIZATION AND DETERIORATION,

JANUARY 1955–SEPTEMBER 1957

As the Thais and Americans moved into their fifth year of military cooperation after the signing of the Manila Pact in September 1954, the friendship between the United States and the Thai military government remained strong. The halcyon days of the previous May when Dulles met a Thai representative almost weekly to discuss air bases, bilateral security pacts, and massive aid increases had passed, but the Thais still had much to praise about American policy. The Manila Pact demonstrated the Americans' commitment to protecting and aiding Thailand, and military cooperation continued undiminished. U.S.-Thai relations were poised for further growth.

The first happy development for the Thais after the Manila conference was the appointment in October 1954 of John E. Peurifoy to replace Donovan as ambassador. In itself, the departure of a friend as powerful as Donovan was regrettable, but the Thais had been aware from the beginning that his term would be brief. When accepting appointment in 1953, Donovan had insisted that financial constraints would limit him to serving no more than a year as ambassador. He asked for special nonofficial status as the president's personal representative so that he could receive income from his Wall Street law firm, but Eisenhower refused. In August 1954, Donovan left Bangkok, a year after his arrival.[1] Under these circumstances, Peurifoy was the best the Thai generals could hope for. Flamboyant, outspoken, and politically ambitious, Peurifoy had already earned a reputation as one of the State Department's premier anti-Communists. He started his ambassadorial career in Greece, where he helped assemble a right-wing government following the civil war, and came to Thailand directly from

Guatemala, where he had directed, just four months earlier, the CIA-led overthrow of the supposedly procommunist Jacobo Arbenz Guzmán government. Such a hardened anti-Communist could be expected to speak up for Thailand when policymakers considered military assistance programs for the country. His connections in Washington, moreover, ensured that his voice would be heard. His friendship with former senator and Secretary of State James F. Byrnes and other congressmen from his home state of South Carolina had already boosted his State Department career. Although a life-long Democrat, his service in Greece and Guatemala had gained him the attention of Dulles and Eisenhower, and his close cooperation with the CIA had won him important friends in the intelligence community. Clearly, John Peurifoy was a player. And the Thais had good reason to hope that he would line up on their side.[2]

More important, Peurifoy was not the only prominent U.S. figure working for Thai interests in late 1954 and 1955. By that time, Thailand was developing a powerful constituency in Washington along the lines of Chiang Kai-shek's China Lobby. During the Indochina crises of 1953 and early 1954, the Thais had earned a prominent position in the administration's regional strategy, and policymakers continued to place overriding importance on the Thai alliance following the Geneva conference and the signing of the Manila Pact. Speaking for the State Department's Bureau of Far Eastern Affairs, Assistant Secretary of State Walter Robertson wrote Dulles in January 1955 that "Thailand remains today the sole secure base for United States counter action against communism on the mainland of Asia. With the changed communist tactics it will become even more important that Thailand remain a friendly Asian voice in Asian councils, and a pioneer of anti-communist Asian unity."[3] Even more so than the State Department, the CIA emerged at this time as a powerful spokesman for aid to Thailand. Outside the administration, former Ambassadors Stanton and Donovan were now mobilizing support among the public and in Congress for a strong Thailand policy. In October 1954, Stanton wrote an article for the journal *Foreign Affairs* advocating full U.S. support for the Manila Pact and increased military assistance for Thailand. Soon afterward, the Thai government hired Donovan as "economic adviser" (i.e., lobbyist).[4] With his vast influence and Washington experience, Donovan did more than anyone else on the American side in the following months to win the Thais increased aid. In return, the Thais made sure that Donovan's finances recovered from his year of privation as ambassador. In January, they gave him $25,000 for his "expenses" and, over the remainder of the year, reportedly added another $75,000.[5] Like his friend Willis Bird, Donovan had learned to combine service for Thailand with moneymaking.

This emerging Thai lobby coalesced and won its first victory during Phao's late 1954 visit to the United States. Following Sarit's success in getting $25 million in increased military aid in the July staff talks, Phao went to the United States in November to request a large loan and $37 million in grants for budget support and the Volunteer Defense Corps. Eisenhower, Harold Stassen of the Foreign Operations Administration, and even State Department officials greeted Phao's proposal cautiously, but Thailand's American constituency made its influence felt almost immediately.[6] Before Phao's arrival, the embassy urged Washington to grant his request, and, in contrast to the coolness of Stassen and State Department officials, CIA director Allen Dulles approved Phao's proposal enthusiastically. The intelligence chief told Phao in their November 10 meeting that he would support the aid increase in the next NSC session.[7] Meanwhile, Phao made a big splash in Congress. Probably thanks to Donovan's influence, Phao met separately with Sen. H. Alexander Smith, Democratic leader Sen. Mike Mansfield, and influential Republican Sen. William F. Knowland, and another senator held a party in Phao's honor. Donovan presented the aid request on Phao's behalf to the senators and congressmen attending the party.[8] As a result of such lobbying, Rep. Albert Morano of the House Foreign Affairs Committee wrote John Foster Dulles soon afterward urging "that immediate steps be taken to reach a decision on supplying United States aid for the strengthening of Thailand."[9] The administration, partly in response to the Thai campaign, granted most of Phao's request. On December 4, Stassen informed Phao that the United States would provide $25 million in budget support and a $3 million supplement for Phao's Volunteer Defense Corps.[10]

While the United States thus added to its already extensive aid programs, developments within the Manila Pact grouping also turned the Thais' way in early 1955. In February of that year, the Manila Pact countries held in Bangkok the group's first ministerial-level conference since the signing of the treaty in September. Dulles continued to reject Thai suggestions that SEATO establish a unified NATO-style command with forces at its disposal and military bases in Thailand, but the Thais won American support on several important points. The conference, on U.S. urging, established a permanent secretariat for the grouping and approved a Thai proposal for a communist subversion surveillance committee. In a clear signal of the continued centrality of Thailand to the grouping, the conferees designated Bangkok as the organization's headquarters. They appointed a Thai its head.[11]

As well, in 1955, American policy toward Indochina shifted further in the Thais' favor. After rebuffing Thai pleas over the previous two years for the United States to take control of matters from France, the Americans, after Geneva, replaced the French as the dominant power in Indochina. The United States intensified its aid to and involvement with the South Vietnamese government in late 1954 and 1955, and, by October 1955, the U.S.-supported prime minister, Ngo Dinh Diem, was able to oust French-backed Bao Dai. While not so forward as in Vietnam, U.S. policy was also making inroads into Laos and Cambodia. When meeting Phao, Dulles explained that the United States planned to begin, as the Thais had long wanted, aiding the two countries directly, bypassing France.[12]

Most important, the United States planned to extend its influence in Laos and Cambodia partly by strengthening Thailand's ties with the two countries. The United States had previously discouraged overly intimate relations between Thailand and its Indochinese neighbors in deference to France, but, once the French had disappointed the United States at Geneva, the Americans reversed course. Hoping to lure Thailand's neighbors away from neutralism and closer to SEATO, the State Department asked the embassies of the region in October 1954 to recommend ways to improve relations among Burma, Cambodia, Laos, and Thailand.[13] In response, the Bangkok embassy advised that the United States make Thailand the focal point of its efforts and "foster Thai leadership" in the region.[14] Agreeing with the recommendations, Dulles approved a plan in February 1955 to circumvent restrictions the Geneva agreements had placed on direct U.S. military aid to Laos by sending Laotian police officers to Thailand for paramilitary training.[15] Later that year, the United States established a "Regional Economic Development" program based in Bangkok to enhance Thailand's commercial ties with Laos and Cambodia.[16] Donovan again laid his prestige on the line on behalf of his Thai clients. Sometime around the new year, he urged the administration to encourage formation of a "Buddhist confederation" of Burma, Laos, Cambodia, and Thailand along the lines of the earlier Thai proposal for a Buddhist Union.[17] At last, the United States was throwing its weight behind the Thai political and economic offensives in the region.

Indicative of his own satisfaction with Thailand's improved relations with the United States, Phibun arranged, in the winter of 1954, a grand, two-month tour of the United States and pro-Western nations in

Europe and Asia over the spring of 1955.[18] No pressing foreign-policy issue needed attention, and he planned to discuss little of importance with the leaders he was to meet, but the field marshal seems to have wanted to celebrate his foreign-policy triumphs of the past year. After suffering politically over the previous ten years from his wartime collaboration with the Japanese, Phibun, recent comments by his surviving relations show, considered the willingness of Eisenhower and Queen Elizabeth to receive him as vindication of his wartime policies.[19] He planned the tour, in the wake of recent favorable developments in Thai relations with the United States and the West, as a diplomatic coming-out party.

THE GENESIS OF DEMOCRATIZATION

Although Thai-American relations remained sound, all was not well in Thailand. In early 1955, Phao intensified his political activities. Vietminh military victories and the need for him and Sarit to consolidate their power bases had stifled conflicts within the ruling clique in 1953 and 1954, but the conclusion of the Geneva conference and passing of the external crisis freed Phao to renew his drive for complete power. Evidence on his plans at the start of the year is scarce, but his later actions and the initiation by Phao's newspaper, *Chao,* of an anti-Sarit campaign that January show that Sarit's ouster was Phao's immediate goal.[20] Ultimately, subsequent events demonstrate, Phao hoped to topple Phibun himself.

Phibun responded to Phao's scheming with a democratization campaign—a campaign that would rock Thai-U.S. relations for the next three years. Ever since the Manhattan Rebellion and the Silent Coup, Phibun had sought a place for non-Coup Group political forces in the government. Then, in early 1955, he decided that if he could transform the political competition from a match of military forces, of which he had few, to a contest for popularity among voters, journalists, and politicians, he could significantly weaken Phao and strengthen his own position. His image as a war hero and statesman, Phibun was confident, would carry him to electoral victory over the brutal, famously corrupt, and widely despised Phao, and his greater political finesse would win points in Parliament. In a speech to high-ranking bureaucrats on January 12, Phibun predicted that conservatives would not be able to stop "ideas [in society] from moving forward."[21] Two days later, he publicly pledged that "in the future greater political power would reside in the people" and promised unspecified reforms.[22] Under different circumstances, such remarks could be dismissed as empty rhetoric, but Phibun's actions following his return from abroad five months later show that he meant business.

Phao recognized the threat and immediately retaliated with his own supposedly democratic initiative. Three days after Phibun's remarks, Phao gave a speech to provincial police commissioners lamenting the lack of democracy in the country and advocating greater popular participation in government.[23] Then, on April 13, the day before Phibun's departure for his world trip, Phao submitted a memorandum to the field marshal proposing decentralization of the local administration system. Phao announced the scheme publicly four days later. He claimed that it would bring the country "full-fledged democracy."[24]

But, while using the same vocabulary, Phao and Phibun could not have been talking about more different matters. When Phao, the police strongman dependent on terror and bribery for his position, spoke of "full-fledged democracy," he really meant "rule by Phao." As political scientist Fred Riggs has observed, Phao's decentralization plan, though appearing at first glance genuinely liberal, actually strengthened provincial governors' control over local affairs and thus, by extension, Phao's Ministry of the Interior.[25] Phibun, on the other hand, had something similar to genuine democracy in mind. He almost certainly did not favor full democracy as it existed in the West and would have known, in any case, that the Coup Group would never have allowed it, but he did hope that a more open political system would make him again, as before the Silent Coup, the indispensable bridge between civilian and military elements of government. Half a democracy, Phibun had concluded, was better than none at all.

Although no American officials suggested it at the time, Phibun's incipient anti-Phao democratization campaign posed serious dangers for the United States. Despite the considerable U.S. aid to Sarit's army and the moral support the embassy provided Phibun, four years of CIA patronage of the police and Phao's friendship with Bird and CIA agents had brought Phao and the CIA closer together than ever. Allen Dulles' strong support for Phao's November 1954 aid request derived from this firmer CIA-Phao partnership. By that time, moreover, the CIA was not the only U.S. agency siding with Phao. An Operations Coordinating Board group in December 1954 recommended shifting the bulk of all future military assistance to Phao's police.[26] Donovan's infatuation with the police had also, for the moment, brought the embassy over to Phao's side. A private researcher commissioned to evaluate U.S. aid programs in the country reported in October 1954 that the "American official establishment in Bangkok had climbed into bed with General Phao."[27] Such intimacy convinced Thais by mid-decade that Phao was the Americans' favorite. As Peurifoy noted in mid-1955, "Close U.S. cooperation with and generous support for Phao have tended [to] create in [the] public mind and possibly in Phao's the not unreasonable impression [that] Phao [is the] chosen instrument [of] U.S. policy."[28] As long as Phao and the military regime retained their grip on the country, the identification of the United States with him presented no threat, but if Phibun ever succeeded in liberalizing the political system, Phao's unpopularity could come to haunt the Americans.

Worst of all for the United States, Phibun's democratization campaign coincided with—and contributed to—a gradual, but stunning, shift toward friendlier relations with China. Because the diplomacy involved in this policy change occurred secretly and involved no official record-keeping, and because Phibun's motives, methods, and aims appear to have changed over time, it is impossible to say for sure what his reasoning was and how far he was prepared to go, but the available evidence suggests that a complex set of factors influenced him.

Helpful here is an examination of Phibun's previous foreign-policy volte-face, his decision during the war to reach out to the Allies and turn on the Japanese. In early 1943, just as Pridi was organizing the Free Thai and sending agents to China to contact the Allies, Phibun secretly dispatched his own representatives to meet Nationalist generals in Yunnan. Over the course of 1943 and early 1944, Phibun sent at least four such delegations. Also, in late 1943, he laid plans to move the capital to remote Petchabun province to mount resistance against the Japanese. The scheme failed, and the missions ended when Pridi ousted him in July 1944.[29] In attempting this foreign-policy reversal, Phibun was responding to Allied victories in the Pacific and the consequent changes in the balance of power in the region. Clearly, he understood by the second half of 1943 that Japanese defeat was likely and that the consequences for Thailand were serious. As well, concern for his personal political survival in the face of these changes certainly entered Phibun's calculations. Were he not to reach a modus vivendi with the Allies—and quickly—his political fate, he realized, would be sealed. In 1955, a decade later, Phibun confronted a different set of problems, but his opening to communist China in the mid-1950s involved similar concerns. In 1955, he perceived, as in 1943, important changes in the international situation. He also felt that his own political career, as before, demanded a change of policy.

Internationally, Phibun foresaw in 1955 no development, such as a Chinese takeover of Southeast Asia, as dramatic as the Allied victories in Asia in 1943 and 1944, but he probably did suspect that important diplomatic shifts could occur. Since Stalin's death in 1953, tensions between the United States and the Soviet Union had eased noticeably, and China had adopted considerably more forthcoming policies toward the West and noncommunist Southeast Asian nations at Geneva and afterward. China, according to Zhou's new policy, would befriend any country that refrained from joining alliances hostile to Beijing.[30] As such, a rapprochement between the United States and China and a more prominent Chinese diplomatic profile in the region appeared possible, and Phibun felt pressure to keep in step, as he had failed to during the war, with the pace of international developments. He did not want to be caught holding to the fiercely anti-PRC policy of 1953–1954 in the event of Sino-American normalization of relations or the emergence of China as the predominant power in the region. At the very least, a limited rapprochement with Beijing could lessen any military threat from the Chinese colossus.

Domestic political considerations, as in 1944, also appear to have weighed heavily in Phibun's mind. As long as his political position depended on support from the military, Phibun's friendship with the Americans strengthened him, but were he to broaden his power base in a more open political system, the U.S. alliance could prove a liability. He knew that anti-American, pro-PRC leftists, as in 1951 and 1952, would be vocal and play a small but crucial role in the press, Parliament, and the government, and that even moderates might support a more independent foreign policy. Under such circumstances, continuance of an undiluted pro-U.S., anti-PRC policy would damage his political and electoral prospects. A shift in foreign policy away from the United States and toward China, conversely, could boost his chances to regain control of Parliament from Phao and win big in elections scheduled for February 1957.

Equally important, Phibun had decided by 1955, later events showed, that, to parry Phao's political attacks, he had to reduce American involvement in Thai politics. In the early 1950s, Stanton had offset the CIA friendship with Phao with embassy backing for Phibun, but Donovan's arrival disrupted the balance in U.S. policy. With the embassy as well as the CIA then relying on Phao, Phibun began to worry that the United States would conspire with Phao to oust him. Peurifoy's arrival especially frightened Phibun. The new ambassador having just overthrown a government in Guatemala, Phibun suspected that

Peurifoy had similar orders in Thailand. So real was Phibun's fear that Peurifoy felt it necessary to ask Phibun's daughter at a private dinner party to tell her father that the United States had no intention of ousting him.[31] Phibun thus felt constrained in his dependence on the United States. A reduction of American influence in the country and exploration of new foreign-policy possibilities now appealed to him.

The African-Asian Conference at Bandung, Indonesia, in April 1955 offered Phibun the possibilities he was looking for. Although proclaiming the event a meeting of nonaligned nations, the conference's primary sponsors, Prime Minister Jawaharlal Nehru of India and President Sukarno of Indonesia, invited communist China as well as pro-Western Philippines and Thailand to attend. This conference, where the Thai representative could not avoid meeting Zhou, was the ideal setting for Phibun to make an opening to China. It is not clear whether he had the Chinese in mind when formally accepting Sukarno's invitation in early February, but by the time of Prince Wan's departure for Bandung in April, Phibun had definitely decided to make contacts with Zhou. Before Wan left, Phibun ordered the prince to try to meet Zhou and sound him out on PRC intentions regarding Thailand.[32] To maximize the political benefits of any success Wan had with the Chinese—given the democratic reforms he planned—Phibun personally paid for a delegation of Thai newsmen to cover the conference.[33] Never before had a large group of Thai journalists gone abroad.[34] Probably to let the newsmen know that they would witness an important change in Thai foreign policy, Phibun told them that Wan was attending "to show the conference that we intend to cooperate with *all sides* in building world peace" (emphasis added).[35] This conciliatory statement contrasted sharply with Phibun's explanation to foreign reporters soon afterward. He told the Western newsmen that he had sent Wan with orders to reject Nehru's and Zhou's Five Principles.[36]

At Bandung, Wan won the opening Phibun had sought. Although Wan delivered a typically hardline introductory speech denouncing the Thai Autonomous Zone in Yunnan, PRC manipulation of Chinese in Thailand, and Chinese collaboration with Pridi, he watched for the chance to make contact with Zhou.[37] Zhou's own speech was remarkably conciliatory, and, when the two met in the corridor afterward, Wan listened eagerly to Zhou. Zhou explained that Pridi was in Beijing, not Yunnan, and that China had established the Thai Autonomous Zone purely for administrative purposes. Wan accepted Zhou's invitation to dinner that night, and, the following morning, Zhou sent Wan silk for his wife. Wan gave Zhou a cigarette case.[38]

In the weeks following Bandung, Phibun and Wan followed a single policy, but spoke with two voices. While Phibun, on tour since early April, issued a stream of anticommunist diatribes in various world capitals, Wan in Bangkok commended the PRC's amicability. Phibun asserted in Los Angeles that, "to halt communism, . . . it will have to be by force," and in Karachi he commented that "I have seen no signs of the Communists stopping their policy of swallowing other countries." Wan, however, praised Zhou back home for having shown "a great deal of conciliatoriness" at Bandung and claimed that Thailand could recognize the PRC "under certain conditions."[39] He had refused an invitation from Zhou to visit China, the prince explained, only because he was "too busy."[40] In Washington, Phibun told Dulles that he did not trust Zhou and claimed that he had cabled Wan from Los Angeles to reject Zhou's invitation.[41] He thus was able to reassure the United States even as Wan continued his overtures to the Chinese.

None of this flirtation with Beijing reflected any dissatisfaction on the part of the Thai military government with American policy, because, as Wan was praising Chinese reasonableness in public, the Thai Lobby was winning the country another aid supplement behind closed doors. By now, the lobby was functioning effectively in both hemispheres. In Bangkok, work on the supplement began in June, when Senator Everett M. Dirksen visited. Ambassador Peurifoy, with his connections with the South Carolina congressional delegation, was no stranger to such congressional powerhouses and, apparently, put on a good show for the senator. Meeting Dirksen with Phao, Peurifoy urged the senator to propose in Congress a special aid appropriation for Thailand. The Thais would use the aid, a Thai memorandum of the conversation explained, "to strengthen relations with Laos, Vietnam, Cambodia, and Burma, by quietly distributing to these countries $50–60 million." Dirksen pledged his support for the plan.[42] Once back in the United States, he presented the proposal to a pleased Eisenhower and, in Congress, abandoned his previous opposition to foreign assistance increases and pushed strongly for aid supplements for both Thailand and Taiwan. The primary purpose of the scheme, Dirksen confidentially explained to Eisenhower and Dulles, was to aid Laos and Cambodia without the French knowing. "If America provides the aid itself directly," Phao reported that Dirksen told the president and secretary of state, "it will not be able to work closely [with the recipients], because France objects."[43]

Meanwhile, the private arm of the Thai Lobby had mustered its own resources in support of the plan. Through Donovan, Bird, or his other CIA connections, Phao had, by that time, hired lawyer Paul Helli-well, the former OSS agent who had incorporated Sea Supply Company in Miami for the CIA in 1950, as a lobbyist in addition to Donovan.[44] Donovan and Helliwell divided the Congress between them, with Donovan assuming responsibility for the Republicans and Helliwell taking the Democrats.[45] To add force to his efforts, Donovan published an article in *Fortune* magazine in July praising Thailand's support for the United States. Donovan identified himself in the article as a former ambassador to Thailand but failed to note his present capacity as a highly paid lobbyist for the Thai government.[46]

In the end, all the hard work paid off, and, although the final figure fell short of the $50 million to $60 million Peurifoy had originally proposed, Congress appropriated Thailand and Taiwan together a special supplement in late July of $12.2 million. Remarkably, Congress granted the supplement despite cutting Eisenhower's worldwide foreign assistance request by $258 million.[47]

PHAO'S POWER GRAB

Although American policy toward Thailand remained overwhelmingly favorable, the internal factors inducing Phibun to democratize and open up to China—Phao's ambition and U.S. support for Phao—intensified that summer. After months of increasing tensions among the triumvirate and press reports in May of army-police rivalry, Phao decided in June to make his move.[48] This time, he turned to the United States for help. On the evening of June 17, Phao arranged, "at his urgent request," in Peurifoy's words, a private meeting at the embassy. During their talk, Phao warned Peurifoy that a coup against Sarit was imminent. Junior officers "trained in [the] United States," Phao claimed, believed that JUSMAG [Joint U.S. Military Assistance Advisory Group, the new name for MAAG] wanted Sarit replaced, and Phao described his brother-in-law, Col. Chatchai Chunhawan of the tank corps, as especially eager to oust the supposedly ineffective army leader.[49] Chatchai's tanks at one point faced Sarit's forces in a tense showdown.[50] While disclaiming any intention of initiating a conflict, Phao asserted that he would have to intervene, along with the navy and air force, if fighting erupted between his brother-in-law and Sarit. Implicitly, Phao was asking for Peurifoy's approval for him to eliminate Sarit.[51]

But Peurifoy rebuffed Phao. He neither believed Phao's claims about widespread dissatisfaction in the army, nor did he want a repeat of the Manhattan Rebellion. He worried that armed conflict in SEATO's anchor would weaken the alliance. Most of all, Peurifoy had no desire to see Phao replace Phibun as national leader. Although Phibun had initially suspected Peurifoy's intentions, by that summer, the ambassador had actually emerged as a Phibun supporter. Justin O'Donnell, who had served briefly as CIA station chief in early 1955, may have helped turn Peurifoy against Phao. The CIA removed O'Donnell in the spring of 1955 because of Phao's unhappiness with his blunt criticism of Phao's corruption and involvement in the opium trade.[52] In any case, the plan to eliminate Sarit, Phibun's main counterweight to Phao, clearly threatened Phibun as much as Sarit. Significantly, Phao claimed that the junior officers would act no later than June 21, the day before Phibun's scheduled return from abroad. Peurifoy, therefore, told Phao unambiguously that the United States would strongly oppose his scheme. "I made it perfectly clear to Phao," Peurifoy recounted, that "JUSMAG is not (repeat not) encouraging any movement against Sarit and that [the] United States is actively supporting [the] Thailand Government [i.e., Phibun]."[53] Taken aback, Phao dropped his coup plans.

Phibun responded to this latest plot by starting his democratization campaign in earnest.[54] On June 22, at the Bangkok airport on his return from abroad, Phibun pledged to newsmen that he would start giving regular press conferences.[55] A week later, at his first press conference, he promised to run for an assembly seat in the 1957 elections.[56] A week after that, he instructed cabinet members to end all involvement in business.[57] Then, in the next two weeks, he announced that the government had approved establishment of political parties and, in a speech before newly commissioned naval officers, condemned coups and military involvement in commerce.[58] Phao, dependent on the use of force in politics, the parliamentary monopoly of his Legislative Study Committee, and corrupt business activities, could not but have viewed these initiatives with alarm. Obviously, Phibun planned to undercut entirely the economic, political, and legislative basis of his power.

As before, Phao reached out to the Americans for help. Soon after Peurifoy rebuffed his coup proposal, Phao returned to the embassy complaining about Wan's recent overtures to the Chinese and claiming that Phibun had rejected Zhou's invitation to Wan to visit China only because Phao had urged it. Although directly criticizing only Wan, clearly, Phao was trying here to impugn Phibun's intentions and show his own loyalty to the United States.[59] Then, on the evening of July 13—several days after Phibun publicly called on cabinet members to resign their military positions[60]—Phao visited Peurifoy a third time. "Jovial" but "not . . . joking," as Peurifoy put it, Phao proposed that he and the United States combine to "start a revolution." Thailand, Phao claimed, "should become a full democracy." To that end, he continued in typical fashion, the police planned to overthrow Phibun very soon in a military coup. Peurifoy, again, however, deflated Phao's hopes, this time expressing himself even more bluntly than before. "Emphatically," Peurifoy cabled Washington, he informed Phao that "my recent advice to him, with reference to the possibility of [a] coup within the Army and its serious implications, held good in this instance." Peurifoy added that he "frankly did not think he [Phao] was now qualified for the job" of prime minister.[61] Clearly, Phao would get no help from this quarter.

But Washington was another story. Although it had won aid packages benefiting the entire military regime, the Thai Lobby was Phao's personal domain. Allen Dulles, the CIA, Donovan, Helliwell, and the senators and congressmen supporting Thai aid requests had all worked exclusively through Phao or more closely with Phao than with Phibun, and, in both the November 1954 and July 1955 aid supplements, Phao, not Phibun, had mobilized Thailand's supporters in the United States. Such connections had already benefited Phao politically. Around the beginning of 1955, Donovan urged the Defense Department to "expand the overt and covert capacities of Phao's forces as rapidly as possible."[62] While Phao's star was thus ever rising in Washington, Phibun's fortunes were dropping. Despite Wan's performance as front man in the opening to China, the State Department concluded that his statements represented Phibun's policy. According to the new Thai desk chief, Rockwood Foster, "Wan's previous devious history, his uncanny facility for sensing the domestic political winds, and his incredible ability to survive for almost twenty years under varying Thai foreign policies" all indicated clearly that he was acting with Phibun's consent.[63] After Peurifoy's first rejection of Phao's coup plot, therefore, Phao made plans for an August trip to the United States, possibly to take his case directly to his boosters in Washington. Phao claimed that he was making the trip to finalize a Bank of America loan for the government, but Peurifoy believed that he had more political aims in mind. "Phao's real interest in visiting [the] United States," Peurifoy opined, "is to consult his counsel [Donovan] and friends he has recently made on Capital [sic] Hill."[64] Indicative of Phao's popularity in Congress, when he finally made the trip, Senator Dirksen traveled one hundred eighty miles to meet him.[65]

As a result, Washington did not enthusiastically endorse Peurifoy's rejection of Phao's second coup proposal. While informing Peurifoy that officials would "give [a] euphemistic answer in support [of] your position should Phao raise [the] matter" of Phibun's overthrow when in Washington in August, the State Department reply to Peurifoy's most recent dispatch claimed that the "ouster [of] Phibun [would be] detrimental [*at*] *this time*" (emphasis added).[66] In a second telegram sent two weeks later at the end of July, the State Department explained to Peurifoy that, although Washington would discourage Phao from overthrowing Phibun, the United States would have to accept, at some point, Phao's acquisition of complete power. Repeating almost word for word the police chief's specious and self-serving claims, the cable asserted that Phao needed to "seek justice from Phibun for junior Army officers" and that the "eventual disposition [of] Sarit and devolution [of the] Prime Ministership to Phao from Phibun will remain causes [of] political instability until resolved." The United States must, the dispatch advised, "be prepared [to] accommodate its policy to realities [of] Thai internal politics over which we can exert only marginal influence."[67]

Peurifoy rejected any such acquiescence to Phao's plans. Although it is impossible to say for certain whether the State Department intended its messages merely to prepare Peurifoy psychologically for what it considered inevitable or to hint that it would give Phao the go-ahead for a coup, Peurifoy clearly believed the worst of Washington. If the sentence on accommodating U.S. policy to Thai political realities, he firmly responded to the second telegram, "should properly be construed [to] mean [that the] U.S. [is] unwilling [to] embarrass its relations with Phao by counselling him against [the] use of force, I respectfully disagree and request [to] be so advised."[68] Having seen firsthand in Guatemala American coup-makers' modus operandi, Peurifoy knew when Washington was planning to overthrow a foreign government. This case had all the markings.

Whatever plans Washington had, however, Phibun gave it no chance to implement them. Aware of Phao's plotting, Phibun moved, as soon as the chance arose, to eliminate the threat Phao posed.[69] On August 2, just as Phao was departing for England and the United States, Phibun announced the beginning of a sweeping cabinet reshuffle aimed at Phao. That day, he replaced Phao's brother-in-law, Praman Adireksan, with a Sarit supporter, Sawai Sawaisaenyakorn, as deputy minister of communications, brought in a Sarit underling, Thanom Kittikachorn, as deputy minister of cooperatives, and assumed for himself the interior portfolio. On August 5, Phibun ousted Phao's father-in-law, Phin, from the deputy minister of defense's office and took from

Phao himself the deputy minister of finance portfolio. In the days immediately before and after the cabinet reshuffle, Phibun also issued a flurry of announcements and decrees aimed at the roots of the Phao political empire. He ordered suppression of the opium traffic, instructed the police to sever all business connections, stepped up his campaign to reshape Phao's parliamentary caucus, the Legislative Study Committee, into a pro-Phibun party, and removed Chatchai from command of the Bangkok area-based Second Cavalry regiment.[70] Later, Phibun declared that only the prime minister could order a police or army alert and announced that he might place the police's armored division under the army.[71] To foster free speech and further liberalize the political system, Phibun transferred Phao's authority to censor newspapers to the governor of Bangkok and initiated a public forum modeled on England's Hyde Park speakers' corner.[72]

All of this severely weakened Phao. His ouster from the Ministry of Finance deprived him of management of the lucrative gold trade, Phibun's assumption of the interior portfolio took effective control over that crucial ministry from him, and the removal of Praman and Phin from the Defense and Communications ministries reduced his influence in the cabinet. The assault on monopolies hit the economic lifeline of Phao's political machine, and the moves to liberalize the regime and reform the Legislative Study Committee threatened Phao with defeat in Parliament and future elections. Phibun's August initiatives dealt Phao a setback that he never entirely overcame. His reaction, while in England, to news of Phibun's cabinet reshuffle demonstrated the gravity of the situation facing him. During negotiations over teak sales in London on August 5—the day Phibun demoted him and Phin —Phao found it impossible to keep his attention on lumber. A British official reporting on the meeting noted that Phao was "much preoccupied with a telegram he had just received. General Phao was very *distrait* during the interview, so much so that at one point he trailed off, took the telegram out of his pocket again, and re-read it."[73]

Phao's setbacks did not disenchant those American officials still favoring some degree of democratic rule in Thailand. Although senior officials in Washington appear to have sided with Phao, the embassy and lower and middle-ranking State Department officials welcomed Phibun's democratic reforms and Phao's demotion. Robert Magill, the embassy's chief political officer, believed that Phibun's moves greatly benefited Thailand and U.S. interests. Describing the field marshal's initiatives as having "rectified the balance of political forces and given promise of certain needed political and economic reforms," Magill opined that Phibun had the "sincere desire to bring about some genuine, albeit gradual, political and economic progress in Thailand." The aging Phibun, Magill speculated, wanted to top off his long political career with "good deeds so as to make a favorable mark in his country's history."[74] Similarly, Chargé d'Affaires and Acting Chief of Mission Norbert Anschuetz praised Phibun effusively. "He [Anschuetz] thinks," Office of Philippine and Southeast Asian Affairs Director Kenneth Young said, "that there is no one in Thailand equal to Phibun in statesmanship and deftness. He also informs me there seems to be an almost universal general satisfaction at Phao's reversal." Young effusively commended Anschuetz' "outstanding ability," thus indicating his likely agreement with the chargé's evaluation.[75]

Because Phibun still considered the United States a threat, however, such initially optimistic assessments of the democratic reforms and political offensive against Phao proved premature. Phibun was well aware—and afraid—of Phao's clout in Washington and the Bangkok Sea Supply offices. The recent opening to China, Phibun also feared, had turned Washington against him. Within a week of his demotion of Phao, Phibun lost his only powerful friend on the American side, Ambassador Peurifoy. On August 12, while Peurifoy was driving his two sons back from a paratrooper display at the PARU camp, a truck ran into his robin's-egg-blue Thunderbird, killing Peurifoy and his son, Daniel.[76] Although the circumstances of the accident indicated no foul play, the Phibun camp, having seen the handiwork of Phao's hired killers time and again in the past, immediately assumed police involvement.[77] Apparently, the CIA also had its worries at first. Phao, in describing to Phibun his trip to the United States in the days following Peurifoy's death, related with undisguised relief that a CIA report had concluded that Peurifoy's death was accidental. "Initially, regarding the death of Ambassador Peurifoy," Phao wrote, "some [in Washington] were suspicious. . . . [But] the report signed by Police Major Jack Shirley and Mr. McCaffery [both CIA workers] from the Hua Hin PARU unit dispelled the uncertainty and doubts of CIA officials. Now matters have unfolded neatly."[78] At the same time, showing how much the field marshal worried over the Americans' reaction to the recent foreign-policy shift, Phao reassured Phibun about U.S. intentions. "Regarding Thai policies toward the United States," Phao reported, "no one [in Washington] distrusts you." "Everyone," Phao concluded, "wants you to remain in charge."[79] Clearly, Phibun was feeling highly vulnerable. And Phao knew it.

Phibun was probably concerned here not only over his personal political position. The United States, that August, had begun low-level negotiations with China in Geneva on the return of U.S. airmen captured during the Korean War. Although Dulles insisted that the United States would talk only about prisoners of war, the Western press speculated at length about the possibility of a normalization of relations.[80] This development probably added to any fears Phibun already harbored that the United States would leave Thailand holding to a strong anti-PRC policy alone.

Phibun, therefore, rounded out his democratization and political offensive against Phao with new moves to distance Thailand from the United States. Publicly, he hinted at a change in policy in statements to the press in July and August. At the opening of a SEATO session in early July, Phibun discounted reports of a threat from the Thai Autonomous Zone in Yunnan and promised to do nothing that could be construed as "a challenge to the Communists."[81] The next month, he told Parliament that the government would have to alter its stance toward China if the U.N. changed its own position.[82] At a reception at the Indonesian embassy, he told reporters that Thailand would recognize Beijing if the U.N. admitted the PRC.[83] Although such responses appear at first glance unexceptional in light of the momentary belief that American recognition of China was possible, they broke sharply with Phibun's previous attitude toward the PRC. All prior statements on the subject since 1950 declared that Thailand would withhold establishment of relations no matter what the Western stance.[84]

Phibun's new policy on freedom of expression also detached him from the American alliance—and showed how he was using democratization to do so. Although the transfer of censorship authority from Phao to the governor of Bangkok would have been sufficient to liberalize the political atmosphere and encourage criticism of the hated Phao, Phibun did not stop there. He also lifted the ban on criticism of Thailand's foreign relations—just two months after Phao had renewed it.[85] As Phibun certainly expected, an outpouring of neutralist articles in leftist newspapers such as *Phim Thai* and *Sayam Nikorn* and much of the Chinese press immediately followed. Although he easily could have maintained restrictions on national security grounds, Phibun chose instead the policy that he knew would antagonize the United States but possibly score points with Beijing, leftists, and neutralists. Meanwhile, speakers at Phibun's new Hyde Park also began criticizing the United States. Since it was well-known that Phibun had hired some of the speakers, such as Phi Bunnag and Thongyu Phutpat, to denounce Phao, it is quite possible that he had also ordered the attacks on the United States.[86]

Particularly worrisome from the U.S. standpoint was Phibun's assault on American programs associated with Phao. When he ousted Phao from the Finance Ministry, Phibun also announced his intention to transfer the CIA-sponsored Volunteer Defense Corps from Phao's Interior Ministry to the Defense Ministry, long headed by Phibun.[87] Later reports claimed that Phibun had instructed all VDC members to turn in their weapons, and journalists speculated that Phibun was considering removing PARU from Phao's control.[88] While Phibun ended up unable to follow through with these initiatives, they must have frightened Washington. Unfortunately, all the State Department documents dealing with the matter, because of its connection with the CIA, have been withheld from the public.

Most ominously, Phibun's democratization campaign sparked a competition between himself and Phao for the affections of neutralists, local Chinese, and the PRC. Already by early July, Phao had begun, in response to Phibun's political challenge, wooing the Chinese community with proposals to reduce the alien registration fee and allow Chinese secondary schools to open.[89] In the first week of September, soon after his return from the United States, Phao moved to distance himself publicly from the Americans. In two meetings at the embassy, Phao told Anschuetz that, although the police would continue cooperating closely with the United States, he would take a less conspicuous role. He now considered it, Phao told Anschuetz, "inadvisable for him [Phao] [to] receive as many prominent foreign visitors as in past."[90] The reason, Phao explained, was "that he [Phao] is frequently charged with having sold Thailand to [the] Americans."[91] The U.S. connection, Phao now realized, could hurt, as well as help, him. A PRC connection, he also saw, could benefit him greatly. At about the same time as his talks with Anschuetz, Phao's ethnic Chinese financial manager, Luen Buasuwan, began making contacts with Beijing.[92] Like Phibun, Phao hoped here to win points with leftists, Chinese, and neutralists. He feared that, were Phibun to establish relations with the PRC before he could distance himself publicly from the United States, he would suffer politically.

But Phibun was not to be topped in the competition for leftist and neutralist support. After assuming the interior portfolio, he took from Phao responsibility for Chinese affairs.[93] In October, he announced that the government would release the following year the thirty-seven political prisoners convicted after the 1952 crackdown.[94] Just as he had competed with Pridi in sending secret missions to China during the war, Phibun, upon learning of Luen's communications with the PRC on behalf of Phao, ordered his own ethnic Chinese confidant, Sang Phat-thanothai, to contact Beijing.[95] At the same time, cheap Chinese goods and propaganda materials began pouring into the country, almost certainly with official connivance.[96] Instead of producing a friendlier government for the United States, therefore, Phibun's democratization was freeing anti-American leftists and leading Thai foreign policy astray from the straight and narrow path of U.S.-sponsored anticommunism.

TRIUMVIRATE POLITICS AND NEUTRALISM

Toward the end of the year, matters worsened between Phao and Phibun —and for the United States. By mid-October, reports of Phibun's plans to transfer PARU from the police to the army had appeared often enough and with sufficient credibility that Anschuetz called on Phibun to warn him off the move.[97] Phibun heeded Anschuetz' protest, but conflicts within the triumvirate—and the threat to the United States— only increased. Phibun's newspapers, "Hyde Park" speakers he hired, and now Sarit's popular newspaper, *San Seri,* attacked Phao mercilessly, and, in late November and early December, tensions nearly boiled over. Reports of clashes between the army and police appeared, and Sarit publicly accused the police of having unjustly arrested soldiers.[98] The *New York Times* claimed on November 23 that Phibun planned to oust Phao.[99] A week later, Phibun moved to take control of all CIA assistance to the police from Phao. In a letter to the Foreign Ministry, Phibun proposed establishing a committee of navy, army, air force, and police representatives chaired by a Foreign Ministry official to manage Sea Supply's police assistance programs.[100] Clearly, he hoped to end Phao's special relationship with the CIA. But Anschuetz, aware that the field marshal was planning some sort of action, again called on Phibun on December 1 and warned him in some of the strongest language yet used with the Thais not to eliminate Phao. "Although I recognized [that] this [is an] internal affair," Anschuetz explained, "I wanted him [Phibun] [to] know [that the] west and [the United States are] ready [to] use such influence as we might command [to] resolve [the] current situation."[101] Phibun, in response, called Phao and Sarit together to ease tensions.[102] The Foreign Ministry, wanting to avoid any political struggle, refused to head the CIA assistance oversight committee Phibun had proposed.[103] Instead, police officers took five of the twelve spots on the committee and the chairman's slot, and Phao retained, in the end, effective control of the Sea Supply programs.[104] Only Anschuetz' timely démarches and Foreign Ministry foot-dragging, therefore, spared PARU a disruptive transfer and saved the CIA covert military assistance programs from a body designed to dismember them.

As Phao and Phibun struggled over control of the CIA police aid, they also, oddly enough, began coordinating their contacts with China. Although they started by competing for Chinese attentions, circumstances compelled them to work together. Only with police acquiescence could Phibun's representatives travel to China without harassment, and Phao had found that PRC officials refused to meet his financial adviser, Luen Buasuwan, to avoid offending Phibun.[105] To get a piece of the China action, Phao then realized, he would have to join hands with Phibun. Phibun's and Phao's confidants, Sang Phatthanothai and Luen, added to the pressures on the two rivals to unite forces. Both ethnic Chinese, Sang and Luen were close friends. When Luen later died, the court appointed Sang executor of his will.[106] From the beginning, the two urged Phibun and Phao to make contacts with the PRC, and their friendship helped ensure that the field marshal and police chief acted in unison. Ironically, therefore, an initiative Phibun had begun partly as an attack on Phao became, at this time of extreme political tension, a joint Phao-Phibun policy.

With Phibun and Phao now cooperating, the opening to Beijing finally got off the ground. In November, the two camps agreed on the composition of a jointly controlled secret mission to Beijing and decided to discuss normalization of relations. Luen, it was determined, would obtain the necessary travel documents and fund the expedition, while Sang enlisted his friend, Ari Phirom, as head of the mission. Ari, owner of a procommunist Chinese school who was briefly jailed in 1952 and 1954, had several important contacts on the mainland. Along with a leftist reporter for Sang's newspaper, Karuna Kusalasai, Ari went on Phibun's behalf, while Phao and Luen arranged for two northeastern MPs they had for some time financed, Amphorn Suwannabon and Saing Marangkun, to represent the Phao camp. Ari and Karuna left Thailand for China ahead of the others in the first week of December 1955.[107]

Ari's mission was a smashing success. Unable to notify anyone in China in advance, Ari and the other representatives experienced some adventures in making their way first to Guangzhou (Canton) from Hong Kong and then getting official permission and help in traveling to Beijing, but, once in the capital, they met with a rousing reception.

Senior officials of the Chinese Foreign Ministry greeted them soon after their arrival. After telling the officials over the course of several meetings the background and objectives of their visit, the representatives met with Mao and Zhou themselves for an hour and forty-five minutes. Urging Thailand to adopt a neutralist foreign policy, the two communist leaders assured Ari and his colleagues that China harbored no aggressive intentions toward Thailand and explained the benefits of trading with the PRC. Mao hinted that terms of any commerce would be favorable to Thailand and offered technical assistance as a sweetener. Trade between the two countries, Mao explained, would not require formal relations.[108] The next day, Zhou gave a dinner for the delegation, and, after two exhilarating weeks in China, Ari led the mission on a circuitous route back to Bangkok. Luen feted them at the Phao-Phin compound on their return.[109]

Ari's mission led immediately to an even more important encounter with the Chinese. While in Beijing, Ari told the Chinese Foreign Ministry that Sang and Luen would accompany Phibun on an official trip to Burma scheduled for several days later. Phibun, Ari explained, wanted the two secretly to meet Chinese officials there. After Phibun's arrival in Rangoon, the PRC embassy tracked down Sang and Luen—traveling incognito—and, in two days of meetings on December 16 and 17, Sang and Luen, in close consultation with Phibun, conducted substantive talks with the Chinese.[110] The Chinese repeated Mao's assurances and commercial proposals, and, on the second day, Luen and Sang signed a memorandum of understanding with the Chinese pledging Thailand and the PRC to establish formal relations. "The two countries," the statement declared, "are willing to adopt, timely and gradually, suitable measures to increase mutual exchange and establish contacts in the spheres of trade and culture in order to normalize their relations in the long run."[111]

As the phrase pledging the Thais to normalize relations "in the long run" implied, Phibun did not envision drastic changes for the near future. Outwardly, he remained staunchly pro-United States, and, on his return to Bangkok, he publicly ruled out all dealings with Communists. "There is no way," he declared at the airport, "to establish friendly relations or an understanding with communist countries." "How can it be possible," he asked rhetorically, "when Communists intend to take over the world?"[112] Phibun moved slowly to avoid frightening the Americans.

Despite his caution, however, Phibun appears to have genuinely intended, at this point, to fully normalize relations with China, and

Luen, Sang, and Phao, in coordination with Ari in Beijing, arranged an additional visit to China. This time, none other than Thep Chotinuchit, the former nemesis of the Coup Group and the United States, acted as the government's representative. Funded by Luen, Thep, along with several leftist MPs, including Khlaew Norapati and Thim Phuriphat, and a journalist from Sang's newspaper, traveled to Beijing in January and, like Ari, met Mao and Zhou.[113] Mao told Thep nothing new, but, significantly, Thep, unlike his predecessors, went openly. Although he never disclosed Phao's role, Thep announced publicly in December the Chinese invitation to visit, and his delegation received massive press coverage on both its departure and its return.[114] When back in Bangkok, the delegation described in detail to reporters its talks with Mao and Zhou. Performing the political theater for which Thais were famous,[115] Phao and other officials publicly warned Thep in advance that the trip was illegal, and Phibun made a show in the cabinet of supposedly trying to confiscate Thep's passport, but the delegation left unhindered.[116] Although Phao jailed the delegation members on their return for the benefit of the Americans, he released them several months later on the excuse that they needed to campaign for the upcoming elections.[117] Likewise, when Amphorn and Sa-ing went public with their own visit, either on orders from Phao or to steal for themselves some of the favorable attention Thep had attracted, the police detained them only briefly.[118] Interestingly, Amphorn and Sa-ing, whether to protect Phao and Phibun or to make themselves appear, like Thep, independent of the government, omitted any mention of the other members of the mission or Phao's and Phibun's support for the trip.[119]

Again, the parallels of this later opening to China with the secret wartime contacts with the Allies are striking. In 1944, four Free Thais the British had airdropped into the country fell into police hands, but, since it then wanted to improve Thailand's image with the Allies, the government made no real effort to punish them. Before the Japanese representative came to interrogate the prisoners, the police coached them, while, to portray the government as tough, jailers also temporarily chained the four.[120] Phao and Phibun, likewise, did not want to arrest Thep, but, just as the government in 1944 had performed a charade for the Japanese, they had to maintain for the United States a facade of official disapproval of contacts with Beijing. Phao and Phibun easily could have stopped Thep. They simply chose not to.

Phibun's democratic reforms had made such charades possible. Phibun could justify to the United States public visits like the Thep mission only by dissociating himself completely from them. With the restrictions on civil liberties of the 1952–1954 period, no one would have believed that private delegations to the PRC lacked official sanction, but, in the wake of his democratic reforms, Phibun could plausibly claim that he lacked the authority to stop unofficial visits. The promotion of open visits by nongovernmental figures, therefore, would later emerge as one of the government's favorite forms of contact with Beijing.

As if all of this was not bad enough for the United States, matters only worsened in December 1955 with the appointment of Max Bishop as Peurifoy's replacement. Bishop gained the Bangkok posting, his first—and last—ambassadorial position, because of his friendship with Under Secretary of State Herbert Hoover, Jr. That dubious asset aside, Bishop brought few qualifications to the job. Loud, blunt, and critical, Bishop refused to adopt the soft-spoken, subtle style of communication valued in Thai society. His abrasiveness and bull-in-a-china-shop diplomatic approach quickly made him enemies in the Thai press. While experienced in Japanese and Northeast Asian affairs, he had had limited involvement with Southeast Asia or Thailand. Though a career Foreign Service officer, he immediately provoked the enmity of almost every American diplomat then working in Bangkok. In Washington, his intimacy with conservative congressional heavyweights had boosted his State Department career, but, in Bangkok, half a world away from the Senate Foreign Relations Committee room, his ridiculous boasts of controlling Congress and past association with Sen. Joseph R. McCarthy only made him seem a traitor to the profession. His authoritarian management style and habit of upbraiding his staff in public alienated his subordinates. "I don't think you'll find many people," one former aide has diplomatically put it, "who were charmed by Max Bishop." Another simply called Bishop "a shit."[121]

Bishop discovered early how troubled relations between the United States and Thailand had become. In mid-February 1956, after Donovan arrived on an unofficial trip to Bangkok, Phibun called Bishop to Government House to explain the nature of the visit. Donovan had notified Phao, not Phibun, of his travel plans, and Phibun, it seems, again worried that Donovan and Phao were plotting a coup. Bishop assured him that Donovan had come for purely personal reasons, but Phibun remained suspicious until Donovan left shortly afterward. When Bishop piously commented that the United States "would not under any circumstances tolerate any interference by American officials in the local political scene," Phibun replied—"with a twinkle in his eye,"

Bishop recounted—that "sometime in the past it had not been possible to tell 'which General to deal with.' "[122]

On into 1956, Phibun distanced himself from the United States, and he and Phao intensified their efforts to woo leftists and China. In February, Wan once more publicly mooted the possibility of recognizing Beijing and, in response to a question about trade policy, implied that the government might lift nonstrategic goods from the export embargo list for China.[123] In April, the navy began showing a PRC-produced film at a fund-raising campaign for the navy welfare fund.[124] In May, the government elevated its relations with the Soviet Union to the ambassadorial level.[125] In March, the police allowed three leftist Pridi-ites in exile in China, Chiap Chaisong, Chom Saeng-ngern, and Nongyao Prapasathit Watanakoman, to return to Thailand.[126] For the Americans' benefit, Phao arrested the three on their arrival in April, but, as with the visitors to Beijing, released them quickly.[127] When Chiap later entered a Buddhist temple in Bangkok to live as a monk for three months, the police sent the abbot a letter absolving Chiap of guilt in any crime. Phibun sent Chiap a monastic robe as a present.[128]

Throughout this time, Phibun exploited the press freedoms democratization had created. In December, Sang's previously hardline anticommunist newspaper, *Sathianraphap*, began urging, concurrently with Phibun's initiation of contacts with the Chinese, a more neutral foreign policy.[129] Phibun's English-language organ, the *Tribune*, started criticizing American military aid to Thailand in January as imposing an unjust financial burden.[130] This semiofficial press campaign encouraged independent anticommunist newspapers, such as *Thai Mai, Prachathipatai,* and *Kiattisak,* to join, for the first time, the leftist press in advocating a reassessment of American aid programs. Phibun apparently aimed here not only to send a friendly message to the Chinese, but also to persuade the United States to shift the emphasis of its material assistance from military to economic aid. Military aid, he seems to have decided, strengthened his foes, while economic aid boosted his standing with the public. When Dulles came to Bangkok for the SEATO meeting in March, Phibun asked explicitly for help with a high-profile housing project for the poor. Echoing the essence of the arguments the *Tribune* was then presenting, the cabinet's aide-memoire to Dulles argued that "the heavy impact of her [Thailand's] military expenditure on her national budget" necessitated the assistance.[131] Wan told a press conference afterwards that Thailand received sufficient military aid but wanted economic assistance increased.[132]

In June 1956, democratization again helped Phibun justify to the

Americans a step in his opening to Beijing, the partial lifting of the trade embargo on China. Phibun had wanted, probably since Luen and Sang signed the statement in Rangoon pledging to increase trade with China, to loosen the export embargo Thailand had imposed on the country at American urging in 1951, but the United States resisted any change in Thailand's stance. Bishop announced in his first press conference in March the United States' firm opposition to any trade between Thailand and China.[133] To circumvent this obstacle, Phibun played up the public demands he faced—partially inspired by his own newspapers, of course—to lift the embargo. He told Dulles in March "that there was a great deal of pressure in this country [Thailand] to trade with Communist China," and Phot later told Assistant Secretary of State Robertson that "pressures [from] businessmen and [the] public" were irresistible.[134] In June, after French and British relaxation of their own embargoes strengthened his hand, Phibun had the cabinet exclude rice and timber from the list of forbidden exports. Robertson expressed his "great disappointment" to Phot, and Dulles later did the same, but Phibun answered that "strong public opinion" had forced his hand.[135]

Additional contacts with the Chinese quickly followed. Within two weeks of the cabinet decision to relax the embargo, Phibun sent Ari Phirom back to Beijing, this time with moneymaking in mind and two businessmen in tow—Uthai Tungkhaplin of the government tobacco monopoly and Prasert Siriphiphat of the Phao-associated Bangkok Bank. Once in Beijing, Ari and his companions negotiated what they considered a very good price for the bales of unsold tobacco then accumulating in the tobacco monopoly's warehouses, and a second trip to Guangzhou a month later finalized the deal. Thailand's most important ethnic Chinese banker, Chin Sophonpanich of the Bangkok Bank, completed the transfer of money in London. Proceeds from the sale went directly to the government party's campaign coffers.[136]

The United States floundered in its response to these developments. Back in November and December 1955, Anschuetz, believing that the neutralist trend derived from Thai fears of an American rapprochement with China, warned Phao and Phibun about the dangers of neutralism and had Dulles assure Phibun by letter that the Geneva negotiations would not lead to U.S. recognition of Beijing.[137] Anschuetz later commented—almost at the very moment Ari was toasting Zhou in Beijing—that these moves had "arrested" the neutralist drift.[138] When that assessment proved wrong, Dulles explained to Phibun in person while visiting Bangkok in March 1956 that the U.S. hardline policy toward China would remain in force. As confident then as An-schuetz had been in December, Dulles proudly reported to Eisenhower that he had settled matters once and for all. "I think now," Dulles wrote the president, "[that] our relationship has been satisfactorily firmed up and that we can continue to count on the Thais so long as they think they can count on us."[139] That same month, Bishop issued his strongly worded public warning against relaxing the embargo also certain that he had ended all Thai consideration of trading with the PRC. Bishop could not have been more mistaken, and, instead of stiffening Phibun's anticommunist resolve, the warning provoked charges of American interference in Thai politics.

Bishop, indeed, raised all sorts of problems for the United States in 1956. Browbeating his subordinates, lecturing the State Department on its foreign-policy failings, and treating SEATO as his private fief, Bishop had within several months of his arrival in Thailand offended nearly every person of importance in the country. At a reception given by the British ambassador, he publicly insulted the widow of the publisher of the *Chicago Tribune*.[140] Word got around, and, within months, *Time* magazine had devoted an entire article to Bishop's failure as an ambas-sador. Describing him as "a truculent, table-pounding career diplomat, who in seven brief months has alienated many responsible Thais, demoralized his own staff and created ill will at SEATO council meet-ings," *Time*, somewhat unfairly, blamed Bishop for Thailand's "drifting to the left."[141] Later, he endured further public humiliation. Aspects of his character appeared in 1958 in the unflattering portrait of the fic-tional American ambassador, "Lucky" Louis Sears, in the best-selling novel, *The Ugly American*. Like Bishop, Ambassador Sears had problems with the press.[142]

In fact, one of Bishop's shortcomings, his excessive reliance on Phibun, may have helped reduce the field marshal's suspicion of the United States. Despite his McCarthyite sympathies, Bishop believed strongly that the United States should uphold constitutional govern-ment in Thailand. For him, that meant that the embassy should shun opposition figures or anyone other than the constitutional head of gov-ernment—Phibun—and the head of government's official representa-tives in the Foreign Ministry.[143] Such restrictions and Bishop's habit of believing implicitly whatever Phibun told him continually frustrated embassy staff, but Bishop's partiality probably restored much of Phibun's trust in the United States. Reportedly, the field marshal referred to Bishop as "my ambassador."[144] The United States, now that Phao was weakened and Bishop was supporting Phibun, probably no longer appeared so menacing.

THE FEBRUARY 1957 ELECTIONS

While Phibun may have perceived less danger of an American-sponsored coup after Bishop's arrival, the electoral political struggle his democratization campaign had provoked pushed him and the government further toward neutralism. By the second half of 1956, the February 1957 elections were only half a year away, and the country's various political forces were engaged in a wild scramble for electoral advantage. Phibun's democratization had revived the Democrats, and a number of new leftist parties began contesting for popularity. Although Phibun, Phao, and Sarit all nominally supported the government party, now called the Seri Manangkhasila Party, their public expressions of unity barely masked an intense political competition among them. Each financed his own party in addition to the government party, and the struggle for control of MPs and candidates within the Seri Manangkhasila grouping grew fierce. Unfortunately for the United States, the three leaders aimed most of their appeals at neutralist-minded leftists.

The leftist politicians of this period in no way resembled the Communists and procommunist intellectuals arrested in the 1952 crackdown. Of the four parties grouped under the so-called Socialist United Front, one, the Social Democrat Party, promoted a sketchily described socialism free of class theory or Marxism, and another, the Hyde Park Party, taking its name from Phibun's Thai-style speakers' corner, had no real organization or program despite being led by former Peace Committee member Phethai Chotinuchit. Thep's Economist Party, the largest of the coalition, also advocated a socialism showing no signs of Marxist influence. Only the tiny Socialist Party spoke of radical economic and social change. Just as avowedly communist MP Prasert Sapsunthorn's ignorance of Marxist theory had prompted the ridicule of the 1948 U.S. regional ambassadors' conference, so these later leftist politicians took only a casual interest in political ideology. Their ideas and platforms were muddled, self-contradictory, and, at times, enigmatic. Although most praised Beijing and criticized U.S. "imperialism," their admiration for the PRC derived more from a vague attraction for something new and seemingly dynamic than a plan to transplant the communist system to Thailand. Some may have cooperated with local Communists, but, if so, a desire for political support from wherever they could get it rather than close ideological affinity motivated them.[145] These politicians are best classified as leftists to distinguish them from centrist neutralists such as the northern MP, Sukit Nimmanahaeminda (Nimanhemin),[146] but most were moderate, not radical, leftists. So uncertain were the leftist parties' platforms that a visiting representative of the Asian Socialist Conference in 1956 could not decide if they were "true socialists."[147] They posed no threat to the country's social and economic order.

The triumvirate focused its political efforts on these leftists precisely because they were so harmless. Now that the United States had pledged itself to defend Thailand with SEATO, the Democrats, the Americans' favorites, had come out in favor of a strong pro-U.S. policy, but the party was too big and, with its backbone of social elites, too cohesive, by Thai standards, for Phibun, Phao, and Sarit to manipulate. Instead, the three directed their appeals toward the more inviting leftists. Rather than a strong commitment to a dangerous ideology, the most notable features of the leftist politicians of the period were their opportunism and willingness to be co-opted. They lacked clear policy agendas, and in some cases, integrity. Acceptance of funding and political positions from the government, as with Thep's receipt of money from Phao, came naturally to many. Even those with clear and strongly held beliefs readily lent their backing to government leaders willing to accommodate leftist aims. Karuna Kusalasai, one of Phibun's delegates on the Ari mission to Beijing, was typical in his ability to regard himself both as a principled leftist and a Phibun supporter.[148] In the lead-up to the elections in the last half of 1956 and early 1957, therefore, Sarit, Phibun, and Phao intensified their efforts to woo leftist politicians. When working together, they tried to win leftist support for the government party as a whole. When working against each other, they attempted to attract leftists to their individual political camps.

Because of his cool relations with the Americans, Sarit was, in some ways, the most forward in campaigning for leftist support. While Bird, Donovan, and CIA agents worked and socialized intimately with Phao throughout the first half of the decade, few American officials befriended Sarit. In comparison to the self-controlled but energetic and outgoing Phao, the dour and apparently dissolute Sarit held little personal appeal. A legendary womanizer and hardened alcoholic, Sarit was already drinking himself to the cirrhosis of the liver that would kill him in 1963. His behavior at a reception Phibun gave in December 1954 for JCS Chairman Radford offended the Americans. "Gen. Sarit," an American observer said of the occasion, "became grossly drunk as he has habitually at most social events since last Aug[ust]. Adm. Radford was shocked and disgusted."[149] Many Americans displayed their dislike of Sarit openly. Citing the failure of embassy personnel to greet him on his return from the United States in July 1954 as an example of American neglect of the army commander, the private researcher commis-

sioned that year to study American aid programs strongly urged the
United States to improve its relations with Sarit.[150] Instead of reaching
out to him, however, Bishop, refusing to deal with anyone other than
Phibun, shunned Sarit. Phao, now working closely with a new CIA station chief, John Hart, suffered little from Bishop's aloofness, but Sarit,
in contact only with the relatively powerless JUSMAG, seems to have
taken Bishop's policy as an insult.

Possibly out of spite, and certainly with leftist politicians and journalists in mind, Sarit mounted in the second half of 1956 a scathing
public relations campaign against the United States. In keeping with
his reserved habits, he said little in public that the United States
objected to, but his popular newspaper, *San Seri,* adopted what independent observers considered the most anti-American and openly pro-
Beijing stance of any publication in the country.[151] *San Seri*'s sensation-
alist treatment of a brawl in September between Thais and American
GIs contrasted sharply with other publications' subdued coverage.[152]
Bishop, in response to the newspaper's criticism of the GIs, told the
deputy foreign minister, Rak Panyarachun, that the United States
might cancel a scheduled visit of U.S. troops to Thailand if the *San Seri*
attacks continued. "Unless prompt remedial measures were taken,"
Bishop informed Rak, the embassy "might feel impelled [to] recommend strongly against allowing these visits."[153] Although Phao agreed
to bury the case brought against the servicemen in exchange for a crate
of American whiskey, *San Seri* kept the brawl in headlines for a week
after Bishop's meeting with Rak.[154] Even then, the newspaper dropped
the issue only because of a new outrage—the movie version of the hit
Broadway play, *The King and I.* For several days, *San Seri* published front-
page photographs of Yul Brynner as Thailand's nineteenth-century
King Mongkut in various supposedly insulting poses.[155]

Phibun and Phao worked hard to match Sarit in the competition
for leftist political support. In August, the two got Phethai Chotinuchit,
the former Peace Committee member now heading the Hyde Park
Party, to join the Seri Manangkhasila Party.[156] Then, in November, Phao
renewed his efforts to make peace with Pridi. That month, he persuaded Chaem Promyong, a Muslim Pridi associate, to join Seri Manangkhasila and announced that Pridi could return to Thailand. Chaem
explained publicly that he had joined the party to help bring Pridi into
the government.[157] Throughout the latter half of 1956, Phao wooed
Chinese leftists. In October, he formed a new government-Chinese relations committee with prominent leftists filling half the Chinese slots.
The next month, he accused Taiwan of having sent a "secret organiza-

tion" "to create unrest in Thailand" and warned local Kuomintang societies that the police would watch them closely to ensure that they did not start a "revolution."[158] Immediately before the election in February 1957, Phao announced that he favored abrogation of the anti-Communist act and commented that "if traders want to do business with Communist China it is their own affair."[159] Particularly arousing Bishop's anger, at the end of 1956, Sang helped organize a strike at the American-owned Standard Oil Company. The strikers demanded that the company buy its crude oil from the Soviet Union.[160]

Phao and Phibun also continued their opening to China. In September, Sang arranged for several Thai monks to visit Beijing, and Phibun soon afterward secretly sent two naval officers there.[161] That same month, the Public Relations Department trumpeted news of a friendly encounter between Phibun's wife, La-iad, and Chinese officials at a Federation of United Nations Associations conference in Geneva.[162] Four days later, Phao announced that a PRC economic mission would stop overnight in Bangkok en route from Rangoon to Phnom Penh. He emphasized the police's role in protecting the important visitors.[163] In November, Phibun got the cabinet to permit Zhou likewise to stop in Bangkok on his way from Phnom Penh to New Delhi.[164] Zhou, for reasons that remain unclear, refused the offer, but Phibun sent another secret trade mission to Beijing in January 1957, again, likely with the aim of raising campaign funds, and, in February, reports appeared that La-iad Phibunsongkhram would herself go to Beijing.[165] La-iad, then chairperson of the World Federation of U.N. Associations, announced in January that she saw no reason why China could not join the group.[166] All the while, moreover, Sang corresponded with Zhou on Phibun's behalf. Phibun urged Zhou in these letters to allow two of Sang's children to study in China.[167] Apparently, as Ari Phirom observed, Phibun borrowed the idea of relative-swapping as a confidence-building measure from the Chinese war stories then popular in Thailand.[168]

All of these disturbing—from the American perspective—developments came in preparation for the February 1957 elections, but the worst was to come with the polls themselves. Leftist parties, though failing to capture any seats in Bangkok, won, by one calculation, twenty of the fifty-three seats up for grabs in the militarily strategic northeast.[169] More important, despite its massive advantage in resources and its efforts to woo the left, the government party suffered an embarrassing defeat. Although Seri Manangkhasila gained a majority of the seats contested, it won far fewer than expected, and the government had to depend on strong-arm tactics to eke out a victory. In Bangkok, where Phibun and eight of his cabinet ministers had run for the nine city seats, Khuang and his Democrat allies pulled ahead of Phibun and several of the cabinet ministers in the initial counts. Only after the government tampered with the ballot boxes did Phibun end up defeating Khuang. Angered by the cheating, student organizations planned massive rallies to protest government tactics. Phibun, in response, declared a state of emergency.[170]

Unfortunately for the United States, while the election results severely weakened Phibun and Phao, Sarit, the most distant, unpredictable, and ostensibly anti-American member of the triumvirate, emerged from the debacle greatly strengthened. Never having maintained a high political profile and always leaving legislative and electoral matters to Phao and Phibun, Sarit escaped public criticism in the days following the elections. Phibun, probably hoping to associate him with the polls and the unpopular emergency measures, charged Sarit with suppressing the demonstrations, but Sarit turned the assignment to his advantage. Instead of ruthlessly squelching the opposition, as he had in the Palace and Manhattan rebellions, he met and talked frankly with student protesters. At Chulalongkorn University, Sarit told students that the elections "were dirty, the dirtiest." "Everybody cheated," he concluded.[171] Sarit thus managed to dissociate himself from the rest of the government and emerged as the hero of the opposition in general and the left in particular. Events had forced Phao, on the other hand, into full-speed political retreat. Phibun told Bishop several weeks after the election that he would probably have to remove Phao from the cabinet.[172]

The United States took some comfort from the lack of any indication in the election results that the Thai public favored neutralism. Despite the leftist parties' focus on Bangkok and the government's concentration of verbal attacks and poll fraud on Khuang, the strongly pro-U.S. Democrats, not leftists, performed best in Bangkok. Even Phethai Chotinuchit, combining a leftist platform with Seri Manangkhasila's resources, lost to the Democrats. Leftists owed their victories in the northeast more to the close personal ties they maintained with their constituents and their antigovernment public stance than their foreign-policy platforms. With no American military presence in the region, leftists' criticism of U.S. imperialism went over the heads of most northeastern peasants.

But among Bangkok students and intellectuals—the most politically active segments of the population at this critical time—the election aftermath told a different story. Because of the United States' close association with Phao and Phibun, students and intellectuals, the social groups most attracted to Sarit, also blamed the Americans for the electoral fraud. On March 2, students marched to Phibun's and Phao's Interior Ministry to protest alleged U.S. interference in the elections and, in May, held an anti-SEATO rally.[173] Even Kukrit Pramoj, the respected and staunchly anticommunist political and social commentator, launched a broadside in his *Sayam Rath* newspaper against U.S. interventionism. Calling Bishop a gangster *(kui)*, Kukrit implied that the ambassador had taught Phao and Phibun how to cheat in elections.[174] Kukrit's attack landed him in jail, and the United States faced additional criticism for allegedly ordering his arrest.[175] All of this so upset the United States that the U.S. Information Service began, for the first time, to survey opinions in Bangkok regarding the United States.[176] To reverse the course of anti-Americanism among students and intellectuals, that spring Washington also shifted the emphasis of its economic assistance and propaganda programs from the rural northeast to Bangkok.[177] Washington now feared that anti-Americanism in the capital would cause the United States to lose everything in Thailand.

Furthermore, rather than ending the competition within the triumvirate for leftist sympathies, the February elections intensified the struggle. Because of the weakness of parties, the periods after elections in Thailand have always seen as much political maneuvering as the run-ups to elections. Leaders compete furiously, with little regard for party or ideology, for the allegiances of members of Parliament, and newly elected MPs shop around for the best deal they can find. In the spring 1957 setting, the deep personal and political differences now dividing Sarit, Phao, and Phibun made the postelection struggle especially heated. Because the competition was so tightly contested, leftists acquired unusual importance.

Instead of sending them back to the Americans' embrace, therefore, the postelection political turmoil encouraged Phibun and Phao to step up their courtship of the left and China. In April, as the government again began allowing the showing of movies from the PRC, this time including unabashed communist propaganda films, three separate private groups—an ethnic Chinese basketball team, a labor delegation, and a cultural troupe—visited Beijing, all with official connivance.[178] The police that month also allowed Pridi's wife, Phunsuk, to return to Thailand from China. Phao, Sarit, and probably Phibun, sources told the U.S. embassy, immediately opened negotiations with her seeking Pridi's political support.[179] Over the summer, the government released the thirty-seven leftist political prisoners from the 1952 crackdown, as Phibun had promised in 1955, in conjunction with the twenty-fifth Buddhist centennial celebration. That same month, Phibun, through Sang, provided thirty thousand *baht* ($1,500) to leftist Thammasat law students printing a commemorative volume for the celebration. The students' final product, consisting mostly of Marxist articles and photographs of the anti-American demonstrations and the recent visits to Beijing, included a progovernment article by Sang and a frontispiece with portraits of university rector Phibun and vice-rector Phao.[180] The head of Phibun's Thammathipat Party, Piam Bunyachot, in the meantime, criticized the United States for, he claimed, supporting Phao in the political struggle. "I am not sure," Piam explained, "what sort of politics the United States is playing."[181]

This latest neutralist shift confused the Americans. At first, policymakers thought that international concerns predominated in Thai thinking and that Phibun planned to establish relations with the PRC. A State Department telegram of May 9 drafted by Young and Bushner and initialed by Robertson speculated that the Thai government was preparing "for [a] possible modus vivendi with Communist China," and Young later commented that the Thais wanted to "have an 'anchor to windward' in case Communist China should achieve greater influence in Asia and the world."[182] Magill, the embassy's chief political officer, agreed. The Thais wanted, he explained, "reasonably profitable and safe relations with Peiping [Beijing]" and "some accommodation to Communist China."[183] But Magill's boss, Bishop, was not so sure. Although Bishop concurred on May 1 that "TG [Thai government] China policy is indeed in [a] preliminary process of change favorable to [the] CHICOMS [Chinese Communists]," two weeks later he claimed that recent gestures toward Beijing and leftists reflected not a determined foreign-policy change but a response to local political developments. The recent visits to Beijing, the Chinese propaganda films, and the semiofficial neutralistic press campaign, Bishop suggested, were "motivated primarily by domestic political considerations and only secondarily by TG desire [to] cast foreign policy anchor to windward."[184] However much Bishop and other policymakers disputed its causes, all on the American side agreed that the latest neutralist trend was dangerous. No one wanted it to continue.

The threat, as the Americans now saw it, was not to Thailand's security. In 1951 and 1952, the Korean War had excited fears that leftist participation in government and leftist press and Peace Committee agitation would open the country to communist attack, but Americans felt no such alarm in 1957. The wars in Korea and Vietnam had ended, Eisenhower and Khrushchev were talking to each other, and China was preaching the five principles of peaceful coexistence. Never at this time did subversion or invasion appear to threaten Thailand. One intelligence report from May 1957 commented that "there is no evidence of increased [Communist Party of Thailand] strength that would endanger the ability of Thai security agencies to maintain the present degree of internal security."[185] No U.S. policymaker ever suggested that the triumvirate would allow leftists to enter the government in large numbers or control important ministries. Even if the leftists were to increase their political influence significantly, American officials no longer greatly feared that they would act as communist fifth columns. Although officials at times referred to leftists as "subversives," the term functioned more as a catch-all label for anyone critical of the United States than as a literal description of leftist motives. An embassy dispatch of early 1956 noted that Thep, "although described as leftist, . . . has never been identified as a Communist. The policies which he now espouses on behalf of his new party are neutralist in the India-Burma style."[186] The United States realized that the majority of leftist politicians of the period had no plan for radical economic, social, or political change.

Rather than because of a perceived threat to Thailand's security, the United States feared the increasing influence of the left and the shift toward neutralism because they endangered American political and diplomatic interests in the country. The easing of the embargo on China weakened American efforts to isolate Beijing, official flirtation with leftists undercut American opposition to the Laotian government's dealings with the communist Pathet Lao, and Thai interest in a rapprochement with China threatened U.S. plans for SEATO. As a May 9 State Department telegram warned, further changes in the direction of neutralism would "undermine our efforts [to] reverse [the] neutralist trend [in] some [of] Thailand's neighbors[,] particularly Laos," and would "likely weaken our attempts [to] strengthen SEATO."[187] In contrast to the 1950–1952 period, U.S. concerns now focused less on communist subversion than on anti-Americanism. The previous September, for example, Bishop had protested *San Seri*'s criticism of the United States in the GI-Thai brawl incident, not the newspaper's praise for the "New China."

Thus recognizing a serious threat to U.S. policy, the Americans made one last desperate attempt that spring to halt Phao's and

Phibun's drift to the left. Dropping all diplomatic niceties, Robertson called Phot to the State Department on May 16 and firmly protested the PRC films, the visits to Beijing, and the continuing anti-American articles in Sarit's and Phibun's mouthpieces.[188] A week later, Bishop issued an identical démarche to Phibun personally in Bangkok.[189] At first, these protests worked wonders, and, four days after Robertson's meeting with Phot, Wan publicly reiterated Thailand's commitment to SEATO, while, on the very day of Bishop's encounter with Phibun, Deputy Foreign Minister Rak Panyarachun delivered a speech on television criticizing communist aggression in Asia and Eastern Europe and pledging cooperation with Thailand's allies.[190] The visits to Beijing abruptly ended. In the end, however, this latest effort to reverse the neutralist trend backfired, as had the others. Within days of Rak's speech, someone from the Thai government, apparently wanting to show that Phibun had reversed policy only because of U.S. pressure, revealed to newspapers an account of Robertson's protest.[191] Another round of press criticism of American interventionism ensued, and all the positive results of the démarche were lost. Robertson strongly protested the latest articles to Phot, but the damage had already been done.[192] The United States was fortunate only in that no one leaked this protest against the leak.

That spring and summer another worrisome development, Sarit's imminent rise to power, confronted the United States. Because of his avoidance of the political spotlight and apparent dissoluteness, the Americans had long underestimated Sarit as a force in Thai politics, but by the summer of 1957, it was clear to all that he was the most powerful man in the country. While Phao had spent the past five years devoting his time, efforts, and money to local administration, manipulation of Parliament, and political assassination, Sarit had consolidated his power base in Thailand's most important military institution, the army. By 1957, Sarit had marginalized the Phao-Phin faction within the army and gained nearly absolute control over the service's forces. The February elections and his adroit handling of the antigovernment demonstrations then won Sarit broad public support and created an image of irresistible political momentum. In a system where only political winners with spoils to distribute can attract followers, this psychological advantage provided him a tremendous boost. That summer, for the first time, Thais and westerners concluded that Sarit had the necessary forces and political support to oust both Phao and Phibun. Control of government, by then, was his for the taking.

Worst of all for the Americans, just as his rise to power was appearing inevitable that summer, Sarit intensified his attacks on the United States. In June, Sarit took his MPs in the government party and, with a number of outsiders, formed a party of his own, the Sahaphum Party. Ominously for the United States, the new party attracted significant leftist support, and Sahaphum leaders directed many of their appeals toward leftist issues, especially opposition to the United States. The party's three leading leftist and neutralist MPs, Yat Waidi, Sa-ing Marangkun (a member of the first mission to Beijing formerly funded by Phao), and party spokesman Ari Tantiwetchakun, were especially vocal in their attacks. Yat told reporters in July that Sahaphum wanted to replace the government because "it is too closely bound to America," and Ari blasted the United States for its support of Phao and Phibun. The United States had provided jeeps, Ari told newsmen, for Seri Manangkhasila MPs to campaign in the countryside.[193] He claimed that the United States "only wants to support the throne Field Marshal Plaek is sitting in. It doesn't at all look out for the Thai people."[194] Even Sahaphum's centrist leader, Sukit Nimmanahaeminda, preached a neutralist line. "We want to be friendly to all countries," Sukit proclaimed when elected party leader in June, "with malice towards none."[195] One of Sarit's two closest aides in the army and deputy minister of the interior, Praphat Charusathian, suggested openly to reporters at the height of a controversy over Thai contributions to U.S. military advisers' operating expenses that JUSMAG helped the army little. Its withdrawal, he claimed, would not affect the army's effectiveness.[196] Disagreements between Thai leaders and the Americans on JUSMAG counterpart fund requirements were nothing new, but never before had a Thai official— especially one so important—gone public with the dispute. Then, toward the middle and end of the summer, the Sarit camp turned its wrath on the most important American aid-providing institution in Thailand, the CIA. In July, *San Seri* began attacking Sea Supply, and by August, the previously obscure organization had become so well-known and controversial that Phibun publicly denied (falsely) that it was still operating.[197] Possibly because of Sarit's spectacular success in winning leftist and neutralist support, Phibun and Phao again began allowing private groups to travel to China. Three such groups left in August and September.[198] Most alarmingly, in late July and August, Sarit himself joined the anti-American, anti-CIA publicity campaign. In the last week of July, he criticized the Standard Vacuum Oil Company for demanding payment of debts from the Thai government, and on August 20, he praised JUSMAG but lashed out at Sea Supply. "We are pleased to have you

[JUSMAG] here," he told newsmen, "because you came to work openly, not like another unit [the CIA] that works underground."[199]

Again, the Americans had great difficulty determining a response to these disturbing developments. At first, opinion in some quarters held that Sarit, if in power, would maintain the substance of Phibun's still largely pro-American foreign policy and that the United States need not alter its approach toward Thailand. Sarit, the State Department's Office of Intelligence Research predicted in an early assessment in May, would take a more neutralist line in public and speak out more bluntly on JUSMAG counterpart fund requirements but would materially change policy toward the United States and China little.[200] As the summer progressed, however, the United States grew more concerned. In June, an interdepartmental National Intelligence Estimate cautioned that the United States should prepare itself for further setbacks. Whoever was in power, the estimate forecast, would "seek to develop a more flexible foreign policy," and the best the estimate's writers could say about Sarit was that he would not change Thailand's foreign policy "radically, at least in the short run."[201] In July, Bishop gave the most pessimistic evaluation of Sarit yet offered. He warned that Sarit's accession to power would force the United States to make "major adjustments" in Thailand.[202]

In the end, after months of debate, the State Department decided to prepare for the worst. A department telegram to the embassy agreed that Phibun remained the "most reliable, constructive and statesman-like leader capable of holding power in Thailand" but instructed Bishop, in light of the likelihood of an army coup, to maintain good relations with Sarit.[203] The department suggested in an earlier dispatch that the embassy yield to Sarit on the JUSMAG controversy. "Unless you [Bishop] think he [is] likely [to] be ousted," a department cable advised, the "constructive course [of] action over [the] long run appears to be [to] attempt [to] meet his objections by taking steps where feasible further to reduce JUSMAG costs to Thai[land]."

The State Department was wise to prepare for the worst, because it was about to happen. In August, after two months of increasingly harsh criticism from the Sarit camp and threats by Sarit MPs to overthrow the government, Phibun made a bold move to stem the tide of political support flowing to Sarit. To retake the moral high ground and deprive Sarit of his income from the national lottery, Phibun ordered cabinet members in the middle of the month to remove themselves from all business activities.[204] But while such tactics had worked wonders against

Phao in August 1955, this time Phibun's gambit backfired. Sarit called Phibun's bluff and, along with three supporters in the cabinet and forty-six appointed MPs, resigned on August 20.[205] As Sarit had hoped, the press and public rallied behind him, and, on September 13, he demanded that the entire government resign immediately and Phao be replaced as police chief.[206] Although Phao and Phin submitted their resignations, Phibun refused to accept the letters. Tensions increased, and, on September 15, a crowd marched on Sarit's house asking him to oust Phibun and Phao. To the demonstrators' cheers, Sarit promised that he would comply with "the popular will."[207] He ordered his men to action, and, on the following morning, army units seized key points throughout the city. Phibun, fearing for his life, fled the country, and Phao, after surrendering personally to Sarit, left for his Swiss bank account in Geneva.

Then, Sarit and popular forces created the single most frightening clash between Americans and Thais in the history of relations between the two countries. As Sarit's troops moved on police bases on the morning of September 16, a column of soldiers, accompanied by a crowd of supporters, marched on the Sea Supply office. CIA agents had already begun burning documents on the roof, but the angry crowd and troops reached the office before the job was complete. Only CIA station chief John Hart's extraordinary heroism—from the American perspective—saved Sea Supply from hostile occupation. When the soldiers and protesters moved on the building, Hart blocked their path and refused them entrance. The soldiers then backed down.[208]

Two years of Phibun's democratization, therefore, had nearly destroyed Thailand's alliance with the United States. Democratization had intensified the power struggle at the top, reduced the government's accountability to U.S. pressure, and contributed to the movement toward a more neutralist foreign policy. New guarantees of civil rights had revived leftists and neutralists as political powers in the country. As all of these new forces converged in the coup of September 1957, the Thais, sworn allies of the United States since 1954, challenged one of the most important American institutions in the country in a dangerous armed confrontation. These events seriously damaged the Thai-U.S. alliance. Both sides needed to make "major adjustments," in Bishop's words, before it could be restored.

Chapter Ten

DICTATORSHIP AND RESTORATION,

SEPTEMBER 1957–DECEMBER 1958

Despite the tensions surrounding the 1957 coup, Sarit and the United States needed each other badly. Although the Americans had by then created a second client state in Diem's Republic of Vietnam, Thailand, because of its greater size, wealth, and stability, remained the United States' most important ally on the Southeast Asian mainland. A National Security Council paper in November called Thailand "the hub of U.S. security efforts in Southeast Asia."[1] Likewise, the United States remained crucial to Thai regional strategy. Sarit, even more than Phibun and Phao, wanted U.S. help in expanding Thai influence in Laos. Raised by an ethnic Lao mother on the Laotian border in northeastern Thailand, Sarit made Laos and support for the right-wing Laotian army commander, Phoumi Nosavan (Sarit's cousin) top policy priorities. Almost immediately after the coup, Sarit began pressing the United States to assist Phoumi. Domestically, Sarit also needed U.S. help. The Thai government, by then, had grown dependent on American economic aid and budgetary support. "If external aid were halted or curtailed," a 1957 Office of Intelligence Research study reported, "Thailand would either encounter fiscal and foreign payments deficits, or have to cut expenditures on development projects drastically, or adopt some combination of these and other measures."[2] Similarly, the army continued to rely heavily on American military assistance. Most of the army's equipment—almost all U.S.-supplied—took only American spare parts, and, although 1957, coming on the tail end of an expansion program, represented a low point in the military assistance cycle, the $26.2 million in U.S. overt military aid provided in 1957 still accounted for 41 percent of all the money reported spent—

Thai and American—on Thai defenses that year.[3] Were the United States to terminate this military assistance, all activities of the Thai army would come to a screeching halt. Sarit's own political position then would likely have become untenable. The press reported widespread dissatisfaction among junior army officers after the coup, and many feared that Sarit's ambitious lieutenant, Praphat Charusathian, would exploit the tensions to overthrow Sarit.[4]

Sarit, moreover, showed little interest in continuing Phibun's and Phao's opening to China. At no point had he become involved in their contacts with Beijing, and, more interested in pursuing his Laotian schemes than in geopolitics, he probably perceived few advantages from association with Zhou and Mao. China, for Sarit, was the ally of Thailand's rival for influence in Laos—North Vietnam—not a land of diplomatic opportunity. The evidence suggests that he ended all official contacts with Beijing after the 1957 coup.[5]

Both Sarit and the United States, therefore, made clear after the coup that they wanted to maintain the friendship between the two countries. Immediately after the takeover, on September 17, Sarit notified the foreign embassies in Bangkok that the new government would respect its foreign obligations, protect foreigners, and remain loyal to SEATO. Made public, the notification implicitly informed the United States and the Thai people that Sarit intended to end the opening to China. The coup was necessary, the note claimed, because the previous government had "allowed secret contacts with communist circles in China."[6] That same day, Washington reciprocated Sarit's gesture. Sarit's takeover, a State Department statement commented, was a domestic affair and would not affect U.S. relations with Thailand.[7] In a meeting with Bishop that Sarit called three days later, both sides made further amends. "U.S. policy," Bishop explained to Sarit, is "based on interests, and attitudes [toward] world problems and not on [the] personality of [an] individual [leader], which was [an] entirely internal matter." Sarit assured Bishop that Thailand would remain firmly in the U.S. camp. He promised that the interim government he planned to appoint the following day would "strictly observe [the] old foreign policy and adherence to [the] U.N. and SEATO" and even pledged that the interim prime minister would be "pleasing to [the] U.S."[8] Indeed, the Americans heartily approved his choice, Phot Sarasin. American-educated, a former ambassador to the United States, currently SEATO secretary-general, Phot enjoyed the Americans' complete confidence, despite having opposed the recognition of Bao Dai in 1950. Again, as with Pridi's appointment of Seni as prime minister in 1945 and Phibun's selection of Khuang in 1947, a newly arrived Thai kingmaker was soothing Washington's anxieties with presentation of an appealing front man.

Nevertheless, serious problems remained to be resolved, the most pressing of which was Sarit's distrust of the CIA. At the same time that Sarit was reassuring Bishop and the State Department, Phao's replacement as police chief, Sawai Sawaisaenyakorn, initiated a loud Sea Supply–bashing campaign on Sarit's behalf. On September 20, the day of Sarit's meeting with Bishop, General Sawai told the press that the government would terminate Sea Supply assistance to the police and might disband the CIA-supported Water Police, PARU, and BPP.[9] A week later, he accused Sea Supply of being "illegal" and "a serious threat to the safety of this country." "If it was sincere" in wanting to help Thailand, he asked rhetorically, "why did it have to burn its documents?"[10] At his most vehement, Sawai announced that he was investigating reports that Sea Supply planned to fly the Hua Hin PARU unit to Bangkok to return Phao to power.[11] Members of Parliament echoed Sawai's complaints in Parliament.[12]

The increased influence of leftists and neutralists, moreover, posed a serious long-term threat to U.S.-Thai relations. Having ridden to power partly on the backs of leftist and neutralist politicians and journalists, Sarit already depended to a significant extent on their support, and all expected the left to play an even more important role in the government formed after the new general elections planned for December. Phot predicted in November that the next government would include Thep's Economist Party, and an NSC paper reported that same month that "we [the NSC] anticipate a period of considerable domestic instability affording opportunities for leftist and neutralist exploitation."[13] Sarit and the Phot government worked hard in the weeks before the elections to maintain leftist and neutralist support. Sarit allowed leftists to remain in his Sahaphum Party, and Phot gave the economics portfolio to centrist, but neutralist, party leader Sukit Nimmanahaeminda. The State Department termed Sukit "unfriendly to the U.S."[14] The press continued its attacks on the United States unimpeded, and, despite the apparent termination of official communications with the PRC, Phot and the Foreign Ministry softened the government's public stance toward Beijing and unofficial contacts with China. Phot's policy statement to Parliament on September 24 proclaimed that the government would "promote friendly relations with *all nations*" (emphasis added).[15] In a press conference two days later, he stated that trade with China in nonstrategic goods was permissible and that journalists could travel to Beijing.[16] When former Peace Committee leader

Kulab Saipradit, now free after the 1957 amnesty, asked to meet Phot to get permission to travel to the Soviet Union, Phot not only agreed to see Kulab and allow the trip but engaged the well-known Marxist in an hour-long, friendly discussion.[17]

The United States responded sharply to these developments. On September 28, the State Department notified Bishop that it was considering stopping aid shipments to increase U.S. "leverage in [the] evolving political situation."[18] Although Bishop rejected the plan, on October 1, he protested to Phot the continuing press criticism of the United States and Sea Supply. Calling leftist and neutralist journalists "subversive elements," Bishop called on Phot to halt the "provocative and irresponsible press campaign against SEATO and [the] U.S."[19] Sea Supply responded in kind to the semiofficial CIA-bashing. Despite Sarit's and Sawai's criticism of Sea Supply as "secret" and "underground," Sarit, of course, had known about Sea Supply, through his membership on the Naresuan Committee, from the beginning. An unnamed Sea Supply official therefore told a *Sayam Nikorn* reporter around October 1 that Sarit had all along been aware of Sea Supply's mission and that the unit had sent all its documents (presumably, those not burned) to Sarit after the coup. The official gave the reporter a photograph of Sarit viewing PARU exercises as proof. *Sayam Nikorn* printed the picture, with Sarit's figure circled, on its front page.[20]

If all of this failed to change Sarit, the Americans were prepared to take more drastic action. On October 22, a cable to Bishop initialed by Robertson and drafted by Young called for direct U.S. intervention to eliminate leftist and neutralist influences in the country. Unless the "subversive malignancy" can be removed, the cable said, the United States "will face [an] increasingly grave situation in Thailand with inevitable adverse consequences throughout Southeast Asia." The cable instructed Bishop to work with "approachable" figures such as the king, Sarit, Phot, Khuang, and "possibly" the less reliable Praphat, Thanom Kittikachorn, and Sukit, to form a pro-American government after the elections. Bishop was authorized to "remind these political elements [that] . . . American aid [to] Thailand cannot be taken for granted if [a] power grouping emerges antagonistic [to] Free World objectives or blind [to] Communist dangers." Then, once the threat of an aid cutoff had helped form a sympathetic government, Bishop was to convince the new leaders to "counter Communist subversion." The cable instructed Bishop to persuade the Thais, in other words, to stifle leftist and neutralist newspapers and politicians. It cited his démarche on press criticism to Phot as an example to follow.[21]

American strategy succeeded, to a large extent, in changing Sarit's stance toward the CIA. At the end of the month, the police announced that reports of PARU plans for a countercoup were a hoax, and, several days after Bishop's démarche to Phot, the director-general of the government's Public Relations Department asked newspapers to stop criticizing Sea Supply.[22] In an October 11 meeting, CIA station chief John Hart and Sawai reached conclusive agreement on the CIA's future. Sea Supply would be disbanded, Hart and Sawai decided, but the International Cooperation Administration (ICA, the predecessor of the Agency for International Development) would be allowed to provide aid to the police in its place, in reduced form. The United States had actually been pushing for such a transfer, to make the police programs less subject to suspicion, for several years, and the CIA, in any case, merely transferred many of its activities to the ICA cover.[23] Although the army temporarily assumed control of PARU and the head of the provincial police took command of the BPP, neither unit was disbanded. To reassure the United States on that point, Sawai announced, when publicly releasing details of his meeting with Hart, that the government planned to "increase the forces and strength" of the BPP.[24] Given the depth of Sarit's distrust of the CIA, the Americans had reason to be pleased with this outcome. BPP and PARU would lose their autonomy, and the United States would no longer provide large amounts of lethal aid to the police, but the CIA's intelligence activities and Thailand-based regional operations would continue unimpeded. Indeed, at this time or soon afterward, the CIA, working partially through the Thai station, began its aid program for Sarit's cousin, Phoumi Nosavan, in Laos.[25] Sarit and the CIA had found common ground.

But the legacy of Phibun's democratic reforms continued to plague the relationship—and Sarit. Unlike Phibun, Sarit felt no emotional attachment to the forms of parliamentary democracy. While Phibun had studied in France and first come to power in 1932 in a "revolution" partly inspired by democratic ideals, Sarit—along with Phao—represented a new generation of Thai military leader lacking foreign experience or exposure to democratic societies. In almost every instance, these younger leaders preferred authoritarianism to liberalism. As much as he would have liked to, however, Sarit dared not tamper with Phibun's reforms. Sarit's carefully cultivated image of himself as an honest, disinterested defender of clean elections and fairness in government remained an important element of his personal political power, and expectations among students, journalists, and intellectuals that he would sponsor new and open elections soared after his coup.

Especially because his liver condition kept him from taking an active role in government, Sarit could not afford to dash these hopes for a more democratic government. Phibun's reforms stayed in place, and civilian influences continued to disrupt relations with the United States.

Press freedoms remained especially troubling. Phot, partly in response to Bishop, imposed censorship on six anti-American and opposition newspapers in late October, but press criticism of the United States persisted through November and December in muted form.[26] Although Sarit and Phibun had encouraged earlier attacks on the United States, the government's loss of control of the press, not official connivance, gave rise to this latest round of anti-American commentaries. Significantly, Thai-language newspapers—including Sarit's *San Seri* —at this time criticized Phot's Sarit-appointed cabinet as vehemently as they attacked the United States.[27] Even in the best of times, Thai political figures exerted less than absolute control over newspapers they owned, and, in the heady atmosphere following the 1957 coup, journalists paid little heed to government requests. By December, his own publications had grown so antigovernment that Sarit ordered the editor of *San Seri,* Thanong Sathathip, to submit all articles for his approval before printing. His letter to Thanong complained that *San Seri* had printed news "about the *Khana Thahan* [the "Military Group" that ousted Phao and Phibun], the Sahaphum Party, and even myself, that repeatedly deviates from the truth."[28] The protest had little effect.

The elections in December—largely free and fair as Sarit had promised—worsened matters for the United States. Leftist candidates won a dozen or so seats, and, because the Sahaphum Party won only forty-five of the one hundred fifty seats contested—just six more than the Democrats—Sarit badly needed their support.[29] He reshaped his Sahaphum Party six days after the elections into a larger grouping of Sahaphum and Seri Manangkhasila MPs dubbed the Chat Sangkhom Niyom Party[30] and included, as he had earlier with the Sahaphum Party, a number of leftists and neutralists. The new prime minister, Sarit's loyal First Army commander, Thanom Kittikachorn, brought three of them, Net Khemayothin, Ari Tantiwetchakun, and Thim Phuriphat, into the cabinet. Net had been a Pridi supporter and *San Seri* editor.[31] Ari, former Sahaphum Party spokesman, had helped found in 1956 the neutralist, left-of-center Free Democrat Party.[32] Thim, a relative of Thong-in Phuriphat, one of the four MPs Phao murdered in 1949, had been a member of the Economist Party and Thep's 1956 mission to China. Although Thep failed to join Net, Ari, and Thim in the postelection government, his Economist Party and other leftist and neutralist opposition MPs were sure to keep up the heat on the United States in Parliament. The State Department's plan of October to bring about formation of a "satisfactory political alignment," therefore, clearly had failed.[33]

The increased influence of leftists and neutralists forced the new government to present an even softer public stand toward Beijing and local Communists than the preelection government had. Although Sarit took little interest in continuing Phibun's opening to China, Thanom had no choice but to tailor at least the packaging of the government's policies to leftist and neutralist demands. During the new government's presentation of its policies to Parliament in early January, Foreign Minister Wan for the first time agreed to consider exempting rubber from the embargo on "strategic" exports to China, and Thanom, while commenting on a promise Minister-without-Portfolio Thim Phuriphat had issued to repeal the anti-Communist act, stated that the government was willing to rescind any law that infringed on people's freedom.[34] Thanom squandered even the limited gains on censorship that Phot had made. Press attacks on the United States increased in intensity and frequency, and, in late March, the U.S. embassy reported that, recently, "the leftist press has made critical charges [regarding the United States] on virtually a daily basis."[35] Such pressures worried not only the United States. In March, the new deputy foreign minister, Wisut Athayukti, complained to U.S. Chargé d'Affaires George Wilson over "growing leftist influence" in the country.[36] He told the embassy in April that, "while Thanom gave him [Wisut] full support and authority in Foreign Affairs he found it increasingly exhausting and onerous to support and defend policies in Cabinet against left-wing and neutralist pressures from some other Cabinet members." Wisut went so far as to urge the United States to press Sarit to oust the leftists from the cabinet.[37] That same month, Thanom made a further gesture to these neutralists and leftists, saying he would consider accepting any aid the Soviet Union offered and would not oppose rubber sales to China.[38]

In allowing government leaders to make such statements, Sarit did not want to weaken the alliance with the United States. On military assistance, CIA aid to Phoumi, and policy in the region, the United States and Sarit saw eye to eye. The neutralist rhetoric was mere verbal posturing. Sarit intended neither to follow socialist economic policies nor to repeal the anti-Communist act, and all sides knew, despite Wan's concession on rubber exports to China, that Thai traders would never sell much rubber to the extremely small Chinese market. At all times, government officials tempered their neutralist statements with strong declarations of support for SEATO.

By the spring of 1958, moreover, the Americans had established the same sort of rapport with Sarit that they had previously enjoyed with Phao and Phibun. After the coup, Washington quickly removed the most serious impediments to American friendship with Sarit—Bishop and Hart. The State Department ordered Bishop to leave his post at the new year, and, not long after that, the CIA removed the Phao-tainted John Hart. Bishop would never receive another ambassadorship. Bishop's and Hart's replacements, U. Alexis Johnson as ambassador and Robert Jantzen as CIA station chief, quickly made amends with Sarit. Jantzen became especially close to the new Thai strongman. In early 1958, after a liver hemorrhage forced Sarit to go to the United States for several months of medical treatment, Jantzen visited his hospital room regularly.[39] An indication of how fully Jantzen earned Sarit's trust in those days came later in November 1958, when Sarit planned to fire and punish a high-ranking assistant, Air Chief Marshal Dawee Chullasappa, for allegedly plotting to overthrow the government. Jantzen's intervention with Sarit saved Dawee's job—and possibly his life. Acting on a tip from CIA contacts in the military, Jantzen informed Sarit that the accusations against Dawee were false, and, on that basis, Sarit exonerated him. Later, Sarit acquired evidence of his own confirming Jantzen's claim, adding to Sarit's confidence in Jantzen.[40]

All this led the Americans to the radically new conclusion that Sarit would help the United States more than even Phibun and Phao had. Despite the new government's need to "show its 'independence' of U.S. influence," an Office of Philippine and Southeast Asian Affairs memorandum noted, Sarit has "reinvigorated Thailand's support for SEATO."[41] A subsequent Operations Coordinating Board report explained that "Thailand's support for SEATO and its opposition to communist subversion appear firmer than before Field Marshal Sarit's coup d'etat."[42] Sarit's goals, the United States now understood, were highly favorable to the United States.

While the Americans had resolved their problems with Sarit himself, however, the "subversive malignancy" of neutralist and leftist journalists and politicians still worried them. On January 15, just six days after Thanom's and Wan's comments in Parliament on the anti-Communist act and trade with China, Chargé Wilson personally protested to Wan the government's continued failure to ban films from the PRC or exile a group of allegedly communist Chinese journalists.[43] In March, when rumors appeared that the government would allow five more Pridi-ites to return from the PRC, Wilson advised Washington to warn Sarit off the move.[44] Although the State Department decided against bothering Sarit, still in the United States recuperating from his operation, it instructed the embassy to express U.S. concerns to Thai officials in Bangkok.[45]

In May, the State Department decided to take the leftist and neutralist problem to Sarit personally. Since January, Sarit had wanted an economic aid supplement, and, in April, he arranged to meet Eisenhower, Dulles, and high-ranking State and Defense Department officials in Washington to present a proposal. Sarit assured the Americans that he would prevent leftists from taking control of the government and promised never to allow Pridi to return, but, instead of getting the generous aid package he hoped for, Sarit received a polite rejection from Dulles and a stern lecture from Robertson on *San Seri*'s criticism of the United States.[46] Turning against him Sarit's argument that increased aid would help the government fight subversion, Robertson interjected that press attacks on the United States "vitiate [the] purpose [of] U.S. aid programs as well as Sarit's own intention [to] counter subversion in Thailand." When Sarit denied controlling *San Seri* or *Thai Raiwan* and noted the irresponsibility of the press in developing countries in general, Robertson retorted that "even in developed [developing?] countries responsible leaders take every means of getting [the] facts before [the] people."[47] The United States agreed to fund several small projects to avoid forcing Sarit to return, in Wilson's words, "empty-handed," but the Americans' rejection of the broader Thai proposal and Robertson's lecture communicated effectively their displeasure with anti-Americanism in Thailand.[48] Since Sarit had told General Erskine that he needed the aid supplement to "strengthen" his political position, the U.S. rebuff must have greatly disappointed him.[49]

By then, Sarit as well as the Americans had begun to lose patience with politicians and the press. From its inauguration, Sarit's new party, the Chat Sangkhom Niyom, troubled him. The former Sahaphum MPs in the party resented the Seri Manangkhasila newcomers, and the two factions fought endlessly over the division of offices and patronage. Twenty-six former Sahaphum MPs ended up resigning from the amalgamated party, and, in February, even Chat Sangkhom Niyom MPs joined in opposition criticism of the government's budget. Several MPs soon afterward protested use of Lottery Bureau funds to pay for Sarit's operation. In March by-elections in Bangkok and the northeast, the government suffered another electoral setback. Of the twenty-six seats contested, the Democrats won thirteen to the government party's nine.[50] His inability to control these politicians and voters as firmly as his army apparently frustrated Sarit. A press report appeared in March that Sarit, complaining that he had given his party more than fourteen million *baht* but still faced demands for "tens of millions more," planned to resign as Chat Sangkhom Niyom Party chief.[51]

American pressure helped convince Sarit to act against the leftists, neutralists, politicians, and journalists troubling him and the United States. Immediately after Robertson's lecture on press criticism of the United States, Sarit sent Thanong Sathathip, the editor of *San Seri*, a hastily written but stern letter ordering the newspaper to end the negative reporting. *San Seri*'s attacks on the United States, Sarit wrote, had brought him "under suspicion, especially from foreigners." He ordered Thanong to "consider correcting [the newspaper's commentaries], especially regarding foreign policy." In response, Thanong led the entire staff of the newspaper in resigning and started a new publication named—apparently to express their anger at American interference in the newspaper's and their country's affairs—*Independence (Ekarat)*.[52] In late June, Sarit made a surprise visit back to Bangkok from the United States to deal with matters personally. Showing his knowledge of U.S. support for repressive methods, he hinted to Robertson before leaving that he might "take action" against the "faults and improper activities" of the government.[53] Once in Bangkok, he wasted no time in letting Parliament and the public know that their freedom to criticize his government had limits. Almost immediately after his arrival, he persuaded thirteen MPs to withdraw their support for an opposition plan to grill the cabinet, thus killing the motion. Sarit, it was rumored, had bribed them. One of the MPs publicly claimed, in addition, that Sarit had threatened to use "de Gaullism" if the motion passed.[54] The politicians momentarily quelled, Sarit then further disciplined the press. *Issara*, a newspaper Phao funded from Switzerland, had been attacking Sarit and the government mercilessly for months, and, just two days after Sarit's return to Bangkok, it linked him to the opium trade. Sarit announced publicly in the first week of July that he could not be held responsible if angry soldiers took revenge on the newspaper and, on July 15, warned its editors in person.[55] Hours after his visit, men in army officers' uniforms ransacked the newspaper's printing room.[56] Several days later, police arrested two *Issara* editors on charges of sedition.[57]

Most important to the United States, Sarit in August moved on the leftist and neutralist cabinet ministers. Proving the efficacy of co-optation, Ari and Thim had, soon after joining the government, already become "more acceptable" to the embassy, and, by the fall, Ari had so changed that the embassy's political counselor described him as "an outspoken anti-Communist," but Sarit still wanted to impress the United States.[58] A cabinet reshuffle had been widely anticipated since his return to Bangkok on June 27, and the *New York Times* reported that the "leftists" would be a target.[59] Eventually, after several weeks of behind-the-scenes political struggles, Thanom, in a series of reshuffles announced from August 5 to August 8, ousted Thim and Ari from the cabinet and demoted Net from his position as deputy minister of communications to the less important (i.e., less lucrative) office of deputy minister of economics. Events were finally turning the Americans' way.

Developments in Thailand's foreign policy were also by then playing into the Americans' hands. For several years, a dispute over ownership of an ancient hilltop temple at Khao Phra Wihan (Preah Vihear) on the Thai-Cambodian border had soured relations between Cambodia and Thailand, and, over the summer of 1958, the controversy heated up to the boiling point. The two sides discussed the issue diplomatically during a Sihanouk visit to Bangkok in mid-July, but, a week later, in a move bluntly designed to pressure the Thais, Sihanouk formally recognized the People's Republic of China. Two weeks after that, he left for a dramatic twelve-day visit to Beijing.[60] Zhou, to cement the new friendship—and possibly to express Chinese displeasure at Sarit's termination of official contacts—issued a harsh condemnation of Thailand on Sihanouk's departure. Beijing radio reported that Zhou "expressed the regret of the Chinese Government at the fact that Cambodian territory was often invaded and blockaded by some of its neighbors [i.e., Thailand and South Vietnam] and deemed these to be unfriendly acts."[61] Thanom accurately described Zhou's statement as having "made a threat" to Thailand.[62] After that, Sarit and Thanom would not even contemplate normalization of relations with Beijing—if they ever had.

Despite the impossibility of pursuing the opening to China, however, pressure from leftist and neutralist journalists and politicians forced the government to maintain its conciliatory public stance. The day before Sihanouk's trip to China, the police allowed five leftist and communist Pridi-ite exiles to return from the PRC.[63] A month after that, in September, Thanom told an MP in Parliament that he would consider amending the anti-Communist act to ease sales of rubber to China and denied that Thailand was giving Taiwan "moral support" in the straits crisis with China.[64] From August to October, the government allowed three groups—comprising a total of thirteen leftist MPs and twelve journalists and writers—to travel openly to Beijing.[65] Sarit had no reason to continue the opening to China, and neutralist pressures within the cabinet were now minimal, but the government, especially because Sarit had gone to England to convalesce, was still too vulnerable to neutralist and leftist criticism to renounce publicly all hopes of improving relations with the PRC. Even within their own party, neutralist pressures on Sarit and Thanom remained strong. Two of the MPs traveling to Beijing, Burana Jampaphan and Banjerd Saicheua, belonged to Chat Sangkhom Niyom.[66]

What finally ended the neutralist statements and flirtation with leftists was not any change in the international environment, but Sarit's seizure of absolute power. While recuperating in England and the United States, Sarit thought broadly about how he should govern Thailand. He looked for ways to impose on the country's greedy, undisciplined, and ungrateful politicians and journalists the same sort of military order he found in the army. In the end, he decided to run the country according to "Thai" principles, not imported Western ideas. He would take as his model, not the representative democracies of Europe and America, but the supposedly benevolent despots of Thailand's ancient past. On October 19, after surreptitiously returning to Bangkok from England, Sarit told his generals in the *Khana Thahan* his plans for a "revolution." The following day, to no one's surprise, he declared martial law. Thanom eagerly gave him the prime ministership.[67]

Sarit's new regime was the most repressive and authoritarian in Thai history. His "revolution" abrogated the constitution, dissolved Parliament, and vested all power in his newly formed Revolutionary Party. Although he pledged to appoint a constituent assembly to act as a legislature and draft a constitution, no one doubted that the body would merely rubber-stamp his orders. In fact, the assembly never functioned as a parliament, and a constitution was promulgated only after a decade. Sarit banned all political parties from the beginning. He imposed a censorship of the press after the coup, moreover, that was stricter than even that of the 1952–1954 period. Immediately, he closed down eighteen leftist, neutralist, and opposition publications, and the Revolutionary Party prohibited new newspapers from opening.[68] "Newspapers that act as the mouthpieces of foreign interests, advocate or uphold such a harmful ideology as Communism, or attempt to sow discord directly or indirectly shall be drastically suppressed," Revolutionary Party Announcement No. 3 proclaimed.[69] Setting the tone for his rule early on, Sarit personally ordered, within two months of his coup, the summary executions of five ethnic Chinese accused of setting fire to their stores.

Sarit badly wanted American approval for his coup and crackdown. Because of his long absence from the country, disputes had arisen within the army, and he then lacked the firm control over that crucial institution that he would later enjoy. An unnamed "ranking" member of the Ministry of Defense General Staff told the embassy in late July that Sarit was having difficulties maintaining order and that he faced a "serious problem of disunity" within the powerful Bangkok-based First Division.[70] In the days after the "revolution," the foreign press reported widespread rumors of a Praphat coup plot.[71] The Dawee incident involving CIA Station Chief Jantzen in November showed clearly Sarit's suspicion of his military underlings. In such an atmosphere of uncertainty, Sarit could not afford to alienate the Americans. In a remarkable display of obsequiousness, he had the ambassador to the United States ask the State Department in November "if [the] U.S. could make some gesture of support for [the] government to be formed."[72]

Sarit, therefore, worked hard to prove that the "revolution" would favor American interests. He gave the United States advance notice of the coup and, from the beginning, emphasized his desire to cooperate diplomatically. A Foreign Ministry letter to the embassy affirmed the day after Sarit assumed office that he intended to "discharge Thailand's duties as [a] member of the South-East Asia Treaty Organisation in every respect."[73] Now that the democratic restraints had been lifted, Sarit made clear to the United States that he would no longer tolerate leftists. When informing the embassy of his plans for the "revolution," he pledged to arrest seventy-two Thai and Chinese communist "agents."[74] Indeed, he delivered the Americans even more than he had promised. In addition to the press censorship, Sarit's "revolution" brought the most intense crackdown on the left Thailand had ever seen. Although real Communists, working underground, proved hard to come by, the mildly socialist but strongly neutralist leftists in Parliament, universities, and the press that so annoyed the United States were easy targets.[75] The police arrested dozens of dissidents and Chinese on the day of the coup, and hundreds, not just seventy-two, followed in subsequent weeks. Sang Phatthanothai, Thep Chotinuchit, Khlaew Norapati, Ari Phirom, Karuna Kusalasai, Thanong Sathathip, Kulab Saipradit, Jit Phumisak, Prasert Sapsunthorn, Chiap Chaisong— all of the Americans' bêtes noire were captured in the sweep. Sarit, passing over neutralists and leftists associated with himself such as Net, Ari Tantiwetchakun, and Thim in favor of those aligned with Phibun or

Phao, served his own interests with the arrests, but most thought that he had initiated the crackdown primarily to please the United States. The day of the coup, the U.S. military attaché commented that the "arrest of communists and other similar actions" are "believed [to] have [the] purpose [of] gaining U.S. support."[76] To ensure that the detainees, unlike those arrested in 1952, would remain in jail, the Revolutionary Party ordered that cases falling under the Anti-Communist Act of 1952 be tried in military courts and allowed police to hold suspects as long as the investigation lasted.[77] Most detained under this decree stayed in prison for years. Those who escaped punishment stayed quiet.

The Americans could ask for nothing better. To be sure, no one on the U.S. side felt comfortable with Sarit's summary execution of arsonists or his rejection of even a rubber-stamp assembly. Johnson cabled Washington after the executions that he thought Sarit should observe "legal norms."[78] Despite the uneasiness the Americans felt in associating themselves with Sarit's new dictatorship, however, they never displayed misgivings or regret. Washington endorsed the coup in private almost without qualification. The State Department's Bureau of Intelligence and Research reported to Acting Secretary of State Christian Herter that "the resignation of the Thanom government will provide the ruling group with the opportunity to form a new cabinet without leftist representation and to institute more vigorous anti-Communist measures, particularly against elements of the press." Sarit's action "does not represent a coup d'etat," the report claimed, but instead was "an orderly attempt by the present ruling group to solidify its position."[79] Likewise, despite distaste for Sarit's methods, even Johnson believed that the ends justified the means. "I was skeptical," he later wrote, "but not instantly critical. I approved of Sarit's arrest of communists and held no particular brief for the corrupt assembly; and although I was not particularly enthusiastic about the way he engineered these changes I felt he was in a much better position than any outsider to judge the necessity of the means he used."[80]

The United States, therefore, gave Sarit the "gesture of support" he so badly wanted. The day after the "revolution," the State Department announced that the coup would not affect the Thai-U.S. relationship. The U.S. government, the statement approvingly noted, had received reports consistent with the Revolutionary Party's claims regarding communist movements in Thailand.[81] On December 18, Dulles cabled a letter thanking Sarit for his support for the West. Embarrassed to identify the United States openly with Sarit's ruthless disregard for democratic principles and civil rights, Dulles asked that the letter be kept secret and clumsily avoided any direct reference to the "revolution," but he made it obvious that the coup pleased him. "In following developments in your country," Dulles wrote, "I have especially noted . . . the steps being taken [by the Revolutionary Party] to maintain the independence of Thailand against the insidious threat of Communist infiltration and subversion."[82] When presenting Dulles' message, Johnson also submitted a formal letter of his own notifying Sarit that, though the worldwide aid budget had been cut, the United States would increase economic aid to Thailand by $20 million. The letters were clear, if understated, endorsements of the coup, and Sarit, taking them as such, released both to the press, despite Dulles' plainly stated desire for secrecy.[83] Local newspapers gave the meeting prominent coverage.

With that, the United States had finally embraced military dictatorship in Thailand. It was a furtive act, given behind a blush and with few words, but it was an embrace nonetheless. After three years of neutralist press attacks, anti-American demonstrations, the confrontation at the Sea Supply office, and the admission of leftists to Parliament and the cabinet, the Americans were willing to suffer a little embarrassment to secure their interests in the country. Those interests, the United States now painfully recognized, were dependent on government repression. The United States had not lost faith in the ability of democratic institutions to govern the country, but it had abandoned all hope that they could protect its policy aims. Here, then, the disputes the Silent Coup and the November 1947 coup had provoked would not trouble the Thai-American relationship. The Americans would deliver no protests of Sarit's disregard for constitutional procedures, submit no demands that he reinstate the parliament, and issue no veiled threats to cut off aid. The Americans' reaction now would be much different from what it had been before, and much more positive. This coup they liked.

CONCLUSION

Military government and the relationship with the United States had progressed in unison in Thailand from 1947 to 1958. When Phibun made his dramatic policy shift in favor of the United States with the Bao Dai and Korea decisions in 1950, civilians in the press, the cabinet, Parliament, and the Foreign Ministry also saw their influence over policymaking drastically reduced. Over the following four years, as the Coup Group consolidated power with the Manhattan Rebellion and the Silent Coup and increased political repression after the late-1952 crackdown, the United States transformed Thailand into an anti-Communist, pro-U.S. bastion. When Phibun's democratic reforms loosened the military's grip on power from 1955 to 1958, the American position within Thailand deteriorated as well. Sarit's imposition of an absolutist dictatorship in 1958 then restored the alliance to its former strength. This correspondence between the level of authoritarianism and intimacy of relations with the United States was much more than mere coincidence. From early on, the fate of military government and American interests in Thailand were linked.

The United States strengthened the military and reinforced its authoritarian tendencies. Phibun's decision to shunt aside the civilian end of the foreign-policymaking apparatus in 1950 derived directly from the American promise of assistance. Once given, this aid dramatically increased the wealth and size of the military. In a country where money and guns made or broke political careers, such an expansion of resources quickly translated into political power, while the emphasis on covert military operations marginalized civilians further. Phao, the main instigator of the Silent Coup, the harassment of dissidents, and the political assassinations, especially benefited from U.S. military assistance. CIA weapons and moral support and the opium-trade profits he gained from participation in the Burmese Kuomintang operation formed the backbone of his political and military empires.

Most important, American pressure continually pushed Phibun and the Coup Group into repressing leftists more harshly than they would have if left to themselves. Throughout the period, the Thai military leadership showed a remarkable facility for co-opting leftists. Phibun appointed a leftist with communist connections, Sawet Piamphongsan, to his very first postwar cabinet, and his governments of the early 1950s included Thep Chotinuchit. Even Phao flirted with leftist publisher Ari Liwira before the 1952 crackdown. The period of increased repression from 1952 to 1954 briefly ended such efforts, but after the institution of democratic reforms in 1955, Sarit, Phao, and Phibun once more reached out for leftist support. The three secretly funded leftist opposition politicians such as Thep, lured others like Thep's brother, Phethai, into joining the government party, and financed private leftist groups such as the Thammasat law student society. All three depended on advice and financial support from leftist or procommunist Chinese. After the 1957 coup, Sarit again brought leftists and neutralists into the cabinet.

Phibun, Sarit, and Phao did not like leftists but felt no special abhorrence for them. Leftists represented merely one of many opposition groups—including conservatives in the Democrat Party, Muslim separatists, and Chinese—that annoyed them. Their co-optation of leftists was consistent with traditional Thai treatment of problem minorities. Just as the Thai-Chinese Krom Tha Sai department of the ancien régime sought to control, not repress, local Chinese, so Phibun, Phao, and Sarit never felt that Thailand's unarmed leftists posed a danger that suasion, bribery, and flattery could not neutralize. When forced to choose between the relatively powerful Democrats and the marginal leftists, the triumvirate often favored leftists.

Rather than the product of deep-seated prejudice, the government's selective targeting of leftists for especially harsh treatment resulted from the relationship with the United States. Because it opened Phibun and the Coup Group to intensified criticism from the left, the American alliance increased leftists' nuisance value. The role of the Peace Committee's October 1952 mission to Beijing in that year's crackdown testified to the government's sensitivity to criticism of its foreign policy. As well, direct, heavy, and incessant pressure from the United States strongly influenced the military's decision to suppress leftists. American complaints after the Manhattan Rebellion about government tolerance of leftists contributed to the 1952 crackdown. Robertson's May 1958 protest of *San Seri*'s anti-Americanism immediately led Sarit to oust Thanong Sathathip from the editorship, and as the U.S. military attaché commented, the arrests of leftists accompanying the October 1958 coup were largely for the Americans' benefit. At no point here did the United States have to teach the Thai generals how to act like dictators. That much came naturally. But American pressure ensured that government repression would target leftists and be harsh.

Simply put, American policy aims were incompatible with Thai democracy. Despite Phibun's decisive leadership, no consensus existed in Thai society in the late 1940s and 1950s on foreign policy. Although the military, largely because it hungered for arms aid, favored the most intimate alliance with the United States possible, civilians involved or interested in foreign-policymaking resisted close identification of Thailand with the United States. Leftists, for ideological reasons, advocated neutralism or alignment with the communist powers, while neutralist sentiments grew among other segments of society in mid-decade. Conservative politicians, such as Khuang and Seni, promoted before 1954 a less exaggerated pro-Western line. The Foreign Ministry, by nature cautious, opposed any bold moves such as Phibun's Bao Dai and Korea decisions. Had the Americans settled for the sort of close but not exclusive relationship that first Pridi and then Phibun had fostered on their own initiative before 1950, this lack of consensus would have posed little problem for the United States, but the Americans demanded much more from Thailand than simple friendship. As well, they expected outspoken support for the United States in the diplomatic arena. Only the military was willing to give such support, and only if civilian influence over foreign-policymaking were curtailed could the generals provide it. The Americans insisted that Thailand present a united public front in supporting the United States diplomatically. Partly out of sensitivity, partly because of the need for Thailand to speak with one voice for it to function effectively as the United States' diplomatic bulldog, the Americans found journalists' and politicians' criticisms of the United States intolerable. Only when military repression artificially imposed a facade of public consensus could Thailand present the united diplomatic front the United States demanded.

Viewed from this perspective, the later, more extensive U.S.-Thai cooperation acquires new meaning. In the 1960s, the Thai government allowed the CIA to run much of its "Secret War" in Laos out of Thailand, sent twenty-five battalions to Laos to fight alongside CIA-supported anticommunist groups, and permitted the United States to operate a string of naval and air bases throughout the north, northeast, and east of Thailand. Fully 75 percent of all American bombing sorties against North Vietnam left from these Thai air bases.[1] Without the firm military rule Sarit's coup had established, none of this would have been possible. Had the cautious civilians of the Democrat Party or the Foreign Ministry controlled the country's foreign-policymaking, the government might have sent no battalions to Laos. Were newspapers and politicians still allowed to discuss CIA activities openly, the United States probably would have found it more difficult to make Bangkok the transportation hub of the "Secret War." And if the press, intellectuals, and students had retained the freedom to criticize Thai foreign policy, the government certainly would not have permitted the United States to station fifty thousand troops in the country's air and naval bases. Thailand was ready to act as a launching pad for the American war against Vietnam only after Sarit's institution of complete dictatorship.

As well, the communist problems of the late 1960s must be considered with the events of the 1950s in mind. In 1965, after pursuing for decades only nonviolent political activities, the Communist Party of Thailand, possibly on orders from Beijing, began an armed insurgency. Quickly, the movement spread in various rural areas, and, by the end of the decade, some foreign observers were predicting that Thailand would become another Vietnam.[2] The fighting ended only in the 1980s. Sarit's abandonment of the policies of the 1955–1958 period—largely in response to U.S. pressure—probably increased the threat that this insurgency posed. Had the United States not successfully opposed Phibun's opening to Beijing, China might not have encouraged the insurgency. And had the government continued to co-opt leftists instead of repressing them, it possibly could have channeled the expression of local and regional grievances fueling the insurgency into less-dangerous activities. The insurgency of the 1960s and 1970s was too deeply rooted in complex social problems for deft diplomacy and minor political compromises to solve completely, but more democratic policies could have made a big difference.

Here, then, lies the tragedy of the Thai-U.S. relationship of the late 1940s and 1950s. The Americans had not embraced military dictatorship in Thailand in 1958 because they had no other choice. In increasing repressiveness and strengthening military control of government, the Americans knew the consequences of their actions. They understood that hundreds of millions of dollars of military aid, support for the most repressive elements of the government, and pressure to

censor newspapers and arrest dissidents reinforced the existing tendency to authoritarianism. They felt, moreover, that military dictatorship hurt Thailand. Although American officials wanted the country to
have strong leadership, they also believed firmly that only with civilian
checks on its power could the military run an effective government.
Otherwise, unbridled corruption and authoritarianism would hinder
development and alienate the people. But Thailand was never important to the Americans in itself. Rather, it mattered only insofar as it
could advance U.S. policy in the region as a whole. When facing the
dilemma of whether to encourage good government in Thailand or
promote American interests, the Americans' decision came easily. They
chose the latter. And Thailand suffered for it.

NOTES

INTRODUCTION

1. Julaphorn Euaruksakun, "Korani Mayakwet: Seuksa Kantatsin Nayobai nai Phawa Wikritkan" [The *Mayaguez* Incident: A Study of Crisis Decision-Making] (M.A. thesis, Chulalongkorn University, 1986), 17–41.

2. Benedict R. O'G. Anderson and Ruchira Mendiones, eds. and trans., *In the Mirror: Literature and Politics in Siam in the American Era* (Bangkok: Duang Kamol, 1985).

3. R. Sean Randolph, *The United States and Thailand: Alliance Dynamics, 1950–1985,* Research Papers and Policy Studies no. 12 (Berkeley: Institute of East Asian Studies, University of California-Berkeley, 1986); Donald E. Nuechterlein, *Thailand and the Struggle for Southeast Asia* (Ithaca, N.Y.: Cornell University Press, 1965); David A. Wilson, *The United States and the Future of Thailand* (New York: Praeger, 1970); Adulyasak Soonthornrojana, "The Rise of United States–Thai Relations, 1945–1975" (Ph.D. diss., University of Akron, 1986); Apichart Chinwanno, "Thailand's Search for Protection: The Making of the Alliance with the United States, 1947–1954" (Ph.D. diss., Oxford University, 1985); Vanida Trongyounggoon Tuttle, "Thai-American Relations, 1950–1954" (Ph.D. diss., Washington State University, 1982); Arlene Becker Neher, "Prelude to Alliance: The Expansion of American Economic Interest in Thailand during the 1940s" (Ph.D. diss., Northern Illinois University, 1980); Chatri Rritharom, "The Making of the Thai-U.S. Military Alliance and the SEATO Treaty of 1954: A Study in Thai Decision-Making" (Ph.D. diss., Claremont Graduate School, 1976); Irvin Marshall Rice, "Thailand's Relations with the United States: A Study in Foreign Involvement" (Ph.D. diss., American University, 1969). One possible exception to the above is Frank C. Darling, *Thailand and the United States* (Washington: Public Affairs Press, 1965). Although writing at the height of the Cold War in Southeast Asia, Darling took interest in the interaction between Thai diplomacy and domestic politics. Unfortunately, however, he lacked access to official documents.

4. Randolph, *United States and Thailand,* 11.

5. Thak Chaloemtiarana, *Thai Politics: Extracts and Documents 1932–1957* (Bangkok: Social Science Association of Thailand, 1978), 803.

6. J. L. S. Girling, *Thailand: Society and Politics* (Ithaca, N.Y.: Cornell University Press, 1981), 92.

7. Thak Chaloemtiarana, *Thailand: The Politics of Despotic Paternalism* (Bangkok: Social Science Association of Thailand, Thai Khadi Research Institute, Thammasat University, 1979). Thak conducted the research for his book in 1971, before archives in Thailand, the United States, and England released classified materials from the 1940s and 1950s.

8. George McT. Kahin, *Intervention: How America Became Involved in Vietnam* (Garden City, N.Y.: Anchor Press, 1987); Bruce Cumings, *The Origins of the Korean War: Liberation and the Emergence of Separate Regimes* (Princeton, N.J.: Princeton University Press, 1981), and *The Origins of the Korean War, 1947–1950: The Roaring of the Cataract* (Princeton, N.J.: Princeton University Press, 1992).

9. Thailand Central Statistical Office, Office of the National Economic Development Board, *Statistical Yearbook of Thailand*, no. 22 (vol. 2), 1945–1955 (Bangkok: Thailand Central Statistical Office, Office of the National Economic Development Board), 426.

10. As Constance M. Wilson, *Thailand: A Handbook of Historical Studies* (Boston: G. K. Hall, 1983), 26, explains, because official statistics on ethnicity and religion from the 1940s and 1950s are unreliable, only approximate figures can be provided.

PART ONE: LEARNING TO LIVE WITH PHIBUN, 1947–1948

1. *New York Times,* November 10, 1947.

2. Bulkley, "The Question of Phibun Again," April 1948, in Stanton, "Fortnightly Summary of Political Events in Siam for the Period April 1 through April 15, 1948," April 29, 1948, 892.00/4-2948, Record Group (RG) 59, U.S. National Archives (USNA).

CHAPTER ONE: PRELUDE TO THE COUP, JANUARY 1947–NOVEMBER 1947

1. Thawatt Mokarapong, *History of the Thai Revolution: A Study in Political Behavior* (Bangkok: Chalermnit, 1972), 4–42.

2. Edward Bruce Reynolds, "Ambivalent Allies: Japan and Thailand, 1941–1945," (Ph.D. diss., University of Hawaii, 1988), 58.

3. Charivat Santaputra, *Thai Foreign Policy 1932–1946* (Bangkok: Thai Khadi Research Institute, Thammasat University, 1985), 211–213.

4. Reynolds, "Ambivalent Allies," 325–329.

5. Thamsook Numnonda, *Thailand and the Japanese Presence, 1941–1945,*

Research Notes and Discussions no. 6 (Singapore: Institute of Southeast Asian Studies, 1977), 21–41.

6. Reynolds, "Ambivalent Allies," 470, 479, 544–545, 585, 591.

7. Ibid., 610.

8. For the peace settlements with the Allies, see Larry Allen Niksch, "United States Foreign Policy in Thailand's World War II Peace Settlements with Great Britain and France" (Ph.D. diss., Georgetown University, 1975).

9. The 1932 constitution provided for both elected and appointed members of parliament. The January 1946 polls filled the elected seats, and the August polls filled the formerly appointed seats, which Pridi's May 1946 constitution made elected. On the 1946 constitution and elections, as well as for the best history of the Free Thai, see Sornsak Ngamkhajornkulkit, *Khabuankan Seri Thai kap Khwamkhatyaeng Thang Kanmeuang phainai Prathet Thai, 2481–2492* [The Free Thai Movement and Political Conflict in Thailand, 1938–1949] (Bangkok: Institute of Asian Studies, Chulalongkorn University, 1988), 209–221.

10. The 1932 Promoters' "People's Party" was what political scientist David A. Wilson, describes as a *khana,* not a genuine party. Wilson defines *khana* as "the Thai term for a semiformal group." Examples of *khana* are the 1932 Promoters Party, the 1947 Coup Group, and the 1957 Military Group. Although *khana* are semiformal, private groups, Wilson explains, their role is public. Membership is initially determined by participation in a coup or some activity involving risk, and vows are exchanged upon formation of the group. Not cliques but aggregations of cliques, *khana* are "exclusive and fraternal in nature" and have something of the quality of secret societies. David A. Wilson, *Politics in Thailand* (Ithaca, N.Y.: Cornell University Press, 1962), 246–248.

11. Sornsak, *Khabuankan,* 38.

12. *Bangkok Post,* August 10 and 21, 1946. Because he could also count on the support of many independent members of parliament, Pridi's majority was actually larger than these figures would suggest. In general, it is hard to be precise about party representation in Parliament in the 1940s and 1950s. Members often switched parties, and party configurations in the assembly changed regularly. Figures cited here and elsewhere on party representation should be taken only as approximations.

13. James C. Ingram, *Economic Change in Thailand, 1850–1970* (Stanford, Calif.: Stanford University Press, 1971), 163–165; Charivat, *Thai Foreign Policy,* 286.

14. Sornsak, *Khabuankan,* 127–128.

15. Suchin Tantikun, *Rathaprahan P.S. 2490* [The 1947 Coup d'État] (Bangkok: Social Science Association of Thailand, 1972), 52–53.

16. Niksch, "United States Foreign Policy," 191.

17. *Luang* Sukhum and Atthakit Phanomyong, "Political Developments in Siam Since the Coup D'Etat of Nov. 8, 1947," September 27, 1948, box 74, document 780, William J. Donovan Papers, U.S. Army Military History Institute, U.S. Army War College, Carlisle, Pennsylvania.

18. Quoted in Norman Britton Hannah, "Power and Politics in Constitutional Thailand," unpublished MS, 1958, 103.

19. Ibid.

20. *Phim Thai,* March 20 and 21, 1947 (unless otherwise indicated, all Thai-language newspapers cited in this study are held in the Thailand National Library).

21. Ibid., March 25, 1947. Although the best translation of *thammathipat* would be "justice," Phibun gave the party the English name "Conservative," probably to appeal to British and American anticommunist sensibilities. Phibun's opponents ridiculed him for the mistranslation. See ibid., March 26 and 27, 1947.

22. Ibid., April 10, 1947.

23. *Rai-ngan Kanprachum Preutthisapha Samai Saman lae Samai Wisaman P.S. 2489–2490,* [Records of the Senate Ordinary and Special Sessions, 1946–1947], series 1, session 10/2489, November 1, 1946, pp. 245–246; Stanton, "Fortnightly Summary . . . March 1–March 15, 1947," March 24, 1947, 892.00/3-2447, RG 59, USNA.

24. Charivat, *Thai Foreign Policy,* 174–175.

25. Stanton to secretary of state, November 13, 1947, 892.00/11-1347, RG 59, USNA; Comments by Anderson, March 31, 1947, on Thompson telegram to Foreign Office (F.O.), March 28, 1947, FO 371/63910, Public Record Office (PRO), London, England.

26. Thompson to F.O., March 28, 1947, FO 371/63910, PRO.

27. Acheson to Bangkok embassy, April 4, 1947, 892.00/3-2747, RG 59, USNA.

28. Stanton to secretary of state, April 19, 1947, 892.00/4-1947, RG 59, USNA.

29. Thompson to F.O., March 29, 1947, FO 371/63910, PRO.

30. Memorandum of conversation by Landon, April 5, 1947, 892.00/4-547, RG 59, USNA.

31. Memorandum of conversation by Landon, April 15, 1947, 892.00/4-1047, RG 59, USNA.

32. Memorandum of conversation by Drumright, April 22, 1947, 892.00/4-2247, RG 59, USNA.

33. Andrew J. Rotter, *The Path to Vietnam: Origins of the American Commitment to Southeast Asia* (Ithaca, N.Y.: Cornell University Press, 1987), 56.

34. Ibid., 56–57. Rotter provides the best discussion available of the relationship between the dollar gap and British and American Southeast Asian policy in the early postwar years.

35. See comments by Anderson, March 31, 1947, on telegram from Thompson to F.O., March 28, 1947, FO 371/63910, PRO, for the clearest explanation of how the British feared Phibun would disrupt their plans for Thailand and the region.

36. Darling, *Thailand and the United States,* 82.

37. In 1947, Thailand's total trade with the United States was worth $18 million, with Hong Kong, $26.6 million, with Singapore, $21.3 million, and with the British empire as a whole, $58.6 million. Thailand Department of Commercial Intelligence, Ministry of Commerce, *Commercial Directory, 1949–1950* (Bangkok: Department of Commercial Intelligence, 1949), 221–225. Dollar figures given here are based on the market, not the official, rate of 24.1 Thai *baht*/U.S. dollar, as provided in Ingram, *Economic Change in Thailand,* 337.

38. For a discussion of the role and structure of the Division of Southeast Asian Affairs in the 1940s, see John F. Cady, Oral History Interview, July 31, 1974, Truman Library. Cady served in the division in the years immediately following the war.

39. For wartime American plans for decolonization, see Christopher Thorne, *Allies of a Kind: The United States, Britain and the War against Japan, 1941–1945* (Oxford: Oxford University Press, 1978).

40. Songsri Foran, "Thai-American-British Relations in the Post-World War II Settlement Period," Paper presented to the 7th Conference of the International Association of Historians of Asia, August 22–26, 1977, Bangkok, Thailand, 16–32.

41. Hilldring, "Memorandum for the Secretary, SWNCC," April 21, 1947, 892.20-MISSION/4-2147, RG 59, USNA.

42. Drumright, "Siamese Developments: Prevention of Coup," April 22, 1947, 892.00/4-2247, RG 59, USNA.

43. *Phim Thai,* March 24, 1947; *Thai Ratsadorn,* March 24, 1947. In the pronunciation of the name of this newspaper, the *sadorn* is silent. Care should be taken to distinguish this paper from the separate, modern paper known as *Thai Rat.*

44. *Phim Thai,* April 9, 1947; *Thai Ratsadorn,* March 31, 1947.

45. *Phim Thai,* April 10, 1947.

46. *Thai Ratsadorn,* March 30, 1947.

47. Comments by Whitteridge, December 1, 1947, on letter by F. C. Everson to the Southeast Asia Department, November 20, 1947, FO 371/63912, PRO.

48. Jin Vibatakarasa, "The Military in Politics: A Study of Military Leadership in Thailand" (Ph.D. diss., University of Oregon, 1967), 144.

49. Thak, *Thailand,* 49–50; Sornsak, *Khabuankan,* 82.

50. My discussion of the Free Thai is primarily drawn from Sornsak, *Khabuankan.* Other studies of the Free Thai are Thamsook, *Thailand and the Japanese Presence,* and John B. Haseman, *The Thai Resistance Movement during the Second World War* (Dekalb: Northern Illinois University, Center for Southeast Asian Studies, 1978).

51. Stanton, "Fortnightly Summary... August 1–August 15, 1947," August 26, 1947, 892.00/8-2647, RG 59, USNA.

52. Stanton, "Fortnightly Summary... August 1–August 15, 1947," August 26, 1947, 892.00/8-2647, RG 59, USNA; Sornsak, *Khabuankan,* 157; Thak, *Thailand,* 28.

53. Landon, "Proposed Reply to the Siamese Government if Requested for Military and Naval Missions for Training Siamese Personnel," April 21, 1947, 892.00-MISSION/4-2147, RG 59, USNA.

54. Ibid.

55. Memorandum of conversation by Landon, May 5, 1947, 892.20-MISSIONS/5-447, RG 59, USNA.

56. Memorandum of conversation by Landon, October 1, 1947, 892.20/ 10-147, and memorandum of conversation by Marshall, October 2, 1947, Lot File 54 D 190, RG 59, USNA.

57. Charivat, *Thai Foreign Policy*, 321, 381.

58. Kobkua Suwannathad-Pian, *Nayobai Tang-prathet khorng Rathaban Phi-bunsongkhram P.S. 2481–2487* [The Foreign Policy of the Phibunsongkhram Government, 1938–1944] (Bangkok: Thai Khadi Research Institute, 1989), 13.

59. Sornsak, *Khabuankan*, 186.

60. Neher, "Prelude to Alliance," 69–71.

61. *New York Times,* July 28, 1948.

62. Neher, "Prelude to Alliance," 73–74.

63. For Doll's relations with the Thais, his activities while adviser to the Finance Ministry, and American attempts to counter his influence, see Thompson to F.O., January 25, 1948, FO 371/69986; Doll to Thompson, June 9, 1948, FO 371/70016; and comments by Palliser, September 14, 1948, on Whittington telegram to F.O., September 4, 1948, FO 371/69997, PRO; Stanton to secretary of state, August 11, 1949, 892.00-(W)/8-1149, RG 59, USNA; *Bangkok Post,* August 4, 1949; Charivat, *Thai Foreign Policy*, 321, 381.

64. Thompson to F.O., April 23, 1947, FO 371/63910, PRO.

65. Neher, "Prelude to Alliance," 235.

66. Bulkley, "The Question of Phibun Again," April [n.d.] 1948, in Stanton, "Fortnightly Summary . . . April 1 through April 15, 1948," April 29, 1948, 892.00/4-2948, and Bulkley, "Present Possibilities for Regional Collaboration with Particular Reference to Southeast Asia League," in Report of the Southeast Asia Regional Conference, June 21–June 26, 1948, Section VII, 890.00-SEA Area/G-2948, RG 59, USNA.

67. Stanton, "Fortnightly Summary . . . November 1–November 15, 1947," December 5, 1947, 892.00/12-547, RG 59, USNA.

68. Stanton, "Fortnightly Summary . . . September 16–September 30, 1947," October 9, 1947, 892.00/10-947, RG 59, USNA.

69. Stanton, "Fortnightly Summary . . . January 1–January 15, 1947," January 20, 1947, 892.00/1-2047, RG 59, USNA.

70. Thompson to F.O., April 23, 1947, FO 371/63910, PRO.

71. Thompson to F.O., June 28, 1947, and comments by Turner, July 23, 1947, FO 371/63910, PRO.

72. *Phim Thai,* March 24, 1947.

73. *Thai Ratsadorn,* August 9, 1947. In a subsequent interview with *Thai Ratsadorn* on September 15, Khuang denied that he had formed an "under-

ground government" with Phibun designed to usurp control of Parliament, noting that he lacked the votes to oust Pridi. But Khuang did not deny that he had established a working relationship with Phibun.

74. Sornsak, *Khabuankan,* 253.

75. Comments by Dennis on interview with Pridi, July 7, 1947, in Thompson to F.O., July 8, 1947, FO 371/63910, PRO.

76. Thompson to F.O., June 28, 1947, FO 371/63910, PRO.

CHAPTER TWO: KHUANG AND THE COUP,
NOVEMBER 1947–APRIL 1948

1. Thak, *Thai Politics,* 558–561.

2. Phibun later revealed this to the press. *Sayam Nikorn,* January 22, 1948; *Thai Ratsadorn,* January 22, 1948.

3. Sornsak Ngamkhajornkulkit, ed., "Adit haeng Patjuban: Bantheuk Lap Jorm Phon P. Beuang Lang Patiwat 8 P.Y. 2490" [Today's Past: The Secret Writings of Field Marshal P. on the Truth behind the November 8, 1947, Coup], *Matichon* weekly, November 5, 1989, 21–22; Stanton, "Fortnightly Summary... November 1–November 15, 1947," December 5, 1947, 892.00/12-547, RG 59, USNA. Stanton's sources on the coup were Thamrong, Phibun's son, Prasong Phibunsongkhram, Phao, Phin's son, Chatchai Chunhawan, and Seni, among others.

4. Stanton, "Fortnightly Summary... November 1–November 15, 1947," December 5, 1947, 892.00/12-547, RG 59, USNA. Atthakit Phanomyong, noting like Stanton that Pridi had foreknowledge of the coup, explained that "failure [of the government] to act on the night of the coup was due to gross miscalculation as to the strength of the forces Pibul [Phibun] could muster." Atthakit to Donovan, December 19, 1947, box 73, document 680, Donovan Papers.

5. Allen to Sargent, November 10, 1947, FO 371/63911, PRO.

6. Everson to Southeast Asian Department, Foreign Office, November 20, 1947, FO 371/63912, PRO.

7. Kenneth Landon, *Siam in Transition: A Brief Survey of Cultural Trends in the Five Years since the Revolution of 1932* (1939; reprint, New York: Greenwood Press, 1968); *The Chinese in Thailand* (1941; reprint, New York: Russell & Russell, 1973).

8. Margaret D. Landon, *Anna and the King of Siam* (New York: John Day, 1944).

9. Telephone interview with Peter Pond (son of Josephine Stanton), October 22, 1991.

10. *New York Times,* November 10, 1947.

11. Stanton to secretary of state, November 17, 1947, 892.00/11-1747, RG 59, USNA.

12. Stanton to secretary of state, November 12, 1947, 892.00/11-1247, RG 59, USNA.

13. Stanton to secretary of state, November 13, 1947, 892.00/11-1347, RG 59, USNA.

14. Memorandum of conversation by Landon, November 24, 1947, Lot File 54 D 190, RG 59, USNA.

15. Thompson to F.O., November 10, 1947, FO 371/63911, PRO.

16. Allen to secretary of state for foreign affairs, November 9, 1947, FO 371/63911, PRO.

17. Comments by Palliser, December 2, 1947, FO 371/63913, PRO.

18. Allen to Dening, November 24, 1947, FO 371/63914, PRO.

19. Comments by Palliser, November 22, 1947, on Thompson telegram to F.O., November 21, 1947, FO 371/63911, PRO.

20. Stanton to secretary of state, March 31, 1948, 892.00/3-3148, RG 59, USNA.

21. G. William Skinner, *Chinese Society in Thailand: An Analytical History* (Ithaca, N.Y.: Cornell University Press, 1957), 279.

22. Allen to Sargent, November 10, 1947, FO 371/63911, PRO.

23. Stanton to secretary of state, November 12, 1947, 892.00/11-1247, RG 59, USNA.

24. Suchin, *Rathaprahan*, 124.

25. "Pridi Panomyong's [Phanomyong's] Last Tense Hours in Bangkok," *Bangkok Post*, November 17, 1974.

26. Stanton to secretary of state, "Departure of Nai Pridi for Singapore and Notification Made Thereof to Nai Khuang," December 12, 1947, 892.00/12-1247, RG 59, USNA.

27. *Thai Ratsadorn*, December 1, 1947.

28. Thompson to F.O., November 17, 1947, FO 371/63911, PRO; Drumright to secretary of state, November 18, 1947, 892.00/11-1847, RG 59, USNA.

29. Atthakit to Donovan, December 19, 1947, box 73, document 680, Donovan Papers.

30. Memorandum of conversation by Landon, December 21, 1947, 892.01/12-2147, RG 59, USNA.

31. Thompson to F.O., December 18, 1947, FO 371/63915, PRO.

32. Thompson to F.O., December 4, 1947, FO 371/63913, and Thompson to F.O., December 8, 1947, FO 371/63914, PRO.

33. F.O. to Bangkok embassy, December 9, 1947, FO 371/63914, PRO.

34. Stanton to secretary of state, December 17, 1947, 892.00/12-1747, and Douglas to secretary of state, December 17, 1947, 892.00/12-1747, RG 59, USNA; Thompson to F.O., December 18, 1947, FO 371/63915, PRO.

35. Comments by Palliser, December 10, 1947, on Inverchapel telegram to F.O., December 10, 1947, FO 371/63914, PRO.

36. *Phim Thai*, December 3, 1947.

37. Suchin, *Rathaprahan*, 125; Sornsak, *Khabuankan*, 283, 297–298; Stanton, "Fortnightly Summary . . . December 15–December 31, 1947," January 16,

1948, 892.00/1-1648, and Stanton, "Fortnightly Summary . . . December 1–December 15, 1947," January 2, 1948, 892.00/1-248, RG 59, USNA.

38. Bird to Donovan, December 20, 1947, box, 73, document 680, Donovan Papers.

39. Memorandum of conversation by Lacy, January 7, 1947, 892.00/1-748, RG 59, USNA.

40. Stanton to secretary of state, January 2, 1947, 892.00/1-248, RG 59, USNA.

41. Gallman to secretary of state, November 12, 1947, 892.00/11-1247, RG 59, USNA.

42. Memorandum of conversation by Landon, November 24, 1947, Lot File 54 D 190, RG 59, USNA.

43. Memorandum by Allen, November 14, 1947, FO 371/63911, PRO.

44. Clarke to Allen, December 19, 1947, FO 371/63915, PRO; memorandum of conversation by Lacy, February 3, 1948, Lot File 54 D 190, RG 59, USNA.

45. Thompson to Dening, November 4, 1948, FO 371/69985, PRO.

46. Thompson to F.O., December 5, 1947, FO 371/63914, PRO.

47. Stanton to secretary of state, January 10, 1947, 892.00/1-1048, RG 59, USNA.

48. Thompson to F.O., January 7, 1948, FO 371/69985, PRO.

49. *Phim Thai,* January 24, 1947; Stanton, "Fortnightly Summary . . . January 15–January 31, 1948," February 11, 1948, 892.00/2-1148, RG 59, USNA.

50. Stanton, "Fortnightly Summary . . . November 1–November 15, 1947," December 5, 1947, 892.00/12-547, RG 59, USNA.

51. Stanton, "Fortnightly Summary . . . November 16–November 30, 1947," December 18, 1947, 892.00/12-1847, RG 59, USNA. The exact number of Promoters appointed is unclear. While Stanton says that ten Promoters were appointed senators, Hannah, "Power and Politics," 123, counts only eight.

52. The Democrats themselves won fifty-three seats, and voting patterns after the election showed that they could count on support from twelve independent MPs. Hannah, "Power and Politics," 124.

53. Nigel J. Brailey, *Thailand and the Fall of Singapore: A Frustrated Asian Revolution* (Boulder, Colo.: Westview Press, 1986), 41.

54. Stanton to secretary of state, January 24, 1948, 892.00/1-2448, RG 59, USNA.

55. Stanton to secretary of state, February 5, 1948, 892.00/2-548, RG 59, USNA.

56. *Sayam Nikorn,* February 9 and 16, 1948; *Thai Ratsadorn,* February 9, 1948; Stanton to secretary of state, February 9, 1948, 892.00/2-948, RG 59, USNA; *Bangkok Post,* February 16, 1948.

57. Stanton, "Fortnightly Summary . . . February 16–February 29, 1948," March 15, 1948, 892.00/3-1548, RG 59, USNA. Prince Rangsit was Stanton's source for this incident.

58. Thompson to F.O., February 29, 1948, FO 371/69987, PRO.

59. Stanton to secretary of state, February 9, 1948, 892.00/2-948, RG 59, USNA.

60. Marshall to Bangkok embassy, February 10, 1948, 892.00/2-948; Marshall to Nanking embassy, February 10, 1948, 892.00/2-548; and Marshall to Bangkok embassy, February 9, 1948, 892.00/2-948, RG 59, USNA.

61. Memorandum by Dening, February 11, 1948, FO 371/69986, PRO.

62. Department of State, *Department of State Bulletin,* 18 (1948): 360.

CHAPTER THREE: PHIBUN'S RETURN, APRIL–JUNE 1948

1. Stanton, "Fortnightly Summary... April 1–April 15, 1948," April 29, 1948, 892.00/4-2948, RG 59, USNA.

2. *Thai Ratsadorn,* April 9, 1948.

3. Stanton to secretary of state, April 8, 1948, 892.00/4-848, RG 59, USNA.

4. Whittington to F.O., April 9, 1948, FO 371/69990, PRO.

5. Stanton to secretary of state, April 13, 1948, 892.00/4-1348, RG 59, USNA.

6. F.O. to Washington, Paris, and Nanking embassies, April 13, 1948, FO 371/69991, PRO.

7. Memorandum of conversation by Landon, April 16, 1948, 892.00/4-1648, and memorandum of conversation by Landon, April 21, 1948, 892.00/4-2148, RG 59, USNA.

8. The Burmese Communists were divided into two factions: the "White Flag" Communist Party and the "Red Flag" Communist Party.

9. Landon to Butterworth, "Siamese Political Situation," April 8, 1948, 892.00/4-848, RG 59, USNA.

10. Lovett to Bangkok embassy, April 9, 1948, 892.00/4-848, RG 59, USNA.

11. Comments by Palliser on conversation with Thompson, April 12, 1948, FO 371/69991, PRO.

12. Comments by Grey, April 14, 1948, FO 371/69991, PRO.

13. Lovett to Bangkok embassy, April 12, 1948, 892.00/4-848, RG 59, USNA.

14. Stanton, "Fortnightly Summary... March 15–March 31, 1948," April 14, 1948, 892.00/4-1448, RG 59, USNA.

15. Lovett to Bangkok embassy, April 12, 1948, 892.00/4-848, RG 59, USNA.

16. *New York Times,* April 12, 1948.

17. Stanton, "Fortnightly Summary... April 1–April 15, 1948," April 29, 1948, 892.00/4-2948, RG 59, USNA. Sawet contributed an article to the August 27, 1947, anniversary issue of the Communist Party newspaper *Mahachon* and was quoted in the September 4, 1947, issue of *Nakorn Sarn* newspaper as saying he considered himself a Communist. Sawet's leftist convictions seem not to have run deep, but his appointment demonstrates Phibun's lack of concern at this point for maintaining an appearance of staunch anticommunism.

18. Whittington to F.O., April 9, 1948, FO 371/69990, PRO.

19. F.O. to Washington, Paris, and Nanking embassies, April 13, 1948, FO 371/69991, and memorandum of conversation by Palliser, April 12, 1948, FO 371/69991, PRO.

20. Douglas to secretary of state, April 13, 1948, 892.00/4-1348, and memorandum of conversation by Landon, April 21, 1948, 892.00/4-2148, RG 59, USNA; F.O. to Washington, Paris, and Nanking embassies, April 22, 1948, and Inverchapel to F.O., April 21, 1948, FO 371/69991, PRO.

21. Stanton, "Fortnightly Summary... April 1–April 15, 1948," April 29, 1948, 892.00/4-2948, RG 59, USNA.

22. Lovett to Bangkok embassy, April 14, 1948, 892.00/4-1448, RG 59, USNA.

23. Stanton to secretary of state, April 22, 1948, 892.00/4-2248, RG 59, USNA.

24. Whittington to F.O., April 23, 1948, FO 371/69991, PRO.

25. Whittington to Pridi Debyabongse, April 30, 1948, cover letter by Whittington, May 1, 1948, and Stanton to Pridi Debyabongse, April 30, 1948, FO 371/69992, PRO.

26. Whittington to F.O., May 10, 1948, FO 371/69993, PRO.

27. Bulkley, "The Question of Phibun Again," April [n.d.] 1948, in Stanton, "Fortnightly Summary... April 1 through April 15, 1948," April 29, 1948, 892.00/4-2948, RG 59, USNA.

28. Stanton, "Fortnightly Summary... June 16–June 30, 1947," July 10, 1947, 892.00/7-1047, RG 59, USNA.

29. Memorandum of conversation by Stanton, March 10, 1948, 892.00/3-1048, RG 59, USNA.

30. Stanton, "Fortnightly Summary... February 1–February 15, 1948," March 8, 1948, 892.00/3-848, and Stanton to secretary of state, December 23, 1947, 892.00/12-2347, RG 59, USNA.

31. Stanton, "Fortnightly Summary... April 1–April 15, 1948," April 29, 1948, 892.00/4-2948, RG 59, USNA.

32. Stanton, "Fortnightly Summary... April 15–April 30, 1948," May 14, 1948, 892.00/5-1448, RG 59, USNA.

33. Stanton, "Fortnightly Summary... December 15–December 31, 1947," January 16, 1948, 892.00/1-1648, RG 59, USNA.

34. Memorandum of conversation by Newbold, September 3, 1948, 892.00/10-148, and memorandum of conversation by Stanton, October 25, 1948, 892.00/10-2548, RG 59, USNA.

35. Stanton to secretary of state, January 3, 1948, 892.00/1-348, RG 59, USNA.

36. Stanton, "Fortnightly Summary... February 1–February 15, 1948," March 8, 1948, 892.00/3-848, RG 59, USNA.

37. Bulkley, "The Question of Phibun Again," April [n.d.] 1948, in Stanton, "Fortnightly Summary... April 1 through April 15, 1948," April 29, 1948, 892.00/4-2948, RG 59, USNA.

PART TWO: U.S. MILITARY AID AND THE TRANSFORMATION
OF THAI FOREIGN POLICY, 1948–1950

1. Stanton, "Siamese-French Relations for the Period July–December 1948," January 3, 1949, 751.92/1-349, RG 59, USNA.

CHAPTER FOUR: MAKING THE CASE FOR MILITARY AID,
APRIL 1948–JUNE 1949

1. Stanton to secretary of state, December 12, 1947, 892.24/12-1247, RG 59, USNA.

2. Ibid.

3. Prince Wan to secretary of state, March 16, 1948, 892.24/3-1648, RG 59, USNA.

4. Reed to Cummins, "Siamese Request for Forty-Two AT-6 Planes," July 9, 1948, 892.24/3-1648, and secretary of state to ambassador of Thailand, July 13, 1948, 892.24/8-948, RG 59, USNA.

5. Memorandum of conversation by Landon, April 1, 1948, 892.2311/4-148, RG 59, USNA.

6. Memorandum of conversation by Landon, April 7, 1948, Lot File 54 D 190, RG 59, USNA.

7. These were the U.S. embassy's calculations. Stone to secretary of state, July 12, 1948, 892.03/7-1248, RG 59, USNA.

8. Stone to secretary of state, July 20, 1948, 892.00/7-2048, RG 59, USNA.

9. *Thai Ratsadorn,* April 10 and 11, 1948.

10. Stone to secretary of state, July 13, 1948, 892.00/7-1348, RG 59, USNA.

11. Stanton, "Fortnightly Summary. . . April 15–April 30, 1948," 892.00/5-1448, RG 59, USNA.

12. Thak, *Thailand,* 41–42.

13. Memorandum of conversation by Stanton, October 25, 1948, 892.00/10-2548, RG 59, USNA.

14. Phin to minister of interior, September 21, 1948, Interior Ministry Papers, M.T.0201.2.1.57/1, Thailand National Archives (TNA).

15. *Luang* Chamnan-aksorn to minister of interior, October 1, 1948, Interior Ministry Papers, M.T.0201.2.1.57/1, TNA.

16. Stone, "Summary of Political Events in Thailand for the Month of February 1950," March 13, 1950, 792.00/3-1350, RG 59, USNA.

17. Benson to secretary of state, October 7, 1948, 892.00/10-748, RG 59, USNA.

18. Thompson to F.O., October 1, 1948, FO 371/69998, PRO; Thorpe to director of intelligence, ID, GSUSA, October 11, 1948, 892.24/10-1148, RG 59, USNA.

19. "Communist Activities in Siam: Siamese Communist Party," p. 3, in

Report of Southeast Asia Regional Conference, June 21–June 26, 1948, Bangkok, Thailand, 890.00-SEA Area/G-2948, RG 59, USNA.

20. Ibid. Later, in the 1960s, Prasert renounced communism and became an important adviser to the army on suppression of that period's communist insurgency. See Kasian Tejapira, "Commodifying Marxism: The Formation of Modern Thai Radical Culture, 1927–1958" (Ph.D. diss., Cornell University, 1992), 556–560, for a short biography of Prasert.

21. Davies et al., "Summary of Communist Activities in Southeast Asia: Siam," p. 2, in Report of Southeast Asia Regional Conference, June 21–June 26, 1948, Bangkok, Thailand, 890.00-SEA Area/G-2948, RG 59, USNA.

22. Bushner, "Communist Activities in Siam: Secret Activities," p. 8, in Report of Southeast Asia Regional Conference, June 21–June 26, 1948, Bangkok, Thailand, 890.00-SEA Area/G-2948, RG 59, USNA.

23. Davies et al., "Summary of Communist Activities in Southeast Asia: Siam," p. 2, in Report of Southeast Asia Regional Conference, June 21–June 26, 1948, Bangkok, Thailand, 890.00-SEA Area/G-2948, RG 59, USNA.

24. McQuillen, "Communist Activities in Siam: Chinese Communists— [by] Colonel F. J. McQuillen," p. 2, in Report of Southeast Asia Regional Conference, June 21–June 26, 1948, Bangkok, Thailand, 890.00-SEA Area/G-2948, RG 59, USNA.

25. Ibid., 3.

26. Alexander MacDonald to Donovan, September 23, 1948, box 74, document 780, Donovan Papers. Siviram wrote a book in 1941 fervently praising Phibun's recapture from France of the "lost" Indochinese territories. See M. Siviram, *Mekong Clash and the Far East Crisis* (Bangkok: Thai Commercial Press, 1941).

27. *Bangkok Post,* June 25, 1948.

28. "Report of the Summary Committee on Regional Implications of the Recent Installation of [*sic*] Phibun Government: Re-emergence of Field Marshal Phibul," p. 1, in Report of Southeast Asia Regional Conference, June 21–June 26, 1948, Bangkok, Thailand, 890.00-SEA Area/G-2948, and Marshall to Nanking embassy, September 10, 1948, 892.20-MISSIONS/9-948, RG 59, USNA.

29. Marshall to Nanking embassy, September 10, 1948, 892.20-MISSIONS/9-948, RG 59, USNA.

30. *Rai-ngan Kanprachum Sapha Phu-thaen Samai Saman* [Records of the House of Representatives Ordinary Session], 2491, series 1, session 28/2491, September 23, 1948, 3226–3228.

31. *Rai-ngan Kanprachum Sapha Phu-thaen Samai Wisaman* [Records of the House of Representatives Special Session], 2491, series 1, session 8/2491, December 16, 1948, 631.

32. Hokmokkhasakdi [pseud.], "Jek Teun Fai kap Jek Prathad" [Panicky People and Firecracker Chinese], *Thahan Ma,* March 1948, 1–11.

33. Kat's thinking on the subject can be seen in his article in *Kiattisak* (weekly), January 31, 1950.

34. Speech by Phibun, "Sathanakan khorng Lok kiow-kae Kanjalajon nai Prathet Thai Yangrai" [The World Situation as It Concerns Rebellion in Thailand], February 16, 1949, Cabinet Papers, [2] SR.0201.4, box 4, file 43, TNA. *Sayam Nikorn,* February 18, 1949, reported on the speech.

35. Memorandum of conversation by Reed, May 14, 1948, Lot File 54 D 190, RG 59, USNA.

36. Lt. Gen. *Luang* Cherdwuthakat, "Thut Thahan Thai Pai Indojin" [Military Diplomats Go to Indochina], *Khao Thahan Akat* [Air Force News], October 1948, 88–94; Stanton, "Siamese-French Relations for the Period July–December 1948," January 3, 1949, 751.92/1-349, RG 59, USNA.

37. *Phraya* Saraphaiphiphat (Leuan Saraphaiwanich), "Thahan Khuan Mi Khwamru Reuang Kanmeuang Khae Nai" [How Much Knowledge Should Soldiers Have about Politics?], *Thahan Ma,* October 1948, 1–10. *Phraya* Saraphaiphiphat certainly did not represent the mainstream of army thinking. Not only was he neither a soldier nor a Coup Group supporter, but he held the aristocratic title of *phraya*. Oddly enough, moreover, he had acquired a sympathy for socialism during the time Phibun had imprisoned him on Tarutao Island for royalist activities in 1939. While held there, he became friends with several Chinese Communists Phibun had also detained. Although *Phraya* Saraphaiphiphat was atypical, it is significant that the cavalry's official journal would print his views. He indicated that the journal's editor had actually asked him to write the article. See Kasian, "Commodifying Marxism," 75–80, for a description of the *phraya*'s unusual political experiences.

38. Kasian, "Commodifying Marxism," 353.

39. Benson to secretary of state, October 7, 1948, 892.00/10-748, RG 59, USNA.

40. Charles B. McLane, *Soviet Strategies in Southeast Asia: An Exploration of Eastern Policy under Lenin and Stalin* (Princeton, N.J.: Princeton University Press, 1966), 345.

41. *New York Times,* July 25, 1948.

42. Thongchai Pheungkanthai, "Latthi Khormmunit lae Nayobai Tor-tan khorng Rathaban Thai P.S. 2468–2500" [Communism and the Thai Government's Anti-Communist Policies, 1925–1957] (M.A. thesis, Chulalongkorn University, 1978), 405–407. The Juridical Council was an arm of the prime minister's office charged with drafting legislation to be presented to parliament.

43. Memorandum of conversation by Stanton, July 26, 1948, 892.00B/7-2648, RG 59, USNA.

44. Memorandum of conversation by Landon, August 30, 1948, 892.00B/8-3048, RG 59, USNA.

45. Thorpe to director of intelligence, ID, GSUSA, October 11, 1948, 892.24/10-1148, and Stanton to secretary of state, October 27, 1948, 892.113/10-2748, RG 59, USNA.

46. Thompson to F.O., October 14, 1948, FO 371/70000, PRO.

47. Department of State, *Foreign Relations of the United States* (Washington: U.S. Government Printing Office), 1950, 6, 156 (hereafter cited as *FRUS*).

48. "The Siamese Military Organization," Southeast Asia Regional Conference—Bangkok, Siam, June 21–June 26, 1948, Papers of John F. Melby, Southeast Asia Files, box 9, folder 1, Truman Library.

49. Phot to Phibun, February 28, 1950, Cabinet Papers, [2] SR.0202.86, box 10, file 40, TNA.

50. Stanton to secretary of state, December 8, 1948, 892.00/12-848, RG 59, USNA.

51. Stanton to secretary of state, February 9, 1949, 892.00/2-949, RG 59, USNA.

52. *Sayam Nikorn*, February 18 and 25, 1949.

53. Thak, *Thailand*, 47–49; Stanton, "Summary of Political Events . . . February and up to March 7, 1949," March 25, 1949, 892.00/3-2549, RG 59, USNA.

54. Stanton, "Transmitting Political Survey of the First Six Months of the Phibun Regime," November 22, 1948, 892.00/11-2248, RG 59, USNA.

55. Memorandum of conversation by Stanton, November 30, 1948, 892.00B/11-3048, RG 59, USNA.

56. Reed to Butterworth, "Siamese Politics," November 30, 1948, 892.00/11-3048, RG 59, USNA.

57. Memorandum of conversation by Stanton, December 7, 1948, 892.00B/12-748, and memorandum of conversation by Stanton, October 22, 1948, 892.00B/10-2248, RG 59, USNA.

58. Stanton to secretary of state, November 16, 1948, 892.00B/11-1648, RG 59, USNA.

59. Stanton, "Summary of Political Events . . . November 1948," December 17, 1948, 892.00/12-1748, RG 59, USNA.

60. Stanton to secretary of state, January 10, 1948, 892.24/1-1049, RG 59, USNA.

61. *Times* (London), November 22, 1948; Stone, airgram (no addressee), August 12, 1948, 892.00/8-1248, RG 59, USNA.

62. Comments by Lloyd, September 1, 1948, FO 371/69997, PRO.

63. Dennis to Thompson, October 29, 1948, FO 371/70001, PRO.

64. Thompson to F.O., October 22, 26, and 29, 1948, FO 371/69999, PRO.

65. See documents in FO 371/69993, PRO. For a history of the Muslim separatist problem in the period, see Sathit Saengsi, "Panha lae Upasak nai Kanpokkhrorng Jangwad Chai-daen Phak Tai: Bot-seuksa chaphor Chao Thai Islam," [Problems and Obstacles in Governing the Southern Border Provinces: A Case Study of Thai Muslims] (M.A. thesis, Thammasat University, 1970), 19–20, 61; Hugh Wilson, "Tengku Mahmud Mahyidden and the Dilemma of Partisan Duality," *Journal of Southeast Asian Studies* 23 (1992): 55–59; Surin Pitsuwan, *Islam and Malay Nationalism: A Case Study of the Malay-Muslims of Southern Thailand* (Bangkok: Thai Khadi Research Institute, 1985), 141–165; and Nantawan Haemindra, "The Problem of the Thai Muslims in the Four Southern Prov-

inces of Thailand, Part One," *Journal of Southeast Asian Studies* 7 (1976): 206, 214, 217.

66. Waterfield to Grey, November 30, 1948, FO 371/70001, PRO.

67. Memorandum for Gen. Schuyler, November 8, 1948, P&O Division 091 Siam, RG 319, USNA.

68. Comments by Ledwidge, June 28, 1949, on Thompson telegram to F.O., June 17, 1949, FO 371/76299, PRO.

69. Lacy to Landon, June 10, 1949, Lot File 54 D 190, RG 59, USNA.

70. Stanton to secretary of state, April 19, 1949, 892.113/4-1949; Stanton to secretary of state, April 20, 1949, 890.00B/4-2049; and Stanton to secretary of state, May 28, 1949, 890.00B/5-2849, RG 59, USNA; *FRUS,* 1949, 7, 53; Thorpe, "Quarterly Military Survey," June 1, 1949, Lot File 54 D 190, RG 59, USNA (emphasis in original).

71. Acheson to Bangkok embassy, April 23, 1949, 890.00B/4-2049, RG 59, USNA. Butterworth drafted the telegram, but since Butterworth expressed his personal support for aid for Thailand both before and after its dispatch, the cable likely represented Acheson's own opinions.

72. *Bangkok Post,* June 23, 1949.

73. Stanton to secretary of state, June 16, 1949, 892.24/6-1649, RG 59, USNA.

CHAPTER FIVE: U.S. MILITARY AID AND THAILAND'S COMMITMENT TO THE WEST, JUNE 1949–DECEMBER 1950

1. *Rai-ngan Kanprachum Sapha Phu-thaen Samai Saman P.S. 2492* [Records of the House of Representatives Ordinary Session, 1949], vol. 2, session 11/2492, February 7, 1949, 1219; *Daily Telegraph,* June 1, 1949, reproduced in Stone to secretary of state, June 3, 1949, 892.00/6-349, RG 59, USNA.

2. *Rai-ngan Kanprachum Sapha Phu-thaen Samai Saman P.S. 2492* [Records of the House of Representatives Ordinary Session, 1949], vol. 1, session 3/2492, July 6, 1949, 133.

3. Stanton to secretary of state, June 27, 1949, 892.00B/6-2749, RG 59, USNA.

4. Stanton to secretary of state, January 21, 1949, 892.00/1-2149, RG 59, USNA.

5. *Sayam Nikorn,* August 30, 1949.

6. Robert M. Blum, *Drawing the Line: The Origin of the American Containment Policy in East Asia* (New York: Norton, 1982), 90–92.

7. Ibid., 128–129, 131. The quotation is from p. 129.

8. Acheson to Bangkok embassy, July 28, 1949, 892.20/7-2849, RG 59, USNA.

9. Blum, *Drawing the Line,* 132–136.

10. *Sayam Nikorn,* August 13, 1950; *Bangkok Post,* August 12, 1950; Wan to

Phot, July 31, 1949, Political Series, International Conferences (Southeast Asia Union), 3.4.3/5, Thailand Foreign Ministry Library (TFML).

11. Evelyn Colbert, *Southeast Asia in International Politics, 1941–1956* (Ithaca, N.Y.: Cornell University Press, 1977), 115.

12. Ogburn, "Chiang-Quirino Proposal for a Pacific Union . . . ," August 14, 1949, 890.00/8-2449, RG 59, USNA.

13. Thailand sent an observer to the conference but took no active role.

14. Phot to Phibun, July 18, 1949, Political Series, International Conferences (Southeast Asia Union), 3.4.3/5, TFML.

15. Memorandum of conversation by Reed, August 17, 1949, 890.20/8-1749, RG 59, USNA; *Liberty* (Bangkok), August 18, 1949, in Political Series, International Conferences (Southeast Asia Union), 3.4.3/5, TFML.

16. Phot to Phibun, August 19, 1949, Political Series, International Conferences (Southeast Asia Union), 3.4.3/5, TFML.

17. *Liberty* (Bangkok), August 18, 1949, in Political Series, International Conferences (Southeast Asia Union), 3.4.3/5, TFML. According to *Sayam Nikorn*, August 19, 1949, Phibun, when referring to the outside aid any Pacific or Southeast Asian Union would need, called on the "United Nations" to provide armaments. Whether he referred to the West, as *Liberty* claimed, or the United Nations, as *Sayam Nikorn* reported, the message was the same. When Phibun spoke of the United Nations, he often meant the West alone. He thus avoided appearing overly dependent on one nation or a single group of nations. Similarly, after the signing of the Manila Pact in 1954, he referred to SEATO when he was really speaking of the United States.

18. Cited in Khab Kunchorn to foreign minister, August 30, 1949, Political Series, International Conferences (Southeast Asia Union), 3.4.3/6, TFML.

19. *Sayam Nikorn*, August 28, 1949; *Bangkok Post*, August 27, 1949.

20. Stanton to secretary of state, August 29, 1949, 892.00B/8-2949, RG 59, USNA.

21. The date on the issue is illegible, but the context shows that Wan made his statement in late August or early September 1949.

22. Stanton to secretary of state, September 23, 1949, 892.00B/9-2349, RG 59, USNA.

23. Stanton to secretary of state, August 30, 1949, 890.20/8-3049, RG 59, USNA.

24. Stanton to secretary of state, August 30, 1949, 890.20/8-3049, RG 59, USNA.

25. Acheson to Bangkok embassy, September 1, 1949, 890.20/9-149, RG 59, USNA.

26. *Sayam Nikorn*, September 13, 1949.

27. Stanton to secretary of state, September 23, 1949, 892.00B/9-2349, RG 59, USNA.

28. *Sayam Nikorn*, September 19 and 20, 1949; *Phim Thai*, September 20, 1949; Stanton to secretary of state, "Prime Minister Phibun's Statements on

Communism," October 13, 1949, 892.00B/10-1349, RG 59, USNA; *Rai-ngan Kanprachum Sapha Phu-thaen Samai Wisaman P.S. 2492* [Records of the House of Representatives Special Session, 1949], vol. 1, session 7/2492, November 24, 1949, 687–689.

29. *Rai-ngan Kanprachum Sapha Phu-thaen Samai Wisaman P.S. 2492* [Records of the House of Representatives Special Session, 1949], vol. 1, session 7/2492, November 24, 1949, 687–689.

30. *Near and Far East News,* October 10, 1949.

31. Stanton to secretary of state, "Prime Minister Phibun's Statements on Communism," October 13, 1949, 892.00B/10-1349, RG 59, USNA.

32. Wan to Phot, September 3, 1949, Political Series, International Conferences (Southeast Asia Union), 3.4.3/5, TFML.

33. *FRUS,* 1949, 7, 930.

34. Thompson to F.O., December 15, 1949, FO 371/76302, PRO.

35. C. M. Anderson, "Probable Reasons for Siamese 'Cooling-off' Towards Us," November 29, 1949, FO 371/76288, PRO.

36. *New York Times,* December 23, 1949.

37. Unsigned memorandum of conversation of Phibun, Phot, Malcolm MacDonald, et al., December 20, 1949, Diplomatic Relations (Southeast Asia) Series, 2.1.1/4, TFML. Phot's chronology is incorrect. The September 1945 riots he apparently was referring to occurred a full year before the arrival of the first ambassador from Nanking in September 1946. Nonetheless, official Thai fear and resentment of what the government viewed as Chinese interference in Thailand's domestic affairs was real.

38. Phot to Phibun, September 30, 1949, Diplomatic Relations (Southeast Asia) Series, 2.1.1/4, TFML.

39. Memorandum by *Luang* Phattharawathi, October 17, 1949, Diplomatic Relations (Southeast Asia) Series, 2.1.1/4, TFML.

40. *FRUS,* 1949, 9, 141.

41. Phot to Phibun, November 15, 1949, Diplomatic Relations (Southeast Asia) Series, 2.1.1/4, TFML.

42. Phot to Phibun, November 26, 1949, and Sunthorn to foreign minister, December 13, 1949, reproduced in Thani Sukkasem, "Khwamsamphan rawang Thai kap Satharanarat Prachachon Jin: Wikhror Naew Nayobai Tang-prathet khorng Thai thi Mi tor Jin P.S. 2494–2515" [Relations between Thailand and the People's Republic of China: An Analysis of Thailand's Foreign Policy towards China, 1951–1972] (M.A. thesis, Thammasat University, 1982), 311–314.

43. Stanton to secretary of state, December 29, 1949, 892.00-(W)/12-2949, RG 59, USNA.

44. Memorandum of conversation by Stanton, September 23, 1949, 892.00B/9-2349, and Stanton, ". . . Summary of Political Events . . . October 1949," November 15, 1949, 892.00/11-1549, RG 59, USNA; Skinner, *Chinese Society,* 326.

45. Stanton to secretary of state, October 4, 1949, 892.04413/10-449, RG 59, USNA.

46. Office of Intelligence Research, "Thailand's Anti-Communist Pronouncements," OIR 5067 (PV), September 30, 1949, USNA.

47. Commander of Santiban [Criminal Investigation Department] to deputy director-general of the police, September 30, 1949, and comments by Phibun, October 6, 1949, Cabinet Papers, [2] SR.0201.77, box 3, file 26, TNA.

48. "Rai-ngan Kanprachum [Report of the Meeting]," October 18, 1949, Cabinet Papers, [2] SR.0201.77, box 3, file 26, TNA.

49. Foreign Ministry, "Reuang Kammakan Phasom Thai-Jin reu Kammakan Krom Tha Sai" [Regarding the Combined Thai-Chinese Committee, or the Krom Tha Sai Committee], November 7, 1949, Cabinet Papers, [2] SR.0201.77, box 3, file 26, TNA.

50. Memorandum of conversation by Hannah, December 17, 1949, 892.00/12-1749, RG 59, USNA.

51. Quoted in Rotter, *Path to Vietnam,* 95.

52. Ibid., 94–99, 169.

53. *FRUS,* 1949, 7, 62–63.

54. Memorandum of conversation by Landon, September 22, 1949, 851G.00B/9-2249, RG 59, USNA.

55. By tradition, the Thai government hired British subjects, such as William Doll, as financial advisers, French as legal advisers, and Americans as foreign-policy advisers. Patton was the last foreign adviser the Foreign Ministry employed. On American advisers, see Kenneth Young, "The Special Role of American Advisers in Thailand, 1902–1949," *Asia* 14 (1969): 1–31.

56. K.S.P. [Kenneth S. Patton], "Memorandum Regarding: 1) Conference at Manila 2) Recognition of Communist Government in China 3) Bao Dai Regime in Indo-China [in English]," July 21, 1949, Diplomatic Relations (Southeast Asia) Series, 2.1.1/4, TFML.

57. Memorandum of conversation by Butterworth, September 22, 1949, 851G.00B/9-2249, RG 59, USNA.

58. The word Wan used, *ruk-ran,* can mean either aggression or invasion.

59. Phot to Phibun, October 15, 1949, Cabinet Papers, [3] SR.0201.13.1, box 1, file 2, TNA.

60. *FRUS,* 1949, 7, 113, and 1950, 6, 697.

61. Phot to Phibun, May 21, 1949, Cabinet Papers, [3] SR.0201.13.1, box 1, file 2, TNA.

62. Phot to Phibun, October 15, 1949, Cabinet Papers, [3] SR.0201.13.1, box 1, file 2, TNA.

63. Phot to Phibun, November 15, 1949, Diplomatic Relations (Southeast Asia) Series, 2.1.1/4, TFML.

64. Phot to Phibun, December 3, 1949, Diplomatic Relations (Southeast Asia) Series, 2.1.1/4, TFML.

65. Memorandum of conversation by Landon, December 21, 1949, 751G.92/12-2149, RG 59, USNA.

66. Phibun comments on Phot memorandum to Phibun, December 2, 1949, Cabinet Papers, [3] SR.0201.13.1, box 1, file 2, TNA.

67. Stanton to secretary of state, December 10, 1949, 892.20/12-1049, RG 59, USNA.

68. Rotter, *Path to Vietnam,* 177.

69. Merchant to Ohly, December 27, 1949, Lot File 60 D 11, RG 59, USNA; *FRUS,* 1950, 6, 5–8.

70. Phot to Phibun, February 15, 1950, Cabinet Papers, [3] SR.0201.13.1, box 1, file 2, TNA.

71. Lacy to Butterworth, March 17, 1950, 792.5-MAP/3-1750, RG 59, USNA.

72. R. K. Jain, ed., *China and Thailand, 1949–1983* (Delhi: Radiant Publishers, 1984), 6–8.

73. Blum, *Drawing the Line,* 188.

74. Thak, *Thailand,* 59–61.

75. Ibid., 44–46.

76. Rotter, *Path to Vietnam,* 169–170.

77. Gary Hess, *The United States' Emergence as a Southeast Asian Power, 1940–1950* (New York: Columbia University Press, 1985), 353–355.

78. *Bangkok Post,* January 9 and February 6, 1950; Stanton to secretary of state, January 19, 1950, 792.00-(W)/1-1950, RG 59, USNA.

79. *FRUS,* 1950, 6, 725; *Bangkok Post,* February 9, 1950.

80. *Bangkok Post,* February 10, 1950.

81. Ibid., January 14, 1950.

82. Ibid., February 14, 1950; Stanton to secretary of state, February 24, 1950, 792.00-(W)/2-2450, RG 59, USNA.

83. *Bangkok Post,* March 7, 1950.

84. *New York Times,* February 14, 1950.

85. Memorandum of conversation by Jessup, February 11, 1950, 611.92/2-1150, RG 59, USNA.

86. Ibid.; *New York Times,* February 14, 1950.

87. Konthi Suphamongkhon, "Bantheuk reuang Kanrap-rorng Rathaban Bao Dai, Khamen, lae Lao" [Memorandum on the Recognition of the Bao Dai, Cambodian, and Laotian Governments], February 11, 1950, Diplomatic Relations (Southeast Asia) series, 2.1.1/3, TFML.

88. Personal interview with Konthi Suphamongkhon, March 9, 1992; Konthi Suphamongkhon, *Kanwithesobai khorng Thai* [Thai Foreign Policy] (Bangkok: Thammasat University Press, 1984), 456.

89. *FRUS,* 1950, 6, 748.

90. *Bangkok Post,* February 14, 1950.

91. Ibid., February 13, 1950.

92. *Kiattisak* (weekly), February 27, 1950.

93. *Bangkok Post,* February 21, 1950.

94. Ibid., February 23, 1950.

95. Konthi, *Kanwithesobai,* 456.

96. Personal interview with Konthi Suphamongkhon, March 9, 1992.

97. Stanton, "Summary of Political Events . . . February 1950," March 13, 1950, 792.00/3-1350, RG 59, USNA.

98. Colbert, *Southeast Asia,* 209.

99. *Bangkok Post,* March 7, 1950.

100. Thompson to F.O., March 1, 1950, FO 371/84363, PRO.

101. *FRUS,* 1950, 6, 42.

102. Acheson, "Conversation with the President," March 9, 1950, 792.5-MAP/3-950, and Webb to Bangkok embassy, March 13, 1950, 792.5-MAP/3-1050, RG 59, USNA.

103. Rotter, *Path to Vietnam,* 191.

104. Edwin F. Stanton, *Brief Authority: Excursions of a Common Man in an Uncommon World* (New York: Harper, 1956), 233.

105. Samuel P. Hayes, ed., *The Beginning of Aid to Southeast Asia: The Griffin Mission of 1950* (Lexington, Mass.: Heath, 1971), 258.

106. *FRUS,* 1950, 6, 60. The Thai program resembled the so-called Point Four technical assistance program provided to other developing countries in Asia, not the capital transfer programs of the Marshall Plan's Economic Cooperation Administration (ECA). The Thai program, therefore, has often been referred to as a Point Four program. In fact, however, the ECA, not Point Four's Technical Cooperation Administration, funded Chinese and Southeast Asian (including Thai) economic assistance programs. See Charles Wolf, Jr., *Foreign Aid: Theory and Practice in Southeast Asia* (Princeton, N.J.: Princeton University Press, 1960), 60–62, for an explanation of the differences between the two agencies.

107. Wan to Worakan, April 10, 1950, and Worakan to Phibun, April 11, 1950, Cabinet Papers, [3] SR.0201.13.1, box 1, file 2, TNA; *Bangkok Post,* April 11, 1950.

108. *FRUS,* 1950, 6, 96–97.

109. Maj. Gen. Plod Plodporapak Phibunphanuwat to Phibun, July 10, 1950, and Phibun comments, July 13, 1950, Cabinet Papers, [3] SR.0201.13.1, box 1, file 2, TNA.

110. Kammakan Jat-tham Prawat Thahan Thai nai Songkhram Kaoli, *Prawatisat Kanrop khorng Thahan Thai nai Songkhram Kaoli* [History of the Fighting of Thai Soldiers in the Korean War] (Bangkok: Kammakan Jat-tham Prawat Thahan Thai nai Songkhram Kaoli, 1981), 48, TFML.

111. Personal interview with Konthi Suphamongkhon, March 9, 1992.

112. *Sayam Nikorn,* July 1, 1950.

113. *Rai-ngan Kanprachum Sapha Phu-thaen Samai Wisaman Chud thi 1 2491* [Records of the House of Representatives Special Session, Series 1, 1948], session 8/2491, December 16, 1948, 631.

114. *Rai-ngan Kanprachum Sapha Phu-thaen Samai Saman Khrang thi 2 P.S.*

2493 [Records of the House of Representatives Second Ordinary Session, 1950], session 9/2493, July 3, 1950, 665–696; *Rai-ngan Kanprachum Rathasapha P.S. 2492 Lem 1 lae Rai-ngan Kanprachum Ruamkan khorng Rathasapha P.S. 2492–2494* [Records of the Sessions of Parliament 1949, vol. 1, and Records of the Joint Sessions of Parliament, 1949–1951], series 1, joint session 8/2493, July 22, 1950, 740–812.

115. *Rai-ngan Kanprachum Sapha Phu-thaen Samai Saman Khrang thi 2 P.S. 2493* [Records of the House of Representatives Second Ordinary Session, 1950], session 9/2493, July 3, 1950, 669–670, 662.

116. *Rai-ngan Kanprachum Rathasapha P.S. 2492 Lem 1 lae Rai-ngan Kanprachum Ruamkan khorng Rathasapha P.S. 2492-2494* [Records of the Sessions of Parliament 1949, vol. 1, and Records of the Joint Sessions of Parliament, 1949-1951], series 1, joint session 8/2493, July 22, 1950, 790.

117. Lacy to Rusk, July 25, 1950, 792.5-MAP/7-2550, RG 59, USNA.

118. Ely to Rusk, August 8, 1950, 792.5-MAP/8-850, RG 59, USNA.

119. Truman to secretary of state, July 14, 1950, 792.5-MAP/7-1450, RG 59, USNA.

120. *New York Times,* August 2, 1950, and January 3, 1951.

121. *FRUS,* 1950, 6, 134–135.

122. Worakan to Phibun, August 28, 1950, Cabinet Papers, [3] SR.0201.13.1, box 1, file 2, TNA.

123. Stanton, "Opening of Communist Propaganda Campaign in the Thai Press," June 27, 1949, 892.00B/6-2749, RG 59, USNA.

124. Stanton to secretary of state, August 24, 1949, 892.00B/8-2449, RG 59, USNA.

125. Stanton, "Review of Communist Propaganda in Bangkok," May 5, 1949, 892.00B/5-549, RG 59, USNA.

126. Stanton, "Opening of Communist Propaganda Campaign in the Thai Press," June 27, 1949, 892.00B/6-2749, RG 59, USNA.

127. Stanton to secretary of state, October 25, 1949, 892B.00/10-2549, RG 59, USNA.

128. Turner, "Monthly Political Report for May 1950," June 15, 1950, 792.00/6-1550, RG 59, USNA.

129. For Phethai's interrogatories on recognition of China, see report on parliamentary debate, October 10, 1949, Diplomatic Relations (Southeast Asia) series, 2.1.1/4, TFML; *Rai-ngan Kanprachum Sapha Phu-thaen Samai Saman P.S. 2492* [Records of the House of Representatives Ordinary Session, 1949], vol. 1, session 8/2492, December 1, 1949, 785. In the July 22, 1950, debate on the dispatch of troops to Korea, Phethai also, of course, opposed the government's policy.

130. *FRUS,* 1950, 6, 96–97.

131. Stone, "Summary of Political Events . . . January 1950," February 20, 1950, 792.00/2-2050, RG 59, USNA.

132. Stone to secretary of state, February 23, 1950, 792.00/2-2350, RG 59, USNA.

133. Stanton to secretary of state, March 16, 1950, 792.00-(W)/3-1650, RG 59, USNA.

134. Thongchai, "Latthi Khormmunit," 385–386; Kasian, "Commodifying Marxism," 438.

135. Phayathai [pseud.], "Mahantaphai jak Khormmunit" [The Great Danger of Communism], *Yuthakot*, May 12, 1950, 31–40.

136. Thongchai, "Latthi Khormmunit," 407.

137. *Phraya* Ramratchaphakdi to permanent secretary, Foreign Ministry, March 2, 1950, Diplomatic Relations (Southeast Asia) series, 2.1.1/6, TFML; Wan to Worakan, April 10, 1950, Cabinet Papers, [3] SR.0201.13.1, box 1, file 2, TNA.

138. Kasian, "Commodifying Marxism," 445.

139. *Ratchakitjanubeksa*, "Reuang Ham Sang reu Nam Sing Phim khao ma nai Ratcha-anajak Thai," June 19, 1950, P.S. 2493, lem thi 67, phak 1, lem 3, torn thi 35, 2721, and "Reuang Ham Khosana reuang thi kiowkap Kanmeuang rawang Prathet," July 20, 1950, P.S. 2493, lem thi 67, phak 2, chabap phiset, torn thi 40, 1.

140. Suwimon Rungjaroen, "Botbat khorng Naknangseuphim nai Kanmeuang Thai rawang P.S. 2490–2501" [The Role of Journalists in Thai Politics, 1947–1958] (M.A. thesis, Chulalongkorn University, 1983), 147.

141. Skinner, *Chinese Society*, 328.

142. Turner, "Monthly Political Report, October 1950," November 22, 1950, 792.00/11-2250, RG 59, USNA.

143. Memorandum of conversation by Stanton, October 4, 1950, 792.00/10-450, RG 59, USNA.

144. Turner, "Chinese Affairs in Thailand, November 1950," December 12, 1950, 792.00/12-1250, RG 59, USNA.

145. Office of Intelligence Research, "Political Opportunities for Chinese Communists in Thailand," OIR 5151, August 21, 1950, USNA.

146. *Luang* Chamnan-aksorn to minister of the interior, March 3 and 22, 1950, Interior Ministry Papers, M.T. 0201.2.1.57/2, TNA.

147. *Phraya* Ramratchaphakdi to permanent secretary, Foreign Ministry, March 2, 1950, Diplomatic Relations (Southeast Asia) series, 2.1.1/6, TFML.

148. Stanton to secretary of state, October 25, 1949, 892B.00/10-2549, RG 59, USNA; "Note on Anti-Communist Law," n.d. [prepared sometime after November 30, 1951, on request of Phibun], bound volumes of law and draft acts, vol. 452, "Kotmai Porngkan Khormmunit" section, "Rang Ph.B.R. Porngkan Kankratham an pen Phai tor Chat" part, Juridical Council Library. I would like to thank David Strechfuss for sharing with me his notes on the Juridical Council anti-Communist act papers.

PART THREE: FORMING THE ALLIANCE, 1950–1954

1. Allison, "Observations of John M. Allison on his Tour of U.S. Missions in the Far East, September 26 to November 16, 1952," n.d., 790.00/12-552, RG 59, USNA.

CHAPTER SIX: THE ESTABLISHMENT OF AN AMERICAN MILITARY PRESENCE, JUNE 1950–DECEMBER 1951

1. Stanton, "Military Assistance Program Fiscal Year 1951," 792.5-MAP/3-3050, RG 59, USNA.

2. For recent scholarship on the impact of the Korean War on American foreign policy, see Robert J. McMahon, "The Cold War in Asia: Toward a New Synthesis?," *Diplomatic History* 12 (1988): 307–327; James I. Matray, *The Reluctant Crusade: American Foreign Policy in Korea, 1941–1950* (Honolulu: University of Hawaii Press, 1985), 247–258; Robert Jervis, "The Impact of the Korean War on the Cold War," *Journal of Conflict Resolution* 24 (1980): 563–592.

3. "Ted" to "John," September 9, 1950, Lot File 52-19, RG 59, USNA.

4. Melby and Erskine, cover letter to "Summary, Report No. 3," Joint State-Defense MDAP Survey Mission, September 15, 1950, Melby Chairman's File 1950 (Sept. 16–30) folder, Melby Papers, Truman Library; "Area Report on Southeast Asia. . . . [Melby-Erskine Mission]," November 22, 1950, 790.58/11-2250, RG 59, USNA.

5. Robert J. Muscat, *Thailand and the United States: Development, Security, and Foreign Aid* (New York: Columbia University Press, 1990), 328.

6. Psychological Strategy Board (PSB), "U.S. Psychological Strategy with Respect to the Thai Peoples of Southeast Asia [PSB D-23]," July 2, 1953, NSC Staff Papers, PSB Central Files series, box 16, Southeast Asia (File 1) (5) folder, Eisenhower Library; Darling, *Thailand and the United States*, 82.

7. Willis Bird Funeral Volume (Bangkok: no publisher, 1991), n.p.

8. After the war, Chennault promoted several covert anticommunist operations that would make use of his struggling Civil Air Transport company. Chennault and Bird had been friends since their service together in China, and they ended up cooperating in Thailand. See William M. Leary, *Perilous Missions: Civil Air Transport and CIA Covert Operations in Asia* (University, Ala.: University of Alabama Press, 1984).

9. Willis Bird Funeral Volume, n.p.; personal interview with Police General Jaroenrit Jamrat-romran, June 1, 1992. It was common for American officials stationed in Thailand to put down roots in the country. In addition to those former OSS officers who operated businesses in Thailand, such as Bird, Alexander MacDonald (owner of the *Bangkok Post*), and Jim Thompson (founder of the world-famous Jim Thompson Silk Company), the wife of a CIA agent sent to the country in the 1950s opened the well-known Polaris bottled water com-

pany. At least one other CIA agent, Jack Shirley, married a Thai, as did Consul William Hussey. Bird remained in Thailand until his death in 1991, and William Lair worked in Bangkok into the 1990s.

10. Melby to Lacy, September 29, 1950, Melby Chairman's file 1950 (Sept. 16–30), box 12, Melby Papers, Truman Library.

11. Personal interview with William Lair, September 24, 1992.

12. Ibid.; Salao Rekharuji and Kamon Jantharasorn, *Waterlu khorng Jorm Phon Plaek* [The Waterloo of Field Marshal Plaek] (Bangkok: Phrae Phitthaya, 1957), 195–200; Willis Bird Funeral Volume, n.p.

13. Stanton to secretary of state, September 19, 1949, 892.00-(W)/9-2949, RG 59, USNA.

14. Phut Buranasomphop, *13 Pi kap Burut Lek haeng Asia* [13 Years with the Iron Man of Asia] (Bangkok: Phonphankanphim, 1981), 166.

15. *Rai-ngan Kanprachum Sapha Phu-thaen Samai Saman, P.S. 2492* [Records of the House of Representatives Ordinary Session, 1949], series 1, session 3/2492, July 6, 1949, 51.

16. The Americans, at least, believed the police better equipped than the army. For an expression of this opinion as well as an estimate of force sizes, see "Report of the Joint MDAP Survey Mission to Southeast Asia: Thailand. Annex A-1. State Department Report," September 30, 1950, Melby Chairman's File 1950 (Sept. 16–30) folder, Melby Papers, Truman Library. The figures cited here, however, should be taken only as approximations. Either because the Thais kept the matter secret or because they themselves did not know the true numbers, force size estimates in this period varied significantly.

17. Stanton to secretary of state, January 25, 1951, 792.00-(W)/1-2551, RG 59, USNA.

18. Thomas Lobe, *United States National Security Policy and Aid to the Thailand Police,* Monograph Series in World Affairs no. 14 (vol. 14, book 2) (Denver: University of Denver Press, 1977), 23–24.

19. *Sayam Rath,* March 28, 1951.

20. Personal interview with William Lair, September 24, 1992; Franks to F.O., October 4, 1951, FO 371/92143, PRO; *Kiattisak,* April 23, 1950.

21. Personal interview with Saiyud Kerdphon, May 1, 1992.

22. Denis Warner, *The Last Confucian* (New York: Macmillan, 1963), 233.

23. Alfred W. McCoy, *The Politics of Heroin: CIA Complicity in the Global Drug Trade* (Brooklyn, N.Y.: Lawrence Hill Books, 1991), 168.

24. *The Pentagon Papers: The Defense Department History of United States Decisionmaking on Vietnam. The Senator Gravel Edition* (Boston: Beacon Press, 1971), vol. 1, 366.

25. Evidence that the United States had already initiated contacts with the Nationalists appeared in August when Burma's army chief, Ne Win, protested to the American embassy in Rangoon that Burmese officials had discovered an American military officer from the Bangkok embassy in northern Burma without authorization and that the American air attaché's plane from Bangkok had

overflown the area. Ne Win added that the Burmese would arrest the U.S. military attaché if, on his upcoming trip to northern Thailand, he crossed the Burmese border. Key to secretary of state, August 10, 1950, 790B.00/8-1050, RG 59, USNA.

26. McCoy, *Politics of Heroin,* 165–166.

27. Confidential interview, Songkhla, Thailand, June 16, 1992. The Malaysian government has long suspected the Thais of tacitly aiding the Malaysian Communists. See Somkiat Suphanchanaburi, *Khwamsamphan rawang Prathet Thai kap Malesia rawang P.S. 2519–2526* [Relations between Thailand and Malaysia, 1976–1983] (Bangkok: Asian Studies Institute, Chulalongkorn University, 1987), 11–12.

28. McCoy, *Politics of Heroin,* 179–180.

29. Thailand continued to provide assistance to minority rebels on the Burmese border on into the 1990s. See *Far Eastern Economic Review,* December 3, 1992, 22–23.

30. Hla Maung to Worakan, August 8, 1950, [3] SR.0201.11, box 4, file 9, TNA.

31. *Department of State Bulletin,* 23 (1950): 986.

32. Whittington, "Siam: Annual Review for 1950," April 23, 1951, FO 371/92952, PRO.

33. Stanton to secretary of state, November 16, 1950, 792.00-(W)/11-1650, RG 59, USNA.

34. D. C. Watt, "Britain and the Cold War in the Far East, 1945–1958," in *The Origins of the Cold War in Asia,* ed. Yonosuke Nagai and Akira Iriye (New York: Columbia University Press), 97.

35. Whether the ambassador here was referring to the Central Peace Maintenance Committee or the National Defense Council is not clear.

36. Whittington to F.O., March 17, 1951, FO 371/92962, PRO.

37. Minutes [author's name illegible] to secretary of state for foreign affairs, May 11, 1951, FO 371/92140, PRO.

38. McCoy, *Politics of Heroin,* 169.

39. Ibid.

40. *Sayam Nikorn,* March 27, 1951; telephone interview with Norman Hannah, October 26, 1991; telephone interviews with Jerry Rucker, October 26 and 29, 1991; Bushner, "Monthly Political Report—September 1951," 792.00/10-2951, RG 59, USNA.

41. Stanton to secretary of state, June 12, 1952, 792.00-(W)/6-1252, RG 59, USNA.

42. Phut Buranasomphop, *Chaichana lae Khwamphaiphae khorng Burut Lek haeng Asia* [The Victories and Defeats of the Iron Man of Asia] (Bangkok: Sun Ruam Khao Ekalak, n.d.), 208.

43. McCoy, *Politics of Heroin,* 169.

44. Wallinger to F.O., September 21, 1951, FO 371/92142, PRO.

45. Wallinger to F.O., October 12, 1951, FO 371/92143, PRO; *FRUS,* 1951, 6, 296, 317.

46. Wallinger to F.O., September 28, 1951, FO 371/92143, PRO; *FRUS,* 1951, 6, 298.

47. Comments [author's name illegible], October 1, 1951, on Wallinger telegram to F.O., September 28, 1951, FO 371/92143, PRO.

48. *FRUS,* 1951, 6, 299.

49. McCoy, *Politics of Heroin,* 170.

50. Ibid., 169–172.

51. Seymour Topping, *Journey between Two Chinas* (New York: Harper & Row, 1972), 129–131.

52. Telephone interview with Norman Hannah, October 26, 1991.

53. Phao complained to an embassy official in September 1952 that, in the official's words, " 'Washington' had some time ago cut off the help which was being sent to the KMT troops." Memorandum of conversation by Brown, in Brown, "Conversation with General Phao," September 18, 1952, 792.00/9-1852, RG 59, USNA.

54. Warner, "Report on Developments in Thailand and Peripheral Areas . . . January 22–28, 1954," March 4, 1954, 792.00/3-454, RG 59, USNA. Sarit told the embassy in 1953 that he was "extremely skeptical" about U.S. plans to evacuate the Nationalists. Memorandum of conversation by Moscotti, in Widney, "Conversation with General Sarit Thannarat . . . ," August 10, 1953, 792.00/8-1053, RG 59, USNA.

55. McCoy, *Politics of Heroin,* 175–176.

56. Later, the Americans renewed their interest in the Nationalists. In the early 1960s, the United States started hiring former Nationalist soldiers in Burma as mercenaries for secret American military operations in Laos. Ibid., 177.

57. Worakan to Phibun, August 14, 1950, and January 8, 1953, Cabinet Papers, [3] SR.0201.11, box 4, file 9, TNA; M. C. Wongsanuwat Thewakun to Phibun, October 30, 1951, Cabinet Papers, [2] SR.0201.77, box 2, file 18, TNA.

58. Memorandum of conversation by Hannah, October 12, 1951, 792.00/10-1251, and Stanton to secretary of state, February 21, 1952, 792.00-(W)/2-2152, RG 59, USNA.

59. *Luang* Han-songkhram to cabinet secretary, November 17, 1951, and Det Detpradityut to cabinet secretary, January 20, 1953, Cabinet Papers, [3] SR.0201.11, box 4, file 9, TNA.

60. Jin, "The Military in Politics," 147. Because covert aid totals remain classified, and because both the Thais and Americans were prone to exaggerate their actual expenditures, these figures should be taken only as approximations. The U.S. administration, to persuade a Congress that preferred military to economic assistance, included much economic and technical aid under the broadly defined category of "defense support." The Thais inflated figures on their own defense spending to impress the Americans. Nonetheless, despite the impossibility of determining an exact ratio of American to Thai expenditures on Thailand's defenses, it is clear that the figure was extremely high.

61. Neilson, "Army Interim Report on Thailand," in "Area Report on

Southeast Asia by the Military Group of the Joint State-Defense Survey Mission to Southeast Asia [Melby-Erskine Mission]," November 22, 1950, 790.58/11-2250, RG 59, USNA.

CHAPTER SEVEN: THE UNITED STATES AND THE MILITARY'S CONSOLIDATION OF POWER, JUNE 1951–DECEMBER 1952

1. Tula Bunnag, Khuang's secretary, told Hannah of the plot. Memorandum of conversation by Hannah, in Bushner, "Current Thai Political Plottings," April 26, 1951, 792.00/4-2651, RG 59, USNA.

2. Bushner, "Attempted Coup d'Etat of June 29–30 and its Aftermath," September 19, 1951, 792.00/9-151, RG 59, USNA.

3. Thak, *Thailand*, 53–54.

4. Phibun made a broadcast conciliatory to the navy soon after his escape, but Phao went ahead and arrested Admiral Sin, and the police and army set about dismantling the navy immediately. The embassy reported receiving "numerous reports" indicating Phibun's opposition to Coup Group plans to eliminate navy power. Bushner, "Attempted Coup d'Etat of June 29–30 and its Aftermath," September 19, 1951, 792.00/9-1951, RG 59, USNA.

5. Office of Intelligence Research, "The Background of the November 29 Coup D'Etat in Thailand," OIR 5701, December 6, 1951, USNA.

6. Turner to secretary of state, October 19, 1951, 792.5-MAP/10-1951, RG 59, USNA.

7. Amrung Sakunrat, *Khrai Wa Phao Mai Di?* [Who Says that Phao was Bad?] (Bangkok: H. J. K. Kitsayamkanphim, 1983), 73–74.

8. *New York Times,* July 5, 1951.

9. Bushner, "Attempted Coup d'Etat of June 29–30 and its Aftermath," September 19, 1951, 792.00/9-1951, and Bushner, "Attempted Coup d'etat of June 29–30; further information . . . ," October 19, 1951, 792.00/10-1951, RG 59, USNA.

10. Memorandum of conversation by Hannah, October 12, 1951, 792.00/10-1251, RG 59, USNA.

11. *FRUS,* 1951, 6, 1,634.

12. Ibid., 1952–1954, 12, 658–660.

13. Brown, "Monthly Political Report for February 1952," March 28, 1952, 792.00/3-2852, RG 59, USNA.

14. Memorandum of conversation by Stanton, March 3, 1951, 792.00/3-351, RG 59, USNA.

15. *FRUS,* 1952–1954, 12, 658–660.

16. The memorandum itself has been lost, but Hannah has described the contents of the document, and it is alluded to in the State Department's response. Telephone and personal interviews with Norman Hannah, October 26 and November 3, 1991; Allison to Turner, January 11, 1952, 611.92/1-1152, RG 59, USNA.

17. Acheson to Bangkok embassy, June 30, 1951, 792.00/6-3051, RG 59, USNA.

18. Personal interview with William Lair, September 24, 1992.

19. *FRUS,* 1951, 6, 1,634.

20. A U.S. embassy dispatch also reported a rumor that British diplomats had told a pro-Pridi Thai that they had seen U.S. military officers giving advice to the army and police during the rebellion, but no clear documentation of involvement by MAAG has appeared. Bushner, "Attempted Coup d'Etat of June 29–30 and its Aftermath," September 19, 1951, 792.00/9-1951, RG 59, USNA.

21. Thak, *Thailand,* 65–69.

22. Bushner, "November 29 Coup d'etat; Comments of Sang Pathanothai," December 11, 1951, 792.00/12-1151, RG 59, USNA. Phibun's close friend, Sang Phatthanothai, described Phao's trips to the embassy. Phibun had known Sang since the war, when Sang wrote and read Phibun's "Mr. *Man* and Mr. *Khong*" (*man-khong* means "security" in Thai) radio propaganda broadcasts. After the war, when the government jailed the two men for war crimes, Phibun and Sang shared a prison cell at Phibun's request. Apparently, Phibun suffered a minor nervous breakdown while incarcerated, and Sang's companionship raised his morale greatly during this trying time. After his return to power in 1947, Phibun often called Sang to his home—usually late at night—to talk over political or personal problems. Sang's account, therefore, can be taken as well-informed and accurate. Karuna Kusalasai, *Chiwit thi Leuak Mai Dai: Attachiwaprawat khorng Phu thi Kerd nai Phaen-din Thai Khon Neung* [Life Cannot be Chosen: The Autobiography of a Person Born on Thai Soil] (Bangkok: Sayam Samai, 1956), 169; personal interview with Jirawat Panyarachun, April 19, 1992.

23. Sang Phatthanothai and Phin's assistant, *Luang* Suchit Pharaphaya, were the embassy's sources for this account of the coup. Because Sang repeatedly proved himself a reliable source, and because Suchit's description, given despite the fact that it reflected poorly on Phin, corroborated Sang's account, the narrative the two provided can be considered accurate. Phibun's subsequent conflict with the Coup Group shows that, indeed, relations between him and the Coup Group were tense at this time. Bushner, "November 29 Coup d'etat; Comments of Sang Pathanothai," December 11, 1951, 792.00/12-1151, and Bushner, "November 29, 1951 Coup d'etat and Plans of the New Government," December 12, 1951, 792.00/12-1251, RG 59, USNA.

24. The Phao supporters were Phao himself, Phao's father-in-law, Phin, Worakan (though later in the Sarit camp, Worakan was at this time aligned with Phao), Phao's brother-in-law, Praman Adireksan, and Phao's former chief of the Criminal Investigation Department, Police General Lamai Uthayananon.

25. Webb to Bangkok embassy, December 3, 1951, 792.00/12-351, RG 59, USNA.

26. Wallinger, "Siam: Political Summary for November 1951," December 7, 1951, FO 371/92953, PRO.

27. *Sayam Rath,* January 12, 1952.

28. Spinks, "Report on Provincial Developments from Special Intelligence Source for Period July 16–September 9, 1952," October 9, 1952, 792.00/10-952, RG 59, USNA.

29. Telephone interviews with Jerry Rucker, October 26 and 29, 1991; Bushner, "Political Report—September 1951," October 29, 1951, 792.00/10-2951, RG 59, USNA.

30. Memorandum of conversation by Hannah, February 2, 1951, 792.00/2-251, RG 59, USNA.

31. Turner, "Political Report for December 1950 and January 1951," February 21, 1951, 792.00/2-2151, RG 59, USNA.

32. Phethai probably was not a Communist but worked closely with Communists in the Peace Committee. His relationship with the Communists in *Kanmeuang* is unclear. For most of the several years he edited the weekly up to 1951, *Kanmeuang* balanced its numerous Marxist and leftist pieces with occasional moderate and conservative columns, but, in mid-1950, while Phethai still was editor, the Communist Party, Kasian contends, began to take over the journal. *Kanmeuang* adopted, at that time, a noticeably more radical, doctrinaire stance, and, by early 1951, the Communist Party had bought out the journal. After that, it served as the unofficial organ of the party and the Peace Committee. Officially, Jaroen Seubsaeng, chairman of the Peace Committee, was new owner, but, actually, Udom Sisuwan, head of the Communist Party's press and publication department, had bought the journal, and party member Atsani Phonlajan acted as behind-the-scenes editor. Phethai's role in the takeover is unclear. The shift toward a more doctrinaire stance occurred under his tenure, and he later joined the Peace Committee, but he lost his position as editor of *Kanmeuang* after the takeover had been completed in early 1951. Kasian, p. 524, notes that Phethai could have been either a casualty of or a collaborator in the takeover. See Kasian, "Commodifying Marxism," 495–533, for a thorough history and analysis of *Kanmeuang*.

33. Memorandum of conversation by Stanton, March 3, 1951, 792.00/3-351, RG 59, USNA. When meeting Phibun, Stanton did not say specifically why he wanted to see the government broadened, but Turner stated clearly that the embassy hoped that inclusion of the Democrats and Tiang would allow Phibun to dispense with Thep, Liang, and Pathom. Turner, "Political Report for December 1950 and January 1951," February 21, 1951, 792.00/2-2151, RG 59, USNA.

34. *Sayam Nikorn*, February 3, 1951.

35. Thak, *Thai Politics*, 675.

36. Turner cabled Washington on July 11 that, "as previously reported[,] [the] Emb[assy] has no good evidence to support [the] thesis [that the] Commies [are] behind [the] coup." Turner to secretary of state, July 11, 1951, 792.00/7-1151, RG 59, USNA.

37. Memorandum of conversation by Hannah, July 16, 1951, 792.00/7-1651, RG 59, USNA.

38. Kasian, "Commodifying Marxism," 270, states that the committee was "largely formed and staffed by the TCP [Communist Party of Thailand]."

39. Craig J. Reynolds, *Thai Radical Discourse: The Real Face of Thai Feudalism Today* (Ithaca, N.Y.: Southeast Asia Program, Cornell University, 1987), 27.

40. Yuangrat Wedel and Paul Wedel, *Radical Thought, Thai Mind: The Development of Revolutionary Ideas in Thailand* (Bangkok: Assumption Business Administration College, 1987), 70. Like many Thai radicals, Kulab retained faith in Buddhism. Although, according to Kasian, "Commodifying Marxism," 345, Jaroen may have belonged to the Communist Party, Kulab never did.

41. Wiwat Khatithammanit, "Kabot Santiphap" [The Peace Rebellion], *Warasan Thammasat* 14 (June 1985): 13.

42. Turner, "Political Report for November 1950," December 26, 1950, 792.00/12-2650, and Turner, "Political Report for December 1950 and January 1951," February 21, 1951, 792.00/2-2151, RG 59, USNA.

43. See Kasian, "Commodifying Marxism," 420–422, for a list and description of leftist publications of the time.

44. Of Ari's political affiliations, Kasian, "Commodifying Marxism," 530, says: "While Ari was a known progressive and showed his sympathy towards Pridi and Communist China, there is no conclusive evidence as to Ari's alleged communist connection. Some [leftists of the time] chose to believe it . . . , others did not."

45. Brown, "Conditions in Northeast Thailand and Their Effect on its Security," April 23, 1952, 792.00/4-2352, RG 59, USNA.

46. *Phim Thai*'s circulation in 1951 is unknown, but a U.S. embassy dispatch of January 1956 described it as "the largest Thai-language daily." Magill, "Thai Press Advocacy of a More Independent Thai Foreign Policy," January 11, 1956, 692.00/1-1156, RG 59, USNA.

47. Bushner, "Reaction of One Coup Leader to U.S. Representations Regarding the November 29 Coup d'etat," December 13, 1951, 792.00/12-1351, RG 59, USNA.

48. Melby to Lacy, September 19, 1950, Melby Chairman's File 1950 (Sept. 16–30), box 12, Melby Papers, Truman Library.

49. Lacy to Rusk, February 13, 1951, 792.00/2-1351, RG 59, USNA.

50. Thak, *Thai Politics,* 677.

51. Bushner, "Reaction of One Coup Leader to U.S. Representations Regarding the November 29 Coup d'etat," December 13, 1951, 792.00/12-1351, RG 59, USNA.

52. Thongchai, "Latthi Khormmunit," 169, 405–406.

53. Deputy secretary of the cabinet to legislative adviser of the Juridical Council, September 16, 1950, bound volumes of law and draft acts, vol. 452, "Kotmai Porngkan Khormmunit" section, "Khormmunit (Latthi)" part, Juridical Council Library.

54. Thongchai, "Latthi Khormmunit," 408–409.

55. Deputy secretary of the cabinet to legislative adviser of Juridical Coun-

cil, March 9, 1951, bound volumes of law and draft acts, vol. 452, "Kotmai Porng-kan Khormmunit" section, "Khormmunit" part, Juridical Council Library.

56. Phichan Bunlayong [Thai alias of René G. Guyon], "Interpretation of the Constitution and the Declaration of Human Rights as far as Communism is Concerned," April 2, 1951, "Kotmai Porngkan Khormmunit" section, "Khorm-munit" part, Juridical Council Library; Thongchai, "Latthi Khormmunit," 408.

57. *Bangkok Post,* September 3, 1951.

58. Minutes of meeting 36/2494, June 5, 1951, bound volumes of law and act drafts, vol. 452, "Kotmai Porngkan Khormmunit" section, "Khormmunit" part, Juridical Council Library; Bushner, "November 29 Coup d'etat; Com-ments by Sang Pathanothai," December 11, 1951, 792.00/12-1151, RG 59, USNA.

59. *Sayam Rath,* January 15 and 16, 1952.

60. "(Preliminary) Draft Act on Control of Subversive Activities," January 18, 1952, bound volumes of law and act drafts, vol. 452, "Kotmai Porngkan Khormmunit" section, "Rang Ph.B.R. Porngkan Kankratham an pen phai tor Chat" part, Juridical Council Library.

61. *Sayam Rath,* January 15, 1952.

62. *Sayam Nikorn,* January 14, 1952.

63. General-secretary of cabinet to general-secretary of Juridical Council, January 18, 1952, bound volumes of law and act drafts, vol. 452, "Kotmai Porngkan Khormmunit" section, "Rang Ph.B.R. Porngkan Kankratham an pen Phai tor Chat" part, Juridical Council Library.

64. *Sayam Rath,* January 15, 1952.

65. "Redraft of section 3 and section 5," February 18, 1952, and Juridical Council to cabinet, March 13, 1952, bound volumes of law and act drafts, vol. 452, "Kotmai Porngkan Khormmunit" section, "Rang Ph.B.R. Porngkan Kan-kratham an pen Phai tor Chat" part, Juridical Council Library.

66. Memorandum of conversation by Hannah, March 7, 1952, 792.00/3-752, RG 59, USNA. The dispute over the promulgation of the constitution extended to the king himself. The king, apparently wanting to assert his inde-pendence of the Coup Group and supported by Phibun, refused to leave his Hua Hin summer home for Bangkok to issue the new constitution to parlia-ment on March 8, as the Coup Group scheduled. The king agreed only after Phao, Fuen, Prayoon Phamornmontri, and Dawee Chullasappa flew to Hua Hin and virtually forced the king to go to Bangkok. *Sayam Nikorn,* March 9, 1952; *Bangkok Post,* March 7 and 8, 1952; memorandum of conversation by Hannah, March 8, 1952, 792.00/3-852, RG 59, USNA.

67. Memorandum of conversation by Hannah, March 8, 1952, 792.00/3-852, RG 59, USNA. *Sayam Nikorn,* March 9, 1952, reported that Phibun publicly announced his intention to resign as prime minister and assume the presi-dency of Parliament instead. Sang told Hannah that Sang himself was responsi-ble for convincing Phibun to make the move. It is interesting to note that, at this early point, Phibun was already considering seeking a popular power base. Several years later, he followed through with the plans.

68. Thak, *Thailand*, 94–97.

69. Several sources, including Phao himself, revealed in later months to the U.S. embassy that Phibun had been pressing Phao to conduct a sweep of leftists but that Phao had resisted. Brown, "Comments by General Phao on Recent Anti-Communist Police Action," December 9, 1952, 792.00/12-952, RG 59, USNA.

70. Brown, "Thai National Elections of February 26," April 15, 1952, 792.00/4-1552; Brown, "Monthly Political Report: August–September 1952," October 27, 1952, 792.00/10-2752; and Brown, "Chinese Affairs in Thailand, March 1952," April 19, 1952, 792.00/4-1952, RG 59, USNA.

71. *Kiattisak*, August 22 and 23, 1952.

72. Wiwat, "Kabot Santiphap," 13–14.

73. President of the cabinet to secretary-general of Juridical Council, September 3, 1952, bound volumes of law and act drafts, vol. 452, "Kotmai Porngkan Khormmunit" section, "Kotmai Porngkan Khormmunit" part, Juridical Council Library.

74. President of the cabinet to secretary-general of Juridical Council, September 3, 1952, draft communist activities act submitted by Nai Yut, n.d., and meeting no. 61/2495 minutes, October 14, 1952, bound volumes of law and act drafts, vol. 452, "Kotmai Porngkan Khormmunit" section, "Kotmai Porngkan Khormmunit" part, Juridical Council Library.

75. *Bangkok Post*, October 27, 1952.

76. *Sayam Nikorn*, October 14, 1952.

77. Spinks, "Anti-Communist Police Action of November–December 1952," January 17, 1953, 792.00/1-1753, RG 59, USNA. Rumors of tensions were so widespread that Phao had to publicly deny reports of problems between the two men. *Bangkok Post*, November 8, 1952.

78. *Sayam Nikorn*, November 5, 1952; *Bangkok Post*, November 4, 1952.

79. Spinks, "Anti-Communist Police Action of November–December 1952," January 17, 1953, 792.00/1-1753, and Stanton to secretary of state, November 14, 1952, 792.00/11-1452, RG 59, USNA; Wiwat, "Kabot Santiphap," 18. The account the government gave the press of the events of November 9 and 10 corroborates the reports the embassy received. The government reported that Phibun did, in fact, go to Sarit and Phin before arranging a meeting with Phao on the night of November 9, and, although they did not participate in the arrests, the army, navy, and air force did go on alert. Because this first batch of detainees consisted of only lawyers, students, and journalists, clearly the three military branches were protecting themselves from something more menacing than the targets of the sweep. *Sayam Rath*, November 11 and 12, 1952; *Bangkok Post*, November 10, 1952.

80. Spinks, "Anti-Communist Police Action of November–December 1952," January 17, 1953, 792.00/1-1753, RG 59, USNA. One legacy of the Peace Committee's campaign and the "Peace Rebellion" was the leftist connotation the word "peace" *(santiphap)* acquired. Because of this new connotation, after the crackdown, the name of the present official residence of the prime minis-

ter (then serving as the offices of the Ministry of Culture), Ban Santiphap ("Peace House"), was changed to its current name, Ban Phitsanulok. Wiwat, "Kabot Santiphap," 34.

81. For an English-language copy of the act, see Thak, *Thai Politics,* 819–820. The above account of the events leading up to the crackdown and the passage of the Anti-Communist Act explains why the act was passed only after the crackdown began, not before, as would be expected. With a rubber-stamp parliament, there was no need, contrary to what Wiwat, "Kabot Santiphap," 31, claims, for a crackdown to provide the excuse for passing the act, but there was real need for a strong law to help with prosecutions. The government failed to pass the law in advance of the sweep because the arrests of the airmen led Phibun to force Phao to act before the law was ready.

82. Wiwat, "Kabot Santiphap," 30.

83. Kasian, "Commodifying Marxism," 349.

84. *Sayam Rath,* November 15, 1952; *Bangkok Post,* November 12, 1952.

85. Spinks, "Anti-Communist Police Action of November–December 1952," January 17, 1953, 792.00/1-1753, RG 59, USNA.

86. Whitteridge to F.O., November 14, 1952, FO 371/101168, PRO.

87. *Sayam Nikorn,* November 11, 1952.

88. *Sayam Rath,* November 13, 1952.

89. *Bangkok Post,* October 10, 1958.

90. Thak, *Thailand,* 87–90.

91. Suwimon, "Botbat khorng Naknangseuphim," 141; Spinks, "Political Reports for the Months of February and March 1953," May 6, 1953, 792.00/3-653, RG 59, USNA.

92. See Kasian, "Commodifying Marxism," 244, for a list of political murders in the period. Phut, *Chaichana,* 274–276, describes fairly openly the police's murder of the southern Muslim activist Haji Sulong in 1954.

93. Stanton, "Review of the Mutual Security Program in Thailand," January 15, 1953, 792.5-MSP/1-1553, RG 59, USNA.

94. Spinks, "Anti-Communist Police Action of November–December 1952," January 17, 1952, 792.00/1-1753, RG 59, USNA.

95. *New York Times,* December 9, 1952; *Bangkok Post,* January 20, 1953.

96. Spinks, "Anti-Communist Police Action of November–December 1952," January 17, 1952, 792.00/1-1753, RG 59, USNA.

97. Stanton, "Summary of Thai Political and Economic Situation as of January 1953," January 23, 1953, 792.00/1-2353, RG 59, USNA.

CHAPTER EIGHT: BUILDING THE BASTION,
JANUARY 1953–SEPTEMBER 1954

1. Kahin, *Intervention,* 38–39, 43.

2. Department of Defense, *United States–Vietnam Relations, 1945–1967* (Washington: U.S. Government Printing Office, 1971), vol. 9, 62.

3. Minutes of the 143rd Meeting of the NSC, May 6, 1953, and Minutes of the 144th Meeting, May 13, 1953, Whitman Files, NSC series, box 4, Eisenhower Library.

4. Psychological Strategy Board, "U.S. Psychological Strategy with Respect to the Thai Peoples of Southeast Asia [PSB D-23]," July 2, 1953, NSC Staff Papers, PSB Central Files series, box 16, Southeast Asia (File 1) (5) folder, Eisenhower Library. Hereafter cited as PSB D-23.

5. Ibid., 4.

6. Ibid., 7.

7. An Office of Intelligence Research report commented that "most indications point to a domestic and defensive pre-occupation on the part of Peiping in creating the new region." Office of Intelligence Research, OIR 6318, July 3, 1953, *Declassified Documents Reference System* (Washington: Carrolton Press), vol. 7 (1981), no. 353A. Colbert, *Southeast Asia,* 306, notes that "no such use [as a base of operations against Thailand or its neighbors] appears to have been made of this particular area, then or later."

8. Linguists refer to the family of languages closely related to Thai, including Lao and Shan, as "Tai" languages.

9. For a review of the considerable anthropological literature on Thailand's supposedly "loosely structured" society, see Hans-Dieter Evers, ed., *Loosely Structured Social Systems: Thailand in Comparative Perspective,* Cultural Report Series no. 17 (New Haven, Conn.: Yale University Southeast Asia Studies, 1969). Also see Jane Bunnag, "Loose Structure: Fact or Fancy? Thai Society Reexamined," in *Modern Thai Politics: From Village to Nation,* ed. Clark D. Neher (Cambridge, Mass.: Schenkman Publishing Co., 1976), 133–152.

10. PSB D-23, 18.

11. Ibid., 19.

12. Some linguists classify the dialect of northern Thailand as Lao; others consider it separate from the dialect of northeastern Thailand and Laos. Northern Thais themselves call their language *khammeuang,* not Lao. Here, the term "Lao" refers to speakers of the language of northeastern Thailand and lowland Laos, and "Laotian" refers to inhabitants of Laos, regardless of ethnicity or language. From one-third to one-half of the population of Laos at that time were non-Lao.

13. PSB D-23, 25. According to Frederick P. Munson et al., *Area Handbook for Cambodia* (Washington: Foreign Area Studies, American University, 1968), 58, about twenty thousand Lao and Thai lived as farmers in Cambodia's Siem Reap and Battambang provinces at the time. This figure may underestimate the true numbers. In addition to the Thai-related groups in Laos, Cambodia, Burma, and China, an estimated 385,000 Tai tribesmen lived in North Vietnam as of 1960. Danny J. Whitfield, *Historical and Cultural Dictionary of Vietnam,* Historical and Cultural Dictionaries of Asia series, no. 7 (Metuchen, N.J.: Scarecrow Press, 1976), 271. PSB D-23 did not specifically discuss the Tai in Vietnam, but the United States included them in covert programs of the period.

14. Guy Morechand, "The Many Languages and Cultures of Laos," in *Laos:*

War and Revolution, ed. Nina S. Adams and Alfred McCoy (New York: Harper & Row, 1970), 31.

15. Charles A. Stevenson, *The End of Nowhere: American Policy toward Laos since 1954* (Boston: Beacon Press, 1972), 13.

16. PSB D-23, 5–6.

17. Ibid., 5.

18. Ibid., 8.

19. Quoted in John Lewis Gaddis, *Strategies of Containment: A Critical Appraisal of Postwar American National Security Policy* (New York: Oxford University Press, 1982), 155.

20. PSB D-23, 29.

21. Ibid., 35. The final portion of this quotation is sanitized, but the context, discussing extension of the plan into Indochina, makes clear where the PSB intended to take the program.

22. Ibid., 35.

23. "U.N. Appeal on Laos Invasion and Threat to Thailand," June 23, 1953, 751J.00/6-2353, RG 59, USNA.

24. Ibid.

25. *New York Times,* May 7, 1953.

26. "U.N. Appeal on Laos Invasion and Threat to Thailand," June 23, 1953, 751J.00/6-2353, RG 59, USNA.

27. Dulles to Paris embassy, May 3, 1953, 751J.00/5-353, RG 59, USNA.

28. *FRUS,* 1952–1954, 12, 664–665.

29. Minutes of 143rd meeting of the NSC, May 6, 1953, Whitman Files, NSC series, box 4, Eisenhower Library.

30. *FRUS,* 1952–1954, 12, 671–672; Wan to Phibun, May 6, 1953, Cabinet Papers, [3] SR.0201.9, box 3, file 21, TNA.

31. *Department of State Bulletin* 28 (1953): 708.

32. Dillon to secretary of state, May 9, 1953, 751J.00/5-953, and memorandum of conversation by Allen, May 22, 1953, 792.00/5-2253, RG 59, USNA.

33. Wan to Phibun, "Sathanakan nai Prathet Lao" [The Situation in Laos], May 11, 1953, and Pun to deputy prime minister, "Sathanakan nai Prathet Lao" [The Situation in Laos], May 12, 1953, Cabinet Papers, [3] SR.0201.9, box 2, file 18, section 2, TNA.

34. Wan to Phibun, May 14, 1953, Cabinet Papers, [3] SR.0201.9, box 2, file 18, TNA.

35. Pun to Phibun, May 12, 1953, Cabinet Papers, [3] SR.0201.9, box 2, file 18, TNA.

36. Wan to Phibun, May 14, 1953, Cabinet Papers, [3] SR.0201.9, box 2, file 18. TNA.

37. Pun to Phibun, May 12, 1953, and Wan to Phot, May 19, 1953, Cabinet Papers, [3] SR.0201.9, box 2, file 18, TNA.

38. Memorandum of conversation by Wan, May 23, 1953, Cabinet Papers, [3] SR.0201.9, box 2, file 18, TNA.

39. Memorandum of conversation by Allen, May 22, 1953, 792.00/5-2253, RG 59, USNA.

40. Memorandum of conversation by McBride, May 22, 1953, 751J.00/5-2253, RG 59, USNA.

41. Lodge to secretary of state, May 27, 1953, 751J.00/5-2753, RG 59, USNA.

42. Department of Defense, *United States–Vietnam Relations,* 9, 44.

43. Memorandum of conversation by Dulles, June 16, 1953, 751H.00/6-1653, RG 59. USNA.

44. Robertson to secretary of state, "Possible Thai Case Before the United Nations Security Council," June 18, 1953, 792.00/6-1853, RG 59, USNA.

45. Memorandum of conversation by Dulles, June 22, 1953, 792.00/6-2253, RG 59, USNA.

46. Department of Defense, *United States–Vietnam Relations,* 9, 69–96; George Herring, *America's Longest War: The United States and Vietnam, 1950–1975* (New York: Knopf, 1986), 76.

47. Stanton's disagreements with the State Department's Indochina policy dated back to 1947, when he pleaded with Washington to pay greater heed to nationalist sentiments in the area. *FRUS,* 1947, 6, 92.

48. Telephone interview with Peter Pond, October 22, 1991.

49. Stanton to Robert F. Woodward, December 1, 1952, and April 13, 1953, Stanton Papers, Stanton Personal Correspondence Box, Ambassador's Personal Folder, University of Bridgeport Library.

50. Anthony Cave Brown, *The Last Hero: Wild Bill Donovan* (New York: Times Books, 1982), 822.

51. Gresham arrived in November 1952.

52. Memorandum of conversation by Matthews, July 16, 1953, Lot File 55 D 368, and memorandum of conversation by Landon, June 22, 1953, Lot File 55 D 368, RG 59, USNA; *FRUS,* 1952–1954, 12, 398.

53. Smith to Cutler, September 11, 1953, Office of the Special Assistant for National Security Affairs (SPANSA) Papers, NSC series, Briefing Notes subseries, SEA folder, box 16, Eisenhower Library.

54. Cited in Brown, *Last Hero,* 822.

55. *FRUS,* 1952–1954, 12, 684–686.

56. Donovan to Smith, August 19, 1953, box 137B, Donovan Papers.

57. *FRUS,* 1952–1954, 12, 697–698; Operations Coordinating Board (OCB) Working Group on PSB D-23, "Progress Report on PSB D-23," January 27, 1954, *Declassified Documents Reference System,* vol. 13 (1987), no. 1163.

58. Memorandum of conversation by Wan, December 19, 1953, Cabinet Papers, [3] SR.0201.17, box 1, file 2, TNA; Wan to Phibun, January 30, 1954, *Luang* Chamnan-aksorn to foreign minister, February 11, 1954, and n.a., "Khrongkan Jat-tang Prachasamphan Jangwat: Jangwat Ubon Ratchathani, Jangwat Udorn Thani, Jangwat Nakhorn Ratchasima, lae Jangwat Lampang" [The Program to Establish Provincial Public Relations in Ubon Ratchathani, Udorn

Thani, Nakhorn Ratchasima, and Lampang Provinces], n.d., Foreign Ministry Papers, KT.81.35, box 2, file 42, TNA.

59. NSC 5405 Progress Report, August 6, 1954, Annex A, p. 8, SPANSA, NSC Series, Policy Papers subseries, NSC 5405 (2) folder, box 9, Eisenhower library.

60. An interesting adjunct to Donovan's anticommunist propaganda program was an effort he made to heighten the profile of Thai Communists. After his arrival in Bangkok in the summer of 1953, Donovan commissioned an American linguist then living in Bangkok, William Gedney, to translate Marx's "The Communist Manifesto" into Thai. Donovan apparently hoped to scare the Thai government into taking more seriously the communist menace. Gedney hired as his assistant, with embassy approval and funding, a bright, young languages and literature student from Chulalongkorn University, Jit Phumisak. Ironically, Jit later became a leading Marxist intellectual and, after his death in 1966, an icon of leftist students. Jit's biographer and translator, Craig Reynolds, therefore comments that Donovan "unwittingly contributed to the education of a Thai radical by placing in front of him a key Marxist work." Reynolds, *Thai Radical Discourse*, 32.

61. PSB D-23.

62. Memorandum of conversation by Wan, December 19, 1953, Cabinet Papers, [3] SR.0201.17, box 1, file 2, TNA; Wan to Phibun, January 30, 1954, *Luang* Chamnan-aksorn to foreign minister, February 11, 1954, and n.a., "Khrongkan Jat-tang Prachasamphan Jangwat: Jangwat Ubon Ratchathani, Jangwat Udorn Thani, Jangwat Nakhorn Ratchasima, lae Jangwat Lampang" [The Program to Establish Provincial Public Relations in Ubon Ratchathani, Udorn Thani, Nakhorn Ratchasima, and Lampang Provinces], n.d., Foreign Ministry Papers, KT.81.35, box 2, file 42, TNA.

63. Randolph, *United States and Thailand*, 22.

64. Jarvis to Young, "FOA Program in Thailand," April 12, 1955, 792.5-MSP/4-1255, RG 59, USNA.

65. Personal interview with William Lair, September 24, 1992.

66. Telephone interview with William J. vanden Heuvel, October 30, 1991.

67. Personal interview with William Lair, September 24, 1992. The Krom was formally founded in January 1954. *Ratchakitjanubeksa,* January 17, 1954, vol. 1:1, part 6, 309–310.

68. A Thai cabinet directive made explicit the obligation of the Krom Pramuan Ratchakan Phaen-din to share intelligence with the CIA. Thailand Cabinet Meeting Topics, "Reuang Kanruammeu kap Rathaban Amerikan" [Regarding Cooperation with the American Government], January 5, 1955, session 2/2498. I would like to thank Profs. Chai-anan Samudavanija, Narong Phuangphit, and Chakhrid Chumwathana for sharing with me these invaluable cabinet papers, which Ajan Chakhrid and Ajan Narong copied by hand.

69. Yut Jaranyanon to permanent-secretary, Interior Ministry, August 15, 1953, Interior Ministry Papers, M.T. 0201.2.1.8, file 47, TNA; Personal interview

with William Lair, September 24, 1992. The BPP was formally established in December 1954. *Ratchakitjanubeksa,* January 4, 1955, vol. 72, part 2, 10–11.

70. Personal interview with William Lair, September 24, 1992.

71. Phao's successor as police chief, Sawai Sawaisaenyakorn, revealed this in 1957. Kulab Saipradit, *Adit thi pen Bot-rian: Khor-khian Thangkanmeuang Yuk 2500* [Lessons from the Past: Political Writings of the 1957 Era] (Bangkok: Saeng Thian, 1979), 199.

72. During his tenure as ambassador, Donovan discussed at length counterinsurgency strategy with Britain's high commissioner and military commander in Malaya, General Sir Gerald Templer. Brown, *Last Hero,* 825.

73. *Rai-ngan Kanprachum Sapha Phu-thaen Ratsadorn Samai Wisaman P.S. 2497 Lem 2* [Records of the House of Representatives Special Session, 1954, vol. 2], session 9/2497, February 4, 1954; *Sayam Nikorn,* July 4, 1954.

74. "Defense Program Approval 54-72," July 30, 1954, Lot File 55 D 480, RG 59, USNA; *FRUS, 1952–1954,* 12, 744.

75. Personal interview with Police General Jaroenrit Jamrat-romran, June 1, 1992.

76. *FRUS,* 1952–1954, 12, 364; Edward Lansdale, *In the Midst of Wars: An American's Mission to Southeast Asia* (New York: Harper & Row, 1972), 126.

77. Herring, *America's Longest War,* 44.

78. Although it began after the departure of Donovan from Thailand in late 1954 or 1955, the Thai hill-tribe program clearly was in the spirit of PSB D-23.

79. Personal interviews with Joseph Smith, November 4, 1991; David Whipple, November 6, 1991; John Hart, November 4, 1991; and Police General Jaroenrit Jamrat-romran, June 1, 1992. Hart, CIA station chief in Thailand from late 1955 to 1957, claims that he devoted the majority of CIA personnel, funds, and equipment to the hill-tribe program.

80. Personal interview with Leonard Unger, November 6, 1991.

81. See Arthur J. Dommen, *Conflict in Laos: The Politics of Neutralization,* rev. ed. (New York: Praeger, 1971), 294–297, for a short biography of Vang Pao.

82. Neil Sheehan et al., eds., *The Pentagon Papers: As Published by the New York Times* (New York: Bantam, 1971), 133.

83. *Bangkok Post,* May 22 and 29, 1953; *New York Times,* May 23 and 28, 1953; Thomson to secretary of state, May 28, 1953, 651J.92/5-2853, RG 59, USNA.

84. Thomson, "Laotian Attitudes on National Defense," March 29, 1953, 751J.5/3-2953, RG 59, USNA.

85. Phot to Foreign Ministry, June 24, 1953, Wan to Phibun, June 27, 1953, and *Luang* Chamnan-aksorn to foreign minister, July 4, 1953, Cabinet Papers, [2] SR.0201.86, box 10, file 40, TNA.

86. Samai Waewprasert, "Reuang Phiset Bang Reuang kiow-kap Khwam-samphan rawang Prathet Thai kap Prathet Lao" [Important Issues Regarding

Relations between Thailand and Laos], September 1953, Cabinet Papers, [3] SR.0201.9, box 2, file 6, TNA.

87. *Bangkok Post,* October 6, 1953.

88. Pun to Wan, October 19, 1953, and Worakan to cabinet secretary, October 22, 1953, Cabinet Papers, [3] SR.0201.9, box 2, file 6, TNA.

89. Memorandum of conversation by director-general of European and American Department, Foreign Ministry, March 4, 1954, Foreign Ministry Papers, KT.87, box 1, file 7, TNA; *New York Times,* December 24, 1953.

90. *Bangkok Post,* January 11, 1954; *New York Times,* January 9, 10, and 15, 1954; *Le Monde,* January 10–11, 1954, cited in Virginia Thompson and Richard Adloff, *Minority Problems in Southeast Asia* (New York: Russell & Russell, 1955), 226.

91. *New York Times,* January 9, 1954, reported that Cambodia, fearful of Vietnamese domination, "at least appeared interested in the alliance," but a week later, the Cambodian foreign minister announced that his country could not join the union without France. Ibid., January 15, 1954.

92. Thompson and Adloff, *Minority Problems,* 224–226.

93. Rives, "Lao-Thai Relations," February 13, 1954, 651J.92/2-1354, RG 59, USNA.

94. Hugh Toye, *Laos: Buffer State or Battleground* (London: Oxford University Press, 1968), 107, states that "the murder has never been explained." Philippe Devillers, "The Laotian Conflict in Perspective," in *Laos: War and Revolution,* ed. Nina S. Adams and Alfred McCoy (New York: Harper & Row, 1970), 42, terms the assassination "rather mysterious."

95. While noting that "blame for the killing is usually put on the Sananikone family," Stevenson speculates that, if any foreigners were involved, "the French or Thais seem more likely sources of the trouble" than the Americans. Stevenson, *End of Nowhere,* 14, 31.

96. Wilfred Burchett, "Pawns and Patriots: The U.S. Fight for Laos," in *Laos: War and Revolution,* ed. Nina S. Adams and Alfred McCoy (New York: Harper & Row, 1970), 285–286.

97. Toye, *Laos,* 71–80.

98. David K. Wyatt, ed., and John B. Murdoch, trans., *Iron Man of Laos: Prince Phetsarath Ratanavongsa, by "3349"* [Prince Phetsarath], Data Paper no. 110 (Ithaca, N.Y.: Department of Asian Studies, Southeast Asia Program, Cornell University, 1978), xiii–xiv.

99. Cremation Volume of Gen. Sawai Sawaisaenyakorn.

100. Documentary evidence of Thai support for Phetsarath is a complaint he lodged with the Thai government in 1957, after his return to Laos, that the landlord of the building the government had long set aside for him had evicted his relatives. Ambassador Sombun Pansathian to Prime Minister Thanom, November 12, 1957, Foreign Ministry Papers, KT.81.1, file 22, TNA.

101. Personal interview with Police General Jaroenrit Jamrat-romran, June 1, 1992. Former Foreign Minister Thanat Khoman says that, again, around

1960, Laotian leader Phoumi Nosavan secretly proposed a union of the two countries. Personal interview with Thanat Khoman, August 17, 1992.

102. See Cabinet Papers, [3] SR.0201.7, box 3, file 51, TNA, for the news clippings. Donovan's personal papers confirm that, at least later in the year, he supported Thai plans for a confederation of Thailand, Burma, Cambodia, and Laos.

103. Khemchat Bunyarataphan to Phibun, July 21, 1954, Cabinet Papers, [3] SR.0201.7, box 3, file 51, TNA. The *Siang Lao* article was from June 23, 1954.

104. Memorandum of conversation by Hall, in Anschuetz, "Memorandum of Conversation with Police Colonel Ratana Watanamahat," February 24, 1955, 651J.92/2-2455, RG 59, USNA.

105. Samai to Foreign Ministry, May 26, 1954, Cabinet Papers, [3] SR.0201.9, box 2, file 2, section 4, TNA.

106. Samai to Foreign Ministry, June 5, 1954, Cabinet Papers, [3] SR.0201.9, box 2, file 2, section 4, TNA.

107. Khemchat to Phibun, June 17, 1954, and Samai to acting foreign minister, June 15, 1954, Cabinet Papers, [3] SR.0201.9, box 2, file 2, section 4, TNA.

108. For various opinions on the complicity of Phetsarath and the Thais, see Talbot de Malahide, "Review of Events in Laos in 1954," October 21, 1955, FO 371/117093, PRO; Heath to secretary of state, October 12, 1954, 751J.00/10-1254, RG 59, USNA; *FRUS*, 1952–1954, 13, 2,298; Warner, "Report on Developments in Thailand and Peripheral Areas for the Periods June 25–July 1, 1954 and July 2–8, 1954," July 28, 1954, 792.00/7-2854, RG 59, USNA.

109. *Deli Me,* January 7, 1955; *Bangkok Post,* October 1, 1954; Wyatt and Murdoch, *Iron Man,* 86–90.

110. *Deli Me,* January 7, 1955.

111. Personal interview with Police General Jaroenrit Jamrat-romran, June 1, 1992. Not surprisingly, General Jaroenrit refused to make any comment on the assassination beyond that statement.

112. Memorandum of conversation by Hall, July 21, 1954, in Warner, "Memorandum of Conversation with Police Colonel Ratana Watanamahat," August 5, 1954, 792.00/8-554, RG 59, USNA.

113. Talbot de Malahide, "Review of Events in Laos in 1954," October 21, 1955, FO 371/117093, PRO; Rives to secretary of state, October 31, 1954, 790.5/10-3154, RG 59, USNA; *FRUS*, 1952–1954, 13, 2,121, 2,192, 2,298.

114. Pun to Phibun, October 18, 1954, Cabinet Papers, [3] SR.0201.10, box 2, file 4, TNA. For Phetsarath's account of events, see Wyatt and Murdoch, *Iron Man,* 86–90.

115. *Bangkok Post,* October 1, 1954.

116. *Sayam Nikorn,* January 15, 1955.

117. *Bangkok Post,* January 31, March 1 and 9, 1955. As late as July 1956, the Laotians still pressed the Thais to return Udom to Laos. "Bantheuk Rai-ngan Kandernthang pai Yeuan Prathet Lao khorng Khana Thut Phiset Thai"

[Report on the Visit to Laos of the Special Thai Delegation, 4–11 July 1956], n.d., Cabinet Papers, [3] SR.0201.20.1.1, box 1, file 11, section 2, TNA.

118. *Bangkok Post,* November 4, 1955.

119. Gage to F. S. Tomlinson, January 19, 1955, FO 371/117346, PRO; Parsons to secretary of state, September 19, 1957, 792.00/9-1957, RG 59, USNA.

120. Unsigned memorandum of conversation of meeting attended by Phao, Dulles, Phot, Sitthi, M. L. Chuancheun Kamphu, and Landon, November 4, 1954, Cabinet Papers, [3] SR.0201.20.1.1, box 1, file 8, TNA.

121. Memorandum of conversation by Hannah, December 2, 1952, in Brown, "Comments by General Phao on Recent Anti-Communist Police Action," December 9, 1952, 792.00/12-952, RG 59, USNA.

122. Katay had long been outspokenly pro-Thai. Like many southern Lao, he felt that the French had arbitrarily divided the two countries and looked forward to the day when relations between the ethnically close nations could be made more intimate. While in exile in Bangkok in the late 1940s, he wrote a tract advocating a reorientation of Laotian trade from Vietnam to Thailand. Katay possibly helped extract the confession from Udom implicating Phoui. Having succeeded his political rivals, Souvanna and Kou, only because of Kou's assassination and facing strong political pressure from Phoui and Souvanna, Katay had good reason to want to see the case buried, and it was widely known at the time of Udom's capture that he did not want Udom returned to Laos, the Foreign Ministry's protests to Thailand aside (Yost to secretary of state, January 18, 1955, 751J.00/1-1855, and Yost to secretary of state, March 16, 1955, 751J.00/3-1655, RG 59, USNA). Udom actually issued his confession to a special investigative commission Katay had sent to Bangkok after Udom's arrest. British Ambassador Berkeley Gage stated explicitly his embassy's opinion that Phao had "succeeded in doing so [covering his own contacts with Phetsarat, which might implicate him in the assassination] cleverly by conniving with Katay to publish an alleged confession by Udom involving the Laotian Deputy Prime Minister, Phoui" (Gage to F. S. Tomlinson, January 19, 1955, FO 371/117346, PRO). For Katay's background and outlook, see Katay [Sasorith Don Katay], *Le Laos* (Paris: Berger-Levrault, 1953); Toye, *Laos,* 107–108; and Nina S. Adams, "Patrons, Clients, and Revolutionaries: The Lao Search for Independence, 1945–1954," in *Laos: War and Revolution,* ed. Nina S. Adams and Alfred McCoy (New York: Harper & Row, 1970), 111.

123. Warner, "Memorandum of Conversation with Police Colonel Ratana Wattanamahat," November 30, 1954, 792.00/11-3054, RG 59, USNA.

124. Yost to secretary of state, January 18, 1955, 751J.00/1-1855, RG 59, USNA.

125. Paddock to secretary of state, January 6, 1955, 751J.00/1-655, RG 59, USNA; Gage to F. S. Tomlinson, January 19, 1955, FO 371/117346, PRO.

126. Phao, in particular, developed an intimate partnership with Katay. Luen Buasuwan, Phao's financial manager, told the U.S. embassy in April 1956 that Phao had contributed nine million Laotian piasters to Katay's election

campaign (Magill, "Effect of the Death of Luen Buasuwan on the Phao-Phin Group and Possibilities for his Replacement," April 17, 1956, 792.00/4-1756, RG 59, USNA), and Katay helped Phao establish the profitable Thai-Lao Trading Association (Parsons to secretary of state, September 19, 1957, 792.00/9-1957, RG 59, USNA). Phao, according to Vietnamese strongman Ngo Dinh Nhu, planted his own men in the Laotian police department and built the department into a force that remained loyal to Katay, even after Katay's election defeat forced him from office in December 1955 (*FRUS*, 1958–1960, 1, 8).

127. Interestingly, a Tai-speaking hill tribe inhabits the village of Dien Bien Phu.

128. Herring, *America's Longest War*, 28–31.

129. *New York Times*, March 30, 1954.

130. *FRUS*, 1952–1954, 13, 1,214–1,217, 1,227.

131. Colbert, *Southeast Asia*, 255.

132. *FRUS*, 1952–1954, 12, 707; Phot to Wan, memorandum on participation in United Action, n.d., American Military Aid 2499-2503 series, 1.6.3/10, TFML.

133. Colbert, *Southeast Asia*, 255.

134. Eisenhower indicated in a May 19 press conference that the participation of appropriate Asian nations would render a British role in United Action unnecessary. *New York Times*, May 20, 1954.

135. Kahin, *Intervention*, 49–51.

136. *FRUS*, 1952–1954, 12, 464.

137. *Sayam Nikorn*, May 12, 1954; *FRUS*, 1952–1954, 12, 709.

138. *FRUS*, 1952–1954, 12, 711, 714.

139. Memorandum of conversation by Wan, May 15, 1954, Cabinet Papers, [3] SR.0201.9, box 5, file 38, section 1, TNA.

140. Landon, "Significance of Bangkok's 2360, May 27," May 28, 1954, Lot File 55 D 480, RG 59, USNA.

141. Thuaithep to acting foreign minister, May 12, 1954, American Military Aid 2499-2503 series, 1.6.3/10, TFML.

142. *FRUS*, 1952–1954, 16, 790.

143. Donovan argued (in the words of an official in Washington) that the air bases would "be an indication [to the Communists] of U.S.-Thai intentions during the Indochina crisis," and a State Department memorandum claimed that increased military assistance to Thailand would "demonstrate clearly to the other nations of the area that the United States does not intend to permit further Communist encroachment in Southeast Asia." Drumright to Murphy, "Possible Mutual Defense and Leased Base Agreement with Thailand and Deployment of One F84G Fighter Wing," May 11, 1954, Lot File 55 D 480, and Drumright to Murphy, "JCS Consideration of Additional Military Assistance to Thailand," June 4, 1954, 792.5-MSP/6-454, RG 59, USNA.

144. *New York Times*, June 6, 1954.

145. *FRUS*, 1952–1954, 12, 724–725.

146. Ibid., 523.

147. Memorandum of conversation by Landon, June 7, 1954, Lot File 55 D 480, RG 59, USNA.

148. Wan to Phibun, May 15, 1954, and Khemchat to Geneva delegation, May 22, 1954, Cabinet Papers, [3] SR.0201.9, box 5, file 38, section 1, TNA.

149. Wan to Phibun, May 15, 1954, and Phot to Foreign Ministry, June 12, 1954, Cabinet Papers, [3] SR.0201.9, box 5, file 38, section 1, TNA; *FRUS,* 1952–1954, 16, 919.

150. Thanat Khoman to the president of the Security Council, May 29, 1954, United Nations series, 1.3.1, TFML.

151. Khemchat to Phibun, May 30, 1954, Cabinet Papers, [3] SR.0201.9, box 5, file 38, section 1, TNA.

152. *Times* (London), June 4, 1954.

153. Fuen to Radford, September 2, 1954, Chairman's File, JCS, 091 Thailand, RG 218, USNA; *FRUS,* 1952–1954, 12, 735.

154. *FRUS,* 1952–1954, 12, 713–714.

155. Ibid., 707.

156. Ibid., 724–725.

157. Ibid., 719.

158. Ibid., 727–728.

159. Ibid., vol. 16, 1013.

160. *The Pentagon Papers: Senator Gravel Edition,* 520.

161. Telephone call from Lodge to Dulles, June 14, 1954, Dulles Papers, Telephone Calls series, box 2, May 1, 1954 to June 30, 1954 (2) folder, Eisenhower Library.

162. Memorandum of conversation by Foster, June 30, 1954, Lot File 55 D 480, RG 59, USNA; *Times* (London), June 17, 1954.

163. *Times* (London), June 19, 1954.

164. France's new prime minister, Pierre Mendès-France, promised, when taking office, to produce a settlement by July 20 or resign.

165. Memorandum of conversation by Key, June 23, 1954, 792.00/6-2354, RG 59, USNA.

166. Colbert, *Southeast Asia,* 264.

167. Department of Defense, *United States–Vietnam Relations,* 9, 559–560.

168. Memorandum of conversation by Landon, July 1, 1954, 790.00/7-154, RG 59, USNA.

169. For a similar argument, see Kiernan, *How Pol Pot Came to Power,* 140–153.

170. Robert F. Randle, *Geneva, 1954: The Settlement of the Indochinese War* (Princeton, N.J.: Princeton University Press, 1969); Colbert, *Southeast Asia,* 238–287.

171. Quoted in Kahin, *Intervention,* 64–65.

172. *New York Times,* May 2, 1954; memorandum of conversation by Foster, June 30, 1954, Lot File 55 D 480, RG 59, USNA.

173. Colbert, *Southeast Asia*, 295–296.

174. *FRUS*, 1952–1954, 16, 803.

175. For a discussion of the background to the formation of the Manila Pact, see Leszek Buszynski, *SEATO: The Failure of an Alliance Strategy* (Singapore: Singapore University Press, 1983), 21–34, and Colbert, *Southeast Asia*, 298–307.

176. For a text of the treaty, see Buszynski, 227–230.

177. Ibid., 228.

178. Jain, *China and Thailand*, 22–23.

179. Wan to ambassador in Washington, July 17, 1954, Phibun Papers, Chulachomklao Military Academy Library; *FRUS*, 1952–1954, 16, 803, and vol. 12, 862–896.

180. *New York Times*, August 27, 1954; *FRUS*, 1952–1954, 12, 880.

181. *Times* (London), August 5, 1954; *New York Times*, August 3, 1954. Wan's bid failed in 1954, but the following year, with American support, he was voted U.N. president.

182. Wan to ambassador in Washington, July 17, 1954, Phibun Papers, Chulachomklao Military Academy Library.

183. Personal interview with Konthi Suphamongkhon, March 10, 1992.

PART IV: DEMOCRACY, DICTATORSHIP, AND THE NEW
ALLIANCE, 1955–1958

CHAPTER NINE: DEMOCRATIZATION AND DETERIORATION,
JANUARY 1955–SEPTEMBER 1957

1. He submitted his resignation letter several months in advance, on the day Dien Bien Phu fell. Donovan to Eisenhower, May 7, 1954, and Donovan to Marcy Dodge, May 7, 1954, box 137B, Donovan Papers.

2. For Peurifoy's career and service in Greece and Guatemala, see Richard H. Immerman, *The CIA in Guatemala: The Foreign Policy of Intervention* (Austin: University of Texas Press, 1982), 136–178; Stephen C. Schlesinger and Stephen Kinzer, *Bitter Fruit: The Untold Story of the American Coup in Guatemala* (Garden City, N.Y.: Doubleday, 1983), 131–140; Gregory F. Treverton, *Covert Action: The Limits of Intervention in the Postwar World* (New York: Basic Books, 1987), 60.

3. Robertson to Dulles, "Visit of Field Marshal P. Phibun Songgram . . . ," January 3, 1955, Lot File 56 D 679, RG 59, USNA.

4. *Liberty*, December 16, 1954, in Foreign Ministry Papers, KT.81.31, box 3, file 50, TNA.

5. Wan to Washington embassy, January 22, 1955, Foreign Ministry Papers, KT.81.35, box 3, file 50, TNA; memorandum of conversation of Dulles and Eisenhower, April 4, 1955, Dulles Papers, White House Memoranda series, box

3, Meetings with the President 1955 (5) folder, Eisenhower Library; *Bangkok Post,* December 18, 1954.

6. Unsigned memorandum of conversation of Phao and Eisenhower, November 4, 1954, unsigned memorandum of conversation of Phao, Puey Ungphakorn, Sitthi, Stassen, et al., n.d. (meeting occurred November 8, 1954), and unsigned memorandum of conversation of Phao, Phot, Robertson, Landon, and Tyson, n.d. (meeting occurred November 12, 1954), Cabinet Papers, [3] SR.0201.20.1.1, box 1, file 8, TNA.

7. *FRUS,* 1952–1954, 12, 737; Phao to cabinet secretary, November 16, 1954, Cabinet Papers, [3] SR.0201.20.1.1, box 1, file 8, TNA.

8. Phao to Phibun, March 28, 1955, Cabinet Papers, [3] SR.0201.20.1.1, box 1, file 8, TNA. The name of the senator giving the party is unclear. Phao called him "Sen. Steinbrick," but no such senator existed. Possibly, Phao was referring to Sen. John Bricker, Republican chairman of the Interstate and Foreign Commerce Committee. Thai memoranda often misspelled American names.

9. Morano to Dulles, November 22, 1954, 792.5-MSP/11-2254, RG 59, USNA.

10. *FRUS,* 1952–1954, 12, 745.

11. Buszynski, *SEATO,* 45; Colbert, *Southeast Asia,* 307; *New York Times,* April 7, 1955.

12. Unsigned memorandum of conversation of meeting of Phao, Phot, Sitthi, M. L. Chuancheun Kamphu, Dulles, and Landon, November 4, 1954, Cabinet Papers, [3] SR.0201.20.1.1, box 1, file 8, TNA.

13. Hoover to Bangkok embassy et al., October 23, 1954, 790.5/10-2354, RG 59, USNA.

14. Parsons, "Relationships Between and Among Thailand, Burma, Cambodia, Laos and Vietnam," October 29, 1954, 790.5/10-2954, RG 59, USNA.

15. Samai to Wan, March 8, 1955, Cabinet Papers, [3] SR.0201.7, box 5, TNA.

16. Muscat, *Thailand and the United States,* 136.

17. W. H. Godel, "Possible Actions in Support of the Pan-Thai Concept Advocated by General Donovan," n.d. (copy sent to Donovan, January 26, 1955), box 9, Donovan Papers.

18. *New York Times,* December 7, 1954.

19. Personal interviews with Jirawat Panyarachun, April 9, 1992, and Rak Panyarachun, April 11, 1992. Jirawat is Phibun's daughter; Rak, his son-in-law, was, for two years, Phibun's deputy minister of foreign affairs.

20. *Chao's* anti-Sarit campaign is noted in Whitteridge, "Annual Review," January 3, 1956, FO 371/123641, PRO. Since no repository holds copies of *Chao,* diplomatic dispatches are the best source regarding the newspaper.

21. *Sayam Nikorn,* January 19, 1955.

22. Farrior, "Remarks on Democracy by Thai Leaders," January 25, 1955, 792.00/1-2555, RG 59, USNA.

23. *Sayam Nikorn,* January 19, 1955.

24. Ibid., April 17, 1955.

25. Fred W. Riggs, *Thailand: The Modernization of a Bureaucratic Polity* (Honolulu: East-West Center Press, 1966), 188–197. Phao exercised effective control over the ministry in his capacity as deputy minister.

26. *FRUS,* 1952–1954, 12, 747.

27. Lloyd A. Free, Director of Research, Research Council, Inc., "Thailand: An American Dilemma," October [n.d.] 1954, NSC Staff Papers, OCB Central Files series, box 55, Thailand (File #1) (4) folder, Eisenhower Library.

28. Peurifoy to secretary of state, August 4, 1955, 792.00/8-455, RG 59, USNA.

29. Net Khemayothin, *Ngan Tai-din khorng Phan-ek Yothi* [The Underground Work of Colonel Yothi] (Bangkok: Feuang Aksorn, 1957), 15–30; Reynolds, "Ambivalent Allies," 470–545.

30. Jay Taylor, *China and Southeast Asia: Peking's Relations with Revolutionary Movements* (New York: Praeger, 1974), 261–268.

31. Personal interview with Jirawat Panyarachun, April 9, 1992.

32. Personal interviews with Rak Panyarachun, April 9, 1992; and Karuna Kusalasai, February 24, 1993. Karuna was an intimate of Sang Phatthanothai and an important figure in Phibun's opening to China.

33. *Phim Thai,* April 1, 1955.

34. Ibid., March 24, 1955.

35. Ibid., April 1, 1955.

36. *New York Times,* April 12, 1955.

37. Wan, Opening speech at Bandung conference, Foreign Ministry Papers, K.T.95.3, box 13, file 57, TNA.

38. *Krommameun* Narathip Phongpraphan (Wan Waithayakorn), "Kanprachum Bandong" [The Bandung Conference], *Rathaphirak* 15, no. 1 (January 1973): 45.

39. *New York Times,* April 16, 1955; *Bangkok Post,* June 18, 1955 (Phibun's comments). *Deli Me,* April 30, 1955; *Bangkok Post,* April 16, 1955 (Wan's comments).

40. *Deli Me,* April 30, 1955.

41. *FRUS,* 1955–1957, 22, 822.

42. Thailand Cabinet Meeting Topics, "Reuang Kanjeraja rawang Phubanchakan Thahan Akat, Athibodi Krom Tamruat, Ek-akharatchathut Amerikan, lae Senator Dirksen" [Regarding Discussions among the Commander of the Air Force, the director-general of the Police, the American ambassador, and Senator Dirksen], Meeting 36/2498, June 22, 1955.

43. Unsigned memorandum of conversation of Phao and Dirksen, n.d. (meeting occurred August 19, 1955), and Phao to Phibun, August 17, 1955, Cabinet Papers, [3] SR.0201.20.1.1, box 2, file 20, TNA. Dirksen did not reveal the purpose of the aid to his congressional colleagues or the press.

44. Phao to cabinet secretary, September 12, 1955, Cabinet Papers, [3] SR.0201.20.1.1, box 2, file 20, TNA.

45. Phao to Phibun, August 17, 1955, Cabinet Papers, [3] SR.0201.20.1.1, box 2, file 20, TNA.

46. William Donovan, "Our Stake in Thailand," *Fortune,* July 1955, 94–95.

47. *New York Times,* July 29, 1955.

48. *Bangkok Post,* May 14, 1955.

49. Peurifoy to secretary of state, June 18, 1955, 792.00/6-1855, RG 59, USNA.

50. Peurifoy to secretary of state, July 2, 1955, 792.00/7-255, RG 59, USNA. Chatchai was foreign minister during the *Mayaguez* incident. Later, in 1991, after having become two years earlier Thailand's first elected prime minister in twelve years, he was overthrown in a coup.

51. Peurifoy to secretary of state, June 18, 1955, 792.00/6-1855, RG 59, USNA.

52. Personal interview with Joseph Smith, November 4, 1991; telephone interview with Jerry Rucker, October 26, 1991.

53. Peurifoy to secretary of state, June 18, 1955, 792.00/6-1855, RG 59, USNA.

54. Press reports would have made it clear to Phibun, if his own sources already had not, that Phao was up to something. Tensions between the police and army were evident, and, in mid-May, Sarit announced that he had received a letter threatening his life. The letter, Sarit claimed, was intended to provoke strife between the army and the national police force. *Bangkok Post,* May 14, 1955; *New York Times,* May 15, 1955.

55. *Sayam Nikorn,* June 24, 1955.

56. *Phim Thai,* July 2, 1955.

57. *Sayam Nikorn,* July 9, 1955.

58. Magill, "Phibun—The New Look," August 24, 1955, 792.00/8-2455, RG 59, USNA.

59. Peurifoy to secretary of state, June 21, 1955, 751G.00/6-2155, RG 59, USNA.

60. *Sayam Rath,* July 10, 1955.

61. *FRUS,* 1955–1957, 22, 827–828.

62. W. H. Godel, "Possible Actions in Support of the Pan-Thai Concept Advocated by General Donovan," n.d. (copy sent to Donovan on January 26, 1955), box 9, Donovan Papers.

63. *FRUS,* 1955–1957, 22, 826.

64. Peurifoy to secretary of state, June 21, 1955, 751G.00/6-2155, RG 59, USNA.

65. Phao to Phibun, August 17, 1955, Cabinet Papers, [3] SR.0201.20.1.1, box 2, file 20, TNA.

66. Hoover to Bangkok embassy, July 14, 1955, 792.00/7-1455, RG 59, USNA.

67. Dulles to Bangkok embassy, July 28, 1955, 792.00/7-1955, RG 59, USNA.

68. Peurifoy to secretary of state, August 4, 1955, 792.00/8-455, RG 59, USNA.

69. Press reports of a coup plot immediately following Phao's second meeting with Peurifoy show that Phibun knew of Phao's activities. *Sayam Rath,* July 17, 1955.

70. *Bangkok Post,* September 3, 1955; Magill, "Phibun—The New Look," August 24, 1955, 792.00/8-2455, RG 59, USNA.

71. *Sayam Nikorn,* September 2, 1955; *Bangkok Post,* September 2, 1955.

72. *Sayam Nikorn,* September 1, 1955. Phibun's forum gave birth to the modern Thai verb "to hyde-park," meaning to speak in an open space on a political topic.

73. Landymore to Whitteridge, August 10, 1955, FO 371/117338, PRO.

74. Magill, "Phibun—The New Look," August 24, 1955, 792.00/8-2455, RG 59, USNA.

75. Young to Robertson and Sebald, "Situation in Bangkok," September 9, 1955, 792.00/9-555, RG 59, USNA.

76. "Rang Kham-torb Krathu-tham thi S.107/2498 Reuang Kanmorana-kam khorng Phana. Ek-akharatchathut Saharat Amerika Prajam Prathet Thai khorng Nai Ari Tantiwetchakun Samachik Sapha Phu-thaen Ratsadorn" [Draft Answer to Interrogatory S.107/2498 Concerning the Death of His Excellency the American Ambassador to Thailand of Mr. Ari Tantiwetchakun, Member of the House of Representatives], n.d., Foreign Ministry Papers, KT.81.35, box 3, file 56, TNA.

77. Personal interview with Rak Panyarachun, April 9, 1992. Rak still suspects that Phao was behind Peurifoy's death.

78. Phao to Phibun, August 17, 1955, Cabinet Papers, [3] SR.0201.20.1.1, box 2, file 20, TNA.

79. Phao to cabinet secretary, September 12, 1955, Cabinet Papers, [3] SR.0201.20.1.1, box 2, file 20, TNA.

80. U. Alexis Johnson with Jef Olivarius McAllister, *The Right Hand of Power* (Englewood Cliffs, N.J.: Prentice-Hall, 1984), 237.

81. *Sayam Nikorn,* July 7, 1955.

82. *Phim Thai,* August 12, 1955.

83. *Sayam Rath,* August 19, 1955.

84. *Bangkok Post,* February 1950; Stanton to secretary of state, March 9, 1950, 792.00-(W)/3-950, and Stanton to secretary of state, September 28, 1950, 792.00-(W)/9-2850, RG 59, USNA.

85. *Sayam Nikorn,* September 1, 1955.

86. Magill, "Thailand's 'Hyde Park'—The Phramane Ground Orations," January 4, 1955, 792.00/1-456, RG 59, USNA.

87. *San Seri,* August 6, 1955.

88. *Sayam Nikorn,* September 3, 1955; *Bangkok Post,* September 2, 1955.

89. *Sayam Nikorn,* July 7, 1955.

90. Anschuetz to secretary of state, September 7, 1955, 792.00/9-755, RG 59, USNA.

91. Anschuetz to secretary of state, October 6, 1955, 792.00/10-655, RG 59, USNA.

92. Ari Phirom, *Beuang-lang Kansathapana Samphanthaphap Yuk Mai Thai-Jin* [The Background to the Establishment of the Modern Thai-Chinese Relationship] (Bangkok: Mitnarakanphim, 1981), 10, 57.

93. Skinner, *Chinese Society,* 341–342.

94. *San Seri,* October 22, 1955.

95. Ari, *Beuang-lang,* 9.

96. *New York Times,* November 19, 1955.

97. Anschuetz to secretary of state, October 6, 1955, 792.00/10-655, and Anschuetz to secretary of state, October 15, 1955, 792.00/10-1555, RG 59, USNA.

98. *Phim Thai,* December 2, 1955.

99. *New York Times,* November 23, 1955.

100. Dilokrit to chief of staff, Ministry of Defense, December 22, 1955, Cabinet Papers, [3] SR.0201.13.1, box 3, file 17, TNA.

101. Anschuetz to secretary of state, December 1, 1955, 792.00/12-155, RG 59, USNA.

102. *Phim Thai,* December 2 and 3, 1955.

103. Dilokrit to chief of staff, Defense Ministry, December 22, 1955, Cabinet Papers, [3] SR.0201.13.1, box 3, file 17, TNA.

104. "National Defense Council Announcement Concerning the Establishment of a Committee of the National Defense Council to Coordinate American Police Aid," n.d., Cabinet Papers, [3] SR.0201.13.1, box 3, file 17, TNA. Because the committee was secret, this announcement was never actually issued to the public. Pun to Phibun, December 29, 1955, same file as above.

105. Ari, *Beuang-lang,* 10.

106. *Sayam Rath,* June 12, 1956.

107. Wanwai Phatthanothai, *Jo-ern-lai: Phu Pluk Maitri Thai-Jin* [Zhou Enlai: The Person Who Established Thai-Chinese Friendship] (n.p.: n.p., n.d.), 4; Karuna, *Chiwit thi Leuak Mai Dai,* 169–174; Ari, *Beuang-lang,* 4–13.

108. Ari, *Beuang-lang,* 14–59, 88–90, 118–129; Wanwai, *Jo-ern-lai,* 4–8.

109. Ari, *Beuang-lang,* 239–240.

110. Ibid., 58, 88, 100.

111. The memorandum of understanding is reproduced in Wanwai, *Jo-ern-lai,* 14.

112. *Phim Thai,* December 20, 1955.

113. Personal interview with Karuna Kusalasai, February 24, 1993; Wanwai, *Jo-ern-lai,* 4, 15–16. Luen later admitted to the U.S. embassy, for unknown reasons, that he had long funded Thep's political activities. He also told the embassy that he had funded the trip of Amphorn and Sa-ing, though he claimed that they had told him that they would go, not to China, but to Japan

and the United States. Magill, "Effect of the Death of Luen Buasuwan on the Phao-Phin Group and Possibilities for his Replacement," April 17, 1956, 792.00/4-1756, RG 59, USNA.

114. *Phim Thai,* December 13, 1955.

115. Theater *(lakhorn)* is one of the metaphors Thais most frequently employ when talking about their politics. Examples are Jamlorng Itharong, *Lakhorn Kanmeuang* [Political Theater] (Bangkok: Upakorn Kanphim, 1949), and Thamsook Numnonda, *Lakhorn Kanmeuang 24 Mithunayon 2475* [The Political Theater of 24 June 1932] (Bangkok: Social Science Association of Thailand, 1992).

116. *San Seri,* December 14, 1955; Chai to permanent secretary, Foreign Ministry, December 31, 1955, Cabinet Papers, [3] SR.0201.20.1, file 1, TNA.

117. *Bangkok Post,* June 13, 1956.

118. *Sayam Rath,* March 27, 1956.

119. Thep, Amphorn, Sa-ing, and the politicians accompanying Thep made their supposed defiance of the government in visiting China one of their main political selling points. Indicative of the importance such MPs attached to their facade of independence from the government, Khlaew Norapati denies to this day any knowledge of official support for his and Thep's delegation, though with some serious contradictions. In a 1986 interview with a Thai magazine, Khlaew claimed that he had called on Phao to get government permission for the trip. Phao refused to sanction the trip and threatened to arrest the delegates on their return, Khlaew asserted, but also handed Khlaew one hundred dollars cash! In an article he wrote for the same magazine two years later, Khlaew contended that Phao refused to meet him at all. In a recent interview, Khlaew reverted to his earlier story, claiming that Phao gave him money but warned him not to go. Clearly, Khlaew, like Thep, Amphorn, Sa-ing, and many other neutralist and leftist politicians of the time, has concealed his connections with military figures to foster an image of himself as a political maverick. *Matichon* weekly, November 16, 1986, special section, 2–6, and April 24, 1988, 27; Personal interview with Khlaew Norapati, October 15, 1992.

120. Puey Ungphakorn, "Thahan Chuakhrao" [Part-time Soldier], in *Bantheuk Patibad Ngan Tai-din khorng Adit Seri Thai* [Accounts of the Underground Work of Former Free Thai], ed. Khana Kammakan Wan Santiphap Thai (Bangkok: Khana Kammakan Wan Santiphap Thai, 1990), 58.

121. The description of Max Bishop comes from interviews with former embassy officials. Because of the personal nature of their statements, the interviewees have asked to remain anonymous.

122. Memorandum of conversation by Bishop, March 16, 1956 [meeting occurred February 21, 1956], 611.92/3-1656, RG 59, USNA.

123. *Bangkok Post,* February 2, 1956.

124. *Phim Thai,* April 21, 1956; *Bangkok Post,* May 10, 1956.

125. *Sayam Rath,* May 22, 1956.

126. *Phim Thai,* March 6, 1956.

127. Ibid., April 11, 1956.

128. *San Seri,* July 23, 1956. It is traditional for Thai Buddhist men to serve as monks at some point in their lives for a three-month rainy season.

129. Magill, "Press Criticism of U.S. Aid Program," January 11, 1956, 792.00-MSP/1-1156, and Magill, "Thai Press Advocacy of a More Independent Thai Foreign Policy," January 11, 1956, 692.00/1-1156, RG 59, USNA. No copies of *Sathianraphap* are extant, but, luckily, the U.S. embassy monitored Sang's publication and occasionally sent extracts to Washington.

130. *New York Times,* January 11, 1956. As with *Sathianraphap,* because no repositories retain copies of the *Tribune,* the best sources on editorial trends in the newspaper are in diplomatic dispatches and foreign correspondents' accounts of local press and political developments.

131. Thai cabinet to Dulles, "Aide-Memoire" [in English], March 13, 1956, Cabinet Papers, SR.0201.17, box 1, file 2, TNA.

132. *New York Times,* March 14, 1956.

133. Ibid., March 4, 1956.

134. *FRUS,* 1955–1957, 22, 864, 892.

135. Ibid., 892, 894; Phibun to Bishop, July 30, 1956, in Bishop to secretary of state, July 30, 1956, 493.929/7-3056, RG 59, USNA.

136. Ari, *Beuang-lang,* 178–179, 189; Wanwai, *Jo-ern-lai,* 21.

137. Anschuetz to secretary of state, November 30, 1955, 692.93/11-3055; Anschuetz to secretary of state, December 1, 1955, 692.93/12-155; and Robertson to Dulles, "Possible 'Neutralist' Trend in Thailand," November 26, 1955, 790.5/11-2655, RG 59, USNA.

138. Anschuetz to secretary of state, December 15, 1955, 692.93/12-1555, RG 59, USNA.

139. *FRUS,* 1955–1957, 22, 861, 865.

140. Gage to Tomlinson, October 16, 1956, FO 371/123648, PRO; personal interview with Theodore Tremblay, November 5, 1991.

141. "Thailand: A Time for Skill," *Time,* July 9, 1956, 25.

142. William J. Lederer and Eugene Burdick, *The Ugly American* (Greenwich, Conn.: Fawcett Crest, 1958), 64. Sears had nothing written about him in *Time,* but, like Bishop, he was criticized in the *New York Times* for having done nothing to stop the neutralist trend in the country he served in.

143. Personal interviews with Robert Cleveland, November 4, 1991, and Theodore Tremblay, November 5, 1991.

144. "Thailand: A Time for Skill," *Time,* July 9, 1956, 25.

145. Because of Beijing's moderate policy of peaceful coexistence between communist and capitalist nations and promotion of neutralism among noncommunist Asian nations, it is at times hard to distinguish between genuine neutralists and pro-Communists in Thailand in these years. Khlaew Norapati's account of the Thep trip to China, *Yiam Pakking* [Visiting Beijing] (Bangkok: n.p., 1957), for example, emphasized Mao's and Zhou's assurances that they accepted Thais' preference for a noncommunist political and economic system

and nowhere advocated establishment of communism in Thailand, but all of this was in keeping with Chinese policy. The book presented a flattering portrait of life in China and expressed sympathy for Thai communist and leftist exiles the delegation met there, such as Prasert Sapsunthorn. Khlaew echoed Mao's claim that the government established the Thai Autonomous Zone for purely administrative purposes and lauded China's foreign policy throughout the account. Typical of the ambiguities in the book—and the stance of leftists as a whole—was a speech of Thep that Khlaew recorded in which Thep greeted his Chinese hosts as *mit-sahai* (p. 152). Combining the neutral word for friend *(mit)* with the communist term for comrade *(sahai),* Thep apparently attempted in the speech to sound similar to, but not exactly like, a Communist. Based on the close adherence of Thep and his allies to policies promoted by the PRC, Kasian believes that Thep's Economists acted as a pro-Communist united front party. Kasian, "Commodifying Marxism," 273, comments that Thep's Economist Party "had a close unofficial working relationship with the CPT [Communist Party of Thailand]." But the Economists'—and other leftist politicians'—uncertain socialism, acceptance of financial support from military figures, and eagerness to join the government at almost any price indicate that they considered Beijing and local Communists—like government leaders—allies of convenience, not ideological soulmates. For many of the leftists of the period, the desire for communist or procommunist support represented merely one aspect of their opportunistic approach to politics.

146. Sukit, an intellectual educated at the London School of Economics, was a former Pridi-ite and Cooperative Party member. Although he described his beliefs as "mild socialism," Sukit at times opposed government intervention in the private sector and favored foreign investment in Thailand. Guthrie, "Elections in Thailand—II—Parties and Prospects," 792.00/12-457, RG 59, USNA.

147. David Wilson, "Thailand and Marxism," in *Marxism in Southeast Asia: A Study of Four Countries,* ed. Frank N. Trager (Stanford, Calif.: Stanford University Press, 1959), 98.

148. Personal interview with Karuna Kusalasai, February 24, 1993.

149. Cowen to G2, December 22, 1954, 792.551/12-2254, RG 59, USNA.

150. Lloyd A. Free, Director of Research, Research Council, Inc., "Thailand: An American Dilemma," October 1954, NSC Staff Papers, OCB Central Files series, box 55, Thailand (File #1) (4) folder, Eisenhower Library.

151. Warner, *Last Confucian,* 237.

152. *San Seri,* September 19, 20, 22, 24, 26, 27, and 28, 1956.

153. Bishop to secretary of state, September 28, 1956, 792.00/9-2856, RG 59, USNA.

154. Memorandum of conversation by Peters, October 8, 1956, in Tremblay, "Memorandum of Conversation with General Phao Sriyanon, Director-General of the Thai Police," October 29, 1956, 792.00/10-2956, RG 59, USNA; *San Seri,* October 2–4, 1956.

155. *San Seri,* October 11–14, 1956. Since then, the play and the movie version have been banned in Thailand.

156. Ibid., September 1, 1956.

157. *Bangkok Post,* November 28, 1956.

158. *Sayam Rath,* November 17, 1956; *San Seri,* November 13 and 15, 1956.

159. *Sayam Nikorn,* February 5, 1957; *Bangkok Post,* February 4, 1957.

160. Thongchai, "Latthi Khormmunit," 373; Bishop, "Matters Discussed During Ambassador Bishop's Call on Major Rak Panyarachun, Acting Foreign Minister of Thailand," January 7, 1957 (meeting occurred January 4, 1957), 611.92/1-757, RG 59, USNA.

161. Wanwai, *Jo-ern-lai,* 23, 31–32.

162. *Sayam Rath,* September 15, 1956.

163. Ibid., September 19, 1956. Originally, the government had planned to allow the mission to stay in Bangkok for several days, but, after Bishop protested the visit to Wan, the Thais arranged, on Wan's urging, for the Chinese officials to stay in Bangkok only one night. Memorandum of conversation by Somjai Anumanratchathon, September 18, 1956, Cabinet Papers, [3] SR.0201.17, box 2, file 24, and various documents in Cabinet Papers, [3] SR.0201.7, box 7, file 190, TNA.

164. *San Seri,* November 27, 1956.

165. Wanwai, *Jo-ern-lai,* 33–36.

166. *Sayam Nikorn,* January 20, 1957.

167. Eventually, Zhou accepted Phibun's proposal, and Sang sent his children to live with Zhou. For an account of the experiences in China of one of Sang's children, see Sirin Phathanothai, *Dragon's Pearl* (New York: Simon & Schuster, 1994).

168. Ari, *Beuang-lang,* 193; Wanwai, *Jo-ern-lai,* 24.

169. Charles F. Keyes, *Isan: Regionalism in Northeast Thailand,* Data Paper no. 65 (Ithaca, N.Y.: Southeast Asia Program, Cornell University, 1967), 44. Thep's Economist Party took all eight of its seats in the northeast, and the more centrist Free Democrat Party won all of its eleven seats in the region. The Hyde Park Party, originally led by Phethai Chotinuchit, won one of its two seats in the northeast. No other leftist party won any seats in this election.

170. Thak, *Thailand,* 106–108.

171. Ibid., 108; *San Seri,* March 2–5, 1957; *Sayam Rath,* March 3–5, 1957.

172. Bishop to secretary of state, March 22, 1957, 792.00/3-2257, RG 59, USNA.

173. *San Seri,* March 5 and 6 and May 19, 1957; Reynolds, *Thai Radical Discourse,* 35. The March 2 protest concerned the embassy's distribution of leaflets condemning the Soviet invasion of Hungary at a student rally. Although the embassy likely intended the pamphlets as straightforward anticommunist propaganda, the students interpreted them as an implicit threat that the United States would support bloody repression of the demonstrations.

174. *Sayam Rath,* March 12, 1957.

175. Thamsook Numnonda, "Khabuankan Tor-tan Amerikan Samai Jorm Phon P. Phibunsongkhram" [The Anti-American Movement in the Field Marshal P. Phibunsongkhram Era], *Ruam Botkhwam Prawatisat*, no. 2 (January 1981): 67. Ironically, while Bishop in part inspired the unflattering portrait of Ambassador "Lucky" Louis Sears in *The Ugly American*, Kukrit, elected prime minister in 1975 after the military government had been overthrown, played the prime minister of the mythical Southeast Asian state of "Sarkhan" in the movie version of Lederer and Burdick's novel. Kukrit was prime minister during the *Mayaguez* incident.

176. USIS (Bangkok), "A Study of Thai Attitudes Toward the Southeast Asia Treaty Organization," March 4, 1957 (mimeo), cited in Randolph, *United States and Thailand*, 35; Research and Reference Service, "A Note on Thai Attitudes toward SEATO, American Aid, and Relations with Communist China," Report no. 12, August 13, 1957, cited in Thamsook, "Khabuankan," 65. The surveys showed strong support for SEATO and the United States. Since they appear to have been designed for public consumption, however, the accuracy of the polls is questionable.

177. Office of Intelligence Research, "Probable Developments in Thailand," OIR 7503, May 13, 1957, 48, USNA; *FRUS, 1955–1957*, 22, 915.

178. Wanwai, *Jo-ern-lai*, 39–44.

179. Bishop to Young, May 20, 1957, 792.00/5-2057, RG 59, USNA.

180. Kasian, "Commodifying Marxism," 379; Reynolds, *Thai Radical Discourse*, 34–35. The commemorative volume is notable for printing, for the first time, Jit Phumisak's famous Marxist analysis of Thai history, "Chomna khorng Sakdina Thai nai Patjuban" [The Face of Thai Feudalism Today]. The essay heavily influenced the student radicals of the 1970s. Reynolds, *Thai Radical Discourse*, translates the essay in full.

181. *Sayam Nikorn*, July 20, 1957.

182. *FRUS, 1955–1957*, 22, 923, 916.

183. Magill to Young, "Some Aspects of the Situation in Thailand," May 29, 1957, 792.00/5-2957, RG 59, USNA.

184. *FRUS, 1955–1957*, 22, 917.

185. Office of Intelligence Research, "Probable Developments in Thailand," OIR 7503, May 13, 1957, USNA.

186. Magill, "Thailand's 'Hyde Park'—The Phramane Ground Orations," January 4, 1956, 792.00/1-456, RG 59, USNA. Of the prominent leftist politicians of the time, only Phethai, described in this report as having "long been identified with pro-communist causes," was linked in any way in U.S. reports with Communists.

187. *FRUS, 1955–1957*, 22, 916.

188. Pun to Wan, May 20, 1957, Cabinet Papers, [3] SR.0201.17, box 1, file 2, TNA.

189. *FRUS, 1955–1957*, 22, 919–920.

190. Tremblay, "Prince Wan's Statement to Press and TV on Thai Govern-

ment Policy Toward the United States," May 24, 1957, 611.92/5-2457, RG 59, USNA; Speech by Rak Panyarachun, May 23, 1957, Supreme Command Papers, vol. 1, box 25, file 671, TNA.

191. *Khao Phap,* June 4, 1957, in Cabinet Papers, [3] SR.0201.17, box 1, file 2, TNA.

192. Phot to acting foreign minister, June 20, 1957, Cabinet Papers, [3] SR.0201.17, box 1, file 2, TNA.

193. *Sayam Nikorn,* July 23, 1957.

194. *Sayam Rath,* September 3, 1957.

195. *Bangkok Post,* June 12, 1957.

196. *Sayam Nikorn,* June 15, 1957.

197. *San Seri,* July 1 and 2, 1957; *Sayam Nikorn,* August 9, 1957.

198. Thani, "Khwamsamphan rawang Thai kap Satharanarat Prachachon Jin," 76.

199. *Sayam Nikorn,* August 1, 1957; *Sayam Rath,* August 22, 1957.

200. Office of Intelligence Research, "Probable Developments in Thailand," OIR 7503, May 13, 1957, 82, USNA.

201. *FRUS,* 1955–1957, 22, 926.

202. Bishop to secretary of state, July 5, 1957, 792.5-MSP/7-557, RG 59, USNA.

203. Dulles to Bangkok embassy, September 3, 1957, 792.5-MSP/7-557, RG 59, USNA.

204. *Deli Me,* August 17, 1957.

205. *Sayam Nikorn,* August 21 and 22, 1957.

206. Ibid., September 14, 1957.

207. *Sayam Rath,* September 17, 1957.

208. *Khao Phap,* September 29, 1957, cited in Kulab, *Adit,* 198; personal interviews with David Whipple, November 6, 1991, and Joseph Smith, November 4, 1991.

CHAPTER TEN: DICTATORSHIP AND RESTORATION,
SEPTEMBER 1957–DECEMBER 1958

1. NSC 5612/1 Progress Report, November 6, 1957, p. 7, SPANSA, NSC series, Policy Papers subseries, box 18, NSC 5612/1 folder, Eisenhower library.

2. Office of Intelligence Research, "Probable Developments in Thailand," OIR 7503, May 13, 1957, 52, USNA.

3. Jin, "Military in Politics," 147. These numbers should be viewed as approximations. Also, were covert aid totals available, the ratio of U.S. to Thai contributions would rise significantly.

4. *New York Times,* December 15, 1957.

5. Because those former leaders in the best position to know of any contacts with Beijing declined to be interviewed, it is impossible to be sure whether

the postcoup governments continued to send official delegations to Beijing, but it is clear that there were no stopovers of PRC officials in Bangkok under Sarit, as had occurred in October 1956. Furthermore, given the eagerness of members of Phibun's delegations to Beijing to go public with their experiences after Thailand officially established relations with China in 1975, it seems likely that anyone involved in similar missions under Sarit would also have made the most of the opportunity to gain public admiration. The lack of such accounts from the Sarit era indicates that no trips were made. Significantly, the United States believed that, unlike the precoup government, Sarit's cabinets had made no covert contacts with Beijing (Office of Intelligence Research, "Thailand's Foreign Relations," OIR 7734, June 11, 1958, 6, USNA). For accounts of the official delegations to Beijing organized under Phibun, see the books by Ari, Wanwai, and Karuna, cited above, Karuna's interview with the *Bangkok Post*, August 3, 1975, and interviews of Khlaew Norapati with *Matichon* weekly, November 16, 1986, special section, 2–6, and April 24, 1988, 27.

6. *Sayam Rath*, September 22, 1957.

7. *FRUS*, 1955–1957, 22, 932.

8. Ibid., 933.

9. *Sayam Rath*, September 21, 1957; *Bangkok Post*, September 20, 1957.

10. *Khao Phap*, September 29, 1957, quoted in Kulab, *Adit*, 298.

11. Salao and Kamon, *Waterlu*, 313.

12. *Deli Me*, September 25, 1957.

13. Wilson, "Intentions of Prime Minister Pote Sarasin with Respect to Returning to Post of SEATO Secretary General," November 18, 1957, 790.5/11-1857, RG 59, USNA; NSC 5612/1 Progress Report, November 6, 1957, SPANSA, NSC series, Policy Papers subseries, box 18, NSC 5612/1 folder, Eisenhower library.

14. Dulles to Bangkok embassy, September 30, 1957, 792.00/9-2757, RG 59, USNA.

15. *Deli Me*, September 25, 1957.

16. *Sayam Rath*, September 28, 1957.

17. Kulab Saipradit, *Pai Sahaphap Sowiet* [Going to the Soviet Union] (Bangkok: Suphapburut, 1958), 8–9.

18. *FRUS*, 1955–1957, 22, 935.

19. Ibid., 936–937.

20. *Sayam Nikorn*, October 4, 1957.

21. *FRUS*, 1955–1957, 22, 940–942.

22. *Deli Me*, September 29, 1957; *Sayam Nikorn*, October 5, 1957.

23. Unsigned memorandum of conversation between Phao and Hollister, August 12, 1955, Diplomatic Relations (America) series, 2.4.1/3, TFML; personal interview with David Whipple, November 6, 1991.

24. *Sayam Nikorn*, October 18, 1957. Sawai's announcement and open discussion of the meeting with Hart was unprecedented.

25. Johnson, *Right Hand of Power*, 296.

26. *San Seri,* October 30, 1957. The censored publications were *San Seri, Sathianraphap, Kanmeuang, Khao Phap, Pituphum,* and *Kiattisak.*

27. In one three-day period in mid-October, *San Seri* attacked Phot on everything from the budget and the Yanhee dam project to, of course, the alliance with the United States. *San Seri,* October 16–18, 1957.

28. Suchat Sawatsi, "Jotmai Lap khorng Jorm Phon Sarit theung Thanong Sathathip" [Field Marshal Sarit's Secret Letters to Thanong Sathathip], *Lok Nangseu,* September 12, 1978, 115.

29. The self-proclaimed socialist parties captured only twelve seats in December, as opposed to twenty-one in the February elections, but, as Keyes, *Isan,* 43, notes, a number of successful independent and progovernment candidates, such as Khrong Chandawong, Pleuang Wansi, and Cheun Rawiwan, ran on leftist platforms.

30. Although the English translation—"National Socialist"—is the same as that of the Coup Group's Chat Sangkhom Party of the first part of the decade, the two were unrelated.

31. Earlier, the United States had considered Net a "conservative" Free Thai and thus friendly to the United States. Only after the initiation of democratic reforms and his assumption of the editorship of *San Seri* did Net show neutralist or leftist sentiments.

32. For Ari, the jump to the government party was especially easy. A U.S. intelligence estimate earlier reported that his Free Democrat Party was "suspected of receiving support from government leaders" (Office of Intelligence Research, "Probable Developments in Thailand," OIR 7503, May 13, 1957, 8, USNA). Amphorn Suwannabon, the neutralist MP Phao had funded and sent to Beijing with Ari Phirom's first delegation, headed the party.

33. Unfortunately, Thai and U.S. documents are silent on the outcome of the October plan to intervene in the formation of the new government. Possibly the plan was dropped, but, more likely, the State Department has not declassified the relevant documents.

34. *Rai-ngan Kanprachum Sapha Phu-thaen Ratsadorn Samai Saman P.S. 2500 lae Samai Wisaman P.S. 2501* [Records of the House of Representatives Ordinary Session, 1957, and Special Session, 1958], Samai Wisaman (Samai thi 1), P.S. 2501, session 1/2501 (wisaman), January, 9, 1958, 83–85, 142.

35. Guthrie, "Socialist Front Parties Protest SEATO Maneuvers, Nuclear Tests, Establishment of Rocket Bases in Thailand," March 28, 1958, 790.5/3-2858, RG 59, USNA.

36. Wilson to secretary of state, March 11, 1958, 792.00/3-1158, RG 59, USNA.

37. Johnson to secretary of state, April 18, 1958, 792.551/4-1858, RG 59, USNA.

38. *San Seri,* April 23, 1958.

39. Personal interviews with U. Alexis Johnson, November 5, 1991, and David Whipple, November 6, 1991.

40. Personal interview with David Whipple, November 6, 1991.

41. Whittington to Parsons and Palmer, "Use of ICA Contingency Fund for Thailand," March 14, 1958, 792.5-MSP/3-1458, RG 59, USNA.

42. OCB Report on NSC 5612/1 and NSC 5809, May 28, 1958, SPANSA, NSC series, Policy Papers subseries, box 25, NSC 58-0 (2) folder, Eisenhower library.

43. Memorandum of conversation between Wan and Wilson by Japhikorn, January 15, 1958, Cabinet Papers, [3] SR.0201.17, box 2, file 24, TNA. Wan suggested sending the journalists to the PRC, but Wilson insisted they be sent to Taiwan. Wilson probably feared that they would prove even more obnoxious to the United States if given a platform for their views in Beijing.

44. Wilson to secretary of state, March 11, 1958, 792.00/3-1158, RG 59, USNA.

45. Dulles to Bangkok embassy, March 21, 1958, 792.00/3-1858, RG 59, USNA.

46. Wilson to secretary of state, January 17, 1958, 792.551/1-1758; Dulles to Bangkok embassy, April 30, 1958, 792.551/4-3058; and memorandum of conversation by Bushner, May 14, 1958, 611.92/5-1458, RG 59, USNA.

47. Dulles to Bangkok embassy, May 17, 1958, 792.551/5-1758, RG 59, USNA.

48. Wilson to secretary of state, January 17, 1958, 792.551/1-1758, and Dulles to Bangkok embassy, June 28, 1958, 792.551/6-2858, RG 59, USNA.

49. Dulles to Bangkok embassy, April 30, 1958, 792.551/4-3058, RG 59, USNA.

50. Thak, *Thailand*, 136–138.

51. *Sayam Rath*, March 27, 1958.

52. Suchat, "Jotmai Lap khorng Jorm Phon Sarit," 116. The Thai word *ekarat* refers to the independence of nations, not individuals, and is often applied to countries that have regained independence after a period of occupation or colonization.

53. Dulles to Bangkok embassy, June 23, 1958, 792.551/6-2358, RG 59, USNA.

54. Thak, *Thailand*, 139.

55. *Sayam Rath*, July 6 and 18, 1958.

56. Ibid., July 17 and 18, 1958.

57. Ibid., July 22, 1958.

58. Bishop to secretary of state, January 4, 1958, 792.00/1-458, and Guthrie, "Transmittal of Memorandum of Conversation with Panit Sampawakoop, National Assemblyman from Petburi," October 15, 1958, 792.00/10-1558, RG 59, USNA.

59. *New York Times*, July 9 and 17, 1958.

60. Memorandum of conversation by Wan, July 12, 1958, Cabinet Papers, [3] SR.0201.17, box 2, file 41, TNA; Watthana Kanjana-akharadet, "Samphanthaphap Thangkanmeuang rawang Prathet Thai kap Kamphucha tangtae Pi P.S. 2489" [Political Relations between Thailand and Cambodia since 1946], M.A. thesis, Thammasat University, n.d., 57–61.

61. *Bangkok Post,* August 25, 1958.

62. *Sayam Nikorn,* August 27, 1958.

63. *Sayam Rath,* August 12, 1958; *Deli Me,* September 4 and 5, 1958. As was now customary with Thai leftists returning from exile or trips to China, the police detained the five on their arrival, but the court soon released them on bail. The five revealed to the court that the police had given permission for them to return.

64. *Bangkok Post,* September 24, 1958; *Deli Me,* September 20, 1958.

65. Thani, "Khwamsamphan rawang Thai kap Satharanarat Prachachon Jin," 77.

66. *Sayam Rath,* August 29, 1958.

67. Thak, *Thailand,* 140, 179–186.

68. Albert G. Pickerell, "The Press of Thailand: Conditions and Trends," *Journalism Quarterly* 37 (winter 1960): 90.

69. "Announcement of the Revolutionary Party, No. 3," October 20, 1958, reproduced in Batson, "Announcements and Directives of the Revolutionary Party," November 5, 1958, 792.00/11-558, RG 59, USNA.

70. Memorandum of conversation by Dobrenchuk, July 27, 1958, in Guthrie, "Transmittal of Memorandum of Conversation," August 5, 1958, 792.00/8-558, RG 59, USNA.

71. *Times* (London), November 5, 1958.

72. Herter to Bangkok embassy, November 13, 1958, 792.00/11-1358, RG 59, USNA.

73. Ministry of Foreign Affairs to U.S. ambassador, October 21, 1958, reproduced in Batson, "Announcements and Directives of the Revolutionary Party," November 5, 1958, 792.00/11-558, RG 59, USNA.

74. Johnson to secretary of state, October 20, 1958, 792.00/10-2058, RG 59, USNA.

75. In later years, the police captured several communist leaders. According to a former agent, the CIA tipped off Sarit to the whereabouts of one prominent Communist (possibly Suphachai Sisati, captured in mid-1959). As the CIA expected, Sarit personally interrogated the suspect and ordered him executed without trial. Personal interview with David Whipple, November 6, 1991.

76. Weld to secretary of state, October 20, 1958, 792.00/10-2058, RG 59, USNA.

77. "Announcement of the Revolutionary Party, No. 12," October 22, 1958, reproduced in Batson, "Announcements and Directives of the Revolutionary Party," November 5, 1958, 792.00/11-558, RG 59, USNA.

78. Johnson to secretary of state, November 10, 1958, 792.00/11-1058, RG 59, USNA.

79. Cumming to acting secretary of state, n.d., 792.00/10-2058, RG 59, USNA.

80. Johnson, *Right Hand of Power,* 275–276.

81. *Sayam Rath,* October 23, 1958.

82. Dulles [Paris] to secretary of state [*sic*], December 18, 1958, 792.00/12-1858, RG 59, USNA.

83. *Sayam Nikorn,* December 24, 1958.

CONCLUSION

1. Kahin, *Intervention,* 334–335.

2. Louis E. Lomax, *Thailand: The War That Is, the War That Will Be* (New York: Vintage Books, 1971).

SELECTED BIBLIOGRAPHY

ARCHIVAL SOURCES

Chulachomklao Military Academy Library, Nakhorn Nayok, Thailand
    Phibun Papers
Dwight D. Eisenhower Library, Abilene, Kansas
    NSC Staff Papers
    Whitman Files
    Office of the Special Assistant for National Security Affairs Papers
    C. D. Jackson Records
    John Foster Dulles Papers
Harry S. Truman Library, Independence, Missouri
    Oral History Interview Collection
    John Melby Papers
Public Record Office, London, England (PRO)
    Foreign Office Records, FO 371
Thailand Foreign Ministry Library (TFML)
    American Military Aid Series
    Diplomatic Relations (America) Series
    Diplomatic Relations (Southeast Asia) series
    Political Series
    United Nations Series
Thailand Juridical Council Library
    Law and Draft Act Papers
Thailand National Archives (TNA)
    Cabinet Papers
    Interior Ministry Papers
    Foreign Ministry Papers
    Supreme Command Papers
Thailand Office of the Secretary of the Cabinet
    Cabinet Topics

University of Bridgeport Library, Bridgeport, Connecticut
    Edwin Stanton Papers
United States Army Military History Institute, Army War College, Carlisle,
    Pennsylvania
    William J. Donovan Papers
United States National Archives, Washington, D.C. (USNA)
    General Records of the Department of State (Record Group 59)
    Records of Foreign Service Posts (Record Group 84)
    Records of the United States Joint Chiefs of Staff (Record Group 218)
    Records of the Army Staff (Record Group 319)

                                                                INTERVIEWS

Norbert Anschuetz, November 5, 1991
Howard Bane, October 29, 1991 (telephone)
Max Bishop, November 8, 1991 (telephone)
Chalermsi Bird, June 23, 1992 (telephone)
Robert Cleveland, November 4, 1991
Norman Hannah, October 26, 1991 (telephone); November 3, 1991
John Hart, November 4, 1991
William Hussey, October 25, 1991 (telephone)
Jaroenrit Jamrat-romran, June 1, 1992
Jirawat Panyarachun, April 9, 1992
U. Alexis Johnson, November 5, 1991
Karuna Kusalasai, February 24, 1993
Khlaew Norapati, October 15, 1992
Konthi Suphamongkhon, March 9, 1992
William Lair, September 24, 1992
Jack Lydman, November 4, 1991
Joseph McManus, October 31, 1991 (telephone)
Peter Pond, October 22, 1991 (telephone)
Rak Panyarachun, April 11, 1992
Jerry Rucker, October 25, 1991 (telephone)
Joseph Smith, November 4, 1991
Joseph Burkholder Smith, October 23, 1991 (telephone)
Thanat Khoman, August 17, 1992
Theodore Tremblay, November 5, 1991
Leonard Unger, November 6, 1991
William vanden Heuvel, October 30 and November 8, 1991 (telephone)
Wanwai Phatthanothai, September 24, 1992 (telephone)
David Whipple, November 6, 1991

PUBLISHED SOURCES (ENGLISH)

Published Government Documents

Declassified Documents Reference System. Washington: Carrolton Press.

Department of Defense. *United States–Vietnam Relations, 1945–1967.* 2 vols. Washington: U.S. Government Printing Office, 1971.

Department of State. *Background: Thailand.* Washington: U.S. Government Printing Office, 1956.

———. *Department of State Bulletin.* Washington: U.S. Government Printing Office.

———. *Foreign Relations of the United States.* Washington: U.S. Government Printing Office.

———. *Foreign Service List.* Washington: Division of Public Services.

The Pentagon Papers: The Defense Department History of United States Decisionmaking on Vietnam. The Senator Gravel Edition. 4 vols. Boston: Beacon Press, 1971.

Sheehan, Neil, et al., eds. *The Pentagon Papers: As Published by the New York Times.* New York: Bantam Books, 1971.

Thailand Central Statistical Office, Office of the National Economic Development Board. *Statistical Yearbook of Thailand,* no. 22 (vol. 2), 1945–1955. Bangkok: Thailand Central Statistical Office, Office of the National Economic Development Board.

Books, Articles, and Dissertations

Adams, Nina S. "Patrons, Clients, and Revolutionaries: The Lao Search for Independence, 1945–1954." In *Laos: War and Revolution,* edited by Nina S. Adams and Alfred McCoy. New York: Harper & Row, 1970.

Adulyasak Soonthornrojana. "The Rise of United States–Thai Relations, 1945–1975." Ph.D. diss., University of Akron, 1986.

Aldrich, Richard J. *The Key to the South: Britain, the United States, and Thailand during the approach of the Pacific War, 1929–1942.* Kuala Lumpur: Oxford, 1993.

Anderson, Benedict R. O'G. "Murder and Progress in Modern Siam." *New Left Review* 181 (May/June 1990): 33–48.

Anderson, Benedict R. O'G, and Ruchira Mendiones, eds. and trans. *In the Mirror: Literature and Politics in Siam in the American Era.* Bangkok: Duang Kamol, 1985.

Anuson Chinvanno. *Brief Encounter: Sino-Thai Rapprochement after Bandung, 1955–1957.* Bangkok: International Studies Center, Ministry of Foreign Affairs, 1991.

———. "Thailand's Policies Towards the People's Republic of China, 1949–1957." Ph.D. diss., Oxford University, 1988.

Apichart Chinwanno. "Thailand's Search for Protection: The Making of the Alliance with the United States, 1947–1954." Ph.D. diss., Oxford University, 1985.

Blum, Robert M. *Drawing the Line: The Origin of the American Containment Policy in East Asia.* New York: Norton, 1982.

Brailey, Nigel J. *Thailand and the Fall of Singapore: A Frustrated Asian Revolution.* Boulder, Colo.: Westview Press, 1986.

Brown, Anthony Cave. *The Last Hero: Wild Bill Donovan.* New York: Times Books, 1982.

Bunnag, Jane. "Loose Structure: Fact or Fancy? Thai Society Re-examined." In *Modern Thai Politics: From Village to Nation,* edited by Clark D. Neher, 133–152. Cambridge, Mass.: Schenkman Publishing Co., 1976.

Burchett, Wilfred. "Pawns and Patriots: The U.S. Fight for Laos." In *Laos: War and Revolution,* edited by Nina S. Adams and Alfred McCoy. New York: Harper & Row, 1970.

Buszynski, Leszek. *SEATO: The Failure of an Alliance Strategy.* Singapore: Singapore University Press, 1983.

Caldwell, J. Alexander. *American Economic Aid to Thailand.* Lexington, Mass.: Lexington Books, 1974.

Charivat Santaputra. *Thai Foreign Policy 1932–1946.* Bangkok: Thai Khadi Research Institute, Thammasat University, 1985.

Chatri Ritharom. "The Making of the Thai-U.S. Military Alliance and the SEATO Treaty of 1954: A Study in Thai Decision-Making." Ph.D. diss., Claremont Graduate School, 1976.

Coast, John. *Some Aspects of Siamese Politics.* New York: International Secretariat, Institute of Pacific Relations, 1953.

Colbert, Evelyn. *Southeast Asia in International Politics, 1941–1956.* Ithaca, N.Y.: Cornell University Press, 1977.

Cumings, Bruce. *The Origins of the Korean War: Liberation and the Emergence of Separate Regimes.* Princeton, N.J.: Princeton University Press, 1981.

———. *The Origins of the Korean War, 1947–1950: The Roaring of the Cataract.* Princeton, N.J.: Princeton University Press, 1992.

Darling, Frank C. *Thailand and the United States.* Washington: Public Affairs Press, 1965.

Devillers, Philippe. "The Laotian Conflict in Perspective." In *Laos: War and Revolution,* edited by Nina S. Adams and Alfred McCoy. New York: Harper & Row, 1970.

Dommen, Arthur J. *Conflict in Laos: The Politics of Neutralization.* Rev. ed. New York: Praeger, 1971.

Donovan, William. "Our Stake in Thailand." *Fortune,* July 1955, 94–95.

Evers, Hans-Dieter, ed. *Loosely Structured Social Systems: Thailand in Comparative Perspective.* Cultural Report Series no. 17. New Haven, Conn.: Yale University Southeast Asia Studies, 1969.

Gaddis, John Lewis. *Strategies of Containment: A Critical Appraisal of Postwar American National Security Policy.* New York: Oxford University Press, 1982.

Girling, J. L. S. *Thailand: Society and Politics.* Ithaca, N.Y.: Cornell University Press, 1981.

Goldstein, Martin E. *American Policy toward Laos.* Rutherford, N.J.: Fairleigh Dickenson University Press, 1973.

Hannah, Norman Britton. "Power and Politics in Constitutional Thailand." Unpublished MS, 1958.

Haseman, John B. *The Thai Resistance Movement during the Second World War.* Dekalb: Northern Illinois University Center for Southeast Asian Studies, 1978.

Hayes, Samuel P., ed. *The Beginning of Aid to Southeast Asia: The Griffin Mission of 1950.* Lexington, Mass.: Heath, 1971.

Herring, George. *America's Longest War: The United States and Vietnam, 1950–1975.* New York: Knopf, 1986.

Hess, Gary. "The First American Commitment in Indochina: The Acceptance of the 'Bao Dai Solution,' 1950." *Diplomatic History* 2 (1978): 331–350.

———. *The United States' Emergence as a Southeast Asian Power, 1940–1950.* New York: Columbia University Press, 1985.

Immerman, Richard H. *The CIA in Guatemala: The Foreign Policy of Intervention.* Austin: University of Texas Press, 1982.

Ingram, James C. *Economic Change in Thailand 1850–1970.* Stanford, Calif.: Stanford University Press, 1971.

Jain, R. K., ed. *China and Thailand, 1949–1983.* Delhi: Radiant Publishers, 1984.

Jervis, Robert. "The Impact of the Korean War on the Cold War." *Journal of Conflict Resolution* 24 (1980): 563–592.

Jessup, Philip C. *The Birth of Nations.* New York: Columbia University Press, 1974.

Jin Vibatakarasa. "The Military in Politics: A Study of Military Leadership in Thailand." Ph.D. diss., University of Oregon, 1967.

Johnson, U. Alexis, with Jef Olivarius McAllister. *The Right Hand of Power.* Englewood Cliffs, N.J.: Prentice-Hall, 1984.

Jordan, Amos A. *Foreign Aid and the Defense of Southeast Asia.* New York: Praeger, 1962.

Kahin, George McT. *The Asian-African Conference: Bandung, Indonesia, April 1955.* Ithaca, N.Y.: Cornell University Press, 1956.

———, ed. *Governments and Politics of Southeast Asia.* Ithaca: Cornell University Press, 1959.

———. *Intervention: How America Became Involved in Vietnam.* Garden City, N.Y.: Anchor Press, 1987.

Kasian Tejapira. "Commodifying Marxism: The Formation of Modern Thai Radical Culture, 1927–1958." Ph.D. diss., Cornell University, 1992.

Katay [Sasorith Don Katay]. *Le Laos.* Paris: Berger-Levrault, 1953.

Keyes, Charles F. *Isan: Regionalism in Northeast Thailand.* Data Paper no. 65. Ithaca, N.Y.: Southeast Asia Program, Cornell University, 1967.

Kiernan, Ben. *How Pol Pot Came to Power: A History of Communism in Kampuchea, 1930–1975.* London: Verso, 1985.

Kobkua Suwannathat-Pian. *Thailand's Durable Premier: Phibun through Three Decades, 1932–1957.* Kuala Lumpur: Oxford University Press, 1995.

Kunstadter, Peter, ed. *Southeast Asian Tribes, Minorities and Nations.* 2 vols. Princeton, N.J.: Princeton University Press, 1967.

Landon, Kenneth Perry. *Siam in Transition: A Brief Survey of Cultural Trends in the Five Years since the Revolution of 1932.* 1939. Reprint, New York: Greenwood Press, 1968.

———. *The Chinese in Thailand.* 1941. Reprint, New York: Russell & Russell, 1973.

Landon, Margaret Dorothea. *Anna and the King of Siam.* New York: John Day, 1944.

Lansdale, Edward Geary. *In the Midst of Wars: An American's Mission to Southeast Asia.* New York: Harper & Row, 1972.

Leary, William M. *Perilous Missions: Civil Air Transport and CIA Covert Operations in Asia.* University, Ala.: University of Alabama Press, 1984.

Lederer, William J., and Eugene Burdick. *The Ugly American.* Greenwich, Conn.: Fawcett Crest, 1958.

Lobe, Thomas. *United States National Security Policy and Aid to the Thailand Police.* Monograph Series in World Affairs, no. 14, vol. 14, book 2. Denver: University of Denver Press, 1977.

Lomax, Louis E. *Thailand: The War That Is, the War That Will Be.* New York: Vintage Books, 1971.

MacDonald, Alexander. *Bangkok Editor.* New York: Macmillan, 1949.

Marks, Thomas A. "The Meo Hill Tribe Problem in North Thailand." *Asian Survey* 13 (1973): 929–944.

Matray, James I. *The Reluctant Crusade: American Foreign Policy in Korea, 1941–1950.* Honolulu: University of Hawai'i Press, 1985.

McCoy, Alfred W. *The Politics of Heroin in Southeast Asia: CIA Complicity in the Global Drug Trade.* Brooklyn, N.Y.: Lawrence Hill Books, 1991.

McLane, Charles B. *Soviet Strategies in Southeast Asia: An Exploration of Eastern Policy under Lenin and Stalin.* Princeton, N.J.: Princeton University Press, 1966.

McMahon, Robert J. "The Cold War in Asia: Toward a New Synthesis?" *Diplomatic History* 12 (1988): 307–327.

Montgomery, John D. *The Politics of Foreign Aid: American Experience in Southeast Asia.* New York: Praeger, 1962.

Morechand, Guy. "The Many Languages and Cultures of Laos." In *Laos: War and Revolution,* edited by Nina S. Adams and Alfred McCoy. New York: Harper & Row, 1970.

Munson, Frederick P., et al. *Area Handbook for Cambodia.* Washington: Foreign Area Studies, American University, 1968.

Muscat, Robert J. *Thailand and the United States: Development, Security, and Foreign Aid.* New York: Columbia University Press, 1990.

Nantawan Haemindra. "The Problem of the Thai Muslims in the Four Southern Provinces of Thailand. Part One." *Journal of Southeast Asian Studies* 7 (1976): 208–225.

Neher, Arlene Becker. "Prelude to Alliance: The Expansion of American Economic Interest in Thailand during the 1940s." Ph.D. diss., Northern Illinois University, 1980.

Niksch, Larry Allen. "United States Foreign Policy in Thailand's World War II Peace Settlements with Great Britain and France." Ph.D. diss., Georgetown University, 1975.

Nuechterlein, Donald E. *Thailand and the Struggle for Southeast Asia.* Ithaca, N.Y.: Cornell University Press, 1965.

Pickerell, Albert G. "The Press of Thailand: Conditions and Trends." *Journalism Quarterly* 37 (winter 1960): 83–96.

Poole, Peter A. *The Vietnamese in Thailand: A Historical Perspective.* Ithaca, N.Y.: Cornell University Press, 1970.

Randle, Robert F. *Geneva, 1954: The Settlement of the Indochinese War.* Princeton, N.J.: Princeton University Press, 1969.

Randolph, R. Sean. *The United States and Thailand: Alliance Dynamics, 1950–1985.* Research Papers and Policy Studies no. 12. Berkeley: Institute of East Asian Studies, University of California-Berkeley, 1986.

Ray, Jayanta Kumar. *Portraits of Thai Politics.* New Delhi: Orient Longman, 1972.

Reynolds, Craig J. *Thai Radical Discourse: The Real Face of Thai Feudalism Today.* Ithaca, N.Y.: Southeast Asia Program, Cornell University, 1987.

Reynolds, E. Bruce. *Thailand and Japan's Southern Advance, 1940–1945.* New York: St. Martin's Press, 1994.

———. "Ambivalent Allies: Japan and Thailand, 1941–1945," Ph.D. diss., University of Hawaii, 1988.

Rice, Irvin Marshall. "Thailand's Relations with the United States: A Study in Foreign Involvement." Ph.D. diss., American University, 1969.

Riggs, Fred W. *Thailand: The Modernization of a Bureaucratic Polity.* Honolulu: East-West Center Press, 1966.

Rotter, Andrew J. *The Path to Vietnam: Origins of the American Commitment to Southeast Asia.* Ithaca, N.Y.: Cornell University Press, 1987.

Schaller, Michael. *The American Occupation of Japan: The Origins of the Cold War in Asia.* New York: Oxford University Press, 1985.

———. "Securing the Great Crescent: Occupied Japan and the Origins of Containment in Southeast Asia." *Journal of American History* 69 (September 1982): 392–414.

Schlesinger, Stephen C., and Stephen Kinzer. *Bitter Fruit: The Untold Story of the American Coup in Guatemala.* Garden City, N.Y.: Doubleday, 1983.

Sirin Phathanothai. *Dragon's Pearl.* New York: Simon & Schuster, 1994.

Siviram, M. *Mekong Clash and the Far East Crisis.* Bangkok: Thai Commercial Press, 1941.

Skinner, G. William. *Chinese Society in Thailand: An Analytical History.* Ithaca, N.Y.: Cornell University Press, 1957.

———. *Leadership and Power in the Chinese Community in Thailand.* Ithaca, N.Y.: Cornell University Press, 1958.

Songsri Foran. "Thai-American-British Relations in the Post-World War II Settlement Period." Paper presented to the 7th Conference of the International Association of Historians of Asia, August 22–26, 1977, Bangkok, Thailand.

———. *Thai-British-American Relations During World War II and the Immediate Postwar Period.* Bangkok: Thai Khadi Research Institute, Thammasat University, 1981.

Stanton, Edwin F. *Brief Authority: Excursions of a Common Man in an Uncommon World.* New York: Harper & Row, 1956.

———. "Spotlight on Thailand." *Foreign Affairs* 33 (October 1954): 72–85.

Stevenson, Charles A. *The End of Nowhere: American Policy toward Laos since 1954.* Boston: Beacon Press, 1972.

Surin Pitsuwan. *Islam and Malay Nationalism: A Case Study of the Malay-Muslims of Southern Thailand.* Bangkok: Thai Khadi Research Institute, Thammasat University, 1985.

Tarling, Nicholas. " 'An Attempt to Fly in the Face of the Ordinary Laws of Supply and Demand': The British and Siamese Rice, 1945–1947." *Journal of the Siam Society* 75 (1987): 140–186.

———. "Britain and the Bandung Conference." *Journal of Southeast Asian Studies* 23 (1992): 77–111.

Taylor, Jay. *China and Southeast Asia: Peking's Relations with Revolutionary Movements.* New York: Praeger, 1974.

Taylor, Robert. *Foreign and Domestic Consequences of the KMT Intervention in Burma.* Ithaca, N.Y.: Southeast Asia Program, Cornell University, 1973.

Terwiel, B. J. *Field Marshal Plaek Phibun Songkhram.* St. Lucia, Queensland: Queensland University Press, 1980.

Thak Chaloemtiarana. *Thai Politics: Extracts and Documents, 1932–1957.* Bangkok: Social Science Association of Thailand, 1978.

———. *Thailand: The Politics of Despotic Paternalism.* Bangkok: Social Science Association of Thailand, Thai Khadi Research Institute, Thammasat University, 1979.

Thamsook Numnonda. *Thailand and the Japanese Presence, 1941–1945.* Research Notes and Discussions no. 6. Singapore: Institute of Southeast Asian Studies, 1977.

Thanet Apornsuvan. "The United States and the Coming of the Coup of 1947 in Siam." *Journal of the Siam Society* 75 (1987): 187–214.

Thawatt Mokarapong. *History of the Thai Revolution: A Study in Political Behavior.* Bangkok: Chalermnit, 1972.

Thompson, Sir Geoffrey. *Front-Line Diplomat*. London: Hutchinson Press, 1959.

Thompson, Virginia, and Richard Adloff. *Minority Problems in Southeast Asia*. New York: Russell & Russell, 1955.

Thorne, Christopher. *Allies of a Kind: The United States, Britain and the War against Japan, 1941–1945*. New York: Oxford University Press, 1978.

Topping, Seymour. *Journey between Two Chinas*. New York: Harper & Row, 1972.

Toru Yano. "Sarit and Thailand's 'Pro-American' Policy." *Developing Economies* 6 (1968): 284–299.

Toye, Hugh. *Laos: Buffer State or Battleground*. London: Oxford University Press, 1968.

Treverton, Gregory F. *Covert Action: The Limits of Intervention in the Postwar World*. New York: Basic Books, 1987.

Vanida Trongyounggoon Tuttle. "Thai-American Relations, 1950–1954." Ph.D. diss., Washington State University, 1982.

Vichitvong na Pombhejara. *Pridi Banomyong*. Bangkok: Siriyod Printing, 1982.

Walker, William O. *Opium and Foreign Policy: The Anglo-American Search for Order in Asia, 1912–1954*. Chapel Hill: University of North Carolina Press, 1991.

Warner, Denis. *The Last Confucian*. New York: Macmillan, 1963.

Warren, William. *Jim Thompson: The Legendary American of Thailand*. Bangkok: Jim Thompson Silk Co., 1986.

Watt, D. C. "Britain and the Cold War in the Far East, 1945–1958." In *The Origins of the Cold War in Asia,* edited by Yonosuke Nagai and Akira Iriye, 89–122. New York: Columbia University Press, 1977.

Wedel, Yuangrat. *Modern Thai Radical Thought: The Siamization of Marxism and Its Theoretical Problems*. Bangkok: Thai Khadi Research Institute, Thammasat University, 1982.

Wedel, Yuangrat, and Paul Wedel. *Radical Thought, Thai Mind: The Development of Revolutionary Ideas in Thailand*. Bangkok: Assumption Business Administration College, 1987.

Whitfield, Danny J. *Historical and Cultural Dictionary of Vietnam*. Historical and Cultural Dictionaries of Asia series, no. 7. Metuchen, N.J.: Scarecrow Press, 1976.

Willis Bird Funeral Volume. Bangkok: n.p., 1991.

Wilson, Constance M. *Thailand: A Handbook of Historical Studies*. Boston: G. K. Hall, 1983.

Wilson, David A. "China, Thailand and the Spirit of Bandung." 2 parts. *China Quarterly* 30 (1967): 149–169, and 31 (1967): 96–127.

———. *Politics in Thailand*. Ithaca, N.Y.: Cornell University Press, 1962.

———. "Thailand and Marxism." In *Marxism in Southeast Asia: A Study of Four Countries,* edited by Frank N. Trager, 58–101. Stanford, Calif.: Stanford University Press, 1959.

———. *The United States and the Future of Thailand*. New York: Praeger, 1970.

Wilson, Hugh. "Tengku Mahmud Mahyidden and the Dilemma of Partisan Duality." *Journal of Southeast Asian Studies* 23 (1992): 55–59.

Wolf, Charles, Jr. *Foreign Aid: Theory and Practice in Southeast Asia*. Princeton, N.J.: Princeton University Press, 1960.

Wyatt, David K., ed., and John B. Murdoch, trans. *Iron Man of Laos: Prince Phetsarath Ratanavongsa, by "3349"* [Prince Phetsarath]. Data Paper no. 110. Ithaca, N.Y.: Southeast Asia Program, Cornell University, 1978.

Young, Kenneth. "The Special Role of American Advisers in Thailand, 1902–1949." *Asia* 14 (1969): 1–31.

Periodicals

Bangkok Post
Economist
New York Times
Time
Times (London)

PUBLISHED SOURCES (THAI)

Published Government Documents

Ratchakitjanubeksa
Rai-ngan Kanprachum Rathasapha

Books, Articles, and Theses

A. Phibunsongkhram. *Jorm Phon P. Phibunsongkhram* [Field Marshal P. Phibunsongkhram]. 5 vols. Bangkok: n.p., n.d.

Amrung Sakunrat. *Khrai Wa Phao Mai Di?* [Who Says that Phao Was Bad?]. Bangkok: H. J. K. Kitsayamkanphim, 1983.

Ari Phirom. *Beuang-lang Kansathapana Samphanthaphap Yuk Mai Thai-Jin* [The Background to the Establishment of the Modern Thai-Chinese Relationship]. Bangkok: Mitnarakanphim, 1981.

Chit Wiphathawat. *Phao Saraphap (Burut Lek haeng Asia)* [Phao Confesses (The Iron Man of Asia)]. Bangkok: Phrae Phitthaya, 1960.

Chamlong Itharong. *Lakhorn Kanmeuang* [Political Theater]. Bangkok: Upakorn Kanphim, 1949.

Julaphorn Euaruksakun. "Korani Mayakwet: Seuksa Kantatsin Nayobai nai Phawa Wikritkan" [The *Mayaguez* Incident: A Study of Crisis Decision-Making]. M.A. thesis, Chulalongkorn University, 1986.

Kammakan Jat-tham Prawat Thahan Thai nai Songkhram Kaoli. *Prawatisat Kanrop khorng Thahan Thai nai Songkhram Kaoli* [History of the Fighting of Thai Soldiers in the Korean War]. Bangkok: Kammakan Jat-tham Prawat Thahan Thai nai Songkhram Kaoli, 1981.

Karuna Kusalasai. *Chiwit thi Leuak Mai Dai: Attachiwaprawat khorng Phu thi Kerd nai Phaen-din Thai Khon Neung* [Life Cannot be Chosen: The Autobiography of a Person Born on Thai Soil]. Bangkok: Sayam Samai, 1956.

Khlaew Norapati. "Botbat Phakkanmeuang 'Sangkhom Niyom' nai Prathet Thai" [The Role of "Socialist" Political Parties in Thailand]. *Matichon* weekly, April 24, 1989, 24–27.

———. *Yiam Pakking* [Visiting Beijing]. Bangkok: n.p., 1957.

Kobkua Suwannathad-Pian. *Nayobai Tang-prathet khorng Rathaban Phibunsong-khram P.S. 2481–2487* [The Foreign Policy of the Phibunsongkhram Government, 1938–1944]. Bangkok: Thai Khadi Research Institute, Thammasat University, 1989.

Konthi Suphamongkhon. *Kanwithesobai khorng Thai* [Thai Foreign Policy]. Bangkok: Thammasat University Press, 1984.

Krommameun Narathip Phongpraphan (Wan Waithayakorn). "Kan-prachum Bandong" [The Bandung Conference]. *Rathaphirak* 15, no. 1 (January 1973): 27–46.

Kulab Saipradit. *Adit thi pen Bot-rian: Khor-khian Thang-kanmeuang Yuk 2500* [Lessons from the Past: Political Writings of the 1957 Era]. Bangkok: Saeng Thian, 1979.

———. *Pai Sahaphap Sowiet* [Going to the Soviet Union]. Bangkok: Suphapburut, 1958.

Manun Makhasira. "Kanraksa Amnat Thangkanmeuang khorng Jorm Phon P. Phibunsongkhram rawang P.S. 2491–2500" [The Maintenance of Political Power of Field Marshal P. Phibunsongkhram from 1948–1957]. M.A. thesis, Sinakharinwirot University, 1986.

Net Khemayothin. *Ngan Tai-din khorng Phan-ek Yothi* [The Underground Work of Colonel Yothi]. Bangkok: Feuang Aksorn, 1957.

"Pert Ok Sam Sork Khlaew Norapati Khon Di Kaen Nakhorn" [Manly Confessions: Khlaew Norapati—A Good Person of the Country]. *Matichon* weekly, November 16, 1986, special section, 2–6.

Phayathai [pseud.]. "Mahantaphai jak Khormmunit" [The Great Danger of Communism]. *Yuthakot,* May 12, 1950, 31–40.

Phut Buranasomphop. *Chaichana lae Khwamphaiphae khorng Burut Lek haeng Asia* [The Victories and Defeats of the Iron Man of Asia]. Bangkok: Sun Ruam Khao Ekalak, n.d.

———. *13 Pi kap Burut Lek haeng Asia* [13 Years with the Iron Man of Asia]. Bangkok: Phonphankanphim, 1981.

Puey Ungphakorn. "Thahan Chuakhrao" [Part-time Soldier]. In *Bantheuk Pati-bad Ngan Tai-din khorng Adit Seri Thai* [Accounts of the Underground Work of Former Free Thai], edited by Khana Kammakan Wan Santiphap Thai. Bangkok: Khana Kammakan Wan Santiphap Thai, 1990.

Salao Rekharuji and Kamon Jantharasorn. *Waterlu khorng Jorm Phon Plaek* [The Waterloo of Field Marshal Plaek]. Bangkok: Phrae Phitthaya, 1957.

Sathit Saengsi. "Panha lae Upasak nai Kan-pokkhrorng Jangwat Chai-daen

Phak Tai: Bot-seuksa chaphor Chao Thai Islam" [Problems and Obstacles in Governing the Southern Border Provinces: A Case Study of Thai Muslims]. M.A. thesis, Thammasat University, 1970.

Sawai Sawaisaenyakorn. *Phon-ngan nai Tamnaeng Athibodi Tamruat* [Accomplishments in the Position of Police Director-General]. Bangkok: n.p., 1981.

Somkiat Suphanchanaburi. *Khwamsamphan rawang Prathet Thai kap Malesia rawang P.S. 2519–2526* [Relations between Thailand and Malaysia, 1976–1983]. Bangkok: Asian Studies Institute, Chulalongkorn University, 1987.

Sornsak Ngamkhajornkulkit, ed. "Adit haeng Patjuban: Bantheuk Lap Jorm Phon P. Beuang Lang Patiwat 8 P.Y. 2490" [Today's Past: The Secret Writings of Field Marshal P. on the Truth behind the November 8, 1947, Coup]. *Matichon* weekly, November 5, 1989, 21–22.

―――. *Khabuankan Seri Thai kap Khwamkhatyaeng Thang Kanmeuang phainai Prathet Thai, 2481–2492* [The Free Thai Movement and Political Conflict in Thailand, 1938–1949]. Bangkok: Institute of Asian Studies, Chulalongkorn University, 1988.

Suchat Sawatsi. "Jotmai Lap khorng Jorm Phon Sarit theung Thanong Sathathip" [Field Marshal Sarit's Secret Letters to Thanong Sathathip]. *Lok Nangseu*, September 12, 1978, 112–116.

Suchin Tantikun. *Rathaprahan P.S. 2490* [The 1947 Coup d'État]. Bangkok: Social Science Association of Thailand, 1972.

Surachai Yimprasert. "Kankhleuanwai Thangkanmeuang thi tor-tan Rathaban Samai Jorm Phon P. Phibunsongkhram" (P.S. 2491–2500) [Political Movements Opposing the Government of Field Marshal P. Phibunsongkhram (1948–1957)]. M.A. thesis, Chulalongkorn University, 1989.

Suwimon Rungjaroen. "Botbat khorng Naknangseuphim nai Kanmeuang Thai rawang P.S. 2490–2501" [The Role of Journalists in Thai Politics, 1947–1958]. M.A. thesis, Chulalongkorn University, 1983.

Thamsook Numnonda. "Khabuankan Tor-tan Amerikan Samai Jorm Phon P. Phibunsongkhram" [The Anti-American Movement in the Field Marshal P. Phibunsongkhram Era]. *Ruam Botkhwam Prawatisat* 2 (January 1981): 50–83.

―――. *Khwamsamphan rawang Thai-Saharat Amerika phai-lang Songkhram Lok Khrang thi Sorng* [Thai-American Relations after World War II]. Bangkok: Social Science Association of Thailand, 1982.

―――. *Lakhorn Kanmeuang 24 Mithunayon 2475* [The Political Theater of 24 June 1932]. Bangkok: Social Science Association of Thailand, 1992.

Thani Sukkasem. "Khwamsamphan rawang Thai kap Satharanarat Prachachon Jin: Wikhror Naew Nayobai Tang-prathet khorng Thai thi Mi tor Jin P.S. 2494–2515" [Relations between Thailand and the People's Republic of China: An Analysis of Thailand's Foreign Policy toward China, 1951–1972]. M.A. thesis, Thammasat University, 1982.

Thongchai Pheungkanthai. "Latthi Khormmunit lae Nayobai Tor-tan khorng Rathaban Thai P.S. 2468–2500" [Communism and the Thai Government's

Anti-Communist Policies, 1925–1957]. M.A. thesis, Chulalongkorn University, 1978.

Wanwai Phatthanothai. *Jo-ern-lai: Phu Pluk Maitri Thai-Jin* [Zhou Enlai: The Person Who Established Thai-Chinese Friendship]. n.p.: n.p., n.d.

Watthana Kanjana-akharadet. "Samphanthaphap Thangkanmeuang rawang Prathet Thai kap Kamphucha tangtae Pi P.S. 2489" [Political Relations between Thailand and Cambodia since 1946]. M.A. thesis, Thammasat University, n.d.

Wiwat Khatithammanit. "Kabot Santiphap" [The Peace Rebellion]. *Warasan Thammasat* 14 (June 1985): 5–38.

Periodicals

Chat
Deli Me
Kalahom
Khao Thahan Akat
Khao Thahan Phan Seuk
Kiattisak
Phim Thai
Pituphum
Piyamit
San Seri
Sayam Nikorn
Sayam Rath
Thahan Ma
Thahan Rap
Thahan Seu-san
Thai Ratsadorn
Thammathipat
Yuthakot

INDEX

250; relations with party, 251, 252; relations with Phao, 164, 209, 215–216, 223, 231, 312 n. 54; relations with Phibun, 231, 241–242; relations with Pridi, 236–237; relations with United States, 232–233, 243–245, 249–250, 255, 256–257; requests for economic aid, 251; requests for military aid, 193, 207; and Silent Coup, 153–155; U.S. view of, 241; visits to United States, 193, 250, 251

Sasorith Don Katay. *See* Katay

Sathianraphap newspaper, 228

Satjatham, 157

Sawai Sawaisaenyakorn, 186, 218, 245, 247

Sawet Piamphongsan, 57, 260, 274 n. 17

Sayam Nikorn, 158, 246

Sayam Rath newspaper, 157, 236

Sayam Samai, 158

Scott, James, 75

Sea Supply Company: aid to police, 223; arms shipments, 134, 135; attack on office, 242; criticism of, 240–241, 245, 246, 247; Donovan and, 181; establishment, 134; lack of control by U.S. ambassador, 150; and Operation Paper, 141; and training camps, 136, 181, 182

SEATO. *See* Southeast Asia Treaty Organization

Senate, Thai, 51, 71, 152

Seni Pramoj, 19; on Bao Dai issue, 110, 114; in government after 1947 coup, 41, 50; on Kat, 60; opposition to Phibun, 26, 50, 71, 110; on Phao, 136; Pridi and, 20; as prime minister, 31; relations with United States, 31, 33, 35; on SEATO, 197

Seri Manangkhasila Party, 231, 233, 234–235, 240, 248

Serm Winitchaikun, 160

Shan States (Burma), 17, 137–143

Shell Oil Company, 22

Shirley, Jack, 220, 288 n. 9

Siam. *See* Thailand

Siang Thai newspaper, 47

Si Ayutthaya, 148, 149

Siddhiphorn, Prince, 48

Siddhi Savetsila. *See* Sitthi Savetsila

Sihanouk, Norodom, 176–177, 185, 253

Si Krung newspaper, 21

Silent Coup, 153–155, 156, 159, 168, 202

Sinat Yotharak, 28, 50, 71–72

Sin Songkhramchai, 39, 42, 46, 52, 54, 55, 58

Sinthu Songkhramchai. *See* Sin Songkhramchai

Sitthi Savetsila, 133

Siviram, M., 74, 277 n. 26

Smith, H. Alexander, 207

Smith, Walter Bedell, 137, 178–179, 191, 192, 193

Social Democrat Party, 231

socialist parties, 231. *See also* leftists

Socialist Party, 231

Socialist United Front, 231

Sor Sethabut, 26

Souphanouvong, 186

Southeast Asia: economic importance to Britain, 23–24; proposals for collective defense treaties, 192, 194, 195; U.S. aid to, 106, 114; and U.S. policies, 24–26, 128, 169, 170–171, 190–192; Western fears of communist advances in, 73–74, 81, 94–95. *See also* Indochina; *and specific countries*

Southeast Asia League, 77

Southeast Asia Treaty Organization (SEATO), 195–197, 198, 238; conferences, 207–208, 228; public opposition in Thailand, 236; Stanton on, 206; Thai role in, 207–208, 244, 250

South Vietnam, 208. *See also* Vietnam

Souvanna Phouma, 186, 187, 189

Soviet Union: Bangkok legation, 57, 73–74; influence on World Peace Movement, 157; relations with Thailand, 57, 66, 79, 80, 167, 249; relations with United States, 143, 195; relations with Vietnam, 108; veto of Thai appeal to U.N., 194

Special Operations Executive (Britain), 18, 25, 31

Standard Oil Company (Standard Vacuum Oil Company), 22, 234, 240

Stanton, Edwin F.: advocacy for Thailand, 206; and anticommunist propaganda, 120–121; attitude toward Free Thais, 47; on Bao Dai, 104, 110, 111, 113; career of, 40, 178; on corruption in Coup Group, 60, 82; on Khuang's government, 43, 49, 52–53; on local Chinese, 100; meetings with Thai officials, 23, 26, 48, 51; and moralism, 40–41, 55, 178; on Phao, 150–151; on Phibun, 22, 60, 70, 95–96, 97, 150; on

About the Author

DANIEL FINEMAN received his Ph.D. in history from Yale University. He is currently an investment analyst at Jardine Fleming Thanakom Securities in Bangkok.